The CIM Student's Practice and Revision Handbook

The Chartered
Institute of Marketing

The CIM Student's Practice and Revision Handbook

For the CIM Professional Diploma in Marketing

Anthony Annakin-Smith
Paul Dixon
Andrew Sherratt

ELSEVIER

AMSTERDAM • BOSTON • HEIDELBERG • LONDON • NEW YORK • OXFORD
PARIS • SAN DIEGO • SAN FRANCISCO • SINGAPORE • SYDNEY • TOKYO

Butterworth-Heinemann is an imprint of Elsevier

Butterworth-Heinemann is an imprint of Elsevier
Linacre House, Jordan Hill, Oxford OX2 8DP, UK
30 Corporate Drive, Suite 400, Burlington, MA 01803, USA

First edition 2007

Notice
No responsibility is assumed by the publisher for any injury and/or damage to persons
or property as a matter of products liability, negligence or otherwise, or from any use
or operation of any methods, products, instructions or ideas contained in the material
herein. Because of rapid advances in the medical sciences, in particular, independent
verification of diagnoses and drug dosages should be made

British Library Cataloguing in Publication Data
A catalogue record for this book is available from the British Library

Library of Congress Cataloging-in-Publication Data
A catalog record for this book is available from the Library of Congress

ISBN-13: 978-0-7506-8331-9

For information on all Butterworth-Heinemann publications
visit our website at books.elsevier.com

Typeset by Integra Software Services Pvt. Ltd, Pondicherry, India
www.integra-india.com
Printed and bound in Italy
07 08 09 10   10 9 8 7 6 5 4 3 2 1

Contents

getting the most from this book

Our aim in writing this book is to help you pass your CIM Professional Diploma in Marketing examinations. It's full of advice, information and study aids which can all make the difference between passing and failing. Each author has years of experience of teaching CIM students so we have a good idea about what the CIM examiners are looking for in successful exam answers.

The book is broken into four main sections, one for each Professional Diploma subject. Each section follows a similar format – here's how to get the best from each one.

SYLLABUS

The Syllabus summarises what the CIM expect you to know. Spend time also looking at the 'Learning Outcomes' – this is what the CIM expect you to be able to do, so make sure you are comfortable with each item.

KEY CONCEPTS – REVISION CHECKLIST

From experience we know that students find it helpful to have a checklist to work through of key topics to know for the exam. We suggest you use this, ticking off each item when you feel comfortable that you could write about it. All the key theoretical concepts that you need to know are there (but bear in mind that the exam is also about *applying* this theory). If you are a bit unsure about any of the concepts, look for a relevant Suggested Answer, study your course notes or textbooks, or use the extensive online CIM facilities described below.

QUESTIONS

We have included a range of questions for each subject – some from actual past examination papers, and many new ones in the same style. The questions cover all, or virtually all, of the syllabus for each subject so if you work through them you should have a pretty comprehensive understanding of what is needed.

SUGGESTED ANSWERS

You may like to simply read through the suggested answers, in order to absorb or revise information. But before you do so we suggest you draft your own answer – in full form or just as a plan. Then compare it against our 'Check Your Answer' section, which is an opportunity for you to see if you have included the points that are likely to appear in a good answer. If you have all or most of these points then you are likely to be delivering an answer that will earn a 'pass', if not better.

It is worth making two important points about these suggested answers.

First, our suggested answer covers material that you could reasonably be expected to know for the exam. However, a good student's exam answer to a Part B question is typically about 700 – 900 words long (Part A answers are typically twice as long), but ours are a bit longer than this as we have covered extra ground to help you with your revision and understanding. *Don't worry if you can't write this much in the exam – passing is down to quality, not quantity!*

Secondly, we have only given you '*suggested* answers': they are simply *examples* of ways to tackle a question. There is *no* 'right' *answer.* Provided you ensure you answer the question that is set, you could answer in many different ways and still get a good mark. Don't forget that originality of thinking, evidence from recent research, and examples of actual marketing practice are all things that are likely to earn you extra credit in the exam – provided they are relevant to the question.

In addition to the four main sections there are two shorter sections.

Mastering the exam

Much of the skill in passing an exam is about using the right technique. Simply knowing the theory is not enough – time management and being able to apply your knowledge to the situation given in the question are just two of the skills you also require. This section tells you all you need to approach your examination with confidence.

CIM information resources to help you

As a member of the CIM you have access to a tremendous range of resources – many students fail to realise this or take advantage of them. These can help with your learning and revision and give up-to-the-minute information and examples that can turn a fair answer into a really good one. We suggest that you make sure you are familiar with all these resources from early in your studies.

In buying this book you have taken a significant step towards gaining the qualification you want. We believe our experience and your enthusiasm and application can make a winning combination.

Good luck!

Anthony Annakin-Smith, Paul Dixon, Andrew Sherratt

research
mation

SYLLABUS – MARKETING RESEARCH AND INFORMATION

Aim

The Marketing Research and Information unit covers the management of customer information and research projects as part of the marketing process. It provides students with both the knowledge and skills to manage marketing information and the more specialist knowledge and skills required to plan, undertake and present results from market research.

Learning outcomes

Students will be able to:

- Identify appropriate marketing information and marketing research requirements for business decision-making.
- Plan for and manage the acquisition, storage, retrieval and reporting of information on the organisation's market and customers.
- Explain the process involved in purchasing market research and the development of effective client–supplier relationships.
- Write a research brief to meet the requirements of an organisation to support a specific plan or business decision.
- Develop a research proposal to fulfil a given research brief.
- Evaluate the appropriateness of different qualitative and quantitative research methodologies to meet different research situations.
- Design and plan a research programme.
- Design a questionnaire and discussion guide.
- Interpret quantitative and qualitative data and present coherent and appropriate recommendations that lead to effective marketing and business decisions.
- Critically evaluate the outcomes and quality of a research project.
- Explain the legal, regulatory, ethical and social responsibilities of organisations involved in gathering, holding and using information.

Indicative content and weighting

Element 1: Information and research for decision-making (15 per cent)

1.1 Demonstrate a broad appreciation of the need for information in marketing management and its role in the overall marketing process.

1.2 Explain the concept of knowledge management and its importance in a knowledge-based economy.

1.3 Explain how organisations determine their marketing information requirements and the key elements of user specifications for information.

1.4 Demonstrate an understanding of marketing management support systems and their different formats and components.

Element 2: Customer databases (15 per cent)

2.1 Demonstrate an understanding of the application, the role in customer relationship management (CRM) and the benefits of customer databases.

2.2 Describe the process for setting up a database.

2.3 Explain how organisations profile customers and prospects.

2.4 Explain the principles of data warehouses, data marts and data mining.

2.5 Explain the relationship between database marketing and marketing research.

Element 3: Marketing research in context (25 per cent)

3.1 Describe the nature and structure of the market research industry.

3.2 Explain the stages of the market research process.

3.3 Describe the procedures for selecting a market research supplier.

3.4 Identify information requirements to support a specific business decision in an organisation and develop a research brief to meet the requirements.

3.5 Develop a research proposal to fulfil a given research brief.

3.6 Explain the ethical and social responsibilities inherent in the market research task.

Element 4: Research methodologies (30 per cent)

4.1 Explain the uses, benefits and limitations of secondary data.

4.2 Recognise the key sources of primary and secondary data.

4.3 Describe and compare the various procedures for observing behaviour.

4.4 Describe and compare the various methods for collecting qualitative and quantitative data.

4.5 Design a questionnaire and discussion guide to meet a project's research objectives.

4.6 Explain the theory and processes involved in sampling.

Element 5: Presenting and evaluating information to develop business advantage (15 per cent)

5.1 Demonstrate an ability to use techniques for analysing qualitative and quantitative data.

5.2 Write a research report aimed at supporting marketing decisions.

5.3 Plan and design an oral presentation of market research results.

5.4 Use research and data to produce actionable recommendations for a marketing plan or to support a business decision.

KEY CONCEPTS – REVISION CHECKLIST

These are the key concepts you should be aware of when you go into the marketing research and information exam. Be able to define or explain each concept and be prepared to discuss key aspects of it. If you have revised this material well then you should be able to cope with the theoretical aspects of the exam.

Syllabus element 1

Information and research for decision making

	☑		☑
Marketing and the marketing concept	☐	Developing information user specifications	☐
Overview of the information age and the knowledge economy	☐	Definitions for and the role of marketing research	☑
The role of information as a marketing asset	☐	Basic concepts of knowledge management (KM) and key terms	☐
Impact of ICT in marketing and business generally	☐	Barriers to KM and how to overcome them	☐
Information needs for the marketing planning process and typical marketing decisions	☐	Overview of marketing decision support systems and components	☐
APIC framework (analysis, planning implementation and control)	☐	Marketing information system (MKIS) model, its use and application	☑
Four roles for information	☑	Stages of development for an information system or MKIS	☐
Decision levels in organisations	☑		

Syllabus element 2

Customer databases

	☑		☑
Overview of customer relationship management (CRM) and its benefits	☐	Appreciation of ACORN and MOSAIC geo-demographic profiling systems	☑
Overview of CRM technology and its components	☐	Appreciation of TGI (Target Group Index)	☐
Setting up a customer database, the database creation process and various maintenance terms	☐	Adding research data to the database – how and the implications	☐
Customer database – sources and uses of the data	☐	Data Warehouses and marts, including advantages/benefits	☐
Importance of a customer database for profiling customers		Appreciation of Data Mining techniques	
Four types of customer data, their importance and application	☐	Relationship between database marketing and marketing research information – very important!	☐
Adding profile data to a database	☐		

Syllabus element 3

Marketing research in context

Structure of the marketing research industry: ☑ ☐

- o Internal research departments – functions. ☐
- o Trend to broaden role – customer insight teams ☐
- o Types of agency and research supplier, with examples and types of activities undertaken. ☐
- o Professional bodies and their role. ☐
- o MRS and ESOMAR ☐

The market research process: ☐

- o Approach and key elements of each stage. ☐
- o Categories of research: exploratory, descriptive, causal. Know the roles of each category and the relationships between them ☐

In-house and external agency approaches to marketing research projects: ☐

- o Advantages and disadvantages of in-house and agency approaches ☐
- o Management issues ☐

Selecting a marketing research supplier: ☐

- o Selection procedures ☑
- o Selection criteria ☑

MR agency presentations: ☐

- o The beauty parade ☐
- o Advantages for agencies and clients ☐

Ethical and legal aspects of marketing research: ☑ ☐

- o Data protection act – know its key areas of importance to marketers ☑
- o Other relevant legislation ☐
- o Regulatory codes relating to communication with prospects: TPS, MPS, FPS, EPS ☐
- o MRS/ESOMAR Code of Conduct – know its content ☐

The marketing information requirements of organisations that marketing research can address including: ☐

- o Market research ☐
- o Product research ☐
- o Price research ☐
- o Sales promotion/marketing communications research ☐
- o Customer service, support and complaints research ☐
- o Distribution channel research ☐

Marketing briefs and proposals: ☐

- o Purpose, content and layout of each document ☑
- o Be able to produce a brief to cover a given problem/ opportunity and an industry context ☐
- o Be able to produce a detailed proposal in response to a brief or mini-case scenario ☑

Syllabus element 4

Research methodologies

Remind yourself of the marketing research process ☑☐

Overview of the various research methodologies: primary, secondary, quantitative, qualitative ☑

Secondary research, internal and external sources ☑

Application of secondary research data to a business problem ☑

Benefits of the Internet for external secondary research ☑

Uses of secondary research, including its use as a backdrop to primary research ☑

Problems and limitations of using secondary data: ☑
- Availability, applicability, accuracy and comparability ☑

Types of primary research:
- Qualitative and quantitative ☑
Observational techniques: ☑
- Various methods and categories ☑
- Advantages and disadvantages of the various methods

Qualitative research methods: ☑
- Unstructured/individual depth interviews
- Discussion or focus groups ☐
- Projective techniques ☑
- Advantages and disadvantages of each qualitative method ☑
- Moderator role, recruitment and skills set ☑
- Discussion guide content, design and preparation ☑

Quantitative research methods: ☑☐

- Questionnaires and surveys: interviewer administered and self-completion, various types (know a good selection) ☑
- Advantages, disadvantages and comparisons of each type ☑
- Use of technology – CAPI and CATI ☑

- Recruiting field workers, training, skills, supervision of ☑
- Questionnaire design: ☑☑☑☑
  - Design process stages
  - Question types
  - Open, closed, scaling types, scale dimensions ☑
  - Advantages and disadvantages of each type ☑☑
  - Wording, design and layout

Sampling Techniques: ☑☑
- Census or sample? ☑
- Sample size determination
- Sampling frames and sampling error
Probability sampling methods: ☑☑☑
- Simple random sample
- Systematic sample
- Stratified sample
- Multi-stage sample ☑☑☑
Non-probability sampling methods:
Judgement, convenience, snowball
Types of non-response and how to minimise the possibility of

7

Syllabus element 5

Presenting and evaluating information

Analysing quantitative data: ☑ ☑ ☑

- o Coding and data entry ☑
- o Data types ☑
- o Tabulation and cross-tabulation ☑
- o Use of descriptive statistics, measures of central tendency, measures of dispersion ☑
- o Statistical significance ☑
- o Hypothesis testing ☑
- o Correlation and regression for measuring relationships ☑
- o Multivariate techniques including cluster analysis ☑

Analysing qualitative data: ☑

- o Process stages ☑
- o Methods including: tabulation, cut and paste, spider diagrams ☑
- o Use of computer software for analysis ☑

Reports and presentations: ☑ ☑

- o Audience needs and thinking sequence ☑
- o Marketing research reports, format and contents ☑
- o Format for an oral presentation ☑
- o Basic presentation techniques and tips ☑
- o Presenting data graphically – know the range of graphs and charting formats along with the advantages and disadvantages of each type ☑
- o Common problems associated with reports and presentations ☑

PART A MINI-CASES

Before attempting the mini cases in this section, please read the Study and Revision Techniques section of this Revision Guide

Mini-Case 1: SeaLux Cruises (June 2006)

Information requirements for marketing decisions, content of a marketing research brief, written research proposal to satisfy information requirements

Syllabus elements 1.1, 3.2, 3.4, 3.5, 4.1, 4.2, 4.3, 4.4, 4.6, 5.1

SeaLux Cruises is a new cruise operator consisting of two ships sailing out of the port of Southampton in Southern England. It has been established for just over one year and provides cruise-based vacations using its 1400 berth ship, Med Blue, around the Mediterranean, and cruises around Scandinavia and the Baltic States on its 1250 berth ship, Northern Blue. The focus is on offering relaxing vacations with an emphasis on 'luxurious discovery' through a wide range of dining, entertainment and excursion choices. A 12-day Mediterranean cruise on the Med Blue with stops in Venice, Barcelona, Rome and five other cities starts at around £2000.

Although the first year has gone well with very satisfied passengers and no technical problems, the cruises have been running at below optimum capacity. The level of bookings for the sixteen cruises scheduled for the next 12 months is also around 35 per cent below target. This is causing the company some concern, particularly when industry sources and the performance of competitors clearly suggest that the UK cruise market is going through a period of tremendous growth. There is a view among the senior management of the company that the product offering is correct for the target market but the promotion and sales activity is failing to raise awareness and attract or convert potential passengers.

Unlike other cruise lines that use travel agents to sell their cruises, SeaLux undertakes direct advertising in national newspapers and magazines leading to customers booking direct with SeaLux through their Internet site or telephone hotline. The senior management is now concerned that low sales may reflect an unwillingness of the target market (over 40 age group) to book cruises on a direct basis, as they may require the advice and reassurance of a travel agent. Alternatively, the poor sales may simply reflect a low awareness of the advertising and the company's offerings. SeaLux is, therefore, keen to undertake a programme of research to examine the effectiveness of the advertising and the attitudes of the target market towards the preferred methods and channels for the booking of cruise-based holidays. The company is willing to spend up to £70 000 on the research project.

(The above data has been based on a fictitious situation drawing on a variety of events and does not reflect the management practices of any particular organisation.)

Mini-Case 2: Colonnade Technologies Limited

Information requirements for marketing decisions, content of a marketing research brief, written research proposal to satisfy information requirements

Syllabus elements 1.1, 3.2, 3.4, 3.5, 4.1, 4.2, 4.3, 4.4, 4.6, 5.1

Colonnade Technologies Limited (CTL) provides computerised alarm management solutions mainly to commercial alarm receiving centres (ARCs) whose business involves the electronic monitoring of fire and security alarms installed in domestic premises, retail outlets and industrial/commercial buildings. The monitoring and tracking of commercial vehicles and lone workers is also becoming popular, given the ready availability of satellite positioning/navigation devices, combined with mobile phone technology. This new strand of business is proving very profitable for the ARCs.

When an alarm is received, operators in the receiving centre use the management system to despatch key holders, the police or fire services and other resources as may be required. The system can also provide live CCTV pictures and other information, including detailed maps and plans, to assist in managing the incident. All activity, including the system operator's response actions, is accurately time-stamped and logged in a database and can be used to provide management reports for the customer and/or provide evidence for legal or insurance purposes.

Traditionally, there were only a few suppliers of alarm management systems in the UK, each of which enjoyed a fair share of the market and healthy profitability. CTL is the oldest supplier and has built a reputation for innovative software, high system reliability and solid customer service.

A number of changes have occurred in the market during the last five years and CTL is finding business increasingly tough. First, significant consolidation has occurred in the ARC market with a number of acquisitions and mergers taking place, resulting in fewer, but much larger, ARCs which have adopted a business model based upon high volume, low margin business and low cost operations. Secondly, CTL has experienced new and aggressive competition from overseas, especially the US. These competitors offer attractive solutions and lower prices. CTL has lost a number of contracts to the new entrants, including three long-standing customers.

Phil Jones, CTL's managing director, recognises that his organisation has failed to keep pace with the changes that have taken place. He believes that a programme of research is urgently needed to inform a new marketing strategy for the company and is prepared to spend up to £30 000 on the research project.

(The above data has been based on a fictitious situation drawing on a variety of events and does not reflect the management practices of any particular organisation.)

Mini-Case 3: Kelvin Council (June 2004)

Information requirements for marketing decisions, content of a marketing research brief, written research proposal to satisfy information requirements

Syllabus elements 1.1, 3.2, 3.4, 3.5, 4.1, 4.2, 4.3, 4.4, 4.6, 5.1

Kelvin Council is a local government authority with a population of approximately 250 000 people. The population is located in approximately 140 000 households within five main settlements (Bearsden, Milngavie, Kirkintilloch, Torrance and Lennoxtown) as well as in rural villages and hamlets. All local authorities have been given a target for recycling domestic waste. Kelvin Council's target is 20 per cent of domestic waste being recycled by the year 2010. This compares with the 8 per cent figure that Kelvin Council is currently achieving. The council has established recycling centres in the car parks of major retail outlets for the recycling of glass, plastic, aluminium, paper and cardboard. They also sell composting bins to the public for the recycling of garden and kitchen waste. However, the proportion of waste being recycled has changed little over the last three to four years.

The council is now keen to find out more about its residents' attitudes towards recycling, for example:

- o Why they recycle/do not recycle?
- o What are their attitudes towards the need to recycle?
- o What items do they find easy/difficult to recycle?
- o Would they recycle more if each household received a bin for collecting recyclable waste?
- o Are financial incentives needed to increase recycling rates?

The council hopes that answers to such questions will help them to categorise residents into different groupings and assist in the identification of new initiatives to increase the level of recycling.

The Council is willing to spend up to £25 000 on the research project.

Mini-Case Questions

This same question applies to each of the MRI mini-cases presented in this revision guide.

1. You are a research executive in a market research agency and have been asked to do the following:

a) Identify appropriate further information that you would require from the organisation prior to writing a proposal. (10 marks)

b) Having made reasonable assumptions regarding the answers to the information required in Question 1a, produce a proposal to address the research needs of the organisation. (For the purpose of this question, your proposal should exclude the sections relating to personal CVs, related experience, references and contract details.) (40 marks)

(Total 50 marks)

PART B QUESTIONS

Syllabus element 1
Question 1

Information needs of managers and marketing information systems

Syllabus elements 1.1, 1.3, 1.4, 3.4

You have just been appointed marketing manager for an organisation and have been asked to produce a report about the process and benefits of integrating various internal information sources along with external data obtained through marketing research. Your report should:

a) Outline the process you would use to determine the organisation's marketing information requirements. (10 marks)

b) Explain the possible contribution of marketing research to an integrated information system. (7 marks)

c) List the key benefits of such a system. (8 marks)

(Total 25 marks)

Question 2

Information and research for decision-making

Syllabus elements 1.1, 1.3

In your new role as marketing manager for an organisation of your choice, you identify the need to undertake an audit of current marketing operations. In preparation for this task, write a report which provides details of:

a) The information requirements for the audit, outlining possible sources of internal and external data. (12 marks)

b) The key elements of a user specification for information. (8 marks)

c) The criteria you would use to assess the value of the information provided in response to a user specification. (5 marks)

(Total 25 marks)

Question 3

Knowledge management

Syllabus elements 1.1, 1.2

You have been asked to make a short presentation at the next monthly management meeting on the subject of knowledge management (KM).

a) Prepare a set of notes for the presentation which introduces the key concepts and explains the potential benefits to the organisation. (15 marks)

You become aware that one or two of the managers who will attend the presentation have heard about KM and are sceptical about whether it can be successfully introduced.

b) In order to address these concerns, add a short final section to the presentation notes which identifies potential barriers to knowledge management and briefly explain how these might be overcome. (10 marks)

(Total 25 marks)

Syllabus element 2
Question 4

Database information, its benefits and ethical issues (June 2006, Question 2)

Syllabus elements 1.1, 2.1, 2.3, 2.5, 3.6

The senior management of **SeaLux** is of the opinion that the company should know much more about the characteristics of their passengers. This would be useful in customer profiling, building loyalty and obtaining repeat business. Currently, basic name, address and billing information are stored on the company's computers. You have been asked as a new recruit to the marketing department to produce a report which sets out:

a) The types of information that could be collected on a database about passengers and the approaches that could be adopted to collect such information. (9 marks)

b) The potential benefits that would result from holding such information. (7 marks)

c) The issues involved in attempting to merge the information from the database with the customer satisfaction surveys undertaken at the end of each cruise. (9 marks)

(Total 25 marks)

Question 5

Database development and enhancement

Syllabus elements 1.1, 2.1, 2.2, 2.3

As a recent graduate recruited to the marketing department of a national laundry and dry cleaning chain serving retail customers, you have received an enquiry from the sales and commercial director concerning the development of a customer database and asking for a report which sets out:

a) An outline of the way in which you would store and process the data for it to be of use in the provision of information for marketing intelligence and customer relationship activity.   (9 marks)

b) The logistics of collecting customer data and the potential weaknesses of the database in the context of the laundry and dry cleaning chain.   (8 marks)

c) The potential benefits of using geo-demographic and lifestyle data to enhance the database.
(8 marks)

(Total 25 marks)

Question 6

CRM, data warehousing and data mining

Syllabus elements 1.1, 2.1, 2.4, 5.1

As the assistant CRM manager for a regional airline, you have been asked to make a presentation to the local CIM branch covering CRM and a number of related topics. Prepare notes for the elements of the presentation which:

a) Identifies the differences between a customer database and a CRM system, emphasising the importance of the CRM system in the airline's strategy for enhancing relationships with its customers.   (10 marks)

b) Explains the purpose of a data warehouse and data-mining tools, using examples to illustrate your presentation.   (8 marks)

c) Outlines the contribution of cluster and CHAID analysis when segmenting customers.
(7 marks)

(Total 25 marks)

15

Syllabus element 3
Question 7

Roles of information, internal research departments and ethics (June 2005, Question 2, modified)

Syllabus elements 1.1, 2.1, 2.5, 3.1, 3.6

As a recent graduate recruited to the marketing department of a large clothing retailer you have received an enquiry from the marketing director asking for a report which addresses the following:

a) The descriptive, comparative, diagnostic and predictive roles that marketing information can provide. (8 marks)

b) Why are some marketing research departments in large organisations widening their remit beyond marketing research? (10 marks)

c) What ethical issues are raised by such a change being made? (7 marks)

(Total 25 marks)

Question 8

Research agency selection criteria and professional codes of conduct

Syllabus elements 3.1, 3.2, 3.3, 3.6

The company you have recently joined has never commissioned a marketing research project before and therefore requires some advice from you regarding the selection of an agency to undertake a new project. They have received proposals from a number of agencies already but are uncertain about the next steps.

Write a report which details:

a) The selection criteria to use in appointing the successful agency. (15 marks)

b) The elements of the professional codes of marketing and social research practice that relate to the relationship between researcher and client. (10 marks)

(Total 25 marks)

Question 9

Research process and industry players

Syllabus elements 3.1, 3.2, 3.6

Your organisation is about to embark on its first marketing research project. In preparation, you have been asked to write a report that

a) Outlines the key stages in the marketing research process, identifying the contribution that the organisation can make to the overall success of the project.   (15 marks)

b) Outlines the role of the various players in the marketing research industry.   (10 marks)

(Total 25 marks)

Question 10

Importance of ethics, social responsibility and legislation in research

Syllabus element 3.6

Write a briefing note to be incorporated in the induction material for new recruits to the marketing research department of a large fast-moving consumer goods (FMCG) company that

a) Emphasises the importance of ethics and social responsibility in collecting, holding and using marketing research data.   (15 marks)

b) Outlines the organisation's key legal and regulatory responsibilities with respect to the use of data collected and held by the company.   (10 marks)

(Total 25 marks)

Syllabus element 4
Question 11

Secondary research to provide information for a market entry decision

Syllabus elements 1.1, 3.4, 4.1, 4.2

As a freelance researcher working with a company making industrial and commercial office furniture, you have been asked to undertake a secondary research project to provide information to assist the board of directors who are considering whether to enter the retail home office furniture market. Prepare a report for the managing director that

a) Identifies the key benefits of secondary research and outlines its role in improving the effectiveness of future primary research.   (8 marks)

b) Identifies the key types of information that will be required for the consumer market entry decision, providing examples of possible sources of the information.   (12 marks)

c) Explains how you would make an assessment of the accuracy of the secondary data obtained during the project.   (5 marks)

(Total 25 marks)

Question 12

Questionnaire design

Syllabus element 4.5

Design a questionnaire to meet the research objectives of the project set out for **Colonnade Technologies**. The questionnaire should clearly demonstrate your knowledge of sequencing, question wording and question/response format (the layout and presentation of the question-naire will not be assessed).   (25 marks)

Question 13

Discussion guides and projective techniques (June 2006, Question 3)

Syllabus element 4.5

a) Design a discussion guide for use in a series of group discussions to address the research objectives of the project set out for **SeaLux Cruises**.   (15 marks)

b) Provide a detailed description of *two* projective techniques that could also be used within the group discussions, alongside the discussion guide, to help address the research objectives.
                                                                                    (10 marks)

(Total 25 marks)

Question 14

Observational research techniques

Syllabus element 4.3

As a market researcher specialising in observational techniques, you have been asked to make a presentation at a catering industry conference, attended by managers and owners of fast food restaurants and restaurant chains.

Prepare a set of notes for your presentation, outlining the possible contribution of a range of observational techniques that might be relevant to the delegates. (25 marks)

Question 15

Group discussions and individual depth interviews

Syllabus elements 4.2, 4.4

Group discussions and individual depth interviews are very popular research methods that can be used to identify and understand the in-depth attitudes and motivations of respondents.

Write a letter to a prospective client outlining:

a) The key advantages and disadvantages of these two methods. (12 marks)

b) How the disadvantages of each method may be overcome. (7 marks)

c) How the Internet might facilitate the running of group discussions, identifying any specific disadvantages imposed by this medium. (6 marks)

(Total 25 marks)

Question 16

Marketing research for website development

Syllabus elements 1.1, 1.3, 3.4, 4.1, 4.2, 4.3, 4.4, 4.6

You are a researcher working for an e-commerce company that is planning to launch a website and online store to sell cooking ingredients and spices to home cooks and amateur chefs. A key part of your role is to provide information about customer attitudes and behaviour as well as other relevant information that will assist in the development, launch and ongoing success of the new site.

a) Provide an outline of the types of marketing information that you would need to support all stages of the project from inception to post-launch. (10 marks)

b) Identify a number of research approaches and methods that you might use to provide the relevant insight. For each research method chosen, briefly explain how it might be used and what information it might deliver. (15 marks)

(Total 25 marks)

Question 17

Sampling techniques, sample size and accuracy

Syllabus element 4.6

Your manager has told you that the size of a sample is vitally important in determining the accuracy of results in quantitative research.

Write a report which briefly explains sampling and examines the various ways in which a sample can be developed. Comment specifically on your manager's assertion about the importance of sample size and accuracy in marketing research. (25 marks)

Syllabus element 5
Question 18

Statistical techniques (June 2004, Question 4)

Syllabus element 5.1

The senior executives of **Kelvin Council** have received an interim report on the study outlined in Question 1. They are unclear about some of its contents and have asked you to write a technical appendix to the report clarifying the following:

a) The difference between statistical significance and mathematical significance. (5 marks)

b) The concept of hypothesis testing. (9 marks)

c) The difference between correlation and regression. (5 marks)

d) Cluster analysis and its uses. (6 marks)

(Total 25 marks)

Question 19

Analysing quantitative and qualitative data

Syllabus element 5.1

As the newly appointed marketing executive at **Colonnade Technologies** in Question 1, you have been asked by the managing director to write a report explaining how data collected by the marketing research agency might be analysed prior to being incorporated in the final report. Your report should include the following:

a) An outline of the key approaches that can be used to analyse and tabulate data taken from a number of structured telephone questionnaires. (15 marks)

b) An explanation of two approaches that can be used to analyse transcripts from a number of unstructured depth interviews. (10 marks)

(Total 25 marks)

Question 20

Research reports and presentations

Syllabus elements 5.2, 5.3, 5.4

You are a marketing research project leader and have the task of briefing new research agency staff about the communication of research results to clients. Set out some guidelines for:

a) Structuring and writing marketing research reports. (12 marks)

b) The approach to presenting research that focuses on the specific needs of the audience. (8 marks)

c) Addressing the potential problems that can arise when presenting research in reports and oral presentations. (5 marks)

(Total 25 marks)

PART A SUGGESTED ANSWERS

Mini-Case 1: SeaLux Cruises (June 2006)
Answer 1(a)

Check your answer

A good answer is likely to:

☑

Ask a series of relevant questions to expand the client's background, rationale, research objectives and other requirements ☐

Use the questions to demonstrate your understanding of the marketing information requirements relevant to the particular problems or opportunities identified in the mini-case scenario ☐

Use questions to help you expand upon key information given in the mini-case, especially in relation to the research objectives ☐

Look for the key information gaps and use questions appropriately ☐

Use the section headings of a research brief to frame the answer ☐

Recognise your role as a research executive working at an agency ☐

Use a letter, e-mail or fax format addressed to the client ☐

* * * * *

E-MAIL MESSAGE

To: Jahanfar Danesh

From: Christine Researcher

Date: XX/XX/XX

Subject: Research Proposal – Request for Further Information

Dear Jahanfar

We were pleased to receive a copy of your research brief yesterday.

We are now in the process of preparing our detailed response and to assist us, we would like to ask you some questions relating to your brief as follows:

Background and rationale

1. Can you provide some information about your direct competitors, including target customer base, their advertising approaches and details of the direct/indirect channels they use?

2. Has the company undertaken any previous research that might provide information on market segmentation, target markets, SeaLux brand positioning, products/services? If so, can we have access to this material?

3. Do you have any published market research reports covering the cruise industry? Can these be made available to our team?

4. Can you supply measurement data for your advertising and direct response channels, including details of responses received via web and hotline and information on sales conversion success rates?

5. Can you supply copies of recent press/other advertising for SeaLux cruises?

6. In addition to advertising, what other marketing activity is undertaken to increase sales, attract repeat booking and generate word-of-mouth referrals?

Research objectives

1. In terms of researching advertising effectiveness, do you have specific criteria that you consider important?

2. In addition to your stated objectives regarding attitudes and awareness of SeaLux advertising and marketing channels, do you want us to include research into the target market's current attitudes and perceptions towards the SeaLux brand and its product offering?

3. Do you want us to research the effectiveness of the SeaLux website and telephone hotline in converting enquiries and generating sales?

Methodology

1. Do you have any particular ideas or preferences as regards the approach and research methods to be used in the project?

Sampling

1. Do you maintain a database of leads, prospects and customers? If so, can we have access to this information to enable us to draw up lists of potential respondents?

2. Does the customer database include geo-demographic or lifestyle profile data?

3. Does the typical SeaLux customer match your target segment profile or does it indicate a response from a broader or narrower market segment?

4. Do you want to extend the research outside the 40+ target market to include a wider demographic?

Report and presentation

1. What are your requirements with respect to final report and presentation?

Timescales

1. What is your deadline for completion of the research project?

Thank you for your help in providing information relating to the above, it will help ensure that our proposal meets your needs.

With kind regards,

(Christine Researcher)

Tourism Research Ltd.

Answer 1(b)

Check your answer

A good answer is likely to:

☑

Background summarise the client's background and rationale, does not simply re-write it. Focuses on the key information relevant to the client's problem or opportunity. Provides some additional insight, which adds value for the client and helps sell the agency's expertise with respect to the sector and business context. ☐

Objectives develop specific and accurately worded research objectives to meet the client's research requirement. Expands each of the main objectives to define the precise information required. Includes a mix of qualitative and quantitative objectives. Does not include too many objectives but concentrates on what is essential to the client's decision and avoids including any 'simply nice to know' objectives. ☐

Approach and methodology present the proposed research design/programme in a clear, logical and appropriately justified manner. Includes clear sub-sections for each type of research. Links the proposed research to the research objectives. Includes specific sub-sections to cover data analysis and sampling. Sampling section states and justifies the sampling approach and methods chosen. Sampling includes numbers of respondents for each type of research. Gives brief explanations of what is proposed and why. Does not try to educate client with lengthy tutorials on tools and techniques. ☐

Report and presentation addresses the client's need but reflects budget available. ☐

Timescales and programme states realistic timescales which reflect the workload of the proposed research design. Provides an outline programme (see SeaLux answer). ☐

Fees are stated and within client's budget. Provides a simple fee breakdown and uses realistic costs, linked to quantities. ☐

All sections make reasonable assumptions about the answers that might be received from the client in response to questions posed in Part 1(a) and incorporates this information, where appropriate, in each section of the proposal. ☐

All sections meet the client's requirements and demonstrate a creative and appropriate solution. ☐

Role adopts the role of a research executive working for an agency and uses appropriate language/tone of voice. ☐

Format presents a marketing research proposal document. ☐

Presentation and layout presents professionally with appropriate layout and content. Sells the solution and the agency's expertise. ☐

* * * * *

MARKETING RESEARCH PROPOSAL
CRUISE BOOKINGS RESEARCH PROJECT

Prepared for

SeaLux Cruises

By

Tourism Research Ltd

Date: XX/XX/XX

Contact: Christine Researcher

Tel: 01234 567890

Contents

1 Background

SeaLux is a relatively new cruise company, having been established about one year and with cruise operations in the Mediterranean and the North Sea and the Baltic. The cruises are positioned as 'luxurious discoveries' with cruises starting at £2000 for a 12-day multi-city cruise in the Mediterranean.

The first year has proved relatively successful although SeaLux bookings are running at 35 per cent below target. This is against a background of tremendous growth in the market and high-performing competitors.

The SeaLux business model relies on press advertising in national papers and magazines with direct response and booking via a telephone hotline or a website.

The company targets the 40+ age group and there is a management concern that the direct booking model is incompatible with this group and that there may be a preference to use travel agents who can offer help and advice. The company is also concerned about the overall level of awareness of its advertising and its cruise products.

The cruise market is evolving rapidly, the market having doubled in size over the last decade, and so too have capacity levels with new and larger vessels being built. The typical customer demographic is also changing, with cruises increasingly appealing to a much wider and younger market, reflecting a growth in the number of consumers who enjoy well above average levels of disposable income and who are willing to use this spending power to escape a busy lifestyle and enjoy some luxury and relaxation. This luxury-seeking segment may also be more comfortable with the Internet and therefore more willing to use this direct channel for bookings. Similar behaviour might also apply to an increasing number of 40+ consumers. This mirrors experience in the luxury package holiday market where consumers are now adept at designing and booking their own itineraries using the web. SeaLux, with its direct channel infrastructure, should be in a good position to capitalise on this consumer trend.

2 Objectives

2.1 To evaluate the level of awareness of the SeaLux brand and its cruise offerings, more specifically to:

- o Measure the level of awareness of the SeaLux brand within the luxury cruise passenger market.
- o Measure the level of awareness of the SeaLux cruise ships and destinations within the luxury cruise passenger market.
- o To explore perceptions amongst cruise passengers about the positioning of SeaLux relative to direct competitors.

2.2 To determine the attitudes of the target market towards the use of direct channels for booking cruises, more specifically to:

- o Describe attitudes with respect to the use of websites and e-commerce for making cruise bookings.
- o Describe attitudes with respect to the use of telephone hotlines for making cruise bookings.
- o Test the preference for the use of traditional travel agencies for making cruise bookings.

2.3 To evaluate the effectiveness of the current SeaLux press advertising, website and telephone hotline in generating leads and growing sales, more specifically to:

- o Measure the level of awareness of current SeaLux press advertisements.
- o Explore perceptions of the current advertising with respect to theme, imagery, colour scheme, message appeals, brand and product positioning and calls to action.
- o Explore perceptions among customers and prospects, with respect to the website and telephone hotline.
- o Evaluate the effectiveness of the website and customer hotline in generating sales.

2.4 To develop detailed profiles of existing SeaLux customers and prospects to assist in generating future advertising and direct marketing appeals and themes

3 Approach and methodology

We propose a comprehensive programme of research to meet the research objectives specified in Section 2 above. The research design includes a number of approaches and methods which are explained and justified in the following sub-sections:

3.1 Secondary research

Secondary (desk) research will be undertaken as a means of generating relevant background information and to assist in satisfying a number of the research objectives.

Secondary research provides a highly cost-effective means of generating relevant information for the research project and for further use within the organisation as proposed below.

The findings will also help focus and shape the primary research phase; this can save time and money as well as improve the overall effectiveness of the research project.

3.1.1 Internal records
We will conduct an information audit to identify reports, records and databases that will assist our understanding of the target market and to ascertain information and metrics that will help evaluate the effectiveness of current SeaLux advertising, the website and telephone hotline. We will also analyse complaints forms and customer satisfaction survey results to assist in determining customer attitudes towards SeaLux products and services.

3.1.2 External secondary sources
We will use the web, trade magazines, consumer magazines, newspapers and other materials in the public domain to help build a profile of the market, competitors, products and services. We will identify competitor advertising, publicity and press coverage in travel supplement articles. We will generate a summary of recent competitor activity and make recommendations about possible future advertising and marketing opportunities for SeaLux.

3.1.3 Database customer profiling
Within the scope of our secondary research, we will analyse the data held in the SeaLux customer database and produce segmentation profiles from the information available. We will add geo-demographic and lifestyle data to assist in this process. The availability of this data will prove immensely useful both for the current research requirement and in future marketing campaigns activity.

This activity will furnish information required for research objective 4 and provide the basis for more precise targeting of advertising, direct mail and other marketing and promotional activity. It will also assist SeaLux in fine tuning the marketing mix to meet the needs of target customers.

The profiling exercise should also reveal any evidence of additional segments and sub-segments that can be targeted, leading to additional sales revenues for SeaLux.

3.2 Mystery shopping

In order to fully evaluate the effectiveness of the website and telephone hotline, mystery shopping will be undertaken. The mystery shoppers will be recruited from the target market, trained and briefed by the agency.

The shoppers will take the same journey as a live prospect and will observe the processes and procedures employed to engage the prospect and make a sale. The shopping activity will be carried out under the guidance of a tight brief and resulting observations will be recorded on a questionnaire by each shopper.

The resulting information will enable SeaLux management to identify and make any necessary changes to the channel processes and procedures in order to improve the sales conversion rate.

3.3 Primary qualitative research

We propose to employ a mix of telephone depth interviewing and discussion groups to furnish the qualitative objectives of this project.

3.3.1 Telephone depth interviews

One-to-one depth interviewing by telephone will be utilised to gain more detailed insights into brand perceptions and attitudes towards booking channel preferences. This methodology is cost-effective and overcomes the problems associated with geographic dispersal. Respondents will be chosen from the target market, and 20 interviews will be undertaken in total.

3.3.2 Executive interviewing

One-to-one depth interviews by telephone with executives from the cruise industry, the press, journalists, travel writers and travel agents. This is an important specifiers and referrals market, and so a positive perception amongst these groups is vital. The objective will be to gain an industry perspective on SeaLux, its brand, image, reputation and cruise products. 20 interviews will be undertaken in total.

3.3.3 Discussion groups

The discussion group is a cost-effective method for gaining a detailed understanding of attitudes, motivations, and feelings and as a means to explore new ideas and concepts, including SeaLux advertising copy. In the discussion group sessions we will employ relevant projective techniques to help furnish useful depth information and insight.

Given the widely dispersed nature of SeaLux customers and prospects, discussion groups will be conducted using specialist third party facilities at relatively central locations; Manchester and London are convenient for this purpose. We recommend a total of six groups, three in each location.

The information generated during the qualitative phase will provide valuable insight and also help shape and complement the quantitative research.

3.4 Primary quantitative research

For the quantitative research phase, we propose the use of a questionnaire. In view of the geographic dispersal of respondents, a postal survey will be employed; these will be carefully designed and then sent to a sample of respondents from the target market.

A number of the research objective elements can be effectively addressed using the postal survey questionnaire, including the measurement of awareness of the SeaLux brand and to quantify the attitudes of consumers towards aspects of the SeaLux business model, advertising and booking channels.

Questionnaires are a very effective means of establishing findings that are representative of the total population of interest. Specific questions will be included to test out findings drawn from secondary research and the qualitative research phases.

Please see sampling section for specific details of respondent selection and sample sizes.

3.5 Data analysis

Discussion group and telephone depth interview recordings, along with any associated field notes, will be transcribed into a common textual format that can be analysed using a range of analysis techniques including spider diagrams and thematic tabulations. Video/audio excerpts from interviews and discussion group meetings will also be supplied on DVD for further study by SeaLux management.

Questionnaires will be pre-coded and, following the data collection phase, will be entered into a computer for analysis. Key information findings will be tabulated and/or represented graphically. Descriptive techniques will be used where appropriate to summarise the volume of data, providing averages and information relating to the spread of the data. Other statistical techniques will be used to make comparisons and test hypotheses drawn from the findings. The agency employs a number of statisticians who use SPSS software tools to undertake sophisticated analysis and modelling techniques.

3.6 Sampling

Due to the impossibility of obtaining a complete list of every individual in the target market, we have ruled out the use of probability (random) sampling. Instead, we propose the use of non-probability sampling methods – mainly quota sampling but also some convenience sampling. These techniques will prove accurate enough for the type of research being undertaken and will also allow some flexibility in the way we generate lists of respondents to participate in the various research activities.

Our sample will mirror the characteristics of the target customer. The database profiles we produce will assist us in defining the ideal characteristics of the respondents. We will use members of the SeaLux customer and prospect lists and, where a wider sample is required, as in the case of postal surveys, we will purchase a specialist mailing list matched to our criteria.

3.6.1 Specific sampling techniques

Mystery shopping – We will carefully select and train a number of mystery shoppers who broadly match the profile of the target market. We do not require a large number of shoppers, probably 6–10 in total, to cover the telephone hotline and website.

Discussion groups – Six groups of ten participants will be recruited from the target market. We will select individuals who are located within reasonable travel distance of London or Birmingham. We will use a screening questionnaire and will use a quota-based approach to achieve a balance of male and female, SeaLux customers, prospects and non-customers.

Telephone depth interviews – We will use a quota sample of customers and prospects taken from the database. We will interview 20 individuals in total, interview length approx. 15–20 minutes.

Executive Interviewing – We will use a judgement-based approach to select 20 individuals from the cruise industry, the press, journalists and travel agents. Interview length will be 40 minutes maximum.

Postal survey – We will use a quota-based approach that will include existing customers and prospects as well as non-customers taken from the target market. We will purchase a list from a specialist list broker, focussed on cruise passengers. A very large sample is not required for the research and we recommend that a total of 400 respondents be invited to complete the questionnaire.

The use of incentive gifts will help improve the response rate for the postal survey. Discount vouchers for a SeaLux cruise would be appropriate as this might also some encourage additional bookings in the short term.

4 Reporting and presentation

SeaLux will be provided with a comprehensive written research report which will be supplemented by an oral presentation at the SeaLux offices.

An interim report will also be made available in the form of a PowerPoint presentation to summarise the findings of the secondary research phase and completion of the customer profiling (research objective 4).

5 Timescales and programme

The research project will be completed within 25 weeks, from date of contract award.

An interim report will be provided within two months. An indicative programme is given below.

Week No.	Activity
1	Contract award, initial client project meeting
2–4	Secondary research
3–5	Database profiling and customer segmentation
6–7	Qualitative research design, production of discussion guide
6	Prepare interim presentation
8–10	Qualitative fieldwork
8	Deliver interim presentation
11–14	Quantitative research design and questionnaire preparation
15	Pilot test questionnaires and print production
16–20	Quantitative fieldwork
21–24	Data analysis and report preparation
25	Final report and Presentation

6 Fees

Our fee for the research programme is £62 500+VAT

Fee breakdown	£
Secondary research and database profiling	6 000
Six discussion group sessions @ £5 000 ea	30 000
Mystery shopping of website and hotline	1 500
20 qualitative telephone interviews @ £250 ea	5 000
20 executive telephone interviews @ £300 ea	6 000
400 postal surveys @ £10 ea	4 000
Project management, consultancy, data analysis, reports	10 000

Mini-Case 2: Colonnade Technologies Limited
Answer 1(a)

Check your answer

A good answer is likely to:

☑

Ask a series of relevant questions to expand the client's background, rationale, research objectives and other requirements ☐

Use the questions to demonstrate your understanding of the marketing information requirements relevant to the particular problems or opportunities identified in the mini-case scenario ☐

Use questions to help you expand upon key information given in the mini-case, especially in relation to the research objectives ☐

Look for the key information gaps and use questions appropriately ☐

Use the section headings of a research brief to frame the answer ☐

Recognise your role as a research executive working at an agency ☐

Use a letter, e-mail or fax format addressed to the client ☐

* * * * *

E-MAIL MESSAGE

To: Phil Jones

From: Johnny Researcher

Date: XX/XX/XX

Subject: Research Proposal – Request for Further Information

Dear Phil

We were very pleased to receive a copy of your research brief yesterday.

We are now in the process of preparing our detailed response and to assist us, we would like to ask you some questions relating to your brief as follows:

Background and rationale

1. Can you provide any further information about the ARC market, its size, growth rate, the share held by each competitor and an overview of the industry structure?

2. Can you provide us with a summary of your ARC customers, ideally with an outline of the value/scope of typical contracts?

3. Can you describe a typical prospect's decision-making unit (DMU) and its membership in terms of the roles represented?

4. Can you provide a list of your close competitors, including the new entrants you mentioned in the brief, ideally with an indicative list of their customers if possible?

5. Do you hold any published research reports that might be relevant to this project?

6. Have you ever undertaken similar research in the past? If so, could we have access to this information?

7. Can you outline your sales process and provide any information to help us understand how you prospect for business, retain customers and grow sales?

Research objectives

1. In your brief, you refer to the need for a new marketing strategy for CTL. Can you provide a list of the key information that you will require to make your decisions? For example:

- o Will you require a detailed competitor analysis to be prepared as part of this project?
- o Will you require a detailed market and customer assessment?
- o Will you require information about customer perceptions with respect to your own and your competitors' strengths and weaknesses? What shall we include and to what level of detail?
- o Would you like the research to investigate future market opportunities and threats?

2. Would you like the research to consider only the commercial ARC market, or should we investigate other sectors such as the corporate and public sector control rooms market too?

3. Would you like us to research the market for vehicle and lone worker tracking?

Methodology

1. Do you have any particular view as to how we should approach the research, or any particular methodologies or the mix of qualitative and quantitative information that you would like us to include?

Sampling

1. Is the research to be focused on the UK marketplace or is there a wider remit?

2. How many customers and industry executives do you consider we should include in the research?

3. Do you have a customer database that we could have access to in order to draw up a list of individuals and organisations to contact?

Report and presentation

1. What are your requirements with respect to final report and presentation?

Timescales

1. What is your deadline for completion of the research project?

Thank you for your help in providing responses to the above questions.

With kind regards,

(Johnny Researcher)

Applied IT Researcher Projects Ltd

Answer 1(b)

Check your answer

A good answer is likely to:

                                                                   ☑

Background summarises the client's background and rationale, does not simply re-write ☐
it. Focuses on the key information relevant to the client's problem or opportunity.
Provides some additional insight which adds value for the client and helps sell the
agency's expertise with respect to the sector and business context.

Objectives develops specific and accurately worded research objectives to meet the ☐
client's research requirement. Expands each of the main objectives to define the
precise information required. Includes a mix of qualitative and quantitative objectives.
Does not include too many objectives but concentrates on what is essential to the
client's decision and avoids including any 'simply nice to know' objectives.

Approach and methodology presents the proposed research design/programme in a ☐
clear, logical and appropriately justified manner. Includes clear sub-sections for each
type of research. Links the proposed research to the research objectives. Includes
specific sub-sections to cover data analysis and sampling. Sampling section states and
justifies the sampling approach and methods chosen. Sampling includes numbers of
respondents for each type of research. Gives brief explanations of what is proposed
and why. Does not try to educate client with lengthy tutorials on tools and techniques.

Report and presentation addresses the client's need but reflects budget available. ☐

Timescales and programme states realistic timescales which reflect the workload of the ☐
proposed research design. Provides an outline programme (see SeaLux answer).

Fees are stated and within client's budget. Provides a simple fee breakdown and uses ☐
realistic costs, linked to quantities.

All sections make reasonable assumptions about the answers that might be received ☐
from the client in response to questions posed in Part 1(a) and incorporates this
information, where appropriate, in each section of the proposal.

All sections meet the client's requirements and demonstrate a creative and appropriate ☐
solution.

Role adopts the role of a research executive working for an agency and uses appropriate ☐
language/tone of voice.

Format presents a marketing research proposal document. ☐

Presentation and layout presents professionally with appropriate layout and content. Sells ☐
the solution and the agency's expertise.

*   *   *   *   *

MARKETING RESEARCH PROPOSAL
ALARM RECEIVING CENTRE MARKET

Prepared for

Colonnade Technologies Ltd

By

Applied IT Research Projects Ltd

Date: XX/XX/XX

Contact: Johnny Researcher

Tel: 09876 554321

Contents

1 Background

Colonnade Technologies Limited (CTL) is a software and IT company operating in the high technology, alarm management systems sector, supplying software, equipment and services to the alarm receiving centre (ARC) market. The technology is complex, having many sub-systems and interfaces including CCTV, mapping systems and communications. CTL is the oldest supplier in the industry and has a reputation for innovation, reliability and customer service.

CTL has enjoyed a healthy share of its core market, a good profitability level and only a few competitors. Over the last five years, however, a number of changes have occurred in the market, including significant consolidation within the customer base which has meant fewer but larger customers. More recently, new and aggressive competition has entered CTL's market, undercutting the established players and offering attractive solutions. CTL has lost a number of contracts to these new players, including a number of long-standing customers.

Despite these changes, new opportunities have arisen, including larger systems contracts and the opportunity to offer new products and enhancements to capitalise on the growth in vehicle tracking and lone worker monitoring solutions.

The growing demand for vehicle tracking and lone worker solutions, fuelled by a ready availability of low cost GPS and GSM technology, is a response to recent changes in health and safety legislation. Employers have a responsibility to ensure the safety and security of their staff member at all times, including when they are off-site visiting clients. This involves all employers, but particularly those with field-based staff or employees who work alone – health and social workers, council and local government workers, delivery drivers and others. Parking attendants and community wardens are also at risk.

CTL urgently needs to reposition itself, to develop a defensive competitive strategy and to take advantages of new developments, whilst playing to its inherent strengths in market share leadership, brand heritage, reputation, innovation, technical expertise and customer service.

2 Objectives

Based upon the original brief and your response to our request for additional information, the proposed research project has been designed to satisfy the following research objectives with respect to the UK commercial ARC marketplace:

2.1 Identify market perceptions and attitudes towards CTL and its key competitors, more specifically to:

- Measure the levels of awareness of each company's brand, products and services
- Explore perceptions, attitudes and beliefs about each company in terms of: reputation, expertise, quality, service and support, accessibility, flexibility and price
- Measure satisfaction levels with the customer's current supplier
- Evaluate the perceived attractiveness of each company as a potential supplier for a future new or replacement system
- Identify gaps in each company's current product/service portfolio.

2.2 Identify a number of future market opportunities for CTL in the commercial ARC market, more specifically to:

- Identify current and future levels of spending for monitoring systems, their maintenance and support
- Identify projected system replacement dates and likely budgets
- Identify and prioritise each ARC's consideration set and preferences with respect to possible suppliers for the replacement system.

2.3 Establish the potential opportunities for CTL as a potential supplier of monitoring software and systems for lone worker devices and vehicle tracking equipment; more specifically to:

- Identify the key users of such monitoring systems
- Describe their existing and future purchase behaviour
- Estimate the size of the market and its future growth prospects
- Identify the competitive set and estimate competitor concentration ratios

3 Approach and methodology

In addressing Colonnade's research requirement, Applied IT Research Projects will undertake the following programme of research, commencing with a period of secondary/desk research followed with a programme of primary research involving executive interviewing and a research questionnaire.

3.1 Secondary/desk research

This is an important phase of the research project and will address a number of the research objectives. This low-cost method is invaluable, not only as a means of acquiring relevant information quickly and often at no cost, but also as a means of defining the market and the various buyers and suppliers. The findings from this phase will focus the primary research and may reduce the length of time taken to satisfy the research objectives.

3.1.1 Internal records

The secondary research phase begins with an analysis of certain internal records including exhibition and marketing generated leads and enquiries, field sales contact reports, sales order intake records, tender documentation, contracts won/lost and other information that provides insight into the prospects and customers as well as the year-on-year sales performance of CTL. The internal phase will also look at complaints and customer satisfaction/feedback sheets, plus any feedback captured on customer maintenance visit documentation to help build a picture of evolving customer attitudes and perceptions.

CTL's sales contact management system will also provide relevant information on who the customers are, their behaviour and past purchases in addition to providing valuable contact information that we can use to select respondents for some of the primary research.

3.1.2 External sources

Competitor information will be collected using a range of sources including Companies House, Dun and Bradstreet and Kompass Directory. Information on US-based competitors will be accessed from these latter sources. The Internet will also be used to access competitor and customer websites; this will enable access to relevant competitor news and press releases, client references, case studies and product information.

Market statistics will be accessed, as available, from security industry associations and research report publishers, such as Key Note and others who specialise in B2B market data.

It may be necessary to pay for some of this material and a contingency sum has been added in to the fees section to cater for this requirement (see later).

3.2 Primary research

The primary research phase will comprise three elements:

- o Executive interviewing, using qualitative telephone depth interviews
- o Telephone interviewing using a structured, quantitative questionnaire
- o E-mail survey, using a quantitative, web-based questionnaire.

3.2.1 Qualitative research – executive depth interviews

Telephone depth interviews are a cost-effective technique for geographically dispersed respondents and are particularly suited to business-to-business research since they can provide particularly detailed insight at a realistic cost.

Discussion group meetings have been excluded for reasons of cost and geographic dispersal of respondents.

Interviews will be arranged by prior appointment, will last approximately 30–45 minutes and will aim to capture mainly qualitative information about CTL and its competitors, particularly the awareness, perceptions and attitudes components of objective 1, but encompassing some of the requirements of objective 2. Open-ended questions, use of probing and the application of appropriate oral projective techniques will be employed.

Interviews will be recorded and transcribed for later analysis. Interviews will be conducted by our own team of highly skilled interviewers.

For number of interviews and respondent selection information, please refer to the sampling section of this proposal.

3.2.2 Quantitative research – structured telephone questionnaire

This approach will be used to address components of objectives 2 and 3 where mainly quantitative data is required. We will conduct interviews using a structured questionnaire and utilising the latest computerised computer-aided telephone interviewing (CATI) and call auto-mation equipment. A benefit of this approach is that data input, coding and analysis can be undertaken very quickly. The CATI system is also capable of modifying the question routing order presented during an interview, taking account of previous responses. Again, the approach is chosen as a cost-effective method for primary business research.

The use of traditional postal questionnaires has been discounted due to the likelihood of low response in a business context.

3.2.3 Quantitative research – e-mail survey

This fast and cost-effective approach will be used to obtain quantitative information for objectives 2 and 3 and will complement the telephone depth interviewing.

Respondents will be invited to participate by e-mail message which is then linked to a web-based survey, hosted via third party web servers – we normally use SurveyMonkey.com. E-mail surveys can generate a good response rate, if the invitation is well written and constructed. We also incentivise response with a gift value that decays over time (the sooner you respond, the bigger the reward).

The use of a web-based survey approach provides for both open-ended and closed question techniques, as well as various rating scale approaches. The system provides for survey design, data collection and analysis. As with CATI (see above), a degree of question routing and modification is possible during online questionnaire completion.

3.3 Data collection and analysis

Telephone depth interviews will be recorded, transcribed and then analysed by hand using techniques such a grouping, tabulation by theme, and cut and pasting techniques. Our quali-tative research team will then draw up a schedule of key findings and conclusions that will be used in the compilation of the final report.

CATI interviews and e-mail survey questionnaires will be analysed and basic tabulation and statistics being produced by the survey software. This data will then be further analysed in order to produce the final report.

We employ relevant statistical techniques to help with insightful analysis. For example, in order to analyse and make sense of customer satisfaction scores, we look for relationships between satisfaction level and its related drivers such as responsiveness, product quality and innova-tion. Well-known techniques for this type of analysis include correlation and regression; these techniques can be used to identify a relationship and determine its strength.

3.4 Sampling approach and methods

We will use non-probability sampling approaches for a number of reasons. First, it would be very difficult to draw up a complete list of all customers and prospects in the market to enable us to establish a sampling frame for probability (random) sampling. Second, the total number of respondents available for interview is relatively small, given the niche nature of the ARC market. As long as we include a sufficient number of respondents, we are confident that the accuracy of the findings will be more than sufficient for our purposes.

For the telephone depth interviews, we will use judgement sampling in the main to ensure that we achieve a balance of respondents, representing an appropriate mix of small and large companies. A Snowball sampling technique will also be used to obtain recommendations for further respondents, by asking each respondent being interviewed to make a referral.

For respondent selection for structured telephone interviews, we will use CTL's database in order to draw up a list of ARC operators. We will also identify suitable lists of contacts, similar to those used for direct mailing. Lists of security exhibition attendees and B2B list brokers may be appropriate, although the ARC market is fairly niche and lists may be difficult to obtain.

The above approach will be used for the web survey, although here we will also rely on the CTL customer/prospect database.

For the web survey to research the lone worker/vehicle tracking market, we will compile a list from purchased lists of safety, security and HR managers in mainly medium and large blue-chip companies.

4 Reporting and presentation

The findings and conclusions drawn from the research will be presented in a written report with supporting data and analysis. Our research project manager will also present a summary of the salient facts in an oral presentation to CTL's management team on completion of the project.

5 Timescales and programme

The report and presentation will conclude the research project and will be delivered 12 weeks following contract and provision of agreed client records.

6 Fees

Our fee for undertaking the research programme and presenting the report is £29 500.

Fee Structure	£
Secondary research, including contingency for purchased reports:	6 000
Executive depth interviewing by telephone (50 interviews)	10 000
CATI survey (80 respondents)	8 000
E-mail/web survey (target 200 responses)	1 000
Project management, report and presentation	4 500

Mini-Case 3: Kelvin Council (June 2004)
Answer 1(a)

Check your answer

A good answer is likely to:

☑

Ask a series of relevant questions to expand the client's background, rationale, research objectives and other requirements ☐

Use the questions to demonstrate your understanding of the marketing information requirements relevant to the particular problems or opportunities identified in the mini-case scenario ☐

Use questions to help you expand upon key information given in the mini-case, especially in relation to the research objectives ☐

Look for the key information gaps and use questions appropriately ☐

Use the section headings of a research brief to frame the answer ☐

Recognise your role as a research executive working at an agency ☐

Use a letter, e-mail or fax format addressed to the client ☐

* * * * *

LETTER

Acme Public Sector Research Ltd

17 The Row

Kirkintilloch

KK3 5MP

XX/XX/XXXX

Mr Tony Client

Marketing and Public Relations Manager

Kelvin Council

Kelvin

KE1 2AL

Dear Tony

Re: Research Proposal – Request for Additional Information

We are delighted to confirm our intention to respond positively to your request for a proposal and quotation for the project.

In order that we can prepare a detailed response to meet your requirement, we would like to ask you for some additional information relating to your research brief, as follows:

Background and rationale

1. When did the domestic recycling programme commence within the council area?

2. What are the penalties for failing to meet the 2010 target?

3. Has any similar research, regarding domestic recycling, ever been undertaken on behalf of the council? If so, can we have access to this information?

4. Do you have any data for proportions of materials currently being recycled and the recycling rates within the council area? Can we have access to this?

5. Do you have access to any comparative data or research reports relating to domestic recycling in other councils?

Research objectives

1. With respect to residents' attitudes towards recycling, do you require each recycling material type to be evaluated separately?

2. Can you explain the residential recycling process in more detail? Do you want attitudes to be measured for each stage in this process?

3. What types of financial incentive might the council consider to encourage recycling?

Methodology

1. Does the council have any particular idea or preferences with regard to the types of research that it would like to be included in the project?

2. We might want to undertake some research at recycling centres in car parks and retail outlets. Can you provide addresses for these sites?

Sampling

1. Does the council maintain a complete database of households/residents, possibly including demographic data from a commercial database such as ACORN or MOSAIC? If so, may we have access to this data to draw up lists of respondents for the research?

2. Does the database include any data on current recycling rates for individual households?

3. In terms of geographic coverage for the research, do you wish to include the whole Kelvin council area or focus on the certain settlements and resident demographics?

4. Within each household, who should be included in the research?

Report and presentation

1. What are your requirements with respect to final report and presentation?

Timescales

1. What is your deadline for completion of the research project?

Thank you for your cooperation in anticipation.

Yours sincerely,

(Edwin Researcher)

Acme Public Sector Research Ltd

Answer 1(b)

Check your answer

A good answer is likely to:

☑

Background summarises the client's background and rationale, does not simply re-write ☐
it. Focuses on the key information relevant to the client's problem or opportunity.
Provides some additional insight which adds value for the client and helps sell the
agency's expertise with respect to the sector and business context.

Objectives develop specific and accurately worded research objectives to meet the ☐
client's research requirement. Expands each of the main objectives to define the
precise information required. Includes a mix of qualitative and quantitative objectives.
Does not include too many objectives but concentrates on what is essential to the
client's decision and avoids including any 'simply nice to know' objectives.

Approach and methodology presents the proposed research design/programme in a ☐
clear, logical and appropriately justified manner. Includes clear sub-sections for each
type of research. Links the proposed research to the research objectives. Includes
specific sub-sections to cover data analysis and sampling. Sampling section states and
justifies the sampling approach and methods chosen. Sampling includes numbers of
respondents for each type of research. Gives brief explanations of what is proposed
and why. Does not try to educate client with lengthy tutorials on tools and techniques.

Report and presentation addresses the client's need but reflects budget available. ☐

Timescales and programme states realistic timescales which reflect the workload of the ☐
proposed research design. Provides an outline programme (see SeaLux answer).

Fees are stated and within client's budget. Provides a simple fee breakdown and uses ☐
realistic costs, linked to quantities.

All sections make reasonable assumptions about the answers that might be received ☐
from the client in response to questions posed in Part 1(a) and incorporates this
information, where appropriate, in each section of the proposal.

All sections meet the client's requirements and demonstrate a creative and appropriate ☐
solution.

Role adopts the role of a research executive working for an agency and uses appropriate ☐
language/tone of voice.

Format presents a marketing research proposal document. ☐

Presentation and layout presents professionally with appropriate layout and content. Sells ☐
the solution and the agency's expertise.

* * * * *

MARKETING RESEARCH PROPOSAL
DOMESTIC WASTE RECYCLING

Prepared for

Kelvin Council

By

Acme Public Sector Research Ltd

Date: XX/XX/XX

Contact: Edwin Researcher

Tel: 01234 567890

Contents

1. Background

2. Objectives

3. Approach and Methodology

4. Reporting and Presentation

5. Timescales and Programme

6. Fees

7. Appendices

1 Background

Kelvin Council serves 250 000 people, covering 140 000 households, located in five urban settlements and a number of rural villages and hamlets.

Kelvin Council has a government target for domestic recycling of 20 per cent by 2010. The recycling programme commenced in 2001 but at present it is falling short, achieving only 8 per cent.

Kelvin Council has a number of initiatives to encourage recycling, including public recycling centres and the sale of composting bins for recycling kitchen and garden waste.

If the 2010 target is not achieved, the EU and the UK government will impose severe penalties and landfill taxes. Other councils, in a similar position, are diverting resources from other services in order to address their underperformance.

Although the residents appear reluctant to participate fully, at a more general level, awareness of the need to recycle is increasing among the general public, helped by global concerns about global warming and environmental sustainability. There is also some evidence to suggest that the public differentiates by type of material and this knowledge may help Kelvin Council trigger a change in behaviour.

Kelvin Council has not yet established targets for individual waste materials, nor does it currently collect relevant data at this time, preferring instead to measure at the aggregate level.

To date the Council has not offered any financial incentives to residents but is willing to consider that there may be a role for this alongside a number of other new initiatives.

The Council wants to understand residents' attitudes in detail and to use this information to devise segmented and targeted initiatives, aimed at radically changing recycling behaviour.

2 Objectives

A number of objectives will be satisfied by this research project:

2.1 To establish the current attitudes and behaviour of residents towards domestic waste recycling, more specifically to:

- o Determine the current level of understanding about the need to recycle.
- o Describe current recycling behaviour of individuals/households.
- o Identify households who currently own a composting/recycling bin.
- o Identify the factors that motivate positive recycling behaviour.
- o Identify any perceived barriers to recycling, including those relating to the stages of the current recycling process.

2.2 To identify those items which are currently being recycled by residents, more specifically to:

- o Generate a list of domestic waste materials that are considered easy to recycle.
- o Identify those materials that are perceived as difficult/inconvenient to recycle.

2.3 To identify a list of initiatives that will increase residents' propensity to recycle, more specifically to:

- o Test the assumption that residents would be more willing to recycle if provided with a free recycling material collection bin.
- o Identify and prioritise a list of initiatives, including financial incentives, that would motivate an increase in recycling behaviour.

2.4 To generate resident and household segmentation profiles and prioritise these for further action

3 Approach and methodology

In providing the information required to meet the research objectives, the following research design will be executed. The research programme will use exploratory and descriptive approaches, involving a range of techniques and instruments as described in the following.

3.1 Secondary research

A programme of secondary research will be undertaken as the first stage in the research as this will provide relevant background and address a number of the objectives. An important function of this phase is to shape the overall content of the primary research and to ensure that the subsequent research is undertaken in a cost-effective manner which avoids unnecessary fieldwork or reinvention of information.

3.1.1 Internal secondary sources

This will involve a search for relevant council records and databases to build a clear picture of the council area, population clusters, resident/household addresses and characteristics, including council tax banding and for geo-demographic profiling, based upon postcode districts. This information will be used to provide an initial segmentation of the residents and also to establish a sampling frame (please see sampling section).

3.1.2 External secondary sources

This will involve data collection using relevant government statistics and reports concerning recycling behaviour and success rates in other councils. A search of waste directories, magazines and conference proceedings will be undertaken to identify initiatives that have proved successful elsewhere. The information collected will also help generate appropriate questions for questionnaires and discussions.

In order to complete the geo-demographic profiling, we would like to use the Council's MOSAIC system.

3.2 Primary qualitative research

We propose the use of discussion groups to explore current attitudes and motivations with regard to recycling and to identify a list of possible initiatives to encourage increased recycling. We will also explore the barriers to further recycling. The discussion group is a cost-effective method not only for gaining a detailed understanding of residents' attitudes, motivations and feelings but also to explore ideas. The information generated will also help shape the questions that will be included in the questionnaire (please see quantitative research section).

Given the need to generate initiatives and to persuade residents to change behaviour, the meetings will use appropriate techniques, including projective techniques, to help furnish useful information and insight.

In total, we will conduct four group discussions. Participants will be carefully selected and screened to ensure a representative cross-section of residents (please see sampling section). Our own trained discussion group leaders will moderate the discussions.

In order to keep costs down, we plan to use council rooms in each of the conurbations and our own portable video/recording equipment.

3.3 Primary quantitative research

For the main component of the research programme, we propose to use questionnaires to address the key quantitative objectives.

Questionnaires will be used to conduct short face-to-face interviews at recycling centres. These interviews will identify the positive and negative perceptions of users towards recycling centres including access, convenience and signage.

Postal survey questionnaires will be designed and sent to a sample of residents, taking into account socio-economic and demographic data and to ensure that each of the five major conurbations is adequately represented. In line with your request, rural populations have been excluded from the current research. The postal questionnaires will identify household characteristics, recycling behaviour, reasons for not recycling and so on. Questions will also be incorporated to test findings from the discussion group sessions.

Specific details of respondent selection and sample size are included in the sampling section of this document.

3.4 Data analysis

Discussion group recordings will be transcribed into written scripts that can be analysed using computer software and manual analysis techniques including spider diagrams and thematic tabulations.

Questionnaires will be pre-coded and, after the data collection phase, responses will be entered into a computer for analysis. Key information findings will be tabulated and/or represented graphically. Descriptive techniques will be used where appropriate to summarise the volume of data, providing averages and information relating to the overall spread of the data. Other statistical techniques will be used to make comparisons and test hypotheses drawn from the findings.

We will use cluster analysis to help identify a number of unique resident/household segments and to prepare profiles based upon the variables in the data. This information will assist the council in understanding residents' behaviour and in providing targeted communications and initiatives to motivate adoption, thus increasing the overall level of recycling activity.

3.5 Sampling

3.5.1 Sampling frame
The population of interest is defined as the individual residents and households of the five key conurbations: Bearsden, Milngavie, Kirkintilloch, Torrance and Lennoxtown.

A sampling frame comprising all households from the five towns will be drawn from the council tax database. Kelvin Council is responsible for ensuring that this database is accurate and up to date and contains no duplicates.

3.5.2 Sampling approach/techniques
Discussion groups – quota sampling with screening questionnaire defining recruitment criteria. Recruitment will be undertaken using street approaches in each of the five conurbations. A mixture of recyclers and non-recyclers will be recruited, totalling 32 participants in all (for a total of four sessions).

Face-to-face interviews at recycling centres – street approaches to users on exit from the re-cycling centres. Selection will be quasi-random, based upon every nth user. A total of 150 users will be interviewed in total, taking five recycling centres at random from the group.

Postal survey – simple random sampling will be employed, using a stratified sampling technique that reflects the proportional population of each of the five conurbations. A total of 350 households will be selected in each conurbation (based upon the assumption that each has a similar population of approximately 28 000 households).

4 Reporting and presentation

As requested, the research findings and conclusions will be delivered in the form of a PowerPoint presentation with supporting notes and appendices.

A full written research report will be available, if required, at an additional cost.

5 Timescales and programme

The research programme will be completed 20 weeks from contract award and provision of access to the householder database.

A programme activity chart is provided in an appendix to this proposal.

6 Fees

The Agency fee for the research programme is £24 750+VAT.

Fee breakdown	£
four discussion group sessions @ £2 500 ea	10 000
150 face-to-face interviews @ £20 ea	3 000
1 750 postal surveys @ £5 ea	8 750
Project management, data analysis, presentation	3 000

PART B SUGGESTED ANSWERS

Syllabus Element 1
Answer 1
Information needs of managers and marketing information systems

Check your answer

A good answer is likely to:

☑

In the introduction, explain the importance of information to marketing decisions and ☐
explain what is meant by 'integrated information'. Link to appropriate theory of MIS
or MKIS.

In Part a, introduce the need for a systematic approach and then outline the process ☐
stages used to determine the organisation's marketing information requirements.

In Part b, define the term 'marketing research' and explain the contribution that marketing ☐
research makes to the integrated system. Link to an MKIS model to explain how
internal records, marketing intelligence and marketing research contribute to the total
information provided for decision-makers.

In Part c, list and briefly explain the key benefits of an integrated information system for ☐
marketing managers and other decision–makers.

Adopt the role of a newly appointed marketing manager. ☐

Use report format. ☐

* * * * *

REPORT

To: Managing Director

From: Marketing Manager

Date: XX/XX/XX

Re: Integration of Various Internal Information Sources and Marketing Research

1 Introduction

Marketing decisions are taken at all stages of the marketing planning process and also on a
continuous basis in response to problems and opportunities as they arise. Effective decisions
are vital to the growth and profitability of the organisation and the marketing decision maker
plays a critical role in determining this growth and profitability.

In order to be effective, decision makers need relevant, accurate and up-to-date information taken from a variety of sources, both internal and external. A systematic, managed approach must be taken to ensure the efficient collection, integration, communication and management of this information. A vehicle for such an approach is known as a marketing information system (MKIS).

This report outlines a process that may be used to determine the organisation's marketing information needs. It identifies various internal data sources and lists the key benefits of information integration within an MKIS. The report also considers the importance and contribution of external marketing research as an input to the system.

2 Determining the organisation's marketing information needs

As already stated in the introduction, marketing decisions are taken during the planning process and on an ad hoc basis in response to changes in organisational objectives, customer needs, competitor actions and the wider PESTEL environment.

In order to determine the types of information likely to be required by decision makers and to be held within an MKIS, the following steps are suggested:

2.1 Step 1 – Identify the decisions taken by managers

To assist in identifying and understanding the types of decision taken, a planning process model can be used; for example, Analysis, Planning, Implementation and Control (APIC).

Using APIC, typical decision areas can be identified. Decision areas include the setting of marketing objectives and determining the marketing strategy by identifying which customers to serve and with which products and services and how to position for the organisation relative to competition. The formulation of an appropriate marketing mix is also a major decision area and is fundamental to the success of the chosen strategy.

2.2 Step 2 – Identify the information required for the decisions

The decisions taken will depend upon a thorough analysis of information relating to both internal and external environments. Information requirements are, therefore, extensive, covering all aspects of the operation.

This step will require analysis to determine the precise information required and also to identify the manner in which it will need to be presented to the manager for the decision(s). Involvement of the users of the information is vital in this analysis.

It is important to ensure that information ultimately collected in the system is 'relevant and of sufficient scope for the decisions to be taken' (Wilson, 2003). The information requirements will change over time; this needs to be recognised and managed on an ongoing basis and may require specific marketing research projects to be conducted.

2.3 Step 3 – Undertake an information audit

This involves a thorough search for the information identified during the execution of Step 2 above, starting with the existing marketing and corporate databases and also examining records held within each department of the organisation, recognising that much information, collected for a different purpose within a department, for example finance, can be utilised for marketing decisions.

Relevant internal information would include customer complaints, call centre records, service job sheets, production and material cost records, quality data, accounts receivable, sales quotation data, order processing records, sales expenses and so on.

Information identified during the information audit will often need translating (standardising) for use outside the source department in order to remove or convert technical jargon that would not be understood by marketing and other managers.

2.4 Step 4 – Undertake an information gap analysis

This involves identifying the additional information required for decision-making that is not available internally. Once a list has been identified, a strategy must be developed which provides the information, thus closing the gap.

2.5 Step 5 – Design a strategy to fill the information gap

Typically, marketing intelligence gathering and marketing research can be used to fill the information gaps identified during the audit.

Marketing intelligence includes everyday information gathered during the normal course of business and might include tacit information learned by sales and service personnel in the field. It also results from reading industry and trade journals.

Marketing research is a more formal undertaking, requiring carefully defined research or information objectives and involving both desk and field research. Please refer to Section 3 below for further information on the contribution of marketing research.

3 The contribution of marketing research to the system

Much of the information routinely collected by the organisation is based upon past events: customer transactions, enquiries and data captured on customer-completed forms. Wilson (2003) refers to these types of information as 'transactional' and 'volunteered'. Such information tells us little about what is happening in the market as a whole, about non-customers or our competitors and their customers. Also, although we collect information concerning own customer's behaviour (what they buy, when, where...), we know little about their attitudes, their motivations (why), lifestyles and future intentions. Marketing research can contribute to the MKIS by filling some of these gaps.

The Market Research Society, in its definition of marketing research, refers to 'the collection and analysis of data from a sample of individuals or organisations relating to their characteristics, behaviour, attitudes, opinions or possessions'.

Research might include information collected during regular customer satisfaction surveys and regular mystery shopping exercises as well as more specific research projects to provide information for new product development, market entry or diversification.

Profile data, for example from the ACORN or MOSAIC geo-demographic databases, can be purchased to help build detailed profiles of customers and prospects to assist in defining segments and in targeting products and marketing communications.

Marketing research can, therefore, provide more detailed insights for users of the MKIS. This should lead to better informed decisions, especially in the areas of new product development, market selection, segmentation and targeting, as well as specific marketing mix combinations, distribution channel selection and so on.

4 Key benefits of an integrated information system

An integrated approach to information collection, analysis and dissemination will require the dedication of resources on an ongoing basis and it will be important to manage the system proactively. As a result of such investment, we should enjoy a number of key benefits:

1. Decision makers will have access to up-to-date and relevant information presented in a timely manner. Decision support tools and reporting mechanisms will also be available within the system. This should improve decision quality and enable greater responsiveness to problems and opportunities as they arise.

2. The more complete nature of the information will assist in assessing and managing risk and ensure that a wider range of factors are considered when assessing opportunities.

3. Managers will be able to identify trends and should be better positioned to identify opportunities or anticipate changes in markets, customer preferences of competitor strategies.

4. Access to a broader range of company-wide internal data and external information will make it easier to accurately identify our most profitable customers/segments (cost to serve and lifetime value) as well as the products that are most profitable for us. This should help focus our decisions on longer-term profitability.

5. The participation of people from different parts of the organisation, in feeding information into the system (and also benefiting from it), should assist us in further developing the degree of market orientation within the organisation.

5 Concluding remarks

The task of combining various sources of internal and external information into an integrated system – involving internal records, marketing intelligence and marketing research – will require a systematic approach, careful management and the cooperation and contribution of people from all departments.

The key to the success of such a project is to follow a systematic process for the specification of the information needs, to adequately identify the information gaps and then design a system incorporating people, processes and IT that will deliver against this requirement in a cost-effective manner.

The potential benefits are considerable, involving better decisions which are not only linked to competitive advantage and profitability, but also lead to improvements in cross-functional working and greater market orientation.

Answer 2
Information and research for decision-making

Check your answer

A good answer is likely to:

☑

In the introduction, explain the importance and context of an audit of marketing operations ☐
as part of a wider marketing audit.

In Part a, outline the types of information required for an audit of marketing operations, ☐
including customers and markets and each of the marketing mix elements. Include
information on internal and external sources of the information

In Part b, define what is meant by a 'user specification for information' and then introduce ☐
and briefly explain the content of each element.

In Part c, list the assessment criteria and link to information acquisition costs ☐
and the benefits accrued. Strong answers will discuss possible difficulties in making
an assessment.

Adopt the role of a marketing manager. ☐

Use report format. ☐

* * * * *

REPORT

To: Managing Director

From: Marketing Manager

Date: XX/XX/XX

Re: Information for Auditing Marketing Operations

1 Introduction

An audit of marketing operations is a part of an overall marketing audit which is defined as a
thorough 'examination of the marketing function including its environment, objectives, strategies
and activities with a view to determining problems and opportunities and recommending a plan of
action to improve the organisation's marketing performance' (Kotler and Armstrong, 2006).

The focus of this report is the marketing activities or operations element of the audit which is
concerned with a comprehensive, systematic and periodic examination of the organisation's
markets, customers and marketing mix.

The aim of the audit will be to determine the current level of marketing performance and to identify opportunities for improvement in order to meet marketing, and hence corporate, objectives.

2 Information requirements

2.1 Markets and customers

Information requirements include market size, growth, share, stage of maturity, profitability, products and competitors in the market, customer attitudes and buying behaviour, distribution channel approaches and preferences and marketing strategies employed by ourselves and the competition.

2.2 Products

Information requirements include analysis of the contribution of existing products in the portfolio, their costs, contribution, lifecycle stage, share and rate of growth. Other information would include customer needs and satisfaction levels and attitudes towards products with a view to undertaking a gap analysis. An important additional area of the audit would examine the success of the new product development process, contribution of new products and innovation rate.

2.3 Pricing

Information requirements include information on our profit objectives, product costs, breakeven volumes, cost/price/volume to determine price levels and demand and competitor pricing and strategies. We also need to understand customer attitudes with respect to price, their budgets and expectations. Another information area affecting price involves an understanding of costs and margins associated with the distribution channels we use.

2.4 Advertising and promotion

Information requirements include advertising and promotional objectives, our performance levels, details of advertising and promotional budgets and expenditure, results and effectiveness of campaigns, awareness levels, brand attitude and reputation, share of voice, customer perceptions concerning advertising messages, language used, analysis of the responsiveness of target segments, geographic and demographic profiling, as well as analysis of particular media channels used.

2.5 Personal selling

Information requirements include details of sales objectives and salesforce targets, details of geographic and vertical sales territories in terms of size, volume, growth rates and profitability, the effectiveness of sales processes, procedures and management and the efficiency of sales personnel (sales to expenses ratios, lead conversion rates, incentive payments and compensation levels). We would also need to determine whether the salesforce is adequately sized and resourced to meet the objectives.

2.6 Distribution channels

Information requirements include details of the distribution objectives, choices and strategy, effectiveness of the various channels and channel members, extent of coverage/penetration, details of competitor channel choices and their effectiveness, details of channel costs and margins, alternatives available but not used.

3 Data sources

Much of the information required to undertake the marketing operations audit will already be available internally, although it should be borne in mind that there may be information gaps, omissions and inconsistencies in certain areas. Within the audit, there is an opportunity to examine information quality and coverage and to flag these for improvement after the audit has been completed.

3.1 Internal sources

Information can be obtained from a wide range of internal sources, including sales records, marketing campaigns data, marketing department databases, sales forecasts and monthly reports, financial accounts data, production and operations data, service records and company annual reports.

3.2 External sources

Other information can be obtained from external sources; for example, published market research reports, business directories, marketing intelligence, trade/industry journals, the Internet, records of discussions with customers, suppliers, competitors, industry experts and primary research previously undertaken for the organisation and now held internally.

The information search will be greatly simplified where the relevant data from various sources has been previously brought together to form a marketing information system (MKIS).

4 Key elements of a user specification for information

A user specification for information provides the key ingredients for a marketing research brief, sharing a number of similar elements, but it is also used to define the information requirements for any decision-making process within the organisation.

The key elements of the user specification are as follows:

- ○ Rationale – explains the reasons why the information is required, the problem or opportunity to be addressed and what the information users will do, and what decisions they will make using the information produced.
- ○ Objectives – sets out the precise information that will be required, specifying each information target and any associated processing, for example:

Prioritise (associated processing) the criteria used (information target) by customers when choosing a mobile telephone.

An important consideration when writing objectives is that each objective incurs a cost – specifiers should therefore omit 'nice to know' questions and focus on the rationale and the decisions to be taken.

- o Methodology – provides an outline of the scale of the project, whether primary research might be required and an indication of possible data collection (research) methods. Sampling approach and customer segments to be researched would also normally be included.
- o Budget – specified in terms of human resource time (internal provider) and expenditure (agency). When setting a budget, it is necessary to consider the benefits to be gained as well as what is affordable.
- o Timescale – specifies when the information will be required, taking into account any lead time that might be required, perhaps for a product launch decision and plan.
- o Information Reporting – specifies how the information is to be delivered, be it a written report, presentation, spreadsheets, charts or others.

5 Criteria for assessing the value of information

A number of criteria can be considered when attempting to assess the value of the information provided in response to a user specification for information. Such criteria would include answers to the following:

- o Is the information relevant to the manager's needs and the decisions to be made?
- o Is it delivered in good time for the decisions to be made?
- o Is the information accurate or, at least, stated to a defined level of accuracy?
- o Is the information up to date?
- o Is it complete – does it meet the user specification provided?
- o Does the information help reduce risk?
- o Does the information have a value beyond the current decision(s)?
- o Do the benefits arising from the decisions outweigh the costs incurred in collecting the information – does it help us make money or save money?

5.1 Potential difficulties

Taking the last point in particular, the value of information is often difficult to fully assess, since a decision made without access to the information might still have led to similar or greater benefits for the organisation. Alternatively, the information might be totally ignored by the decision maker in favour of 'gut feel' or past experience but lead to similar or superior benefits being enjoyed.

Finally, there is an opportunity cost which might be considered. Could the resources used in obtaining the information have been better applied elsewhere? To minimise the risks and cost, it is important that the user specification is prepared with the full cooperation and agreement of the users and that non-essential or 'nice to know' questions are not included.

**Answer 3
Knowledge management**

Check your answer

A good answer is likely to:

☑

In the introduction, state the purpose of the presentation and then introduce the need to ☐
manage knowledge as an asset.

In Part a, define knowledge management and related terms. Introduce and explain the ☐
key concepts, the process and potential benefits for the chosen organisation, providing
examples set in context.

In Part b, cite typical reasons for KM failure, introduce the key barriers to implementation and ☐
demonstrate how these can be overcome. Stronger answers will take a cross-functional
and market-oriented approach in presenting both the barriers and the solutions.

Adopt the role of the marketing manager. ☐

Use Presentation Notes format. ☐

* * * * *

PRESENTATION NOTES

Presentation to Management Team – Metal Projects Limited

Date: XX/XX/XX

Knowledge Management (KM)

Welcome

Slide 1 – Agenda

- ○ Purpose
- ○ Introduction
- ○ Definitions
- ○ Concepts
- ○ Benefits
- ○ Barriers
- ○ Overcoming the barriers

Slide 2 – Purpose

The purpose of this presentation is to introduce the key concepts of knowledge management
(KM) and to promote a future discussion about the appropriateness of a KM strategy for the
Company as a route to competitive advantage, innovation and growth.

Slide 3 – Introduction

We are said to be living in the information age – an age in which the competitive environment is driven more by the application of superior knowledge and competences and less by the traditional industrial inputs such as buildings, manual labour and capital.

Here at Metal Projects, we create value for our customers, not directly through manufacturing but by the careful way in which we solve manufacturing and construction problems for our customers – our engineers apply superior knowledge every day!

An immediate benefit of KM would be the pooling of solutions by means of a solutions database and then to make these solutions available via an Intranet as a resource to all of our engineers who may be faced with similar problems – continual reinvention of the wheel is wasteful and we know this goes on in Metal Projects. Over time, these solutions would be continually improved and refined and become of greater value to the business.

A sustainable competitive advantage can be developed through the sharing and development of this superior knowledge; we may then use this knowledge to create further unique value for customers with a resulting increase in profitability.

Knowledge is a driver of innovation. Everyone in this meeting recognises the vital importance of innovation to our projects and to our continued market leadership.

Slide 4 – Definitions

Slide 4.1 – A formal definition

'Organisational knowledge is the collective and shared experience accumulated through systems, routines and activities of sharing across the organisation' (Johnson et al. 2005).

Knowledge is naturally accumulated in organisations. The J & S definition suggests that there is a need for systems, routines and activities for sharing the knowledge throughout the organisation. A level of knowledge sharing goes on in every business but, if left purely to chance, it will never be perfected and considerable value will be lost. Like any other organisational asset, knowledge needs to be systematically managed and developed over time.

Slide 4.2 – Another definition

'The leveraging of collective wisdom to increase responsiveness and innovation' (Delphi Consulting Group website).

This less formal definition really captures the essence of what we should be trying to achieve!

Slide 5 – Concepts

KM is concerned with proactively capturing, creating, sharing and using organisational knowledge throughout the business and beyond, into the supply chain.

Unless it is managed and developed, organisational knowledge can become 'lost', either in the mountains of data held in various departmental information bases (called explicit knowledge) or exported to competitors, carried in the minds (individual and tacit knowledge) of employees who eventually leave the Company.

KM requires the integration of various information systems within the Company as well as an effective means of capturing and documenting tacit knowledge, encouraging its transfer between individuals, departments and other stakeholders.

KM is concerned not just about existing knowledge but also about the creation of new knowledge, which, in turn, is further developed over time and applied to new problems as they are presented.

Slide 5.1 – The KM implementation process

Step 1 – Identify where knowledge resides

Step 2 – Develop processes, procedures and systems for KM

Step 3 – Use the systems to capture, document and add value to knowledge

Step 4 – Share and continually build onto existing knowledge

The process of developing a KM strategy involves the above steps; it is a continuous and long-term process as suggested by Step 4.

Slide 6 – The benefits of KM

- o   Brings organisational knowledge into an integrated system which is readily accessible
- o   Captures and shares individual/tacit knowledge, enabling transfer of 'know-how'
- o   Enables knowledge to be developed as an appreciating asset
- o   Enables existing knowledge to be re-used and improved upon
- o   Knowledge becomes a basis for innovation and competitive advantage
- o   Organisational learning (and individual learning) is greatly enhanced.

A number of the benefits of KM have already been suggested during this presentation. The key benefits of KM are summarised in Slide 6.

Slide 7 – Barriers

Despite the cited benefits of KM, many organisations that have attempted to introduce it have failed to accrue any major benefits; projects have taken longer than anticipated and the IT systems have been hampered with problems.

Reports of such problems in the management and technical press are naturally a concern, but there are also many success stories demonstrating how organisations have harnessed knowledge across the organisation and gained a competitive advantage.

So, what are the key barriers to the implementation of KM?

Slide 7.1 – Key barriers

Barriers arise from the following:

- o People
- o Processes
- o Technology

Slide 7.2 – People

Many of the failures or poor performances in KM arise because the people, at all levels, have not been fully considered and engaged in the knowledge management process.

Buy-in has often been poor and often there is a failure to recognise the cultural barrier that may exist.

Culture – people often believe that holding on to their knowledge makes them more valuable; remuneration schemes usually reinforce this thinking. Senior managers sometimes believe that they will lose control of the organisation; some feel insecure in having to share their own knowledge and by having to become more open and less secretive.

A lack of inter-departmental cooperation is the enemy of KM projects. Power and politics often dominate, rather than an emphasis on a common goal – serving the market.

Resistance to change and uncertainty about the future are normal reactions and need to be overcome.

Skills gap – Managers may view KM as a difficult, costly and time-consuming exercise, involving complex IT systems. At the same time, they fail to recognise the need to fully engage their people, who, after all, must contribute their own knowledge to the system and then use the knowledge pool to add value to their work. In short, lack of expertise and inexperience can make it very difficult to know where to start. Little importance is accorded to staff training.

Slide 7.3 – Processes

Objectives or outcomes from the project may be poorly defined with no clear strategy for implementation.

Timescales – Managers often see KM as a quick win/fix-all recipe and they fail to realise that it is a long-term process.

Budgets are often set without looking at the accruable long-term benefits and without recognising the need for investment in training and internal marketing to assist in bridging the skills gap and helping sell the benefits to ensure buy-in.

Ownership – KM is often not owned by any individual manager with the responsibility to make it happen. KM needs a high priority within the organisation if it is to succeed and this requires proactive management.

Systems, processes and procedures are not always fully aligned to ensure that KM and organisational learning are fully integrated within the organisation's activities.

Slide 7.4 – Technology

Information Technology is so often the main emphasis in a KM project, that other important aspects, such as integration of business processes and the need for a change of mindset, staff training and positive culture are often overlooked.

A Lack of Integration of information, systems and people within the organisation often results in a failure of KM to deliver the benefits it is capable of.

Slide 8 – Overcoming the barriers

If the potential problems outlined above are to be overcome, then a proactive, long-term approach must be taken to a KM project.

Slide 8.1 – A KM success checklist

Here is a list of the key factors that will need to be in place if we are to be successful in KM:

- o Total commitment top–down
- o Recognition of the true value of knowledge
- o Long-term perspective of the project
- o A senior manager appointed as sponsor
- o KM viewed as an integrated business process
- o A positive culture for learning and working together
- o Reward scheme aligned to creating and sharing knowledge
- o IT seen as the <u>enabler</u>, <u>not</u> the goal

Slide 9 – Any questions?

I will happily try to answer any questions that you may have.

Can we agree a further discussion with a view to developing a number of objectives and a strategy for developing KM within Metal Projects?

Syllabus Element 2
Answer 4
Database information, its benefits and ethical Issues

Check your answer

A good answer is likely to:

 ☑

In the introduction, introduce the concept of a customer database and outline the key ☐ benefits for the marketing department and for SeaLux in terms of growing sales and building loyalty.

In Part a, introduce and explain the key types of information held in the database. ☐

Use an appropriate framework (e.g. Alan Wilson's 'four types of information') for the ☐ answer.

In Part b, list and briefly explain the key benefits of a customer database in terms of what ☐ it can be used to accomplish.

In Part c, explain why data from the research might be merged with information in the ☐ database. Highlight and explain the ethical and legal implications with reference to the professional codes and relevant legislation.

Use examples set in the context to support the information presented in the report. ☐

Adopt the role of a newly appointed marketing executive at SeaLux. ☐

Use Report format. ☐

*   *   *   *   *

REPORT

To: Marketing Manager – SeaLux Cruises

From: Database Marketing Executive

Date: XX/XX/XX

Re: Customer Database Development for Enhanced Customer Insight

1 Introduction

A customer database has the capability to be a huge asset to the Company and an incredible marketing tool. Before we can fully benefit though, we will need to bring together various sources of information and then enhance these by extending the types of information we collect about our customers in terms of their behaviour, attitudes, opinions, preferences and lifestyles.

The resulting database will greatly assist us in creating targeted marketing campaigns that grow sales in the short term to enable us to meet our targets and, for the longer term, help in identifying, anticipating and meeting customer needs, as well as identifying new customers.

Superior customer insight is a source of competitive advantage and, in an industry such as ours, which is enjoying tremendous growth, the more we know about our cruise customers, the more likely we will be able to retain them as 'loyal stayers'. This will be vital as we see more new competitors enter the marketplace at all levels (e.g. easyCruise).

2 Purpose of report

Currently, little has been formally collected about our customers, beyond the very basics of who they are and what they spend with SeaLux. This report describes how a customer database can be developed and enhanced, the approaches we can use to collect the data and the potential benefits we might enjoy. The report also includes an outline of the legal and ethical implications of collecting and using customer data.

3 Types of customer information and the approaches used to collect it

Alan Wilson (2003) describes four types of information that can be used to build a customer database: behavioural data, volunteered data, profile data and attributed data:

3.1 Behavioural data

This relates to the various transactions that our customers engage in and which we record in bookings, accounting records and operational files. This information helps build a picture of customer buying behaviour but, at SeaLux, it is currently very limited.

In terms of how we extend the range of behavioural data, we need to focus on all interactions with the customer or prospect. At SeaLux, this would include visitor behaviour on the website, via the call centre and with each customer interaction/transaction with the Company.

A good example would be to record the various activities and services that each cruise passenger partakes of during each voyage. This might be achieved electronically, using a loyalty card. We could then use this information not only to gauge the popularity of each service, but also to build a profile of each customer's preferences.

3.2 Volunteered data

This describes the information provided by customers using our web-based enquiry and booking forms and in telephone conversations that take place in our hotline call centre. At present, we have name and address data, but we can extend this significantly, with both the website and the call centre providing an opportunity to capture data relating to customer characteristics, opinions and preferences.

Using behavioural data and volunteered data together, in the customer database, we can build a reasonable picture of what, when and how our customers buy from us and also have some understanding of why they buy, based upon information that we ask them to volunteer.

3.3 Profile data

Profile data takes our insights even further by linking our database with information taken from an external geo-demographic or lifestyle database. Using this bought-in database of common characteristics, we can make inferences about our customers that we can later test and use to build a more detailed understanding of who the customers are and what motivates them. We would also have a better understanding of their income levels, interests and recreational activities which we can link directly to new service development.

A number of commercially available consumer profiling products can be purchased, for example ACORN or MOSAIC. These products provide information on age, geographic location, income level and profession. The use of a specific lifestyle database would also prove useful in being able to help us predict behaviour regarding influences on lifestyle decisions such as luxury cruise holidays.

3.4 Attributed data

This is data that we 'merge in' to the database, based upon findings and conclusions derived from marketing research projects such as the one we are about to initiate. It would also include research we undertake internally, including the customer satisfaction surveys undertaken at the end of each cruise.

Although we cannot add respondent information directly to the individual's record for ethical reasons (please see Section 5), we can make inferences in the database, which we can then test using targeted direct mail and other marketing activities.

By way of an example, we might find that married couples aged 50+ and with a joint income of more than £40 000 are more likely to purchase a luxury cruise, based upon editorial recommendations given in the weekend travel supplements of national newspapers.

We might use this insight to focus our PR activity and to send article reprints about SeaLux to existing customers who meet the age/income profile.

Our ability to use marketing research data will depend very much on the quality and detail of the research findings and conclusions presented in research reports.

4 Potential benefits

In order to benefit from the types of data described above, we will need to develop a customer database and dedicate sufficient resources to its ongoing maintenance and enhancement. Possible benefits might include the following:

- o An ability to develop a greater understanding of customer needs, giving us an opportunity to develop services and marketing mixes that meet their requirements more precisely.
- o An ability to improve our customer service level, by using our database knowledge to develop the sales and support channels that customers want to use.
- o An ability to personalise and more precisely target our marketing communications activity by incorporating offers/messages that meet the recipients' needs, resulting in less wastage and better sales response rates.
- o An ability to personalise/customise the service we provide to customers, by using behavioural and preference data to pre-empt their requirements and requests.

All of the above will greatly assist in building loyalty and repeat sales.

We can use campaign data to monitor and measure the effectiveness of our marketing activity, especially any direct marketing campaigns, as well as the effectiveness of our distribution channels. Based upon this knowledge, we will be able to spend marketing budgets more effectively.

5 Ethical considerations

Marketing research relies on the trust, goodwill, continued understanding and cooperation of respondents who willingly participate in research projects by providing information. Respondents are more likely to provide honest, truthful answers if they believe that the information they give will be held in confidence, that their identity will not be disclosed and that their research information will not be used for sales approaches and direct marketing campaigns.

As well as being a matter of ethics, it is also about being professional. The Market Research Society (MRS) binds its members to a code of professional conduct, which is designed to ensure that standards of professionalism are maintained throughout the industry.

The MRS Code of Conduct (MRS, 2005) requires that 'the anonymity of the respondent must be preserved unless they have given consent for their details to be revealed or attributable comments to be passed on'. This implies that comments made by customers in the course of research cannot be attributed to an individual's database record, unless they have given express consent.

In addition, the MRS provides specific guidelines for what it terms 'mixed purpose projects' involving research and sales/marketing activity. In relation to this, the MRS has a number of mandates including:

- The purpose for which the data will be used must be explained to the respondent.
- Respondents must not be misled about how their data will be used.

UK data protection legislation also impacts on the use of such data collection, since living individuals can be identified from the records made. Although the legislation is too involved to be fully explored in this report, it is important to remember two aspects that would apply:

- Individuals should have a clear and unambiguous explanation of why the data is being collected and to what purpose it will be put.
- Individuals must give their consent to it being collected and be given the choice to opt out of any subsequent use to which the data may be put.

In theory, the above implies that we can use the information provided by respondents in our customer satisfaction surveys directly for sales or marketing purposes, provided that this usage was made explicit in the survey form, that we did not mislead the respondent in any way and that individual respondents did not opt out of subsequent mailings. In practice, using research in this way might serve to reduce the number of survey responses we actually receive and it might impact on the quality of response and degree of honesty with which such feedback is given.

The information given in our satisfaction survey forms is best used solely for the purpose of gauging the performance and quality of our operation and for identifying opportunities to improve our services.

We could certainly provide another form for passengers to use if they would like us to contact them regarding future cruises. On this form we could elicit information that the passenger would like us to consider in designing future communications.

6 Concluding remarks

Without doubt, the creation of a dedicated customer database, holding data collected from a number of sources and using additional information volunteered by customers, as well as the extrapolation of purchased profile and marketing research data, would be of significant benefit to the organisation, enabling closer, more insightful relationships to be built with customers, fostering repeat purchasing and loyalty. The database would help in increasing sales, meeting targets and building a competitive advantage for SeaLux Cruises.

Answer 5
Database development and enhancement

Check your answer

A good answer is likely to:

☑

In the introduction, define what is meant by a customer database and briefly outline its content and key benefits. ☐

In Part a, explain the process for setting up the database and how to maintain it, with particular emphasis on data entry, validation, verification and de-duplication. ☐

In Part b, identify the sources and types of data to be collected and explain how the data will be captured. Identify key weaknesses of a customer database, focusing on information gaps and limitations. ☐

In Part c, define what is meant by geo-demographic and lifestyle profiling; explain briefly the process and tools used. State and then explain the benefits of profiling. ☐

Use examples set in the context of a national laundry and dry cleaning chain. ☐

Adopt the role of a newly appointed marketing executive. ☐

Use Report format. ☐

*   *   *   *   *

REPORT

To: Sales and Commercial Director

From: Marketing Executive

Date: XX/XX/XX

Re: Customer Database Development for Apex (Dry Cleaning and Laundry Services) plc.

1 Introduction

A customer database is simply a collection of inter-related records, containing information about who our customers are and what, when and where they buy. If carefully constructed and developed, such a database can also provide deeper, richer information about customer attitudes, behaviour and lifestyles.

A customer database is an asset that provides the basis for understanding customer purchasing patterns, improving communications through personalisation and improving customer service – it is also a recognised aid to loyalty and retention initiatives. In addition, we can use tools to manipulate, mine and analyse the data for marketing intelligence and sales forecasting purposes. Such a database can also support our need to measure the effectiveness of sales promotions and other direct marketing activities.

This report briefly outlines the process for setting up a database, the logistics of collecting the data and the possible weaknesses that might exist in a customer database. It also considers the possible benefits of using geo-demographic and lifestyle data to enhance the database.

2 Database storage and processing

When building a customer database, it is important to ensure that the information is entered into the system using tried and tested data capture techniques and that processes and procedures for the use and upkeep of the database are fully documented and the users adequately trained. All activity associated with data entry, editing and deletion needs to be consistent, as any lapses will increase the likelihood for errors, duplication or inadvertent corruption or deletion of information.

A number of points are important:

- o The database should be built using proven and easily supported database software. Our IT department will be able to advise as to what might be appropriate, bearing in mind the need for a high degree of compatibility with other existing systems within the Company.
- o A database administrator should be appointed who will assume responsibility for the upkeep of the database and ensure that users observe the procedures.
- o The data should be correctly formatted, based upon a set of defined conventions, taking into account number of characters for each field, use of upper/lower case and so on. The software can be written to enforce these rules during data entry either by automatically converting the input or by advising the user or system administrator of any violations that cannot automatically be corrected.
- o Each database record will need to be thoroughly checked to ensure that it is complete and accurate. Addresses need to be checked, ideally during entry, for correctness, perhaps with the help of a commercial postcode address file validation product such as Experian's QAS system. The use of pick lists on data entry forms and online reference tables can greatly assist in ensuring that data entries are valid. Again, software can be written to assist with this record validation stage.
- o The database must be regularly checked for duplicate records, using pre-defined rules for merging and/or deletion of duplicates. We will also need to consider whether to allow some duplicates to exist (called underkill) or to be particularly onerous and apply overkill. Dealing correctly with duplicate records is particularly important for direct-mail activity, since it can adversely affect perceptions of the Company, be detrimental to our reputation and erode customer loyalty.

3 The logistics of data collection

Most of the data we can easily capture for our database will consist of name, address, contact telephone number and details of individual items each customer leaves with their home branch for cleaning, along with the dates and the amount spent on each occasion. This basic transactional data can be captured in electronic tills installed at each branch. This data is sometimes called behavioural data since it describes what, when, where and how much a customer has spent.

In our business, we have only a very limited opportunity to capture additional data from customers as generally they spend very little time interacting with us, are often in a hurry to drop off or collect and it can, therefore, be very difficult to get them to volunteer information, beyond name, address and telephone number, plus their preference day(s) and times for picking up their cleaned items.

The introduction of a loyalty card scheme, with incentives based upon repeat purchase behaviour and amount spent, would provide us with an opportunity to collect further information from those customers who join the scheme. This volunteered data would supplement the behavioural data and assist our understanding of 'why', since we can include questions on the application form that will help us understand member attitudes, opinions and lifestyles.

We can collect further information on an ongoing basis as we begin to use the database for direct marketing and customer communications activities.

4 Possible weaknesses of the database

A customer database only provides a limited view of the marketplace in which we operate. This limited view reflects a number of problems or weaknesses in the data:

- o The information relates to current and lapsed customers but not to non-customers or customers that purchase from our competitors.
- o The database does not provide any insight into purchasing that our customers might choose to do with our competitors.
- o The data tells us what, when and in which branch our customers transact with us, but not why.
- o The data is historical and, although we can use it as a forecasting aid, it does not have any real predictive power regarding a customer's future intent to use our service.

5 Potential benefits of geo-demographic and lifestyle data

A geo-demographic or lifestyle profile describes a number of attributes shared by 'typical individuals' living in a geographically defined residential neighbourhood or grouped set of postcodes. The whole of the UK is divided into a number of profile groups and subgroups of residential neighbourhoods and the resulting information is provided commercially in the form of a database that can be used to assist with market segmentation studies and target marketing. Two popular profiling systems in current use are ACORN and MOSAIC.

Profile data, taken from one of the above sources can be used to enhance the information that is known about each individual held in our database. Given that, based on transaction data and limited volunteered information, we will initially know very little about our customers, the addition of profile data can greatly extend our knowledge of each customer, effectively helping to build a picture of where they live, type of housing, their interests, income, profession, attitudes, lifestyle and so on.

To give a simple example of how this might help us, we can undertake an analysis of our database, taking into account the profile data added to each record. We should be able to identify correlations in the database and make inferences about, for example, the attributes of our high net worth customers. We can then use this information to segment our database and target others with similar profile attributes to these big spenders. We can then design a targeted direct mail campaign to encourage these potential big spenders to use our service more frequently.

Profile data can be used in a number of ways in addition to the rather obvious example above:

o We can link the geo-demographic/lifestyle profiles to the geographic catchment area for each of our branches. Using financial data for each branch, we can then identify the profiles for our most profitable/highest turnover branches and investigate the reasons why other, low performance branches with similar profiles are not doing so well. Once the reasons are identified, action plans can be developed to improve branch performance.

o Using a similar approach to the above, taking the profiles for the catchment areas around our most successful branches, we can identify suitable locations for new branches, looking for locations with similar profiles to our high performers. Other factors, for example local competition and population size, will need to be factored in, but this should assist our planners and improve the probability of the new branch being successful.

o Using the profile data taken from our list of high networth customers as the basis, we can purchase mailing lists and target non-customers who have a similar profile. In this way, we could increase the number of customers who use each branch.

o Using lifestyle data and behavioural information taken from our customer data, we could investigate the opportunity to offer customised, value-added services and new products to customers who match a given lifestyle profile. This might include garment collection and in-home services.

6 Concluding remarks

As outlined above, the contribution of a customer database to our business has great potential, both as a short-term, tactical tool to improve sales by getting existing customers to buy more and, in a more strategic way, through segmentation studies, branch studies and so on.

Provided that the database project is carefully planned, takes into account a wide range of data sources and is meticulously maintained, it should prove a reliable and valuable asset to Apex.

Answer 6
CRM, data warehousing and data mining

Check your answer

A good answer is likely to:

 ☑

In the introduction, Introduce self and state purpose of presentation ☐

In Part a, identify, define and clearly distinguish a customer database from a CRM system. Explain the importance of a customer relationship management strategy to the airline and show how a CRM system can support this strategy, on an organisation-wide basis. ☐

In Part b, define terms, explain the overall purpose of each and underpin with good examples from within the airline context. ☐

In Part c, define the terms and relate to statistical techniques and data mining. Show how these techniques will help with customer segmentation, using airline specific examples. Stronger answers will specifically cover CHAID analysis, demonstrating wider knowledge and reading. ☐

Adopt the role of a CRM database manager. ☐

Use Presentation Notes format. Demonstrate an awareness of the likely interests and needs of a CIM audience. ☐

*   *   *   *   *

PRESENTATION NOTES

Presentation to CIM Central Eastern Branch

Date: XX/XX/XX

Presentation Notes

Assistant CRM Database Manager – Central Eastern Airlines

The Importance of CRM and Related Technologies For Enhancing Customer Relationships and New Product Development

Welcome audience and introduce self and Central Eastern Airlines

Slide 1 – Agenda

- o Introduction
- o Customer database or CRM system?
- o The importance of CRM to Central Eastern Airlines

o The purpose of a data warehouse and data mining tools
o Statistical analysis and segmentation
o Any questions?

Slide 2 – Introduction

This evening, my aim is to give you some insight into how a regional airline like ours uses key technology tools to help it develop and retain customers and to show how we use the insight gained to develop new segments, new products and new services.

Slide 3 – Customer database or CRM system?

'A customer database is a manual or computerised source of data relevant to marketing decision making about an organisation's customers' (Wilson, 2003).

A customer database is usually maintained by the marketing department in support of its own activities and objectives. It is used mainly for marketing intelligence, segmentation studies, sales forecasting and for testing customer reactions to offers and for use in direct marketing activity. Although much of the data held in the database originates from outside the marketing department, for example transactional and financial data relating to individual customers, the database may or may not be readily accessible for use by other departments.

A CRM system is also essentially structured around a customer database but with one key difference – it receives its data from sources across the organisation and is accessible to anyone who has direct contact with customers or a need to access customer information. Moreover, it is a primary tool used by customer contact personnel in sales, customer service/ call centre and marketing. Its customer-centric database structure builds a history of all inter-action between each individual customer and every point of contact within the organisation.

Senior management have access to the CRM system, usually via executive information tools and a management reporting suite and have greater visibility of customer data, right down to individual transaction records, if required!

The CRM system can also be extended beyond the organisation to distribution channel partners, who can interrogate some of the data and document all these interactions with customers. In addition, some restricted CRM data is available directly to the customers themselves, via their own individualised web pages or other secure access point.

Slide 4 – The importance of CRM to central eastern airlines

Before we look at the role of CRM at Central Eastern Airlines, we should be certain that we all understand that running a CRM system does not mean the organisation necessarily practises customer relationship management – it might just be deceiving itself!

At Central Eastern Airlines we do practise CRM – we just happen to use a CRM system to help us do so! Of course, we cannot build a one-to-one relationship with every single individual who flies with us, but we do focus on developing and maintaining strong relationships with our corporate customers and our gold and platinum frequent flyers. These groups represent about 20 per cent of our customer base but account for more than 80 per cent of our profits.

We need relationships much more than they do!

From a marketing perspective, our CRM strategy allows us to devote considerable resources to communicating with and serving those customers that represent most value to us in the long term. We mine the data and use the analysis to develop deep insights into the behaviour, needs and opinions of these customers. We then work hard to retain them over the long term by anticipating their travel and business needs and having a service ready, just before they need it!

'What about the little people?' I hear you say.

We don't neglect them – we encourage them to join our frequent flyer programme; we monitor their flying behaviour; we make them offers via our direct mail system and our website. We give them value for money when they choose to fly with us and we look for signs in the data that indicate that they are becoming more active as travellers. We can then respond appropriately to this change in their behaviour.

I would also like to focus for a moment on our corporate customers. This business-to-business market is critical to us. We not only use our CRM skills here, but we practise key account management techniques, we assign an account manager, a senior member of our team, and we develop close working relationships with decision makers in each corporate account. We make ourselves available to solve their business travel problems, 24/7/365! The CRM system helps us manage these accounts and acquire new ones.

Slide 5 – The purpose of a data warehouse and data mining tools

A data warehouse is a large database which contains data aggregated from a number of disparate sources within the organisation. This data would typically include operational data, supplier information, sales and financial accounting data. A key feature is that the data held in the warehouse has been standardised for use across the organisation, which means that it is in a format that can be easily understood by non-specialists. The warehouse is normally structured around customers. External data can also added to the warehouse, relating to competitor activity, economic trends and general market conditions.

Data mining is a broad range of descriptive and predictive modelling and analytical techniques used to identify and interpret hidden patterns within the data held in a database, CRM system or data warehouse. Later in the presentation, we will examine two specific techniques that are often included in data mining projects.

Data mining is a very computer-intensive process and is carried out using specialist software tools. We use Clementine from SPSS, but a number of other good products are also available.

Slide 6 – Some of the applications of data mining within the airline include the following:

o Improving customer retention by monitoring rate of change in individual card usage in our frequent flyer membership. The data mining tools flag customers who are 'at risk' so that we can send them details of a promotional offer to bring them back into the fold.
o Running individual customer usage trend analyses to reveal month-on-month variations in travel mileage and to assist with forward demand forecasting.
o Understanding the impact of various internal or external events and trends, including marketing activities, on sales, profit and customer retention. We can use this insight to help us make predictions about the future.

○ Improving the quality of our direct marketing initiatives through micro-segmentation and the creation of customised offers, linked to actual customer needs (we will look at this in more detail later).

It is important to realise that, whilst these tools are very powerful and can reveal deeply buried patterns in a very large database, it is still down to the human to determine the importance, if any, of what is revealed! At Central Eastern Airlines, we employ statisticians to program the tools, undertake the analysis and make sense of the results. A final point, the outcomes must be actionable, in commercial terms and data miners would do well to remember this – a pattern in the data might be interesting, but can we exploit it for competitive advantage?

Slide 7 – Statistical analysis and segmentation

One of the key challenges in marketing terms for the airline is to identify unique and meaningful customer segments from literally terabytes of customer data. With this knowledge, we can build a unique offer or service for a group of customers and often command a premium price in the process.

The data mining tools we talked about earlier include statistical tools that are perfect for segmentation studies. In this section of the presentation, we will outline two related techniques: Cluster Analysis and CHAID.

Slide 7.1 – Cluster analysis

This is the name given to a broad group of statistical techniques used to identify and classify groupings of people (clusters) on the basis of two or more common variables, with a high degree of association within a group, but with very weak or non-existent associations between the groups.

The traditional way of undertaking a cluster analysis is to create a scatter diagram involving the plotting of similar characteristics amongst individual customers with respect to the variables of interest. The clusters can then be identified visually. This manual approach is impractical, especially if large data sets are involved and more than a few variables are being plotted. Instead, software tools, such as SPSS, are used to achieve quick and accurate results from a volume of data.

Cluster analysis is a descriptive modelling technique that can be used with a customer database or a data warehouse to discover hidden and actionable associations in the data and to identify unique segments.

Once the clusters have been determined and the standard tests for segment attractiveness have been applied, the airline's direct marketing team can produce a customised communication or service offering for each segment.

Slide 7.2 – CHAID analysis

(Chi-squared Automatic Interaction Detection)

CHAID is used as an alternative to cluster analysis and also as a supplemental technique; at Central Eastern, we use CHAID as a means of fine-tuning a segmentation project for direct marketing purposes and to help predict the response.

CHAID analysis uses a predictive modelling approach and examines all of the variables involved in a segment to determine which variable or variables are likely to have most influence on the response rate of a group chosen for a direct marketing campaign. It does this by continually sub-dividing segments until there are no more statistically significant sub-divisions to be made. We are looking for the few high impact characteristics that all group members share and will be most responsive to.

If anyone is interested in knowing more about CHAID, there is a great article in a recent *Harvard Business Review* (April 2006, pp. 88–89).

Slide 8 – Any questions

I will be pleased to answer any questions that you may have.

Syllabus Element 3
Answer 7
Role of information, internal research departments and ethics
(June 2005, Question 2, modified)

Check your answer

A good answer is likely to:

 ☑

In the introduction, set the scene, stress the need for accessible and accurate information ☐
in clothing/fashion retailing and then pave the way for the content of the report.

In Part a, introduce and explain each of the four roles of information, giving examples set ☐
in the context of a clothing retailer.

In Part b, start with the traditional role of the internal research department; introduce the ☐
environmental and commercial drivers of change and outline the research department's
response. Outline some of the activities of this wider role.

In Part c, identify the nature of the divided responsibility that the wider remit introduces ☐
and then discuss the ethical implications, explaining how these might be addressed.

Adopt the role of a newly appointed marketing executive. ☐

Use Report format. ☐

*   *   *   *   *

REPORT

To: Marketing Director

From: Graduate Marketer

Date: XX/XX/XX

Re: The Role of Information and the Widening Remit of Internal Research Departments

1 Introduction

Marketing and business decision makers require accurate and timely information, relating to customers, markets and competitors as well as other data relating to wider environmental factors that may have an impact on our business.

As a large, leading clothing retailer, we operate in a fast-paced, fashion led marketplace where 'long term' usually means one year.

We need to continuously track consumer trends and developments in the fashion world, analyse consumer behaviour and monitor competitor activity. We gather this information from multiple sources, both internally and externally and constantly use this knowledge and our expertise to make decisions that drive future growth and profitability in our stores.

This report examines the various roles of information and the widening remit of internal marketing research departments. It also considers the ethical impacts arising from this evolution in the research profession.

2 The key roles of marketing information

It is vitally important that decision makers obtain the right information for the decision in hand and that the providers of such information understand the uses (or roles) to which this information will be put. It is acknowledged that there are four key roles of information in marketing decision-making (Wilson, 2003):

1. Descriptive role – information used to determine *what*, *where*, *when*. For example, we are facing some competition from web-based retailers, so what types of clothing products are consumers buying from the web and from which sites?

2. Comparative role – information that helps answer the *How* questions. Often this information is used for performance benchmarks. Example – How does our average retail sales/m^2 compare with the XYZ Company?

3. Diagnostic role – information that satisfies the *Why* questions, designed to explain the reasons why something went wrong (or possibly went much better than expected). Example – Why did our recent national late summer promotion fail to achieve target in the northern region?

4. Predictive role – information that helps determine answers to the *What would happen if* or the *What if* questions. Example – What would happen to sales and profit if our major city stores stayed open until 9.00 pm?

Although the examples given for each role are quite straightforward, they typify the questions that we ask almost every day and serve to illustrate the four roles.

3 The widening remit of internal research departments

Traditionally, marketing research departments have been responsible for identifying and defining research requirements with internal information users, designing research programmes, conducting and supervising field work, managing projects, sub-contracting to specialist agencies, buying data, carrying out data analysis and writing reports.

The major focus has traditionally been on primary research that creates new knowledge for the organisation; this is often expensive to collect and then frequently under-utilised by the user.

Ever-increasing competitive pressure on firms and a need to reduce budgets and overheads has raised questions about the costs and benefits of maintaining an internal research department: Could the work be outsourced?

In recent years, possibly linked to the information explosion and the information age, there has been an increasing focus on leveraging existing customer knowledge and mountains of other information available on internal databases and internal information storage areas. A prevalence of information technology and highly stressed managers, who are overloaded with data, has actually created a new opportunity for research professionals.

Research departments are reinventing themselves as 'Insight Teams' with a particular emphasis on customer insight and demonstrating the value that the insight team can add cross-functionally by leveraging existing information and by data mining databases and data warehouses.

This wider role now involves:

o Helping information users, now called clients, to define their specific information requirements.
o Bringing the information together from a range of sources, at low cost, and making maximum use of the many existing internal sources.
o Helping users to analyse data, interpret it and to make better decisions.
o Being proactive in developing and managing customer databases that provide real insight into behaviour, trends and future requirements.
o Developing sophisticated customer segmentation profiles and providing information to enable effective targeting and positioning.
o Mining hidden patterns in customer data, as increasingly sophisticated tools become accessible.
o Training staff, including marketing staff, to be able to get the most out of the available systems.
o Working in cross-functional project teams to solve problems, capitalise on opportunities and develop new products and services and so on.

Internal researchers are capable of adding significant value to the organisation whilst simultaneously saving money by reducing the level of unnecessary primary research – unnecessary, because, often, the information is already available in-house and simply needs to be re-discovered. Primary research still has an important role to play, but it may not be the first port of call for the research professional.

4 Ethical issues arising from this wider role

The marketing research industry, and the organisations that use research, rely wholly on the continuing trust, goodwill and cooperation of the individuals that take part in research projects as respondents. Research professionals are bound by a professional code of conduct (Market Research Society) and also by legal requirements relating to the use of customer data and need for confidentiality as detailed in UK/EU Data Protection Acts.

The internal customer insight professional is working both in the camp of the professional market researcher (and must therefore work within the ethical, legal and professional frameworks to protect the respondents from misuse of information that they have given) and in the company of the database marketer, who naturally wants to use information for use in marketing campaigns, direct selling and so on.

The overriding requirement of all marketing and research professionals is to be both legal and ethical in all activities and undertakings. Our own brand values are based upon an ethical approach to business, which protects the consumer and our supply chain workers from harm or neglect. It is appropriate, therefore, that this philosophy encompasses both the information supply chain and all of the marketing activities of the Company.

Our obligation will require as a minimum that all data collected as 'research' be made anonymous at the point of use and only used to assist in data profiling and data attribution. It must never be used directly to engage in selling or direct marketing activity with respondents.

We have an opportunity to gain an advantage by proactively demonstrating the highly ethical nature of all of our business processes as well as our retail clothing products and accessories.

Answer 8
Agency selection criteria and professional codes of conduct

Check your answer

A good answer is likely to:

☑

In the introduction, stress the importance of selecting the right agency for a research project; mention the possible consequences of getting it wrong. ☐

In Part a, provide a brief overview of the selection process and then list and explain the importance of the selection criteria; explain how the agencies will be screened against the criteria. ☐

In Part b, introduce the code of conduct, outlining its purpose. Focus on the elements that are relevant to the relationship between research agency and client. Stronger answers will also reference and relate this agency/client relationship to the research contract document. ☐

Adopt the role of a newly appointed marketing executive. ☐

Use Report format. ☐

* * * * *

REPORT

To: Marketing Manager

From: Marketing Executive

Date: XX/XX/XX

Re: Process for Selecting a Marketing Research Agency and the Implications of the Code of Professional Conduct

1 Introduction

The selection of the most appropriate marketing research agency for our project is a vital process as the outcomes of the project can be very beneficial to our organisation, but it can be a financial disaster if it goes wrong.

A suitably skilled, experienced and knowledgeable agency can make a big difference to the quality of the findings and conclusions drawn from the research which, in turn, impact on the quality of the decisions we will take.

This report outlines the process for making the final agency selection and considers the impact of the code of professional conduct with respect to its implications for the relationship between our organisation and the chosen agency.

2 Criteria for appointing a research agency

We have received marketing research proposals from four agencies in response to our brief. All of these agencies are members of the Marketing Research Society and have the necessary competences to undertake our research project. The initial work to draw up a list of agencies who were invited to respond to our brief has certainly paid off, as the proposals are all of a high quality and appear to meet our research objectives.

We now need to put into place a final selection procedure that will differentiate the four agencies and enable us to select the one which, objectively, we will be confident to work with over the coming months and beyond.

It is recommended that the selection procedure incorporates the drawing up of a matrix of selection criteria which we can use to score each of the proposals.

2.1 The importance of agency presentation to support proposals

We should invite each of the agencies to formally present their proposals to our team. This will enable us to fully understand each proposal and to ask questions. There are a number of criteria items we can assess during this presentation, including:

- The competence of the agency to deliver our project.
- The level of communication and explanation skills.

We will also get to know the people behind the project – subjectively speaking, we need to be sure that we and they can work together harmoniously and productively.

The presentation, sometimes referred to as 'the beauty parade', is considered a formal part of the selection procedure and will provide us with useful additional information to help complete the assessment matrix and make a decision.

2.2 Criteria to be included in the assessment matrix

In addition to the criteria indicated above under Presentation, the following are suggested as being appropriate to be included in the matrix:

- The quality of the written proposal and presentation and the extent to which our requirements (set out in the brief) have been understood and addressed in the proposal documents.
- The extent to which the agency has interpreted our brief and demonstrated additional industry/customer understanding and insights into the current market environment.
- The extent to which they understand our organisation and the rationale driving the research.
- The appropriateness and justification of the proposed sampling methods and research approaches.
- Evidence of innovation/creativity in the approaches and methodologies proposed for the project.
- Relevant experience or expertise that will reduce their learning curve and add value to the research.
- Evidence that they have the resources to meet our requirements and have identified any sub-contractors that will be involved (such as a field work agency).
- Evidence that our project will be allocated sufficient resources and priority and that it will not merely be a small project amongst many large ones.

- ○ Our stated timescales and budgets can be met.
- ○ Supply of adequate references/testimonials from previous projects and at least one client that we can approach directly.
- ○ Introduction to the research project manager who will run our project.
- ○ Current membership of relevant professional bodies is held.

Once we have drawn up the matrix and allocated weighted scores for the criteria to each agency, based upon the research proposal and the supporting presentation, we will need to invite the top-scoring agency to negotiate a contract for the project. We should keep the second highest scoring agency in reserve until the negotiations are complete and a contract is awarded.

3 Codes of professional conduct

The Market Research Society (MRS) has published a code of professional conduct which all professional researchers, who are members, must observe on the basis of self-regulatory compliance. The MRS can also take disciplinary action against members who are in breach of the code.

This code of conduct (recently updated and re-published in December 2005) is based upon, and incorporates, the code of conduct published by the international research body – ESOMAR.

The code of conduct is designed to ensure that minimum requirements are met with respect to social and ethical standards and that the rights and responsibilities of respondents and clients are safeguarded (or met).

In this section, we will consider one key aspect of the ESOMAR code of conduct which is especially relevant to our organisation as we move forward with our first research project. This element relates to Section D of the ESOMAR code, which details 'the mutual rights and responsibilities of researchers and their clients'.

Note: This is especially important, as when we sign the contract with the research agency, we will be bound-in as 'client' to this element of the code.

The relevant rules from the ESOMAR code are summarised below:

1. The rights and responsibilities will be governed by a written contract. Some of the rules may be modified in writing, if required, but certain others may not be modified.

2. If any of the work carried out on the project is to be syndicated with work for other clients, this must be made known, although we are not entitled to know the identity of the other client.

3. Any work to be sub-contracted outside the agency must be notified to us as client. We can request identity details if required.

4. As client, we do not have the right to exclusive use of the agency's services. The agency must avoid possible clashes of interest between services provided for other clients.

5. A number of documents/records remain the property of the client and contents are held in confidence by the agency. This includes briefs and other documents supplied by us to the agency as well as the research data and findings (unless syndicated). The client has no automatic right to know the identities of the respondents unless respondents have given explicit permission (which must be obtained by the researcher).

6. A number of records/documents remain the property of the researcher. These would include: research proposals and quotations (unless paid for by the client) – we cannot disclose details of these to a third party; syndicated reports – again, the client cannot disclose the contents of such research to a third party without the permission of the researcher; other documents not paid for by the client.

7. The researcher must keep records (for an appropriate period of time) to current professional standards. Duplicate copies of such records shall be supplied to the client (at reasonable cost) upon request, provided that confidentiality or anonymity is not breached.

8. The identity of the client shall be held confidential by the researcher, along with confidential information about the client's business.

9. The client has reasonable rights to make quality checks of fieldwork and data preparation, provided that the client pays any additional costs incurred.

10. The client must be supplied with technical details of the project carried out for him.

11. When reporting on research results, findings shall be clearly differentiated from interpretations of these findings, as well as any recommendations based on such interpretations.

12. If the client publishes details of any of the research findings, these shall not be misleading. The researcher shall be consulted in advance to agree form and content of publication.

13. Researchers must not allow their names to be used in connection with any research unless all aspects of the research have been undertaken in accordance with the requirements of the code.

14. Researchers must make their clients aware of the code and the need to comply with its requirements.

Full details of the MRS/ESOMAR codes can be obtained from the MRS or ESOMAR websites.

Answer 9
Research process and industry players

Check your answer

A good answer is likely to:

☑

In the introduction, introduce the concept of a formal research process, explain the ☐
importance of understanding the contribution that the organisation should make to a
number of the stages to help ensure the quality of the research report.

In Part a, introduce and briefly describe each stage of the process, highlighting the role of ☐
the organisation in providing input to relevant stages.

In Part b, introduce and describe the role of the various industry players. Provide ☐
examples where possible.

Adopt the role of a marketing manager or executive. ☐

Use Report format. ☐

*　*　*　*　*

REPORT

To: Marketing Manager

From: Marketing Executive

Date: XX/XX/XX

Re: The Marketing Research Process and an Outline of the Research Industry

1 Introduction

As we are about to embark upon our first marketing research project, it is pertinent to consider
the formal research process and the importance of our involvement in and contribution to a
number of key stages in this process to ensure the success of the research project.

This report outlines the stages of the process, highlighting our contribution to it for the success of
the project. The report also provides an overview of the research industry and introduces the types
of agency that may become involved in our projects, depending upon the approach we take.

2 The marketing research process, including our contribution to it

The activities in a marketing research project follow a sequential process, which is well
known and observed by the marketing research industry. Although some minor variations do

exist, the following description defines the process we are likely to be engaged in as we embark upon our research project.

2.1 Stage 1 – Defining the problem or opportunity

This is the crucial first stage as the resulting outcome has a major influence on the quality of the content in the finished research report.

We should be mindful that all research costs money and the research should help us make decisions to solve problems or capitalise on opportunities. We will therefore need to ensure that we adequately and precisely define the problem or opportunity. We must take the time to ensure that we fully understand (and define in the next stage) the specific information we need from the research project.

2.2 Stage 2a – Formulate the research objectives

In this stage, we need to precisely define the information that we will require as inputs to our problem solving and decision-making process. This information is specified as a series of research objectives or information targets. The objectives should cover all that we require but without any additional 'nice to know' elements as these will cost money and not actually help us.

The research objectives are written in a precise fashion so as to be clear and objective. It is important to involve a number of people at the objective writing stage in order to get buy-in to the project and to identify any information that we might already have available somewhere in the Company.

2.3 Stage 2b – Write the research brief

Once the objectives are written and agreed, the client organisation prepares a marketing research brief. This document describes the research requirement from the client's perspective.

The research brief is an important document which contains details of the problem or opportunity (in the rationale section) and a list of the research objectives created at stage 2a above. Other key information will include a brief situation analysis and an outline of our envisaged research approach as well as details of our timescales, budget and reporting requirements.

The completed brief is 'signed off' internally and supplied to a number of research agencies who are invited to prepare a response in the form of a research proposal.

2.4 Stage 3a – Creation of the research design and preparation of the proposal

In preparing their responses, the agencies will construct the basic research design and document this persuasively within their research proposals. This design includes appropriately justified details of the research approach and the methodologies proposed along with sampling techniques, data collection, analysis and reporting. It also covers timescales, key milestones and the price.

2.5 Stage 3b – Receipt of the proposal by client, selection, negotiation, contract

The proposals are given to the client, usually accompanied by an oral presentation, in a ritual known in the industry as 'the beauty parade'.

The client then makes an objective assessment of each proposal, negotiates with the selected agency and awards a contract.

2.6 Stage 4 – Collection of secondary data

This is a phase of the research data collection aimed at identifying and collating information that assists in addressing the research objectives. It is important as it acts as a backdrop to primary (field-based) research and can save time and money.

2.7 Stage 5 – Collection of primary data

This involves the collection of data from a sample of respondents, using a mixture of qualitative (e.g. unstructured interviews and group discussions) and quantitative (survey questionnaires) methods. Observational techniques (e.g. mystery shopping) may also be incorporated.

This is the most detailed and lengthy phase of the process and usually involves the creation of discussion guides, questionnaires and other research instruments, depending upon the specific research specified in the research design.

2.8 Stage 6 – Data analysis

This stage involves a period of data preparation which, depending upon the actual data collection methods used, might involve the transcription of discussion group recordings, codification of answers on computer, validation of the data, data tabulation, graphs and charts, statistical analysis and so on.

2.9 Stage 7 – Report and presentation of findings

Once the data has been analysed, a series of findings and conclusions are drawn up; the information is documented in a written report and/or a slide presentation and usually then presented orally to the client.

3 Players in the marketing research industry

Careful selection of the most appropriate agency to undertake our project – based upon their size, capabilities, industry experience and other factors – will have a major influence on the overall success of the project.

The following information is an overview of the research industry, starting with the professional/ regulatory bodies.

3.1 The market research society (MRS)

The MRS is the world's largest membership organisation for the industry and represents both the suppliers of research and the client organisation. It also protects the interests and rights of members of the public who act as respondents or participants in research projects.

The MRS provides formal qualifications, training, publications and various events and seminars and is the professional face of the industry.

The MRS publishes a code of conduct which all members and partner companies agree to follow. This code also impacts on clients as we will be bound-in to some of its clauses when we contract with a research agency or consultant.

The MRS also manages the online Research Buyer's Guide; this will prove a useful resource as we identify possible research suppliers for our project.

3.2 Full-service market research agencies

These tend to be the larger supplier organisations, although not exclusively so, who provide a full end-to-end solution to a research requirement. As the term implies, they offer a full range of services and products themselves, although they may sub-contract some specialist work if they do not have resource internally. These agencies often have extensive experience across a range of industries and sectors.

In addition, a full-service agency may well have international marketing research capabilities and resources.

Examples: AC Nielsen and GfK NOP

3.3 Specialist research agencies

Specialists either focus on particular markets, industries or geographic regions or, possibly, in particular types of research. Some of the specialist agencies focus on particular elements of a research project, for example in undertaking questionnaire design.

Examples: B2B International (B2B specialists), Everyday Lives (ethnography/observational research)

3.4 Independent consultants

These tend to handle smaller research projects and offer a particular industry focus or offer a specialised research activity. The consultants might have originally worked for large agencies or as researchers in client organisations.

Examples: Brand Planning and Research (BP+R), Increment Ltd (agricultural market research).

3.5 Fieldwork agencies

Field agencies focus on data collection which might include face to face, telephone inter-viewing and postal surveys. They either use their own staff or recruit and manage free-lancers or operate using a mixture. Use of freelancers is popular and provides flexibility for the agency not only as it reduces costs but also enables fieldwork to be carried out in any part of the country or region in which they operate.

Examples: Ace Fieldwork Ltd, Fieldwork International.

3.6 Data analysis agencies

Here, the focus is on data conversion, validation, transcription, statistics and analysis.

3.7 Syndicated research agencies

These organisations undertake regular research in high-profile consumer and commercial areas and then offer the research as a report to any organisation that wishes to purchase it.

Examples: Mintel, Key Note.

4 Concluding remarks

In order to ensure the success of our project, we will need to undertake some initial preparatory work to identify our problem/opportunity, define our research objectives and then write a research brief that provides a good basis for marketing research agencies to use to prepare their proposals. We also require some knowledge of the industry itself, as this will help us position the agencies and the sub-contractors that they might use to deliver our project.

We will also need help and advice from the industry, from the MRS itself, and from colleagues in other organisations who have commissioned research projects themselves and who can point us in the right direction.

Answer 10
Importance of ethics, social responsibility and legislation in research

Check your answer

A good answer is likely to:

☑

In the introduction, stress the importance of a legal and ethical approach to all research and information-related undertakings. Pave the way for the content of the briefing note and motivate new recruits to read and observe. ☐

In Part a, explain the terms and relate these concepts to the process of collecting, holding and using market research data. ☐

In Part b, identify relevant legal and regulatory instruments and codes and relate these to the information collection activities of the organisation. Emphasise the risks and penalties of getting it wrong. ☐

Use relevant examples set in the context of an FMCG company. ☐

Adopt the role of a newly appointed marketing manager. ☐

Use Briefing Note format. ☐

* * * * *

BRIEFING NOTE

Peacock & Ramble plc

ETHICS, SOCIAL RESPONSIBILITY AND LEGISLATION RELEVANT TO MARKETING RESEARCH

Purpose

This briefing note has been written as part of the induction pack for graduates who are joining the research department as marketing research professionals.

Contents

This briefing note covers the following important topics which relate to the collection, holding, storage and use of marketing research and customer data:

1. The importance of ethics and social responsibility

2. Key legal and regulatory responsibilities.

Requirement for signature

Please ensure that you read this document fully and that you understand its content. Only then should you sign off this element on the induction process card. Your signature confirms both your understanding and your willingness to practise your profession to the highest standards of ethical conduct; that you will be bound by all elements of the Market Research Society (MRS) Code of Conduct and will observe the requirements of relevant legislation at all times.

1 The importance of ethics and social responsibility

As a researcher at Peacock and Ramble you will be expected, by your internal clients, research respondents and departmental colleagues, to act in a professional manner at all times, to be trustworthy and to respect the confidentiality of both respondents and clients when practising your profession. In all of your undertakings, you must be ethical and socially responsible.

1.1 What is ethics?

Ethics is concerned with discriminating between right and wrong behaviour; it is a reflection of the values of our society and it imposes a set of guidelines to be observed in our everyday lives and in our dealings with others.

1.2 Why is ethics so important in marketing research?

In marketing research, ethics is about acting in a socially responsible manner so as to protect the rights of the client and the respondent as well as those external agencies that we use as sub-contractors in the field.

Ethical and socially responsible behaviour is a mandate at all stages of the research process as well as before the project begins and afterwards, when data is communicated and used internally within marketing and other corporate databases.

1.3 What are the ethical responsibilities towards our internal client?

Our clients and other colleagues in the Company at large deserve to be treated in an open, fair and honest manner at all times. We must not allow our own goals and interests to influence the formulation of the client's research problems or objectives; we must remain objective at all times. We must never over-promise, nor must we mislead the client when communicating research findings.

The relationship between researcher and client is a mutual one and, as researchers, we expect that our clients will be honest in communicating their research problems and will not deliberately withhold relevant information from the researcher.

1.4 What are the ethical responsibilities towards individual respondents?

Both the research industry and its client organisations rely on the goodwill and cooperation of respondents and participants; without them we would not be able to function. We must be considered trustworthy and professional in all aspects of the research. Respondents expect us to respect them and to use the data we obtain from them in a professional way with due regard for confidentiality. Respondents do not want their information to be used to sell products to them as individuals; they do expect the purpose of the research to be made clear. They have a right to opt out, if they so wish.

1.5 What are the ethical responsibilities regarding the storage of information?

From an ethical perspective, we must hold and store the information we collect in such a way as to protect the respondents from the possible misuse of the data.

When producing research reports for our clients, we must not disclose the identities of individual respondents. When merging research data into a marketing database, again, the anonymity of the respondent must be protected. Inferences may be drawn from the research findings and extrapolated throughout the database to improve consumer insight.

Response forms identifying the respondent by name may be required for quality control purposes, but such records shall be subject to restricted access.

1.6 What are the ethical responsibilities regarding the use of information?

The key ethical responsibility here is to ensure that the data collected from respondents is only used for the purpose made explicit to the respondent. This means that it will be used in aggregate form to increase knowledge of consumer attitudes, behaviour, opinions and lifestyles. This knowledge can be used for multiple purposes, including segmentation, distribution channel design, packaging design, new product development and advertising message/creative design. It cannot be used directly for selling or direct marketing purposes in connection with the named individuals who are the respondents.

2 Key legal and regulatory responsibilities

This section provides you with some information about the Market Research Society's code of professional conduct as well as relevant legislation that relates to your professional role as marketing researcher with Peacock & Ramble.

2.1 The code of conduct

The Market Research Society (MRS) has a published a code of professional conduct, which all professional researchers must observe on the basis of self-regulatory compliance. Peacock & Ramble is a professional partner company of the MRS and fully embraces this code of conduct.

Peacock & Ramble will take disciplinary action against any researcher who is found to be in breach of this code. This action will be additional to disciplinary action which may be taken by the MRS itself.

The MRS code of conduct (recently updated and re-published in December 2005) is based upon, and incorporates, the code of conduct published by the international research body – ESOMAR.

The code of conduct is designed to ensure that minimum requirements are met with respect to social and ethical standards and that the rights (and responsibilities) of respondents and clients are safeguarded (met).

A full copy of the MRS Code of Conduct is attached as an appendix to this briefing note. Please ensure that you have a thorough working knowledge of this code.

Some of the key elements relating to ethical and social responsibility were covered in Section 1 of this briefing note.

2.2 The data protection legislation

Peacock & Ramble is registered with the Information Commissioner's Office and comes under the terms of the UK Data Protection Act (1984, 1998). This Act incorporates the related EU directive and regulates the processing of data pertaining to any identifiable, living individual, held either in paper records or electronically in a database within the Company.

The Act is designed to protect the privacy of individuals and is concerned with the rights and responsibilities of three entities:

Data controllers – the holder of the data.

Data processors – third party organisations that process information for others.

Data subjects – each consumer or other identifiable, living individuals.

We are termed a 'data controller'. Consumers who register with us via our branded web sites or using reply coupons on our packaging are referred to as 'data subjects'.

Named respondents in research questionnaires are also data subjects and come under the protection of the Act.

We collect and process all of our customer data directly, although we do receive limited data from various supermarket loyalty scheme systems. For Peacock & Ramble, this falls outside the legislation, as the data we receive does not include customer name or address data, apart from postcodes.

As a data controller, we must ensure that data is:

- o processed lawfully and fairly
- o processed only for specific limited purposes
- o relevant and not excessive
- o adequate for the purpose and accurate
- o destroyed when no longer required*
- o processed in accordance with the data subjects rights
- o held securely
- o not transferred outside the EU without consent (exceptions apply).

There are also eight 'sensitive' data categories which relate to content of records held about individuals. Explicit consent is required to hold information relating to these categories; we must also demonstrate a real need to collect such data.

Data subjects have a right to request access to the data we hold about them and they have a right to request that their information not be used for direct marketing.

---

*Certain exemptions are allowed for with respect to marketing research data; since we do not identify research respondents by name/address in any of our electronic databases, this only applies to the original survey forms. These are held in a secure storage facility and held for two years in case of a need for re-processing.

A consumer who registers with us via one of our websites has full access to the data we hold relating to them; they also have the option to opt in and out of various marketing communication and direct marketing activity categories.

A data subject has a right to compensation if we cause him/her any harm due to our contravention of the Act.

2.3 Preference services – TPS/MPS

Consumers have a right to opt out of direct marketing mail shots (or junk mail, as they might call it) using the mail preference service (MPS) or telesales calls using the telephone preference service (TPS). At Peacock & Ramble, we purge all outgoing mailing and telephone lists against the TPS/MPS databases to ensure that we do not include someone who has registered.

Similar preference services cover any B2B leads or prospects (the wholesalers and retailers we use to reach the end consumers). This does not apply to organisations that have traded with us or made a recent request for information.

If you are in any way unsure about what is or is not permissible under the legislation, PLEASE ASK our legal and compliance team for advice (Ext 8000) – better to be safe than sorry.

Syllabus Element 4
Answer 11
Secondary research to provide information for a market entry decision

Check your answer

A good answer is likely to:

  ☑

In the introduction, introduce and define the term 'secondary research'   ☐

In Part a, identify the key benefits of secondary research to the organisation and to improving the effectiveness of the primary research process.   ☐

In Part b, identify the information that will furnish a decision to enter the retail office furniture market. List possible sources of this information both internally and externally.   ☐

In Part c, identify the limitations of secondary data that affect accuracy. Explain how these limitations can be overcome.   ☐

Use examples set in the context of the furniture manufacturer and market entry considerations.   ☐

Adopt the role of a freelance researcher.   ☐

Use Report format.   ☐

*   *   *   *   *

REPORT

To: Managing Director

From: Andy Freelancer

Date: XX/XX/XX

Re: Secondary Research – Its Role in Market Entry Assessment

1 Introduction

Secondary research, also called desk research, may be defined as 'the collation and analysis of data, sourced either internally or externally, previously created for another purpose and now re-used to provide information for decision-making'.

It is an important element of any market or marketing research project and is normally under-taken prior to any primary (field) research that might additionally be required. Secondary research can:

- ○ act as an exploratory phase for a larger research project incorporating primary research. Secondary research helps identify the areas of importance for primary research.
- ○ be used instead of primary research and/or as a means of reducing primary research project costs.

In the context of whether or not Super Office Furniture Ltd should make a decision to enter the retail office furniture market by offering home office furniture mainly to consumers, secondary research can provide the majority of information required. The secondary research will also help identify any primary research that might be required – this latter point will be amplified later in the report.

2 Benefits of secondary research

A number of the benefits of undertaking secondary research have been indicated in the introduction; the key benefits or advantages are as follows:

It is low cost or free to obtain, depending upon the sources used. Internal data is usually free, but a longitudinal (trends over time) market study from Mintel or Euromonitor International might cost several thousand GBP.

It is very good for accessing historic/comparative data – market, price, demand and competitor trends; also comparisons with other markets and sectors over time. These are all important factors in a market entry decision. Such trends may help with making future forecasts.

It can reduce or eliminate the need for primary research – if so, this saves money and cuts down the time period before a decision can be made. In the case of a market entry decision, a significant amount of information on customers, competitors, channels, pricing and other marketing mix factors can be identified and defined using external secondary sources.

It may provide a warning of potential problems – these might make market entry unattractive and allow the decision maker to seek other strategies for growth.

2.1 How secondary research improves the effectiveness of primary research

As already indicated, secondary research can replace, supplement or enhance primary research. In terms of improving the effectiveness of primary research, it contributes in a number of ways:

- ○ It helps clarify the research problem and the research objectives – as secondary research can be used as an exploratory method, which helps 'paint a picture' of the market and highlights the key factors to be investigated.
- ○ It helps confirm that the primary research methods chosen in the research design are appropriate or indicates that other methods might be preferable.
- ○ It can provide useful background information to supplement the research report's findings and conclusions and/or provide endorsement to what has been discovered in the field.

2.2 Weaknesses of secondary data

In considering the above, it is important to remember that the materials used were not created for the specific project and, therefore, there are potential weaknesses associated with secondary research data: information may not be available, it may prove insufficient or irrelevant for our needs and it could be outdated. It might also be inaccurate or biased (please see Section 5).

3 Types and sources of secondary data relevant to a market entry decision

The types of information required for a decision about entry into the UK retail furniture market relate to all of the common areas of marketing information, including the macro- and micro-environments, as well as an understanding of the capabilities and resources needed by the firm to be able to operate effectively and profitably in the marketplace. The following key question areas are potentially addressable using secondary sources:

3.1 Retail office furniture market – Its size, growth rate, maturity stage, future prospects and stability.

3.2 Customers – Who they are, how they segment, what they buy, how much they spend, where they prefer to buy, how frequently they purchase, what are the initiating factors (new house, new job etc.)?

3.3 Industry and Competitors – Its size and structure, barriers to entry, who are the competitors, what share does each have, what are the cost structures and margins. How much rivalry is apparent?

3.4 Distribution Channels – Who are the wholesalers and retailers? Are they accessible to us? Are there any gaps? How should we enter the market? Would a direct channel approach be suitable?

3.5 Product and Price – What is available, competitor product information, emerging trends, gaps in market? What are the pricing levels, pricing objectives and strategies of key competitors and retailers? Discounting tactics? Can we be competitive and is there a potential for us to be profitable?

4 Information sources

Sources of information for secondary research can be found either internally or externally.

For the current decision, almost all of the information is likely to be sourced externally. However, it is always worthwhile considering whether any relevant information might be available in-house, perhaps in the form of reports or presentations that might have formed part of an earlier initiative in this area. Such information would need updating, but might assist in identifying sources and information types.

Also of importance is the need to undertake some informal 'field research' by asking questions and talking to some of the players, suppliers, retailers, wholesalers, retail customers and so on. This can be invaluable, even essential!

4.1 Sources of information would typically include the following:

Trade Associations – the relevant furniture manufacturer and retailer associations can provide industry and market statistics, information on future trends, lists of suppliers (competitors), retailers and so on.

Trade Magazines/Industry journals – as above, perhaps spread out over several issues. Some of these offers back issue archives for free on the web, making this a fast and effective approach for familiarisation and background.

Published Reports – usually at a price, but can deliver accurate and up-to-date information on market, customers, competitors, future trends and so on. Euromonitor, Key Note and Mintel provide good examples of such reports.

Trade Directories and Yearbooks – product information, company information and distribution channel information.

Annual Reports and Accounts – easily accessible for plcs via the Financial Times report request service. For privately held companies, see below.

Companies House, Dun and Bradstreet – for detailed financial and other information such as annual reports of competitors, especially those that are not publicly listed.

Retail office furniture catalogues – for product information, ranges and prices.

The Internet – a rich, easily accessible source for desk research. Use of search engines and directories can speed access to company competitor websites, trade journals, report publishers lists and so on.

Business Libraries – especially business library services in big towns/cities with access to Mintel reports, trade directories, CD-ROMs, company reports.

5 Data accuracy assessment

One of the weaknesses introduced at the end of Section 2 concerns the potential for inaccuracy. The researcher should try to determine the accuracy of each source used or considered.

In determining the accuracy of information, a number of questions should be answered by the researcher:

1. Who commissioned the original research and what was its purpose? Did they have a hidden agenda that might indicate bias?

2. Who undertook the research? Was it a well-known research organisation (and a member of a professional body such as the MRS)?

3. Does the report give details of the research methodology, sampling approaches, respondent descriptions, data collection and analysis (including information on statistical techniques used). Ideally, apply an acid test question – is there enough information to enable a researcher to repeat the study if so desired?

4. Can the accuracy of the information be confirmed or improved by locating additional corroborative evidence from other reports and databases to 'triangulate' with?

If any of the above cannot be confirmed satisfactorily, then ideally the data should be rejected.

Accuracy can be a particular concern when undertaking international secondary research, especially in some of the developing countries. Since the current decision initially concerns our home market, the risk of such inaccuracy is somewhat reduced. Care should still be taken, however, by answering questions 1–4 above.

6 Concluding remarks

There is no doubt that secondary research can contribute positively to the decision regarding entry into the UK retail furniture market. As explained, the secondary research might provide a very large proportion of the information that will be required. Any primary research that might be identified through the secondary phase will almost certainly be reduced and will be focused on the important areas we have been able to identify through our desk research efforts.

Answer 12
Questionnaire design

Check your answer

A good answer is likely to:

☑

Demonstrate the application of the questionnaire design process, especially with respect to choice of question topics, wording, question types/response formats and sequence. ☐

Address specific quantitative objectives from the proposal. ☐

Present the questions in a respondent-centric sequence. ☐

Use clear and unambiguous wording and language appropriate to the respondent. ☐

Employ a variety of different question types. ☐

Incorporate skip or jump questions for routing and screening. ☐

Use Questionnaire format – form design, layout and appearance will not be assessed but do keep it neat and use white space, etc. ☐

* * * * *

WEB SURVEY QUESTIONNAIRE

Lone worker monitoring systems

Thank you for agreeing to take part in this web survey. You have been selected because we believe that you have a leading involvement with the products and services that are the subject of this marketing research.

The information you provide will greatly assist us in improving our knowledge of the lone worker/vehicle tracking industry and the needs of the organisations that manage and monitor these systems.

The information you provide will be used purely for marketing research purposes; the information that you provide will be treated in confidence.

As a thank you for taking the time to answer the questions, we will send you an e-gift voucher which you can exchange for a book or other product at Amazon. The quicker you complete the survey, the larger the value of the e-gift.

Click start to begin the questionnaire. [START]

S0 Screening questions

S1 Within your organisation, do you personally have responsibility or involvement with any of the following activities? (Tick all that apply)

Lone worker monitoring/tracking ☐

VIP/executive protection ☐

Electronic monitoring systems for the above ☐

None of these apply to me ☐

<< If answer submitted = 'none of these apply to me' then ask the following additional question (S2), otherwise jump to Section 1, Q1 >>

S2 Please help us by identifying the name(s) of those within your organisation who have a responsibility for one or more of the activities listed in the previous question

Name: [   ] E-mail address: [   ]

Name: [   ] E-mail address: [   ]

Name: [   ] E-mail address: [   ]

<< On completion of S2, jump to quality check questions at end of survey >>

Section 1 – Information about you and your organization

Q1 Please select the option that best describes your main role within your organisation

[<< primary role pick list >>]

Q2 Please select the option that best describes the *main* industry or sector that your organisation operates in:

[<< UK SIC/industry sector pick list >>]

Q3 What is your organisation's approximate annual turnover? (Please tick one box)

Less than £1M ☐

£1M–£9.99M ☐

£10M–£49.99M ☐

£50M–£99.99M ☐

£100M–£500M ☐

More than 500M ☐

Q4 How many people are employed in your organisation? (Please tick one box)

1–199 ☐

200–499 ☐

500–999 ☐

1000–1999 ☐

2000–4999 ☐

5000 or more ☐

Q5 Approximately how many vehicles are owned, leased or managed by your organisation? (Please tick one box)

none ☐

1–49 ☐

40–99 ☐

100–199 ☐

200–499 ☐

More than 500 ☐

Section 2 – Safety and security of personnel/lone workers

Q6 How many of your organisation's employees regularly work alone or in are in vulnerable roles, where their safety or security may be at risk? (Please tick one box)

none ☐

1–199 ☐

200–499 ☐

500–999 ☐

1000–1999 ☐

2000–4999 ☐

5000 or more ☐

<< If answer submitted = 'None' then jump to quality check questions >>

Q7 Are your organisation's lone or vulnerable workers currently provided with any form of emergency distress signalling device? (Please tick one box)

Yes ☐

No ☐

<< If answer submitted = 'No' then jump to quality check questions >>

Q8 What type or types of emergency distress device(s) are currently issued to staff within your organisation? (Please enter the approximate number of each type in use)

Personal audio attack alarm   [＿＿＿＿]

Standard mobile telephone   [＿＿＿＿]

Mobile phone with integral dedicated panic button   [＿＿＿＿]

Covert tag or identity card with integral GSM transmitter   [＿＿＿＿]

Two-way radio (walkie-talkie)   [＿＿＿＿]

Other, please specify type and number in use   [＿＿＿＿]

103

Q9 Do you currently track the location of any employees using satellite positioning system (GPS) signals? (Please tick one box)

Yes ☐

No ☐

Not sure ☐

Q10 What is the approximate annual budget for supply and maintenance of lone worker and/or satellite tracking devices? (Please specify in £'000s)

	£

Q11 Who is the current provider of your lone worker devices?

Enter the supplier name in this field	

Section 3 – Facilities for computerised monitoring

Q12 How does your organisation currently monitor the location and alarm status of its lone workers and GPS monitored employees? (Please tick one box)

We use a third party alarm receiving centre (ARC) and are happy to do so ☐

We currently use a third party alarm receiving centre but plan to do it ourselves ☐

We currently undertake monitoring using our own facilities ☐

<< If answer submitted = 'We currently undertake monitoring using our own facilities' then jump to Q19 >>

Q13 If you currently use a third party alarm receiving centre but plan to do it yourselves, what is your timescale? (Please tick the first option that applies)

Within the current financial year ☑

In the next financial year ☑

Within two years ☑

Within three years ☑

Not known or planned ☑

Q14 What is your approximate budget for monitoring lone workers? (Please specify in £'000s)

	£

Q15 If you use a third party monitoring centre for lone worker and/or vehicle tracking, please enter the name of the monitoring company in this field

Q16 If you are using a third party monitoring service at present, please rate the service you receive in overall terms (Please tick one box only)

Excellent ☐ Good ☐ Poor ☐ Very poor ☐

Q17 If you currently use a third party but plan to establish your own monitoring facility, please identify a list of possible suppliers in order of likely preference

Probable first choice supplier	<< organisation name >>

Probable second choice supplier	<< organisation name >>

Probable third choice supplier	<< organisation name >>

Other supplier, please specify	

Other supplier, please specify	

Q18 Please complete the following sentence:

If I was choosing a supplier of a monitoring system today, the most important consideration in the decision would be:

....

....

Q19 If you currently monitor your lone workers/vehicles using in-house facilities, please specify the name of the supplier of your monitoring system/software

Q20 What was the approximate total cost of your in-house monitoring system and software? (Please specify in £'000s)

	£

Q21 Please rate the service you receive from the monitoring system vendor in overall terms. (Please tick one box only)

Excellent ☐　　　Good ☐　　　Poor ☐　　　Very poor ☐

Q22 Please consider your attitudes towards your current supplier of the monitoring systems and software you use in-house

Listed below are pairs of statements that could describe your supplier. For each pair, place an *X* between the two statements in a position that best reflects your view of your supplier.								
Expensive								Inexpensive
High quality								Low quality
Market follower								Market leader
Inflexible								Flexible
Innovator								Imitator
Small player								Big player
Accessible								Inaccessible
Collaborative								Adversarial
Product emphasis								Service emphasis

Quality check questions

Thank you for taking the time to participate in this survey.

In case we need to contact you to check any of the information that you have provided or for our internal quality assurance purposes, please provide:

Your name	

Your telephone number	

Organisation name	

Post code from organisation's address	

You will receive your e-gift voucher by e-mail shortly.

Answer 13
Discussion guides and projective techniques (June 2006, Question 3)

Check your answer

A good answer is likely to:

	☑
Adopt a three-phase discussion guide format with timings annotated for each phase.	☐
Address specific qualitative objectives from the proposal.	☐
Cater for the type of respondent taking part, making the content and objectives appropriate.	☐
Present material in a logical sequence that is easily accessible to the moderator during the session. Use a thematic and topic-oriented approach, not just a list of questions.	☐
Use topic headings, open-ended questions and probes.	☐
Use props or exhibits where appropriate.	☐
Incorporate appropriate projective techniques (but not too many), make their use relevant to the objectives and the client context.	☐
Deliver length and detail according to the marks allocated to the question. The discussion guide could be one part of a question, as is the case here, or it could also be a full Part b question, requiring more detail in terms of the question areas, probes and projective techniques used.	☐

* * * * *

DISCUSSION GUIDE

SeaLux Cruises Project

(Tourism Research Ltd)

Date: XX/XX/XX

This discussion guide has been prepared for use by moderators who will lead the series of focus groups to take place in London and Birmingham to address the qualitative objectives for SeaLux Cruises.

1 Introduction phase (15 mins max)

Welcome – Welcome participants, introduce yourself as moderator.

Housekeeping – Safety, security, toilets, refreshments.

Purpose – Explain purpose and importance; outline key objectives of session, topics. Importance of getting involved, no right answers.

Recording – We will be video/audio recording the discussion, for research purposes only.

Duration – Approx. $1\frac{1}{2}$ hours.

Warm-up – Group introductions (introduce neighbour). Warm-up group exercises 'why we cruise' brainstorm.

Questions – Elicit any questions or concerns, then move into discussion phase.

2 Discussion phase:

2.1 Attitudes and perceptions regarding SeaLux and competitors (30 mins)

- o Explore reasons why participants choose cruise holidays in preference to other options
- o Explore perceptions about the range of cruise products available
- o Identify and prioritise criteria for selection of a cruise company
- o Identify which cruise companies they would consider <u>and why</u>
- o Identify which companies they would not consider <u>and why</u>
- o *Projective Technique* – brand mapping chart – get group to position individual cruise companies on chart according to important and linked criteria – please see notes at the rear of this discussion guide.

2.2 Booking channel perceptions and media perceptions (10 mins)

- o Identify and discuss (eliciting reasons) the preferences for cruise booking channel alternatives:

  - – Direct methods – website, telephone, DRTV, magazine page ads
  - – Traditional travel agency.

- o Explore specific benefits of using a direct booking approach by web or telephone.
- o *Projective Technique* – photo sorts – get group to sort photo set according to channel preference most likely to be used – please see notes at rear of this discussion guide.

2.3 SeaLux Advertising Effectiveness (20 mins)

- o Which cruise companies advertise regularly? Rank in terms of visibility in media.
- o Thinking of SeaLux specifically, what advertising have you seen recently?
- o Thinking about advertising themes, what do members like/think most appealing?
- o Show copies of current SeaLux press advert. Discuss strengths and weaknesses of the material in terms of:

  - – Theme
  - – Imagery, colour scheme and style
  - – Message
  - – Brand, visibility and consistency
  - – Call to action
  - – Competitive standout

3 Summary phase (10 mins)

Summary of discussion – conclude discussion, summarise the key discussion outcomes, confirm with audience, capture any final points/corrections.

Thank you – thank everyone for taking the time to participate. Involvement is important to SeaLux.

Confidentiality – mention code of conduct, privacy, data protection, ethical approach.

Incentive gifts and expenses – ensure that expenses payments are made and provide SeaLux holiday gift vouchers to all participants.

Safe journey – close meeting.

* * * * *

NOTES TO DISCUSSION GUIDE
DESCRIPTION OF PROJECTIVE TECHNIQUES

1 General

A number of relevant projective techniques have been incorporated in the SeaLux group discussions. The following notes are intended to assist in conducting these activities.

2 Definition and purpose

Projective techniques are often incorporated within the programme for a discussion group or depth interview as a vehicle for drawing out and deeply exploring the attitudes, opinions and motivations of participants towards a product, brand or situation. The technique often involves the use of an ambiguous object or image that participants use to project their ideas, attitudes and perceptions.

Many of the individual techniques are also quite enjoyable and novel and so they act as a means of breaking up the discussion, adding interest and getting participants talking.

3 Some issues to be aware of

A number of projective techniques are perceived as questionable, since they have been borrowed from the field of clinical psychology and have not been validated for the type of research we undertake in marketing.

There are also concerns relating to the ethical aspect of some of the techniques, given their ability to probe the unconscious mind and reveal feelings that, consciously, the respondent might not wish to provide.

Finally, some of the techniques are so bizarre as to be viewed sceptically by both respondents and clients. There may also be a tendency on the part of some respondents to sabotage an exercise containing a projective technique.

The techniques used by this agency are selected for their proven ability to provide insight. We avoid those techniques that are controversial or have dubious intentions.

We conduct all exercises in an ethical manner.

4 Brand mapping

Alan Wilson (2003) defines brand mapping as 'a projective technique involving the presentation of a number of competing brands and then asking the participants to group them into categories based upon certain dimensions'.

The mapping dimensions can either be elicited from the participants themselves or provided by the moderator, according to the specific client objectives.

Brand mapping is also called perceptual mapping and can be used as the basis for pairing-off important variables and then scoring a product or brand in terms of each.

In a group environment, brand mapping, if done using a wall chart or felt board, can be a great exercise for getting everyone involved in a debate and arriving at a consensus.

For SeaLux, the client wishes to establish the positioning of a number of cruise companies, including the SeaLux brand itself. Relevant comparables include:

- o Luxury level vs. price
- o On-board service quality vs. price
- o Booking options vs. service/advice available

5 Photo sorts

This technique uses photographs or sketch cards, each showing a different individual in terms of age, gender and lifestyle characteristics. Participants are asked to sort the photographs according to which brand the subject would be most likely to choose. The technique is related to brand mapping/perceptual mapping, but specifically attempts to segment individuals according to relevant criteria.

For SeaLux, the client wishes to segment cruise passengers according to the type of cruise and type of booking channel preferred. The photo sort exercise will be employed to explore participants' perceptions without asking direct questions.

Photo Sort Exercise 1 – Categorise subjects according to their most likely cruise brand choice

Photo Sort Exercise 2 – Categorise subjects according to their most preferred and least preferred booking channel option: Web, Telephone, DRTV, Advertising direct response.

Note to moderators

It is important that the group members are encouraged to argue and debate the various possible positionings that they develop in these exercises. We need to understand the rationale and the emotions that lead to the final placement of each brand or character on the charts. Moderators are, therefore, asked to use these techniques as the basis for broader discussion and debate, not just as a mechanical exercise to be achieved as quickly as possible.

Answer 14
Observational research techniques

Check your answer

A good answer is likely to:

☑

In the introduction, introduce self and explain the purpose of the presentation. Build rapport and 'sell the benefits' to the audience, recognising their importance and likely needs. Introduce the concept of observational research and show how it relates to other forms of marketing research. ☐

Introduce and explain a number of relevant observational research techniques. Use examples set in the context of the restaurant industry; illustrate how the techniques could be used and what information might be obtained. ☐

Use a logical approach to presenting the material. ☐

Adopt the role of a market researcher. ☐

Use Presentation Notes format. ☐

* * * * *

PRESENTATION NOTES

Presentation for: CaterEX Conference

Fast Food Restaurateurs Conference Track

Date: XX/XX/XX

The Contribution of Observational Research

Welcome and introduce yourself

Slide 1 – Agenda

- o Introduction
- o Marketing research and observational techniques
- o Observational techniques for researching consumers
- o Researching service quality – mystery shopping
- o Concluding remarks
- o Any questions

Slide 1.1 – Introduction

The purpose of my presentation today is to introduce you to a number of popular research techniques that can assist in understanding your consumers and their needs and also in assessing the performance of your staff in the service delivery process.

Our focus is on relevant observational research techniques, but we will also look at how observational methods can be used with other research techniques, for example focus group meetings.

Slide 2 – Marketing research and observational techniques

Perhaps, as a way of setting the scene, we should begin by briefly looking at marketing research in general terms, starting with a definition.

Slide 2.1 – A definition of marketing research

The collection, analysis and communication of information undertaken to assist decision-making in marketing.

(*Source*: Alan Wilson, 2003)

The marketing decisions we refer to in this definition are often concerned with improving the customer visit experience, speeding the sales process, reducing queues, increasing sales, identifying a staff training need, deciding on a new layout for a restaurant and so on.

Marketing research techniques can provide information to help answer all of these questions and more.

The most common research technique in use today is the questionnaire; I am sure that you are already familiar with this research instrument and I imagine that the majority of you will use customer satisfaction or feedback questionnaires in your restaurants.

Slide 2.2 – Introducing a much older technique – observational research

A data gathering approach where information on the behaviour of people, objects and organisations is collected without any questions being asked of the participant.

(*Source*: Alan Wilson, 2003)

Observational approaches have been in use in retail environments from the very early days of marketing research; initially to track stock movement and sales turnover (wholesale or retail audits) or, with the later development of self-service retail environments, as a means of observing the behaviour of consumers as they move through a store space.

This research was originally undertaken using human observers who made notes on a detailed pro forma. Today, electronic methods such as bar-code readers, scanners, counters and CCTV cameras are more often employed for routine, observational research. Mystery shopping is also commonplace in retail and I will return to the role of this shortly.

Slide 2.3 – Advantages of observational techniques

A number of advantages are claimed including:

- ○ It records exactly what happened, does not rely on a respondent's memory, their verbal skills or their own interpretation of their behaviour.
- ○ The potential for bias is reduced either in an interviewer asking a question or in the respondent's answer.
- ○ Mechanical and electronic methods can be used to improve accuracy of recording, by reducing error in manually recording an observed event or behaviour. With CCTV recording, for example, the event is recorded faithfully and can be replayed many times and be viewed by a number of different experts.
- ○ Observation can identify the behaviour prior to and following a particular purchase or action.
- ○ Observational techniques do not interfere with the life of the respondent and the observer can be either visible or hidden from the view of the respondent.

Slide 2.4 – Disadvantages

- ○ Observation captures behaviour and events but cannot *explain* them, so we will still need to undertake other research or investigation to understand the attitudes and motivation leading to the behaviour.
- ○ The observed event or behaviour may be a 'one-off'; there is no guarantee that this behaviour will be repeated.

As with all things, there are some disadvantages and observation is no different.

Slide 3 – Observational techniques for researching consumers

We will focus here on the observational techniques that you can use in your fast food restaurants, as a method of understanding the behaviour of consumers as they interact with the environment, the promotional materials, food products and the staff.

We will examine the options, based upon a number of different observational techniques.

Slide 3.1 – Electronic point-of-sale equipment

This is already available in the majority of restaurants and can gather data that can later be analysed to determine purchase behaviour. Additionally, software in the tills might be capable of being re-programmed to provide additional information. For example, the till operator could be prompted to classify the age/gender of each person ordering food.

Data from the tills can certainly tell you the order value, number of items and range of items purchased in each transaction. You already use this information for re-ordering products on a just-in-time basis. How many of you have really considered just what the till might be able to tell you about your clients and what they purchase?

Slide 3.2 – Electronic people counters

These can be fitted at the entrance to determine the total number of visitors to each outlet per day. You could use this information in conjunction with the till data to estimate group size.

You can also use counting devices to look at traffic levels in the car park, children's play areas and toilets.

Slide 3.3 – CCTV monitoring

CCTV is usually fitted in each outlet for safety and security purposes but this equipment is also capable of being used to capture and record activity and behaviour in the restaurant.

Cameras could be located behind the tills to enable customer ordering behaviour to be observed. Audio recording could be used to monitor order requests and special orders; this might help with new product development and service delivery improvements and is much more efficient than relying on the memory of the till operator.

Cameras could monitor the seating areas and be used to identify size of group, in which zones are most popular. You could also observe what people do to occupy themselves whilst eating: reading papers, listening to music, chatting with friends and so on. Such information might assist with restaurant redesign, fittings, themes, availability of newspapers, ambient music and so on.

Cameras could also watch the counter area where promotional offers are displayed (and posters elsewhere too) to see whether customers are visibly looking at the promotions. This information could be integrated with till data later to determine the success of such offers relative to the number of opportunities to view.

Traditionally, the fast food industry has been concerned with achieving throughput. Now, there is an increasing emphasis on getting customers to stay longer and to spend more on each visit. The information collected via CCTV might contribute to decisions in support of these goals.

Slide 3.4 – Use of human observers

Human observers will be needed to analyse CCTV footage, but they could also operate visibly in the restaurants. Whether or not this might affect the customer behaviour would need to be carefully considered.

Human observers could be used to count people in and out of the store, monitor queue sizes and movement and observe behaviour and size of group at each table as well as record length of stay.

Another human observational method might involve a waste audit. This looks at the quantity and type of leftover food items from each visitor or group. The method of collection and the logistics of doing this would require some thought, but this information might help to identify additional research to determine ideal portion sizes, food popularity and quality.

Slide 3.5 – Ethnography

In this fast food culture, the use of total immersion observation techniques might have a role by using video recording of the life of a subject, akin to the approach taken in the documentary film – 'Super Size Me'.

Such techniques could look at the total eating, shopping and recreational behaviour of typical fast food consumers over a period of days. This specialised observational research approach is called ethnography and the insights gained through expert analyses of video recordings could be very useful for new product development and as a way of understanding how best to communicate with and engage the typical fast food restaurant customer.

Slide 3.6 – Using other research techniques to understand the behaviour

Remember that observational techniques will tell you what the behaviour is but not why it takes place. To understand the motivational drivers of the behaviour and the attitudes and opinions of the consumer, other research approaches will be required. Focus groups are useful as a means of understanding your customers in these terms. In addition, observation is used within the focus group to help build a fuller picture of the consumer.

Slide 4 – Researching service quality – the use of mystery shopping

Probably the most well known of observational methods, mystery shopping can be very productive in a restaurant environment and is regularly carried out in the large fast food chains and most retail environments.

Slide 4.1 – What is mystery shopping?

The collection of information from retail outlets, showrooms and so on by people trained to observe, experience, record and measure the customer service process by posing as members of the public.

(*Source*: MRS, 2005)

Slide 4.2 – What can mystery shopping do?

Mystery shopping is concerned with collecting objective facts not opinions. Facts can include details of the retail environment, staff dress, staff adherence to procedure and so on.

As the name suggests, the mystery shopper experiences the customer journey just as any real shopper would. On completion of the shopping exercise, the mystery shopper completes a questionnaire to record the observations made.

Mystery shopping can be used as a diagnostic tool to identify areas for improvement in the service delivery or associated procedures to identify staff training needs, to score restaurant performance and to provide motivational incentives to branch staff.

Another important use of mystery shoppers is in competitor evaluation. Please remember, though, that it is the process that is being measured. Competitor shopping is an ethical and legal activity, provided that the mystery shopper does not take up the time of competitors' staff or interfere with normal store operation in any way. As long as the mystery shopper orders and consumes restaurant food products just as a real restaurant customer would, then the activity is ethical.

Slide 4.3 – What are the attributes of a good mystery shopper?

Mystery shoppers require training and need to be selected carefully, as they will have to fit the profile of a typical restaurant customer and be able to memorise a checklist (and the answers to fill in later). They also need to be neutral or, at least, not exhibit the traits of someone who is cynical or overly critical, as this will introduce bias.

Slide 5 – Concluding remarks

I hope that this short presentation has convinced you of the contribution that marketing research, and observational techniques in particular, can make in providing valuable information regarding the behaviour of your consumers and the service delivery in each restaurant outlet. Used with other techniques, such as questionnaires and focus groups, the information will enable you to make a range of product, service and marketing decisions.

Slide 6 – Any questions?

Answer 15
Group discussions and individual depth interviews

Check your answer

A good answer is likely to:

☑

In the introduction, explain the reason for writing the letter, emphasising the relevance □
of qualitative research and discussion groups, and individual depth interviews in particular,
as a means of obtaining in-depth information on attitudes and motivations of
respondents.

In Part a, list and explain the advantages and disadvantages of each method. □

In Part b, identify the disadvantages of each method and explain how these might be □
overcome.

In Part c, explain how the web might be used to host group discussions, outlining possible □
advantages. Identify the disadvantages inherent in this approach.

Adopt the role of a marketing research executive. □

Use letter format. □

* * * * *

LETTER

GroupTek Dynamic Research Ltd

The Green

Middletown

HJ45 8XZ

XX/XX/XXXX

Mrs Jenny Client

Marketing Manager

AT Industrial Engineering

Uptown

HJ34 5TH

Dear Jenny

Subject: Group Discussions and Individual Depth Interviews

Further to our telephone conversation earlier today regarding the possible relevance of group discussions and individual depth interviews, we thought that it might help if we provided you with some additional information detailing the key advantages and disadvantages of these two methods and explained their possible contribution to the overall design for your research project.

We recognise that, as a business-to-business customer, it can often prove difficult to hold group discussions because of the logistics of getting busy engineers and managers to travel to a central venue to take part in a discussion. We have, therefore, included a short section towards the end of the letter which explains how we might address this difficulty by using the Internet to hold online discussions.

Qualitative and quantitative research

Group discussions and individual depth interviews are both forms of qualitative research. This type of research is very popular and can make a considerable contribution to a research project.

In our proposal, we have explained how we will use both methodologies to achieve your objectives. A key aspect of these qualitative methods that distinguishes them from quantitative approaches is their ability to provide very detailed insights into the attitudes, motivations and feelings of the respondents. These insights, although they cannot be considered statistically true for an entire customer base, are very beneficial to you as they help you understand why your customers think or behave in a certain way.

Advantages of Group Discussions and Individual Depth Interviews.

Both methods provide:

o Rich and detailed insights into attitudes, motivations, feelings.
o An opportunity to explore areas that may not have been obvious to the researcher but are deemed important by the respondent(s).
o An opportunity for the respondent(s) to be viewed remotely and also recorded for later analysis.
o The client with an opportunity to hear, first-hand, the respondents' ideas, opinions and feelings.
o An opportunity for the body language of respondents to be observed/recorded.
o An opportunity for props and other stimuli to be included in the discussion or interview; this can be very helpful in drawing out subconscious feelings and as a means of generating and evaluating ideas for new products.
o An opportunity for new questions to be introduced to the respondent(s) during the discussion.

Individual depth interviews have some additional advantages over discussion groups:

o The one-to-one, face-to-face environment can be very good for examining body language and for probing and exploring real depth and personal insights that might be inhibited in a group environment.
o No special 'focus group' settings are required, any comfortable room is sufficient.
o Recruitment tends to be easier, given the generally smaller number of participants involved overall.

In comparison with depth interviews, group discussions:

- o are much less expensive to run and make better use of time, since they involve many more participants, typically 8–10 per session.
- o offer an opportunity for the discussion to benefit from the dynamics of the group; one comment might trigger many others.

There are, however, a number of disadvantages to both methods, which include:

- o They both require highly skilled interviewers/moderators with training in psychology or the social sciences.
- o Sessions can be derailed by powerful individuals and can be hard to control.
- o Transcripts for sessions require skilled analysis and interpretation.
- o There is a high degree of subjectivity in any findings.
- o They rely on small samples of a total population of interest and are not therefore representative of the population as a whole.

Overcoming the disadvantages of both methods

The stated disadvantages of these methods can be largely overcome and where this is not 100 per cent possible, the advantages of the methods are still of great value in terms of the contribution that they can make to the overall project.

The need for highly skilled interviewers/moderators cannot be overcome but, by choosing an agency that employs such specialists, the client has access to a great deal of expertise that can skilfully run and analyse each session.

To avoid the possibility of strong personalities derailing a session, a number of precautions are taken by our staff:

- o The sessions are conducted by moderators/interviewers who are highly experienced in working with groups and can 'manage' and take advantage of the stronger personalities, whilst also being able to draw out contributions for weaker participants. In B2B projects, respondents can be carefully chosen by the client, given that the client knows each customer and can avoid those who might be purely disruptive.
- o A moderator's guide or discussion guide is used to help keep the discussion running within agreed boundaries and to support a list of topics.
- o Screening questionnaires are used to filter out 'professional participants' who will be excluded from the project.

Session transcripts do require skilled analysis; this is ensured by video recording all sessions and then using this material, along with written transcripts, to first sort and then thoroughly analyse responses, using a range of techniques. Again, we draw upon our in-house expertise (psychologists and social scientists) to help us.

The subjective nature of the methodology is acknowledged – again, relevant expertise and experience helps to confirm any ambiguous or subjective response during the session itself as it might in the later analysis, ensuring that any subjectivity does not bias the outcomes significantly.

Small sample size and the corresponding impact on being representative are also acknowledged. Where this is an issue, the conclusions drawn from the qualitative research can be 'tested' using quantitative methods. The quantitative methods are seen as an integrated part of the overall project.

The value of depth interviewing in business-to-business research

It is worth emphasising the value of individual depth interviewing in a business-to-business context such as yours. These interviews can be conducted by making appointments to visit customers at their offices or, where it is impractical to visit the respondents at their place of work, by means of telephone. In our proposal, we have detailed the specific approaches we will take to depth interviewing for this project.

Using the Internet to host group discussions

Where group discussions might prove difficult because of the geographic dispersal of participants, as is often the case in b2b projects, it is possible to use the Internet and specialist software. This approach can never be a replacement for a physical meeting but is nevertheless becoming increasingly popular.

Advantages are obvious:

1. Much lower cost to host than a physical meeting.

2. Removes the need for respondents to travel to a central location, reducing expenses costs.

3. International respondents can take part 'alongside' those who are more local.

4. Business professionals are more likely to participate if they do not have to give up time away from the office.

5. Business people are very comfortable using computers and many already use PCs for teleconferencing, online training and chat sessions.

6. Respondents may be more willing to be totally honest when they are not face to face with other respondents or a moderator.

Disadvantages include:

1. A lack of real interaction and group bonding, since respondents are not physically together.

2. Body language is difficult to monitor, even if web cameras are fitted on each respondent's PC.

3. It is not so easy to use props and other stimuli, although pictures can be shown. Group activities, such as collage making, might also be difficult to facilitate, although, again, specialist software is becoming available.

4. The moderator will have less control over the proceedings and may not have the skills to handle technology issues.

A possible alternative to an online discussion group, where the involvement of all respondents is synchronised in real time, would be to consider the use of forum or bulletin board software. Such tools can be very effective to promote ideas and rolling discussions with respect to product enhancements and new service development.

We trust that the above will help you understand the role of qualitative techniques such as individual depth interviews and discussion groups. If you have any further questions, please feel free to contact us.

Yours sincerely,

(Debbie Researcher)

GroupTek Dynamic Research Ltd

Answer 16
Marketing research for website development

Check your answer

A good answer is likely to:

☑

In the introduction, create the need for marketing information and research to support all
stages of the project; justify your reasoning. ☐

In Part a, outline the types of marketing information that would be needed to support
decisions during the concept development: site design, prototype testing, launch, go
live and operational management of the e-commerce website. ☐

In Part b, identify a number of qualitative and quantitative research methods that could be
applied at the various stages of the web site development process and when
operational. Explain how each chosen technique might be used and what insight it
could deliver. ☐

Adopt the role of a researcher working in the e-commerce company. ☐

Use Report format. ☐

* * * * *

REPORT

To: Web Marketing Manager

From: Research Executive

Date: XX/XX/XX

Re: Use of Qualitative and Quantitative Research Methods to Support the New 'Cook n' Spicy'
E-commerce Site Development and Launch

1 Introduction

As we are well aware, our business operates in a fast-moving and highly competitive environment, where online businesses compete fiercely with one another to capture and retain
customers. This is a world in which the online proposition and experience also competes with
the traditional bricks and mortar business. Customers have enormous choice and the freedom
to decide what they buy, when and how they buy and with whom they make purchases and
build relationships.

In order to ensure that the new Cook n' Spicy proposition is successful, we must understand
our target customer in depth and then determine what we need to do to make the process of
buying cooking ingredients quicker, easier and more pleasurable.

2 Marketing information and website development

Marketing research is an essential element of the new development project. Well in advance of the launch date and, as a key feed to the decision-making process, it can provide information to comprehensively identify and define both the off-line and online aspects of:

2.1 The market

- ○ Its size, growth, stability, profitability.

2.2 The customer

- ○ The target customer groups.
- ○ Profiles for each customer group, providing deep insight into their needs, wants, behaviour, attitudes and motivation.

2.3 The competition

- ○ The competition based upon where the customer currently shops, both online and off-line.
- ○ The shopping experience, including competitor site usability testing and marketing mix.
- ○ What gaps exist, given the current offerings and websites.

2.4 The Cook n' Spicy proposition and website

- ○ The unique value we need to build into our selling proposition/marketing mix.
- ○ Web site design and functionality, user interface design and site prototype testing.

2.5 After the site is launched and operational, marketing research can continue to provide information to help develop and refine the site itself, as well as the products and services provided to the user. Information gathering activities would include:

- ○ Profiling the customers, their user behaviour and deepening our knowledge of them.
- ○ Using user/site behaviour analysis to look for deficiencies in the site and identify ways of improving site effectiveness and sales.
- ○ Undertaking customer satisfaction surveys.
- ○ Identifying relevant information for promotional campaigns and advertising.

3 Review of research approaches and methods

A number of research techniques may be used to gather the types of information identified in Section 2 above.

3.1 Secondary research

Secondary research will be useful at the outset of the project to explore the market, the customers, the industry and the competition. It will help paint a picture of the marketplace and its potential, as well as serve to focus our attention on the key information that we will need to gather using primary research.

The Internet will prove a most valuable resource for our research, but we must not overlook business libraries and marketing research companies that publish reports.

Information can be obtained from trade and consumer cookery magazines, cookery clubs and societies, competitor sites and TV cooking programmes (especially those featuring amateur and home cooks in competitions and in the home). Cookery shows are immensely popular and can provide insight into our target customers.

3.2 Observational techniques

A number of observational research techniques can be used to gather information on behaviour and to observe processes.

3.2.1 Observing users in action

During the development of the Cook n' Spicy site, typical customers could be observed during concept testing of the website. This observation could be conducted using trained observers and/or the use of eye cameras located in the computer monitors and linked to specialist software and the web browser to track eye and mouse movements for later analysis.

This information would help us understand what aspects and features of the site lead to improved usability, including its navigation, site functions, ingredient shopping catalogue, shopping cart, check out and so on.

Once the site is live and operational, software tools (including click stream analysis) running on our web servers can be used to build a picture of user behaviour and to determine how they use and navigate through the site, frequency of visit and so on. With the permission of each user, we could also install cookie software on the user's computer. This could be used to record site visit behaviour.

3.2.2 Mystery shopping

Mystery Shopping could be used to test out the processes and effectiveness of competitor website and e-commerce facilities. This would be carried out using trained mystery shoppers who would resemble typical users and would provide information on the ease of use, convenience and effectiveness of each competitor's site and the off-line service and support processes, including speed of delivery and so on.

In the same way, the Cook n' Spicy website could be mystery shopped at intervals to gather similar information.

Mystery Shopping could also be conducted over the telephone, targeting our customer call centre.

3.3 Qualitative research

3.3.1 Discussion groups

Traditional (off-line) discussion groups could be used to help understand the needs, wants, attitudes and behaviour of the target customer and as an effective method for exploring the current ways in which home cooks and amateur chefs purchase for their cooking needs. This research will need to be conducted at an early stage in the development project and would also contribute to demographic and lifestyle profiling.

The discussion group programme would identify the gaps in the existing offerings in the marketplace and then explore possibilities for the Cook n' Spicy proposition, which would include both the site and its facilities. Qualitative information could also be collected about the proposed cooking products and ingredients that would be available from the brand.

Off-line discussion groups could be used in conjunction with site user observational research (see Section 3.1 above) as a means of obtaining feedback about the site and to gather ideas for improvement and additional features.

Group members would be recruited from the population of interest and then asked to attend meetings at a central location. A computer, running the website software and screenshots of the various parts of the site, would be used as a prop for examination and discussion.

3.3.2 Use of projective techniques
The discussion groups could include a number of projective techniques to help develop aspects of the discussion.

Collage making could be used to explore the world of the home cook/amateur chef to gain insight into their underlying motivations and attitudes.

Perceptual maps could be created to examine competitor brands positionings.

3.4 Quantitative techniques

3.4.1 Questionnaires and surveys
Questionnaires could be designed to collect relevant information about the purchase behaviour of home cooks and amateur chefs. This survey would be conducted at an early stage in the project and used with qualitative information, taken from focus group transcripts as a basis for profiling and segmenting potential customers for Cook n' Spicy.

The information would provide considerable insight into what these customers buy, when they buy, where and why they do so and how frequently. It could also research their needs with respect to how the customer typically accesses technical information about ingredients and recipes.

3.4.2 Online survey and e-mail surveys
Once the site is operational, users can be invited and incentivised to participate in online questionnaires that would have the objective of:

- Collecting information from site visitors and customers to assist in building detailed site user profiles.
- Running satisfaction surveys and tracking studies.

Information can be collected in a number of ways:

Site registration forms Some users (but certainly not all) will be willing to register with the site in order to obtain newsletters, offers and access to promotional offers. As part of this registration process, limited but useful information can be collected that will help us build user profiles.

Pop-up survey invitations Some users will be willing to take part in online surveys during their visit to the site, especially if incentivised to do so. Invitations can be delivered using a pop-up message with a click through to a web-based survey questionnaire.

An element of randomness can be introduced into the recruitment process by serving the invitation only to every nth site visitor to the site. Again the information will help build detailed profiles of the users.

E-mail surveys   These can be used to research those users/visitors who have registered with the Cook n' Spicy website, as well as anyone who has made a purchase from the site. In all cases, a valid e-mail address will be required. Again, the invitation should be incentivised in some way in order to maximise response levels.

Both the profile-seeking research and the customer satisfaction surveys would be conducted at regular intervals in order to track changes in the profile of the typical visitor or user over time and also to measure any user response to changes made to improve the site, changes that might have been driven by feedback from previous surveys.

4 Concluding remarks

Marketing research can make a valuable contribution to all stages of this development project and encompasses both the off-line and online aspects. Research will help us understand the potential customer; identify the best design and feature set for the site itself; help us research the brand, the products and the services we will need to provide in order to be a success in the market.

Once the site is fully operational, ongoing research will continue to provide information to assist in the development and improvement of our products and services, as well as to provide regular satisfaction feedback from customers – we can use this to continuously improve our processes and our products.

In the competitive environment of the web, such research is vital to ensure that our R&D and marketing budgets are justified and underpinned by real market information. This will ensure that funds are spent effectively.

Answer 17
Sampling techniques, sample size and accuracy

Check your answer

A good answer is likely to:

☑

In the introduction, introduce the concept of sampling, define terms, state purpose and link to quantitative methodologies. Mention the role of sampling and accuracy. ☐

In Section 1, provide an overview of the various sampling approaches and techniques. ☐

In Section 2, introduce and briefly explain the various probability and non-probability methods. ☐

In Section 3, discuss the relevance of sampling in determining accuracy. Restate the need for a probability method to be employed. Outline the difficulties that probability samples often present. Explain how sample size is determined. Introduce level of confidence and accuracy. Relate sample size to population size. Relate sample size to cost and time. Explain impact of sampling errors and non-sampling errors on accuracy. State that high accuracy is not always required. Managers willing to trade accuracy for speed and lower costs. ☐

In Section 4, comment specifically on the manager's assertion and reference material already presented to argue a case. ☐

Adopt the role of a marketing or research executive. ☐

Use Report format. ☐

* * * * *

REPORT

To: Marketing Manager

From: Marketing Executive

Date: XX/XX/XX

Re: The Importance of Sampling and Sampling Techniques for Accuracy

1 Introduction

Sampling involves the collection of data from a subset (a sample) of the total group of people (the population of interest) who are relevant to the research project. A subset is usually preferred, since it would usually be cost-prohibitive, even unnecessary, to carry out a survey of the total population of interest (a census).

Once a sample has been determined and the research conducted using the sample group as the respondents, the data can then be analysed and the findings taken as being representative of the population of interest as a whole.

Sampling is most usually associated with quantitative research, for example when using a questionnaire, since the data produced is objective in nature and can easily be processed numerically or using statistics. Depending upon the type of sampling involved, statistical techniques can also be used to determine the level of accuracy represented by the data.

Sampling approaches are also often used in qualitative research although, in reality, this form of research is not credited with being representative, since only a small number of respondents are asked to take part. Any findings can only be linked to the participants and not the population as a whole.

2 Sampling techniques

Sampling involves taking a limited subset of the population in order to be able draw conclusions from quantitative research data about the population of interest as a whole.

There are two broad sampling approaches: probability (or random) sampling and non-probability (or non-random) sampling. A number of specific sampling techniques are available for each broad approach. An overview of these approaches and techniques will be covered below.

2.1 Probability sampling

Probability sampling is so called because every member of the population of interest has a known and equal probability of being selected. Statistical methods can be used to determine accuracy and level of confidence in the data.

In order to be able to undertake a probability sampling approach, we need to be able to construct a sampling frame. This is essentially a numbered list of the entire population of interest. If such a list cannot be constructed, then a non-probability approach must be used.

Four probability sampling techniques are in common use:

1. Simple random sampling – respondents are selected entirely at random (using a random number generator or printed tables). This is the purest form of probability sampling, but it is not perfect. A census is the only approach which approaches perfection.

2. Systematic sampling – a quasi-random method which selects every nth entry in the sampling frame after a random start point in the list has been determined.

3. Stratified random sampling – a quasi-random method, whereby the sampling frame is first divided into a number of meaningful groups (or strata). A number of respondents are then chosen at random from each group. This is a useful approach that would take account of different levels or segments in the group.

4. Multistage sampling – a quasi-random approach which is especially useful where the population is geographically dispersed.

2.2 Non-probability sampling

This approach is employed where a sampling frame is not available or where it would be cost-prohibitive or impossible to obtain. It is also employed where smaller samples are to be used for reasons of speed or cost.

If this approach is used, then statistical techniques cannot be used to determine accuracy and level of confidence in the data.

A number of techniques are in use, including:

1. Convenience sampling – as the name suggests, respondents are chosen for the convenience of the researcher.

2. Judgement sampling – respondents are selected on the basis of the skill and judgement of the researcher, as being deemed appropriate for the research. This technique is often used in B2B research, where customers are chosen as being representative of an industry or segment. Important customers can be included in the research too!

3. Quota sampling – respondent characteristics are first identified, then the researcher recruits a given number (or quota) within each characteristic set.

3 Sample size and accuracy considerations

It is a common perception that the larger the sample size, the more accurate the research results, since the study is thought to be more representative of the total population. This is true only for small populations and up to a certain sample size for larger populations. Beyond a certain point, a law of diminishing returns becomes active. Only a relatively small number of interviews (typically hundreds of respondents) are actually required to achieve acceptable accuracy. To go beyond this number would just add to cost without a justifiable return – to achieve 2x the accuracy you would need to interview 4x as many respondents and incur nearly a quadrupling of costs.

Sample size is not determined by the size of the population in the sampling frame but is an absolute number of respondents and is determined/calculated on the basis of three factors:

1. The degree of variability in the data – a measure of how evenly distributed the characteristics we wish to measure are within the population. The term used is standard deviation from the mean.
2. The level of accuracy required by the decision maker – the greater the accuracy, the more interviews required (subject to the comment made above about doubling accuracy).
3. The degree of confidence required that the results seen in the data will be within a certain range.

Using this information, sample size can be calculated using statistical formulae or by means of sample size tables or a sample size calculator.

Research results will be expressed in terms of accuracy and level of confidence, for example:

95 per cent confidence level +/–3 per cent.

This means that the sample has a 5 per cent chance (1 in 20) of being wrong and that a data result of, say, 50 per cent will actually fall between 48.5 and 51.5 per cent.

3.1 Other factors affecting accuracy of the data

A number of other factors affect the accuracy of the data obtained from the sample, including problems with the way in which the sampling frame was constructed and bias in either the survey questions or in the way the answers were recorded. There is also the possibility of non-response error.

The actual number of samples chosen for interview will be a factor of time frame, cost and the degree of accuracy actually required by the client.

As indicated above, calculation of accuracy is only possible when a probability sampling approach is chosen, since only in this case is the probability of being selected equal and known; this in turn depends on the availability of a valid sampling frame.

4 Further factors to consider

It is important to realise that, whilst accuracy is undoubtedly important, total accuracy (if at all achievable), imposes a very high cost on the research, since it requires many more respondents to be involved in the project with a correspondingly larger data collection and analysis task.

Such accuracy is rarely required to make an informed and appropriate marketing decision. Marketing managers, working to a budget, are more than usually willing to trade accuracy in order to reduce costs and speed up the research process. An exception to this would be where a high level of risk is involved in the decision, for example, in the case of a pharmaceutical company researching/testing a new drug.

The experience of the research agency also plays a role in working out how many respondents will be required for a project and statistical calculation of the optimum sample size is by no means a mandatory aspect of the sampling process.

5 Concluding remarks

Deciding on how to sample the respondents who will participate in a research project is an important element in the research design and it can be seen that accuracy is only one of the considerations, along with whether a valid sampling frame can be generated and the importance of questionnaire design and interviewer skills in reducing bias and non-response errors.

There is a link between sample size and accuracy, but this is not as strong as is generally believed. Accuracy depends upon the precision with which a sampling frame is produced and also upon the sampling approach chosen, probability samples being the only statistically accurate methods.

Client needs, time available for the research and budget factors also need to be considered when developing a sampling plan.

Answer 18
Statistical techniques

Check your answer

A good answer is likely to:

☑

In the introduction. briefly explain the purpose and content of the appendix, emphasising the importance of statistical techniques in analysing research data. ☐

In Part a, introduce and explain each of the terms and state the importance of the difference and the implications for marketing research. ☐

In Part b, define the term and state the purpose. Introduce concept of the null and alternative hypotheses. Outline various methods for testing. Mention errors and their possible implications. Discuss use of correction factors. ☐

In Part c, introduce and explain each of the techniques, discussing the principle and purpose of each. ☐

In Part d, introduce and define. Outline the principles involved and list possible uses. ☐

Use examples relevant to Kelvin Council to illustrate each technique discussed. ☐

Adopt the role of a research executive employed by an agency. ☐

Use the format of an Appendix to a research report. ☐

* * * * *

RESEARCH REPORT – APPENDIX XX
DESCRIPTION OF STATISTICAL TECHNIQUES

1 General

In preparing the findings of this marketing research report, a number of statistical techniques have been used to analyse the data. Statistical techniques are frequently used to summarise, compare, test and understand relationships within the data obtained from the research.

A brief explanation of the common statistical techniques is provided in this Appendix.

2 Mathematical significance vs. statistical significance

2.1 Mathematical significance

Mathematical significance is concerned with the difference in value between two numbers or results. Any difference is of significance from a mathematical perspective. For example, if we consider that Kelvin Council residents were asked the question:

Would you recycle more if you were provided with a bin for collecting recyclable waste?

In the survey, 48 per cent said that they would recycle more, 52 per cent said no, they would not.

Clearly, the numbers represent a difference of 4 per cent, and, although relatively small, the difference is mathematically significant.

Would it be worth making an investment in recycling bins for free issue to residents based on this difference?

To answer this question, we first need to determine whether the two values are statistically significant. If so, Kelvin Council would then be able to look at the business case for investing in recycling bins.

2.2 Statistical significance

Marketing research data is usually obtained from a sample of the total population of interest and is, therefore, subject to a level of error, so we cannot be certain that the difference is important or real enough for management decisions to be made. We can, however, determine whether the difference is statistically significant.

A test for statistical significance can be conducted to determine whether the difference in the two values is large enough to be important and unlikely to be accounted for by natural variations in the population, by chance or through sampling error.

Significance testing can be carried out using hypothesis-testing techniques.

3 The concept of hypothesis testing

A hypothesis is simply an assumption (it could be a guess, hunch or gut feel) about some aspect of the population of interest to the decision-maker. This assumption is referred to as the Null Hypothesis (labelled H_0).

Using the example from the research data in Section 2 above, let us make the assumption that:

H_0 – the two values are not statistically different.

The other possibility, of course is that the two values are statistically significant – this is called the alternative hypothesis, H_1.

H_1 – the two values are statistically different and not due to chance or sampling error.

A number of statistical methods can be used to prove (or accept) the H_0 hypothesis or to disprove (or reject) it. Hypothesis testing enables the researcher to calculate the probability of observing a particular result in the actual population of interest.

Statistical methods for testing hypotheses are manifold and include:

Goodness of fit testing – using a Chi-Square test (or χ_2).

Hypotheses about means – using a Z-test, t-test or analysis of variance test.

Hypotheses about proportions – using a Z-test.

In our example, a Z-test would be appropriate, since we are interested in the two proportions of the population who said they would/would not recycle more if they were provided with a dedicated recycling bin.

Hypothesis testing is a multi-stage process involving setting up the H_0 and H_1 hypotheses, selecting the appropriate test technique, calculating a result and then using this result to accept or reject the null hypothesis.

3.1 Errors

Hypothesis testing is in itself an imperfect approach and is subject to errors; these are referred to as Type I and Type II errors.

A Type I error – causes a rejection of the null hypothesis when it is actually true.

A Type II error – causes an acceptance of the null hypothesis when it is actually false.

When conducting the Z-test, a correction factor (based upon probabilities) called a standard error is factored in to the equation to minimise the potential risk of a type I or a type II error from occurring, depending upon which one is the more important.

For Kelvin Council, the type II error would be most serious, since it could potentially result in a major financial investment in recycling bins without good reason.

4 Correlation and regression

A number of statistical techniques are available for measuring relationships (or associations) between individual variables represented in the research data.

A good example, from the perspective of the Council, would be to understand the relationship between financial incentive payments to residents (variable 1) and recycling rates (variable 2).

In order to identify a possible link between the two variables identified above, techniques such as correlation and regression may be used.

4.1 Correlation

Identifies the strength of a relationship between two variables by examining the degree to which changes in one of the variables, variable 1 (recycling rate), are associated with changes in a second, variable 2 (incentive payments).

Correlation can be shown by plotting instances of the two variables on a scatter graph. Perfect correlation is said to exist when all of the plotted points can be joined by means of a straight line. No correlation would exist where the plots are randomly scattered around the chart.

Correlation, where it exists, can be either positive in direction (low values of one variable are associated with low values of the other and also high values of one are associated with high values in the other) or negative in direction (low values of one variables are associated with high values of the other and vice versa).

The strength and direction of the correlation is normally calculated using a formula and expressed as a coefficient, having a value between $+1$ and -1. The closer to unity the coefficient is, the stronger the relationship between the variables.

4.2 Regression

Identifies the nature of the relationship between the two variables and uses an equation to describe the relationship. Once the equation has been derived, it can be used for forecasting purposes.

As with correlation, regression can be achieved graphically, using a line of best fit to approximate the data and derive values for the equation. A straight line is used for this purpose (having the equation $y = a + bx$, where a is the intercept of the y axis and b is the estimated slope of the best fit line).

In addition to graphical methods, the values for a and b can be calculated using formulae.

It should be noted that, where more than two variables are to be studied, multivariate analysis techniques, such as perceptual mapping and cluster analysis, can be used. Perceptual mapping will be familiar to the marketing team at Kelvin Council. Cluster Analysis is briefly described in the next section below.

5 Cluster analysis and its application

Cluster analysis is a broad term for a group of statistical techniques used to identify and classify groupings of people or objects (clusters) on the basis of two or more common variables, where a high degree of association exists within a cluster, but where very weak or non-existent associations exist between the clusters.

The traditional way of undertaking a cluster analysis is, again, by means of a scatter diagram, involving the plotting of similar characteristics with respect to the variables of interest. Individual clusters are then identified visually, by looking for distinct groupings within the plotted data.

This manual approach is impractical and time-consuming, especially where large data sets are involved and more than a few variables are being plotted. Instead, tools, such as the SPSS software we maintain at this agency, are used to achieve faster and more accurate results from a mass of data. The computer techniques use complex algorithms and iterative techniques to establish patterns in the data and to exhaustively define the unique associations within each identified cluster.

5.1 Application of cluster analysis

In the Kelvin Council area, residents and businesses could be segmented on the basis of relevant criteria they have in common. Cluster analysis could be used to identity important segments using the data set created from the research project. These segments, once properly identified and profiled, could then be used as the basis for future targeted campaigns aimed at changing resident/business behaviour with respect to recycling.

Further, more detailed information on any of the statistical techniques used in marketing research can be obtained by contacting our statistics team.

Answer 19
Analysing quantitative and qualitative data

Check your answer

A good answer is likely to:

☑

In the introduction, state the need for thorough and rigorous analysis of research data in ☐
order to be able to derive the findings and draw conclusions.

In Part a, introduce and describe the various types of quantitative data and explain ☐
the approaches for analysis including: tabulation, cross-tabulation and a number of
descriptive statistical methods.

In Part b, introduce and outline the approaches that can be used to analyse transcripts ☐
from unstructured qualitative interviews. Take two of these methods and describe in
further detail.

Adopt the role of marketing manager. ☐

Use Report format. ☐

* * * * *

REPORT

To: Managing Director

From: Marketing Manager

Date: XX/XX/XX

Re: Techniques for Analysing Quantitative and Qualitative Data

1 Introduction

For it to be useful and meaningful, the data collected during the course of a research project
requires skilful manipulation and analysis, often by statisticians or appropriately trained
researchers. There are a number of techniques that can be used to reduce the quantity of
data and to help make sense of it, so as to enable findings and conclusions to be drawn.

2 Analysing quantitative data

Before the quantitative data obtained from the postal questionnaires can be analysed, it is first
entered into a computer in a format that will make it easier to count or manipulate the data.
There are two separate steps to be undertaken here: coding, where each response is effectively translated into a machine-readable format by allocating a number to each response
(yes = 1, no = 0, etc.); and data entry, where the data is actually entered into the computer

either manually or via a scanner. Coding has to be designed and implemented for each of the different question types employed in the questionnaire including open, closed and scaling type questions.

It is quite normal to code the questionnaires at the design stage; this pre-coding makes the process much easier and reduces the likelihood of errors, especially if the forms are capable of being machine read. The importance of pilot testing of the questionnaire cannot be overstated; such testing would include data collection, coding and analysis stages and any errors should then be indicated and corrected prior to the full-scale data collection phase.

Once the data is in the computer, it is checked for accuracy and cleaned to ensure that there are no errors or inconsistencies in it. Manually coded and entered data is particularly susceptible to such problems.

2.1 Data types

Once the data is clean and complete, it is ready to analyse. For analysis purposes, there are four different types of data:

Nominal data – where numbers are used to represent names or objects, for example: 1 = male, 2 = female.

Ordinal data – where numbers are used to signify order or ranking, but have no other meaning.

Interval data – as ordinal data, but with a fixed and equal interval between values.

Ratio data – where each value is expressed relative to an origin, often 0.

Two key approaches are available to analyse this data: data tabulation and statistical techniques. Each approach has a number of underlying techniques.

It is important to realise that not all of the techniques of analysis are suitable for every data type, although this detail is deemed beyond the scope of this short report.

2.2 Data tabulation

Data tabulation involves the construction of tables containing important data taken from the dataset. Available techniques include frequency distribution and cross-tabulation.

Frequency distribution indicates the number (or frequency) of respondents who gave particular responses to a question, as shown in Table 1.1.

Table 1.1 Market share by number of installed systems (Dec/XX)

Who is the supplier of your current alarm management system?	Sample = 90 (100%)
ABC Computers Ltd	40 (44%)
Colonnade Technologies Ltd	38 (42%)
Tritec Ltd	10 (11%)
US Alarm Dynamics Inc.	2 (2.2%)

2.3 Cross-tabulation

This approach combines the responses from one question with those from another. In the case of the Colonnades research, we could combine the data from Table 1 with that relating to the size of the user organisation. This would provide some insight into which vendors are currently strongest in supplying the small, medium and large customers.

Using the data from Table 1.1 in isolation, ABC would appear to be the market leader with 40 customers. The cross-tabulation provides a different picture, with Colonnade appearing to have a larger share of the total market by size of system. There is also some evidence that US Alarm Dynamics is targeting the large ARC.

Although the simple tables are easy to read, the use of graphs and charts is also popular. The information contained in Table 1.1 could be represented in a pie chart whilst that from Table 1.2 could appear in a donut chart with three rings, with one to represent each size of ARC operator.

Table 1.2 Market share by size of ARC operator (Dec/XX)

	Sample = 90 (100%)	Small ARC	Med ARC	Large ARC
ABC Computers	40 (44%)	38	2	0
Colonnade Technologies Ltd	38 (42%)	3	20	15
Tritec Ltd	10 (11%)	2	7	1
US Alarm Dynamics Inc.	2 (2.2%)	0	0	2

3 Statistical techniques

A large number of statistical techniques are available to the researcher when analysing quantitative data. Such statistics would include techniques for describing (or summarising) the data in a set, hypothesis testing, correlation and regression techniques.

To illustrate the use of some simple statistical approaches, this report will consider descriptive techniques. Sample customer satisfaction scores are used to illustrate a number of techniques.

3.1 Descriptive statistics

Basic statistical methods can be used to summarise large datasets in terms of central tendency (mean, median and mode) and dispersion or degree of the spread of the data (range, variance and standard deviation).

The Mean is easily calculated by adding up the numbers in the set and then dividing by the number of values in the set. This will indicate the average value. Using the following data, the average is 5.3.

4 1 7 5 8 6 2 7 6 7

The Median is the middle case in the set, so for example, the above data has been assembled in ascending order and the middle case is 6.

1 2 4 5 6 6 7 7 7 8

The Mode is the value in the set that appears most frequently in the data, for example in the data above, 7 appears most frequently.

If the above data represented the customer satisfaction scores for a number of Colonnade Technology customers, then which value we should take as representative – 5.3, 6 or 7 – will depend on what we are aiming to achieve.

The Range is represented as the interval between the highest and lowest values, in the above data this is:

$$8 - 1 = 7$$

The Variation is the spread of the data, calculated using the average squared deviation of each number from its mean. Using a statistical function calculator, for the above data, this value is 5.34.

Standard Deviation is the square root of the variance; for this data the value is 2.31.

4 Analysing qualitative data

Qualitative data, from depth interviews, discussion group meetings and ethnographic recordings, is usually video-or audio-taped, but might also include handwritten notes, covering the entire interview or discussion. The various types of material for a number of depth interviews have to be assembled or brought together into one place.

The assembled data may have to be reduced to avoid duplication and additional work in the next stages.

Before the content of the telephone depth interview research can be analysed, the audio recording tapes will need to be transcribed into a written form. This transcription is normally performed by trained audio typists, although direct audio/video analysis software is also available, and results in a detailed script, not unlike that of a theatrical performance. The transcription includes descriptions of tone of voice and gestures (if an interview or discussion is video-taped) to help in the analysis. The tapes themselves are retained to enable further detailed analysis at a later time and in order to be able to copy interesting segments for incorporating into the research presentation.

The written transcripts, usually in a word processor file, are then available for detailed content analysis using either manual or computerised methods, or a combination of the two. The purpose of this content analysis is to extract meaningful information for further analysis and reporting.

A number of manual approaches for content analysis are available to the researcher, all of which involve detailed reading and coding of the transcripts by marking, annotation, grouping, topic classification or highlighting keywords and recurring phrases in order to bring together the information under common themes.

The researcher has the option to code on the basis of predetermined themes and ideas, and/or by simply waiting to see what emerges from the transcript analysis and then grouping the data according to these findings. According to Wilson (2003), common manual techniques include:

- Cut and paste
- Script annotation

    o   Spider diagrams

    o   Data tabulation.

4.1 Cut and paste methods

As the name suggests, the researcher copies short sections of speech from the transcription texts and pastes these into any one of a number of pre-prepared thematic sections, creating a dedicated word processor document.

This technique can also literally be carried out by cutting out parts of a copy of each transcript and sticking them onto large sheets of paper, each labelled with a theme. Typical themes used might include 'brand perceptions', 'attitude towards price' and so on.

The resultant output will consist of a number of grouped or similar phrases and excerpts brought together under related headings, topics or themes.

The output will often still be quite large in volume, but will now enable the researcher to undertake a detailed analysis, looking for contrasting opinions, making comparisons with other sections, summarising and so on, in order to derive a set of findings which can then form part of the final report.

4.2 Spider diagrams

This is a graphical or pictorial approach to coding and displaying the data extracted from the transcripts. A theme or topic is placed in the centre of the diagram and the various responses are then added as radials (or spider's legs) from the centre. Typically, one diagram per theme or topic will be produced.

5. Concluding remarks

Data analysis is a vitally important step in the research process, since it is the stage that links the data collection to the research objectives and results in the researcher identifying a set of findings.

Separate approaches and techniques exist for both quantitative and qualitative data, requiring specific knowledge and skills on the part of the researcher. The results from both types of data analysis then have to be brought together and considered carefully in order to produce the research findings that will appear in the report and from which the conclusions will be made.

Answer 20
Research reports and presentations

Check your answer

A good answer is likely to:

☑

In the introduction, introduce the purpose of the guidelines and motivate new agency staff ☐
to adopt them.

In Part a, introduce and describe the structure and content of each section of a marketing ☐
research report.

In Part b, describe the approach and procedure to be taken when writing a research ☐
report or preparing an oral presentation so as to recognise and satisfy the needs of the
audience.

In Part c, identify a list of common problems that can arise and need to be avoided when ☐
preparing and making research reports and presentations.

Adopt the role of a research project leader. ☐

Use a format to simulate project guidelines. ☐

* * * * *

PROJECT GUIDELINES

Prepared by: Project Leader

Date: XX/XX/XX

Structuring and writing marketing research reports

In order to ensure a consistent and effective approach to the production of written marketing
research reports, the following guidelines have been prepared and are to be followed when
preparing the final documents for the client.

When writing a research report, it is important to appreciate that, from the client's perspective at
least, the report represents the product for which he/she has spent £30 000 to £100 000. The
quality of the findings, its conclusions and the underpinning material are the key attributes of
the product he/she is buying. Ultimately, the quality of the decisions he/she will make largely
depend upon the contents of this report. A high level of professionalism and accuracy is,
therefore, required in its production.

Our agency will adopt the format suggested by Alan Wilson (2003):

1 Research report structure and content

This section of the guidelines document briefly lists and describes the major sections and content of the report. For production purposes, a Microsoft Word template has been created to help you format each report that you produce.

2 Title page

As defined in the Word template, this contains a title for the research project, details of the client and report publication date and uses our corporate house style for presentation. We also routinely include a contact point within the agency in the event that the client needs to contact us.

3 Contents page

Provides rapid access to various pages, sections and sub-sections of the report. Again, this is provided for in the template.

4 Executive summary and recommendations

This section provides an overview of the objectives, research methodology and a summary of the key findings and their implications. Our recommendations to the client should also appear here, unless requested otherwise by the client organisation.

The executive summary and recommendations section may be the only part of the report read by the majority of readers, especially senior managers. Please try to keep this section fairly short, 3–5 pages maximum.

5 Introduction and problem definition

This section is based upon information given in the client brief and expanded in the background and objectives section of the research proposal. The content of the section is a summary of the rationale and research objectives.

6 Research methods and limitations

This section should contain a detailed and justified description of the research methodology, including approaches and methods employed, sampling process, methods for data collection and analysis and details of any statistical techniques employed.

Any limitations imposed by the sampling technique, research methods, low response rates, timing and cost should be highlighted as these will have an impact on the findings and conclusions.

Deep technical information should be relegated to an appendix in order to ensure readability of the content of this section.

7 Research findings

The findings of the research are presented clearly, logically and unambiguously in this section. The material should be structured around each of the research objectives so that the reader may relate the two.

If the research is concerned with customer segmentation, then it is appropriate to format the findings under the segment headings.

The material should be presented with the needs of the client in mind and must be presented in a reader-oriented fashion (see later in these guidelines).

Quantitative research findings should be supported by graphs, charts, tables and cross-tabulations, as appropriate. Again, this material should be presented with the reader in mind.

Qualitative research findings can be supported with quotations taken from transcripts of interviews, although respondents must not be identified by name.

8 Concluding remarks

This section should contain a concise list of the main implications and conclusions drawn from the research findings. Such implications and conclusions should be justified.

Note: Where a finding has been interpreted by the researcher in order to draw an implication or conclusion, this interpretation shall be clearly indicated and delineated from actual findings as required in the MRS/ESOMAR code of conduct.

9 Appendices

Copies of all research instruments – questionnaires, moderator guides, show cards and projective technique materials should be included in the appendices, together with the data tables and technical data referenced in the main body of the report. A list of data sources used for any secondary research should also be incorporated.

Presentation of research with a focus on audience needs

The information in this section of the guidelines is relevant to both written and oral presentations.

The quality of our reports and presentations is a clear indication of our professionalism and communications skills. Because we are usually working with marketing staff within the client organisation, our presentation standards will be judged by the extent to which we both understand and anticipate the needs of the audience or reader and then provide a product that meets these needs.

Alan Wilson (2003) offers an 'audience thinking sequence' as a suitable framework for the presentation of information, based upon the needs of the audience. The following six points reflect this thinking sequence:

- ○ Respect the importance of your audience or reader
- ○ Know what each audience member or reader needs from a presentation

- o Ensure that your report/presentation helps
- o Use evidence to support key information and findings
- o Use recaps and summaries to remind the audience about key points
- o Provide actionable recommendations.

Audience

The readers or audience members at a presentation are usually time-pressured and will only want to read or attend if they believe that the material will help them with their problem solving or opportunity developments. Apart from delivering the right content, a professional, well-structured and logical delivery that is not too long and meets the objectives is what is required. Meet the audience's needs and structure the material so that they can understand it – this is key.

To ensure that we can achieve this, we need to understand the individual readers/members of the audience. This requires research on our part at all stages of the project and during the sales cycle.

Needs

Reports and presentations should provide facts that come from the research and which meet the research objectives.

The facts should be presented in a clear format, using graphs, charts, tables and other pictorial devices in order to convey potentially complex material in a form which is easy to assimilate, but which does not insult the recipient.

Evidence

Our reports and presentations are designed to communicate accurate facts or findings drawn from the research project. Demonstrate that we are using facts, by providing ample supporting evidence, supplemented with explanations as necessary. The client must be convinced by what we communicate.

Conclusions and recommendations

Our report/presentation should provide the client with some help in the form of conclusions and recommendations that are realistic and based upon the evidence contained in the research.

Written research report

This should be capable of standing alone from the oral presentation and should be complete in itself. This will ensure that the report has longevity and can be used as a future reference document within the client organisation. Future readers will not have a direct understanding of the rationale, nor the benefit of a presentation.

Potential problems in research reports and oral presentations

A number of common problems should be considered and avoided by careful preparation. Problems commonly arise in the following areas:

1. Planning – insufficient planning, when preparing a written report or an oral presentation will increase the risk of failure.

2. Length – should not be too long, as this will discourage reading attention. Be aware of unnecessary detail creeping in.

3. Presentation – should not be elaborate or gimmicky, detracting from the purpose and confusing the communication content.

4. Overall content – must be suitable for reader/audience. Do not assume knowledge. Explain technical material, charts, graphs and tables. Make the content interesting too.

5. Technical content – precise but not tediously accurate to 20 decimal places. Explain the analysis and statistical approaches used in the project, but remember that the average manager is not a statistician and will not be impressed with deep detail. Accurate findings and conclusions with supporting evidence and realistic recommendations is what clients quite reasonably expect from a research report or presentation.

The audience thinking sequence, summarised in the previous section, provides a good framework for planning out the report or presentation and for ensuring that the above are avoided.

marketing planning

SYLLABUS

Aim

The Marketing Planning subject provides the essential knowledge and understanding in the creation and use of operational marketing plans and the marketing process. It aims to provide you with an understanding of the differences in the internal and external contexts, within which operational marketing planning and marketing are carried out, and the different models of marketing used to meet these contingencies. The subject aims in particular to ensure that the knowledge and understanding can be applied in the practical construction of appropriate and realistic marketing plans.

Learning outcomes

By the end of this subject you will be able to:

- Explain the role of the marketing plan within the context of the organisation's strategy and culture and the broader marketing environment (ethics, social responsibility, legal frameworks, sustainability).
- Conduct a marketing audit considering appropriate internal and external factors.
- Develop marketing objectives and plans at an operational level appropriate to the internal and external environment.
- Develop the role of branding and positioning within the marketing plan.
- Integrate marketing mix tools to achieve effective implementation of plans.
- Select an appropriate co-ordinated marketing mix incorporating appropriate stakeholder relationships for a particular marketing context.
- Set and justify budgets for marketing plans and mix decisions.
- Define and use appropriate measurements to evaluate the effectiveness of marketing plans and activities.
- Make recommendations for changes and innovations to marketing processes based on an understanding of the organisational context and an evaluation of past marketing activities.

Knowledge and skill requirements

Element 1: The marketing plan in its organisational and wider marketing context (15 per cent)

- Describe the roles of marketing and the nature of relationships with other functions in organisations operating in a range of different industries and contexts.
- Explain the synergistic planning process – analysis, planning, implementation and control.
- List and describe the components of the marketing plan.
- Evaluate the role of the marketing plan in relation to the organisation's philosophy or business definition.
- Assess the potential impact of wider macro-environmental forces relating to the role of culture, ethical approach, social responsibility, legal frameworks and sustainability.

Element 2: Marketing planning and budgeting (20 per cent)

- o Explain the constituents of the macro-environmental and micro-environmental marketing audit.
- o Assess the external marketing environment for an organisation through a PESTEL audit.
- o Assess the internal marketing environment for an organisation through an internal audit.
- o Critically appraise processes and techniques used for auditing the marketing environments.
- o Explain the role of marketing information and research in conducting and analysing the marketing audit.
- o Evaluate the relationship between corporate objectives, business objectives and marketing objectives at an operational level.
- o Explain the concept of the planning gap and its impact on operational decisions.
- o Determine segmentation, targeting and positioning within the marketing plan.
- o Determine and evaluate marketing budgets for mix decisions included in the marketing plan.
- o Describe methods for evaluating and controlling the marketing plan.

Element 3: The extended marketing mix and related tools (50 per cent)

- o Explain the role of strategy development in relation to developing market share and growth.
- o Explain how strategy formulation and decisions relating to the selection of markets impact at an operational level on the planning and implementation of an integrated marketing mix.
- o Explain the role of branding and its impact on the marketing mix decisions.
- o Describe methods for maintaining and managing the brand.
- o Explain how a product or service portfolio is developed to achieve marketing objectives.
- o Explain the new product development process (including innovative, replacement, re-launched and imitative products) and the role of innovation.
- o Explain pricing frameworks available to, and used by, organisations for decision-making.
- o Describe how pricing is developed as an integrated part of the marketing mix.
- o Determine the channels of distribution and logistics to be used by an organisation and develop a plan for channel support.
- o Explain how the marketing communications mix is co-ordinated with the marketing mix as part of a marketing plan.
- o Explain the importance of customer relationships to the organisation and how they can be developed and supported by the marketing mix.
- o Describe how a plan is developed for the human element of the service encounter, including staff at different levels of the organisation.
- o Explain how the physical evidence element of the integrated marketing mix is developed.
- o Explain how a plan covering the process or the systems of delivery for a service is developed.

Element 4: Marketing in different contexts (15 per cent)

○ Explain how marketing plans and activities vary in organisations that operate in an international context and develop an appropriate marketing mix.

○ Develop a marketing plan and select an appropriate marketing mix for an organisation operating in any context such as FMCG, business-to-business (supply chain), large or capital project-based services, voluntary and not-for-profit sales support (e.g. SMEs).

○ Explain how marketing plans and activities vary in organisations that operate in a virtual marketplace and develop an appropriate marketing mix.

○ Determine an effective extended marketing mix in relation to design and delivery of service encounters (SERVQUAL).

KEY CONCEPTS – REVISION CHECKLIST

These are the key concepts you should be aware of when you go into the exam. Be able to define or explain each concept, and to discuss key aspects of it. If you have revised this material you should be able to cope with the theoretical aspects of the exam.

Syllabus element 1

The marketing plan in its organisational and wider marketing context

☑

The role of marketing ☐
Models of marketing ☐
– sales support ☐
– marketing communications ☐
– operational marketing ☐
– strategic marketing ☐
Marketing and other functions ☐
Marketing plans and corporate strategy ☐

☑

Marketing plan elements ☐
– Situation ☐
– Objectives ☐
– Strategy ☐
– Tactics ☐
– Action ☐
– Control ☐
Marketing plan process ☐
Marketing ethics ☐
Corporate social responsibility ☐

Syllabus element 2

Marketing planning and budgeting

☑

The marketing audit ☐
Internal elements ☐
– strengths and weaknesses ☐
Internal audit ☐
– organisational capabilities and resources ☐
Marketing audit ☐
– marketing systems ☐
– marketing structure ☐
– marketing organisation ☐
– marketing orientation ☐
– marketing mix audit ☐
Micro-environment audit ☐
– industry analysis ☐
– competitor analysis (five forces) ☐
– market and customer analysis ☐

☐

Macro-environment audit ☐
– Political ☐
– Economic ☐
– Social ☐
– Technological ☐
– Environmental ☐
– Legal ☐
Opportunities and Threats ☐
Segmentation ☐
Targeting ☐
Positioning ☐
Gap analysis ☐
Benchmarking ☐
Budgets ☐
Plan evaluation and control ☐

Syllabus element 3

The extended marketing mix and related tools

Ansoff's growth matrix ☑ ☐

7 Ps ☑ ☐
- market penetration ☐
- market development ☐
- product development ☐
- diversification ☐

Porter's generic strategies ☐
- cost leadership ☐
- differentiation ☐
- focus ☐

Brands ☐
Brand equity ☐
Brand strategy ☐
Brand management ☐

7 Ps
- Product
  o life cycle
  o portfolios
  o new product development
- Price
  o Pricing theories
  o Pricing objectives
- Place
- Promotion
  o Covered in Marketing Communication module
- People
- Physical evidence
- Process

Syllabus element 4

Marketing in different contexts

International marketing ☑ ☐
FMCG marketing ☐
Business-to-business (supply chain) marketing ☐
Capital project-based marketing services ☐
Not-for-profit marketing ☐
Small and medium enterprise marketing ☐

Marketing virtual enterprises ☑ ☐
- e-commerce ☐
Delivering service excellence ☐

153

PART A MINI-CASES

Mini-Case 1: Liverpool John Lennon Airport in the UK (December 2005, Question 1)

External audit, marketing communications mix, internal marketing

Syllabus elements 2.2, 3.4, 3.10, 4.4

Liverpool Airport, formerly known as Speke Airport, was established in the 1930s and was used as a Royal Air Force (RAF) base during the Second World War, but returned to commercial use when the war ended in 1945. It has been renamed Liverpool John Lennon Airport (LJLA) and faces a significant challenge in sustaining its recent revival and growth in passenger traffic, particularly against a background of strong competition from nearby Manchester Airport and other regional airports.

The LJLA is located 8 km to the Southeast of the city of Liverpool in England and although it is accessible by road, there has been no dedicated rail or metro links for passengers. However, plans are now in hand to develop a new rail link from Liverpool to the airport.

This airport has been overshadowed by its larger competitor, Manchester Airport, which has grown steadily over the past two decades to become the UK's third largest airport servicing both domestic and a growing range of international destinations. In contrast, until recently, Liverpool Airport has seen its business decline steadily over the past 20 years.

In many ways, LJLA's decline has mirrored that of the City of Liverpool (home of the Beatles pop group), which saw its population fall by over 10 per cent during the 1980s as a result of a steady erosion of its traditional industrial base. While Manchester has also experienced a decline in its traditional base in the textile industries, it has been able to diversify into a wide range of new industries, professional services and commerce. During the 1990s, Manchester continued to strengthen its position as the northwest of England's commercial capital and has also seen its cultural infrastructure transformed in recent years.

However, during the latter half of the 1990s, Liverpool had begun to turn its fortunes around, reinventing itself as both a cultural and a commercial centre, partially on the back of significant new investment from government regeneration funds and European Union (EU) grants. Liverpool's population decline has been arrested and the population actually increased by around 2 per cent between 1998 and 2002. With the development of the local attractions, such as the Albert Dock and other cultural areas, Liverpool has begun to challenge Manchester once again as a thriving centre for popular culture, commerce and retailing. And perhaps most notably, Liverpool has built on its pop music heritage and has marketed itself as Britain's 'Capital of Pop Music'. This revival in the city's fortunes has undoubtedly helped the LJLA in halting what had been a steady decline in trade that might have threatened its survival.

The airport's position

The turnaround in LJLA's fortunes has been largely due to the arrival of Easyjet (which is a low cost airline), which has established its UK northern base at LJLA. The success of Easyjet's operations has contributed significantly to the recent growth of traffic through LJLA, and Easyjet expects to handle over 1.5 million customers by the end of the current year. Indeed, the recent marked growth in passenger numbers (up 50 per cent) has made LJLA airport one of Europe's fastest growing airports, which has been built from a relatively low base.

The planned improvements in the local transport infrastructure, which will see a new rail link established between the city and LJLA, is expected to provide a further stimulus to the growth of passenger traffic. The LJLA airport has, however, struggled to shake off its rather old-fashioned, down-market image. Moreover, recent consumer research has revealed that some 65 per cent of respondents had little understanding of the airport's location, how to reach the airport, or the range of destinations it currently serves.

Existing customer base

Analysis of LJLA's current customer base has shown that over 80 per cent of passengers using the airport live within a 25 km radius or have relatives/friends within this catchment area. The majority of passengers using the airport tend to have been drawn from C1, C2 and E (retired) social classes, although there has also been a significant increase in business travellers (up 25 per cent) over the past 15 months. Obviously, the September 11th terrorist attack in New York may still affect public confidence on the safety of flying, which must be considered.

Re-launch

To help maintain this turnaround in its fortunes, the airport tried to change its former poor image to replace and was been renamed 'The Liverpool John Lennon Airport' (LJLA), after the former member of the famous Beatles pop group at a ceremony attended by John Lennon's partner Yoko Ono. The name change was seen as an important step in losing the negative associations attached to the old name.

(The data has been based on a real case, but details may have been changed for assessment purposes and do not necessarily reflect the current management practices.)

Questions

There is a need to improve the business performance of the airport. As marketing manager, you have been asked to write a report for your marketing director covering the following areas:

a) Conduct an external marketing audit to identify the key issues currently facing the Liverpool John Lennon Airport.   (20 marks)

b) Discussion of how the marketing communications mix, as part of the marketing plan, should be utilised to build on the new identity and encourage growth in passengers.   (20 marks)

c) Discussion of how internal marketing can be used to deliver improved service quality at Liverpool John Lennon Airport.   (10 marks)

(Total 50 marks)

Mini-Case 2: Carmunicate

Environmental forces and planning, business expansion, segmentation and internal marketing

Syllabus elements 2.1, 2.2, 2.8, 3.1, 4.1

Carmunicate is a micro-business founded around a unique, patented, hands-free kit for mobile phones, designed by the company, for use in cars. Five years ago the three founders of the business developed the product because they were convinced that it was possible to improve on the products available at the time – primarily there were two types:

- ○ Fully installed kits made by the manufacturers of phones which were dedicated to one phone model, were expensive and could not easily be moved to other cars.
- ○ Simple wires incorporating a microphone and earpiece which were available relatively cheap.

The product developed by Carmunicate utilised a cassette adapter rather than the earpiece. When the cassette was inserted in the cassette player of a car stereo it enabled the voice of the person the user was talking to via the phone to be heard through the car speakers. Whilst the product was very well accepted by all those who tried it, sales were limited and Carmunicate did not generate the levels of business forecast or hoped for.

Utilising a direct marketing strategy, promotion was limited to a very small amount of advertising and a limited amount of publicity gained in various magazines and newspapers (both local and national). Additional, generic, mobile phone accessory products were added to the range sold by Carmunicate, these being purchased from various sources but primarily from the company exclusively appointed to manufacture their own designed product. These suppliers are all based in the Far East.

The major distribution chains for mobile phone products were not interested in dealing with the product due to their existing agreements with buyers, and the size of Carmunicate as a supplier to them – barriers to entry were very high.

Keeping up to date with the rapidly changing mobile phone market was difficult for a company as small as Carmunicate with regular new model introductions from all the manufacturers – many of which had different connectors giving difficulties in ensuring the right balance of stocks for the market requirements.

A database of customers who purchased the product was built up through direct sales, but the nature of the product meant that it was typically a one-off product, although many customers purchased replacements when they changed their phones if the new model required a different connection.

Legal help

The legal situation changed in the UK regarding the use of mobile phones in cars – from a situation where it was not directly illegal to use a hand-held mobile phone whilst driving, the law changed to ban this activity. This should have given Carmunicate an opportunity. However, the timing of the law change related to the decline in the popularity of cassette players in cars – these were being replaced by CD players which the product was not compatible with. It has also been widely reported that the law regarding driving and using mobile phones is largely ignored.

In addition to this, the cost of the simple hands-free kits was reduced massively due to the ready availability of supplies from the Far East and sales through channels such as online auction sites. These simple devices became available for less than 10 per cent of the price of the Carmunicate product.

New markets

In common with many other music-related equipment, the in-car entertainment market has changed recently due to the popularity of MP3 players, and this has led to many car manufacturers including a facility to connect MP3 players to the car stereo. After-market suppliers of car audio equipment are also responding to this change and manufacturing equipment which allows MP3 players to be plugged into them for playback through the system in the car.

This change has allowed Carmunicate to produce a new product which utilises the inputs for MP3 players to connect the mobile phone, and therefore reproduce the sound of telephone callers through the car stereo equipment.

Whilst there is now a range of competitive products due to changes in technology in recent years, including Bluetooth wireless headsets and simple plug-in devices, the simplicity of use of the new Carmunicate product gives it many advantages. The company are hoping to use this advantage to gain access to distribution channels, in addition to their established direct sales which are predominantly conducted via the interweb.

New applications

A major advantage with the new product is that it can also be used in conjunction with laptop computers to turn them into hands-free speaker systems for mobile phones – even giving a conference call facility.

Carmunicate still has only the three founders working for it, and resources are limited.

(The above data has been based on a real-life organisation, but details may have been changed for assessment purposes and the case does not reflect the current management practices.)

Questions

a) Considering the micro- and macro-environmental forces, develop a marketing plan for Carmunicate to stimulate an increase in business.   (20 marks)

b) With reference to appropriate theory, explain how Carmunicate could expand their business over the next two years.   (10 marks)

c) Outline the process for segmenting the market for Carmunicate and provide a profile of a typical Carmunicate user.   (10 marks)

d) Recommend marketing mix decisions for potential international expansion of Carmunicate.   (10 marks)

(Total 50 marks)

Mini-Case 3: The 2008 Olympics in Beijing (June 2004, Question 1)

Macro-environmental forces and the marketing plan, the importance of branding, the concept of service quality

Syllabus elements 2.2, 3.3, 3.4, 4.4

In 2008, China will be hosting the Olympic Games. China is calling these games the 'People's Olympics', and they are to be hosted in Beijing, which is ready to become a truly international city. Beijing is showing a new, vigorous image through its ongoing economic reforms.

By hosting the People's Olympics, there will be an emphasis on the value of human talent, ambition and achievement. Indeed, the organising Committee sees the Olympic Games as a catalyst for exchange and harmony between various cultures and people.

China aims to strengthen public awareness of environmental protection and promote the development and application of new technologies via the Olympics. The Chinese people love sports, and the nation's athletic enthusiasm is evident in wide participation in sports activities among its 1.25 billion population with distinctive achievements of Chinese athletes at previous Olympic Games.

Celebrating the Games in Beijing in 2008 will offer a unique opportunity to inspire and educate a new generation of Chinese youth with the Olympic values, and to promote the Olympic spirit and the cause of sport in China and the world.

The Olympic organising committee

The Beijing 2008 Olympic Games Bid Committee (BOBICO) is in charge of all matters related to Beijing's bid for the 2008 Olympic Games. BOBICO was founded on 6 September 1999. The committee is made up of 10 departments. Its members include athletes, personnel from the education, science and culture circles and contributors from other social sections, as well as officials from the Beijing municipal government, the State General Administration of Sport and departments of the Central Government.

Sponsorship

More than US$600 million is expected to be raised from the international sponsorship of the 2008 Games. A similar amount could be expected to be raised from domestic sponsorships within China from companies wanting to become anything from the official airline, bank, insurance company, telephone company, petrol company and travel agent, to the official supplier of ice cream and waste management services. The committee aims to have the major corporate sponsors signed up before the 2004 Games in Greece, well ahead of the event.

Indeed the games are seen to be the biggest ever-marketing opportunity for China and they are currently starting to develop the marketing plan. The plans for the marketing programme include a nation-wide contest in China to design a new logo for the 2008 Olympics to replace the well-known logo which was used for the Beijing bid. It aims to generate a new look with fresh marketing potential.

Preparation for the games in Beijing is everywhere in evidence from signs in shop windows to pins on the lapels of shoppers. New roads, bridges and stadiums are planned; a massive environmental protection programme is underway; and technological modernisation from cell phones to Internet access is expanding to every corner of the city.

'The Olympics have already speeded the pace of change in Beijing and across China' says Mr Liu Jing-min, Vice Mayor of Beijing and Executive Vice President of the Beijing 2008 Olympic Games Bid Committee. 'The survey demonstrates that the people of Beijing embrace these changes, welcome the world to our city, and are prepared to host a great Olympics.'

(The above data has been based on a real-life organisation, but details may have been changed for assessment purposes and the case does not reflect the current management practices.)

Source: Olympic Games website

Questions

You have been appointed as a Marketing Consultant to assist the Beijing Olympic Organising Committee. Write a report for the Committee that

a) Assesses the potential impact of macro-environmental forces on the marketing plan for the Beijing Olympics, specifically considering the role of culture, ethical approaches and social responsibility.   (15 marks)

b) Explains the role of the Beijing Olympic brand and explains the importance of the brand in attracting the targeted sponsorship required, critically identifying the methods, which could be used to develop the Beijing Olympic brand.   (15 marks)

c) Explains the concept of service quality and recommends an effective extended marketing mix in relation to the service delivery and service encounters for the consumers during the Olympic events.   (20 marks)

(Total 50 marks)

Mini-Case 4: Moving Times

The micro-environment, barriers to marketing planning, customer relationships, competitive advantage

Syllabus elements 1.1, 1.3, 1.4, 2.2, 3.1, 3.2, 3.12

Moving Times is an Estate Agency chain based in the north of the country. The chain was started 20 years ago and has specialised in larger, more exclusive properties, although they do handle properties of all types.

Through mainly organic growth, Moving Times have increased in size to their current situation where they have 45 branches, making them the largest regional agency in the country, with only those having full national coverage having more outlets. Four years ago Moving Times did acquire a competitor who was located at what at the time was the Southern edge of the region covered by Moving Times – this company added eight branches to Moving Times portfolio.

The house market

The house market in the country is variable in the levels of business it sees, being very dependent upon the economy. In the best times, houses can sell within hours of being placed on the market, but during quieter times when the economy is suffering, and particularly if interest rates are high it is common for houses to remain on the market for many months.

The major factors influencing the housing market are the state of the economy and the interest rate (and predictions about it). In addition to these factors, the market is seasonal with the Spring being the busiest time for purchase of houses, and also, for estate agents the time when more people actually place their houses on the market.

With average house prices in the UK now nearing £200 000 and recent reports that first-time buyers are typically needing nearly £30 000 as deposits, many analysts have suggested that the traditional increases in prices may slow down or even go into reverse. So far (at the time of writing) there is no evidence of this actually happening however with prices increasing above expectations.

Marketing estate agents

Estate agents have a poor reputation generally for the levels of service they provide, and there is a general feeling that they cannot be trusted – whether rightly or wrongly. This feeling has arisen because of the tendency by agents to exaggerate the details about property they are selling to make it more attractive to potential buyers.

Estate agents are unusual for high-street outlets in the way they do business – they have two customers for every transaction. The first is the seller of the house who actually pays for the service of the agent, the second being the purchaser of the house who receives the services of the agency free.

Promotion is a major part of the estate agents marketing activity – advertising the property they have on their books, and also promoting their services to encourage people who are considering selling houses to use their services.

Moving Times operate in the same basic way as most agents, but due to their specialisation in exclusive properties they aim to always provide very honest descriptions of properties they are handling, and to provide customers – whether those buying or selling houses – with very high levels of service.

The marketing function within Moving Times has to date been co-ordinated by the Commercial Director without a specific marketing department. Each branch manager is responsible for the advertisement they place in local press on a weekly or monthly basis – although this is done within guidelines set out across the organisation to ensure consistency of image, which is also reflected in the appearance of the branches and all signage.

Moving Times have a website which has details of all the properties they are handling, and which has the facility to enable people to request viewings of houses, although this is not a fully automated system – it is completed manually as the branch normally has to contact the house seller to confirm a convenient viewing time.

Additional services

As most people buying houses require finance of some type to enable them to purchase the property, Moving Times, in common with many agencies, are able to recommend and organise mortgages for their purchasing customers. This service has got harder recently due to increasingly strict regulations in the financial services industry.

In addition to this, Moving Times have agreements with a range of solicitors who can help their customers (either buyers or sellers) with the legal issues of the house transactions. Moving Times receive a commission from these solicitors for business referred to them.

(The above material has been based on a fictitious company for assessment purposes.)

Questions

You have recently joined Moving Times as Marketing Manager. Write a report to the Commercial Manager, which advises on the following.

a) The challenges Moving Times face in the micro-environment – which are the main areas to assess when formulating a marketing plan for the organisation? (20 marks)

b) The barriers to marketing planning which may exist within Moving Times. (10 marks)

c) The importance of customer relationships to Moving Times and how they can be developed and supported. (10 marks)

d) Establishing a competitive advantage for Moving Times. (10 marks)

(Total 50 marks)

PART B QUESTIONS

Question 5

External environment monitoring, information and communication technology

Syllabus elements 2.2, 2.4

As the marketing consultant working on behalf of a not-for-profit organisation of your choice you have been commissioned to:

a) Identify and illustrate the significance of monitoring the external environment when developing marketing plans.   (15 marks)

b) Indicate how recent developments in information and communication technology (ICT) have affected environmental monitoring and the creation of marketing plans.   (10 marks)

(Total 25 marks)

Question 6

Stakeholder relationships, extended marketing mix, international marketing

Syllabus elements 2.1, 4.1, 4.2

You are the Marketing Manager for a not-for-profit service organisation of your choice.

a) Explain the importance of developing and maintaining relationships with your stakeholders.   (10 marks)

b) Recommend an appropriate extended marketing mix for your organisation to ensure that relationships are developed and managed.   (10 marks)

c) Explain how the marketing activities for this organisation may vary in an international context.   (5 marks)

(Total 25 marks)

Question 7

Segmentation, profiling and targeting

Syllabus elements 2.8

As a brand manager for a technology product manufacturer of your choice you have been asked to identify distinct groups of customers in your market.

a) Evaluate the range of variables that may be employed to segment the market.   (10 marks)

b) Using these variables, profile three possible target market segments and explain how you would evaluate their attractiveness.   (15 marks)

(Total 25 marks)

Question 8

Innovation and new product development

Syllabus elements 3.6

Your organisation is planning to develop a new range of products to be targeted at an international market of your choice. Using examples:

a) Explain the role of innovation within organisations. (10 marks)

b) Propose and justify an approach to new product development. (15 marks)

(Total 25 marks)

Question 9

Distribution channels (place) and strategy

Syllabus elements 3.9

As Marketing Manager of a holiday company of your choice, you have been asked by your Marketing Director to review your distribution strategy.

a) Outline and evaluate the various channels of distribution available. (15 marks)

b) Recommend and justify an appropriate distribution strategy. (10 marks)

(Total 25 marks)

Question 10

Product development, marketing mix (December 2005, Question 2)

Syllabus elements 3.1, 3.2, 3.3

a) With reference to appropriate theory, explain how a product development strategy could be implemented to expand sales within a Fast-Moving Consumer Goods (FMCG) organisation. (15 marks)

b) Explain the role of the brand for the above organisation and select an appropriate marketing mix to implement the product development strategy. (10 marks)

(Total 25 marks)

Question 11

Ethics and social responsibility issues

Syllabus elements 1.5, 2.2

You have recently been appointed marketing manager for a large food retailer. You have been asked to advise the Chief Executive on the importance of ethics and social responsibility in food retailing. You should consider:

a) The range of specific ethical and social responsibility issues that could affect the organisation. (10 marks)

b) How the organisation may need to change its marketing activities in response to such issues and how best to benefit from some of the opportunities presented. (15 marks)

(Total 25 marks)

Question 12

Devising marketing budgets, marketing plan evaluation and control (December 2005, Question 3)

Syllabus elements 2.9, 2.10

You work for a chain of international restaurants, as a marketing manager, and are required to offer your advice about the management of the marketing plan for the chain.

a) Critically evaluate *two* different methods of devising a marketing budget for the company's marketing plan, explaining the problems, which could be encountered when setting the marketing budget for this organisation. (10 marks)

b) Assess the different methods for evaluating and controlling the marketing plan. (15 marks)

(Total 25 marks)

Question 13

Marketing budget influences, budgets and mix elements, controlling the plan

Syllabus elements 2.9, 2.10

You are the marketing manager for a car retail group with four outlets and are rather concerned about the current marketing budgets that have been set.

a) Explain the factors which are likely to have influenced the marketing budget for this organisation. (10 marks)

b) Explain and evaluate the different approaches for setting the marketing budget for the mix elements of the marketing plan. (10 marks)

c) Recommend methods for controlling the marketing plan for this retailer. (5 marks)

(Total 25 marks)

Question 14

Pricing and international distribution channels (December 2005, Question 4)

Syllabus elements 3.7, 3.9, 4.1

You are the newly appointed marketing manager for a small company manufacturing agricultural chemical products, such as pesticides, which are marketed as new innovations because of their unique abilities to perform in a range of different geographic climates.

a) Explain and evaluate the different pricing frameworks, which could be used by this company for international market segments. (10 marks)

b) Discuss and justify the channels of distribution and logistics, which could be used by this company to take their products to international markets and suggest a plan for channel support. (15 marks)

(Total 25 marks)

Question 15

The planning gap

Syllabus elements 2.6, 2.7

A health club finds that it has not been able to recruit as many members as normal and it has not achieved the growth objective set by senior management. It has identified a wide gap between the projected and actual member numbers who have fully paid annual membership.

a) Explain the concept of the 'planning gap' and the impact for this health clubs marketing department.   (15 marks)

b) Explain what the club will have to consider in order to close the gap from an operational and strategic perspective.   (10 marks)

(Total 25 marks)

Question 16

The marketing planning process, analysis tools (December 2005, Question 5)

Syllabus elements 1.2, 2.4

As a new marketing manager in an organisation, you have been asked to explain the marketing planning process to your marketing and sales team.

a) Explain the synergistic marketing planning process relating your discussion to the analysis, planning, implementation and control issues.   (10 marks)

b) Discuss and evaluate at least *four* analysis tools, which could be employed to undertake a marketing audit.   (15 marks)

(Total 25 marks)

Question 17

Marketing plans and mix for online business

Syllabus elements 4.3

An established business training company has developed a range of courses suitable for self-study which it intends to distribute via the Internet using a new brand name created specifically for the products.

a) What differences would there be for the marketing plans of the online business as opposed to the more traditional training programmes offered.   (10 marks)

b) Outline a marketing mix for the new course range.   (15 marks)

(Total 25 marks)

Question 18

Small business marketing plans and measurements

Syllabus elements 2.10, 4.2

You are a marketing consultant advising a commercial manager who has recently joined a company of 25 employees her job role contains specific responsibility for marketing.

a) Contrast the factors which affect the development of the marketing plan of the small company (SME) with those faced by a larger organisation. (15 marks)

b) Explain how appropriate measurements could be introduced within the company to evaluate the effectiveness of their marketing plans and activities. (10 marks)

(Total 25 marks)

Question 19

Positioning, communications mix, and plan evaluation (June 2004, Question 5)

Syllabus elements 2.8, 2.10, 3.10

You are a Brand Manager for a consumer product of your choice, which appears to be in decline. You plan to revive and reposition this product in the market.

a) Explain how you will reposition this product and justify which segments will be targeted.
(10 marks)

b) Explain how you will integrate the marketing communications mix to achieve this new positioning. (10 marks)

c) Explain one method for evaluating your marketing plan. (5 marks)

(Total 25 marks)

Question 20

Marketing plans and business objectives (June 2004, Question 2)

Syllabus elements 1.2, 1.3, 1.4

You have been appointed as a Marketing Consultant to a small business-to-business company which is looking to gain financial funding.

a) Explain the components of a marketing plan which the company will need to write, discussing the synergistic planning process. (15 marks)

b) Explain the role of the marketing plan in relation to the company's business objectives.
(10 marks)

(Total 25 marks)

Question 21

Environmental audits; macro-environmental issues; segmentation, targeting and positioning (June 2004, Question 3)

Syllabus elements 1.5, 2.4, 2.8

You are a Marketing Management Consultant and have been asked to undertake a marketing audit for a double-glazing and window frame company.

a) Explain the different processes and techniques used for auditing the marketing environment.
(9 marks)

b) Explain the potential impact of wider macro-environmental forces on the business, such as ethical and social responsibility issues.
(6 marks)

c) Explain the concept of segmentation, targeting and positioning which this company could consider.
(10 marks)

(Total 25 marks)

Question 22

Market penetration and development strategies, pricing decisions (June 2004, Question 4)

Syllabus elements 3.1, 3.8

During a recession, an organisation of your choice has an objective to expand its market share by developing a market penetration strategy.

a) Explain how such a strategy could be achieved at an operational level and contrast this with a market development strategy.
(15 marks)

b) Explain how pricing decisions can help to achieve the organisation's objective. (10 marks)

(Total 25 marks)

PART A SUGGESTED ANSWERS

Mini-Case 1: Liverpool John Lennon Airport (December 2005, Question 1)

Check your answer

A good answer is likely to:

	☑
Link auditing to the marketing plan	☐
Explain the micro- and macro-analysis elements	☐
Produce an analysis based on data given in the case	☐
Consider issues raised by the audit	☐
Discuss the role of communication for new brand values and awareness	☐
Discuss how communications fits into the marketing mix	☐
Explain how the communications mix will be created	☐
Relate communications to issues identified and objectives set	☐
Explain the concept of service quality	☐
How service quality can be delivered in a service organisation	☐
Recognise a role as author – Marketing Manager within company	☐
Use appropriate format – Report format requested	☐

*   *   *   *   *

REPORT

To: Marketing Director

From: Marketing Manager

Date: XX/XX/XX

Re: Marketing Audit, Communication and Service Quality

1 Introduction

In order to move forward and improve the business performance of Liverpool John Lennon Airport (LJLA) we have to create a plan – the first step of which is understanding where we are now through an audit. This knowledge of the environment linked with the corporate objectives will help us to consider where we should be going, setting market objectives and strategies. The final stage is to determine how we are going to get there – the implementation of the plan and its budget and control.

This report will identify how we can use auditing to determine where we are now, also how we should use marketing communication to build our new identity and encouraging passenger growth.

Finally, I will look at how we can use internal marketing to improve the service quality for passengers at the airport.

2 Marketing audit

When evaluating where we are now there are two elements of the environment which we have to consider – these are classed as micro and macro. The micro-environment is an element of the environment which influences LJLA and over which LJLA have influence. The micro-environment includes customers, shareholders, suppliers, the local community, competitors and other liked stakeholders.

The macro-environment, on the other hand, is made up of the elements of the environment which affect LJLA but over which LJLA have little influence – typically classified as Social, Legal, Economic, Political and Technological factors (SLEPT) but for our situation it is important to consider the natural Environment in addition to the main five areas.

2.1 Micro-environment audit

○ *Customers* – Over 80 per cent of our customers live, or know well someone who lives, within 25 km of the airport facility and they mainly come from the C1, C2 and retired social classes. In recent years we have had an increase in the numbers of business passengers that is probably related to the increase in traffic through Easyjet (see below).

We do have a situation, however, where our image is not particularly good – 65 per cent of respondents to a survey knew little about our location, facilities and destinations served – obviously something which has to be addressed if we are to improve the performance of the airport.

○ *Local community* – This is a very important area for us as the airport produces a lot of local traffic and obviously the operation of the airport can be seen as being noisy and disruptive to the local population – a problem which could get worse when we grow our business.

The planned improvements to the local infrastructure, such as the new rail link from Liverpool to the airport, will also affect the community, hopefully providing them with benefits as well as any perceived negative impacts. The increasing levels of business should bring economic benefits such as more jobs for the local community.

○ *Competition* – There are many regional airports in the UK, which offer similar services to ourselves, and there are also larger airports such as our local one at Manchester, which offer passengers a greater range of facilities than we can provide. The main aspect of our competition, however, relates to the airline partners we work with. We gain competitive advantage from the fact that Easyjet have their northern UK base at LJLA. The growth in air travel is partly due to low cost operators such as Easyjet – they attract passengers to the airport through their low cost flights, but this also means that we only attract relatively local customers as the cost of travel to the airport can easily be higher than the cost of the flight from the airport.

The research mentioned above also highlighted that we have a rather old-fashioned, downmarket image compared with other airports – again something which needs to be addressed.

2.2 Macro-environment audit

o *Political* – The main political threat comes from the continuing threat of terrorism following the September 11th attack on New York. The airline industry is very susceptible to potential attacks and they can adversely affect our business wherever in the world they take place.

Additional political factors may include the potential for an international tax on aviation fuel which would increase the costs of air travel – this would be a response to environmental pressure groups.

o *Economic* – The state of the economy has a major influence on our activity as for most customers air travel is a luxury which they will stop if money becomes tight as would be the case during a recession or during periods of high inflation.

o *Social* – The current trend is very much towards more experience which air travel helps to produce, therefore we should be in a situation to benefit from this.
In addition, closer links with Europe are increasing both business and leisure trips within Europe, which Easyjet are well served to provide.

o *Technological* – Companies such as Easyjet have thrived through the use of technology such as the Internet. We have to ensure that we have a great presence on the Internet, as many people who are aware of us will look there to gain more information.

In addition to this, the operations of the airport are very reliant on technology so we have to keep up to date with our systems for passenger and aircraft handling.

o *Environmental* – The reverse of the social trends is that there is increasing awareness of the negative impacts air travel can have on the natural environment which may lead to reduced number of passengers – this can be linked to the political situation of a possible fuel tax. In addition, as already mentioned the airline has some negative environmental impacts for the local community.

o *Legal* – We have to comply with many aspects of the law, from employment law through to those relating to passenger safety principally linked to the terrorist threat already mentioned.

As we currently have a negative image amongst many potential customers, we can use the re-launch of LJLA to change perceptions and ensure we take advantage of the opportunities presented by the environment, whilst minimising the negative impacts.

3 Marketing communications mix

As we have changed our name recently from Speke Airport to Liverpool John Lennon Airport we have a great opportunity to create new brand values and raise awareness and change the negative attitudes to create positive perceptions of the airport.

Marketing communications is just one part of the marketing mix, and as such we have to ensure that the other elements of pricing, product and place are correct for any promotional activity we undertake. The elements of the mix have to be integrated and complementary to each other with consistency throughout. Some of the areas we need to consider are as follows:

- ○ *Pricing* – What are the opportunities for us as regards to price? We are currently seen as downmarket and therefore have to be careful with pricing, but we have an opportunity to use price to show a move upmarket. How we price things such as the parking has to reflect the image portrayed in the promotion.
- ○ *Product* – What is the actual airport environment like (this is also an element of physical evidence)? Within product the airline operators form a major part of our product offer, as do the concessions within the airport.
- ○ *Distribution* – How will we get information to people about the airport – online access is an avenue we have to exploit here.

In addition to these areas, as we are providing a service, we have to consider the extended marketing mix elements of people, process and physical evidence. I will cover this later.

3.1 Communications mix

We need to consider the objectives of our marketing communications activities – at present due to the lack of awareness about LJLA and our poor image we need to concentrate on changing perceptions and getting people to come and use the airport.

As *awareness* has to be generated about LJLA, I suggest we should start off with a television advertising campaign, particularly focused on the Northwest of England and North Wales, as this is where the majority of our customers will come from. To a lesser extent we can advertise nationally, but this would need to be carefully targeted to ensure it is cost-effective.

We could also advertise throughout the region using other media such as posters and transport-related adverts including bus and railway station advertising, and using appropriate local newspaper and other printed media. Leaflets place in local hotels and tourist information offices would also assist with awareness.

The advertising would need to be backed up through PR activity – building on the good publicity which was generated when Yoko Ono attended the renaming ceremony.

We also have an opportunity to work with our airline partners on the promotion of the airport – it is in both our interests to increase passenger numbers and they can play an important part in our activity.

Having generated awareness, we need to get people *interested* in the airport – at this stage a good website becomes essential. Many potential customers will use the Internet to find out more about us – and the website should provide them all the information they need, as well as being attractive and giving a reason to return and check on developments. We can use the website to capture information about people – maybe through an online questionnaire asking about destinations they would like LJLA to offer in the future.

If people are interested in the airport, we need them to *desire* the airport – sales promotion activity can be used for this. We should consider introducing an airport loyalty scheme whereby frequent users could get rewards from free drinks in the airport through to free flights with operators using the terminal.

The desire needs to be followed by action – people who come back and use the airport. The business travellers need to be encouraged to use us regularly, and to tell colleagues about us – we should consider rewarding word-of-mouth advertising. We can collect data about passengers and use carefully targeted mail shots to them to keep them informed about the airport and the changes taking place – new destinations, new facilities and so on. This can be done by e-mail and post.

4 Internal marketing and service quality

As I identified above, critical parts of our marketing include those areas of the marketing mix which are specific to our role as a service – the people, process and physical evidence. We are providing an experience for our customers – the airline passengers – and as such they do not have anything physical to take away for their money, but they will still make judgements about the quality of the 'product' they receive, which will affect future decisions about which airport to use.

We need to ensure that all our staff are aware of how involved they are in the delivery of the service – this can be achieved through internal marketing, the process of selling the marketing plan to the staff. According to Berry (1981), 'The most important contribution the marketing department can make is to be exceptionally clever in getting everyone else in the organization to practice marketing.' This is essentially what internal marketing is concerned with.

As we are a service, the production of the service is inseparable from the consumption of it – our staff produce and provide our product simultaneously (as the customer is consuming it) and therefore they are essential for the provision of the image we wish to portray. The service quality is very dependant on and influenced by the staff and their attitudes.

Internal marketing, therefore, needs to be used to ensure our staff all buy into, and deliver, the levels of service which we want our customers to experience. We need to communicate our targets and motivate the staff to deliver them. This will involve training the staff to ensure they have the necessary skills to delivery the required service quality. To do this we will need to work with other departments within the airport, in particular the Human Resources department to ensure that the staff are available for and receive the training necessary. We should also consider our internal communication programmes to provide the staff with the required information about what is expected of them, and why, and also to inform them of success stories which should assist motivation.

A key element in the delivery of our service is the service encounter between the airport and our passengers – this is interactive marketing. In order to change the way our staff deliver service we could consider adopting the Ericsson Quality culture which they refer to as EQ for enhancing customer service. This would involve concentrating on employees and changing quality statements:

- from a product quality to a total quality concept where every function contributes to quality, whether people directly interact with our customers or not;
- from quality being assessed by a supervisor or the deliverer to the customer being the judge of quality;
- from focus on errors and their appraisal and remedy to focus on prevention, ensuring we do it right from the start;
- from accepting a certain ratio of complaints being normal to aiming for zero errors;
- from the notion that high quality leading to high costs, to the notion that high quality leads to increased business levels, increased customer satisfaction and increased profits.

This final point is critical in that internal marketing can be used to get this message across to employees.

The EQ programme can be summarised as follows:

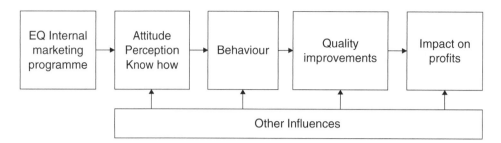

Throughout this process we need to ensure that we motivate, monitor and reward the service levels our staff provide, remembering that as stated, the customer should be the judge of the service quality.

5 Conclusion

Through the understanding of our environment and using this information to produce a plan of where we need to be, the creation of a promotional mix to ensure potential customers are aware of what we offer and then use our facilities, and the management of the service which we deliver to our customers we can be in a position to ensure the business performance of LJLA improves dramatically.

Mini-Case 2: Carmunicate

Check your answer

A good answer is likely to:

                        ☑

Explain the marketing planning process   ☐

The impact on the marketing plan of micro- and macro-environmental forces   ☐

Define growth strategies for organisations   ☐

Identification of the most appropriate growth strategies   ☐

Consideration of role of branding in relation to planning for growth   ☐

Identify segmentation variables for Carmunicate with a typical customer profile   ☐

Apply an appropriate marketing mix for international expansion   ☐

Relate to the context – a micro-business   ☐

Recognise a role as author – Suggest marketing consultant   ☐

Use appropriate format – Report format requested   ☐

*   *   *   *   *

REPORT

To: Carmunicate

From: Marketing Consultant

Date: XX/XX/XX

Re: Marketing planning and growth

1 Introduction

Marketing planning, even in micro-businesses such as yours, is very important to provide a full understanding of the situation you are in, and knowing where to go in the future, and how to get there. The main sections to include in a marketing plan are:

- Where are you now? This should include the corporate objectives and the marketing audit.
- Where are you going? Setting marketing objectives, the strategy to take and segmentation decisions along with positioning.
- How are you going to get there? Considering the implementation of the plan through the marketing mix, the budget, and how to evaluate and control the plan.

175

2 A marketing plan for Carmunicate

2.1 Where are you now?

This section of the plan includes the micro- and macro-environmental forces that impact on the organisation and on the marketing plan.

2.1.1 Micro-environment

As a micro-organisation you have limited resources – both human and financial. However, you do have close relationships with your existing customers through the personal service offered. Suppliers have been helpful, but they will not respond as quickly to you as they might for larger organisations who are more valuable to them.

2.1.2 Macro-environment

The macro-environmental forces can be considered in five areas:

- o *Social*: Usage of mobile phones has reached a level where there are now more phones than adults in the UK – they have become an accepted part of life, and the people who do not have phones have largely chosen that they do not want a phone. In addition, car and computer ownership is high so the environment conditions are good for the products sold.
- o *Legal*: The law at present favours the product, and the implication is that it will be further tightened in the future which should provide benefits. The only legal threat is that the use of mobile phones in cars may be banned completely due to the distraction they are perceived as causing, although this has been rejected in the past. For potential overseas business the legal situation should be considered in each country.
- o *Economic*: With offering a relatively inexpensive product the economic situation is not likely to have a major impact on Carmunicate; however, it is not a necessity so if the economy suffers there could be a downturn in business. Also, as the products sold are all imported the exchange rate needs to be monitored as costs could change dramatically.
- o *Political*: A change in political system is unlikely to affect Carmunicate, although the decisions to change the law may be politically based.
- o *Technology*: As already experienced, the product is affected by technology in two areas – mobile phones and music reproduction – both of which are changing rapidly. It is vital to keep up to date with the trends in these areas to ensure products are relevant to the market needs.

2.1.3 Competition

Whilst your product may be unique, and protected by a patent, there are many forms of competition. The main competition comes from the simple in-car hands-free kits which are readily available from a variety of sources. In addition, for in-car use there is a large variety of products customers could buy instead of the Carmunicate products.

Despite the patents you hold, it is possible for other companies to make products which are very similar so the originality of the design needs to be protected.

Additional competition comes from the car and audio equipment manufacturers themselves who do in some instances make their products available with integrated phone connectivity.

2.2 Where do you want to be?

This section of the marketing plan sets objectives for the plan period. The following needs further discussion with yourselves, but the objectives I propose you consider are as follows:

2.2.1 Market penetration
You should aim to increase the turnover of direct business to £x by the end of the year, representing the opportunity your new product represents.

2.2.2 Market development
You should increase sales through new channels of distribution, which will reach new customers. This should include the computer user market and the less technologically aware customers.

2.2.3 Brand awareness and positioning
At present awareness of the product and brand is low, you should have an objective to increase this and ensure that potential customers understand that the brand represents innovative thinking.

2.3 How are you going to get there?

This section of the marketing plan deals with the strategies which will be used to achieve the objectives.

For this, the following areas should be considered for the marketing mix:

2.3.1 Product
You need to ensure the product is available for all popular models of mobile phone. Extensions to the product range should be considered within the fit of the car and computer usage markets.

2.3.2 Promotion
Obviously, your promotional budget is limited so the emphasis should be on generating as much publicity as possible at low cost. This means taking all possible opportunities to get editorial coverage in the media, and this should focus on the benefits of your product.

Online promotion is important for direct sales, so developing your inter-website to gain good search engine rankings is important.

2.3.3 Place
As you have already emphasised, getting the product on sale through a national retailer is very important for the growth of Carmunicate. An exclusive distribution strategy may be considered, although this could involve compromising your brand through the use of the retailers branding.

The direct distribution should be continued, with improvements to the website and distribution process.

2.3.4 Price
Whilst the product is unique there are competitive products available at very low prices. It is important to price the product at a level which reflects its value in use related to other competing products in the marketplace.

Whilst we would normally suggest a marketing budget be set on an 'objective and task' basis, we understand that your financial situation currently does not allow for this, and therefore would recommend an 'all you can afford' principle. As your organisation is still relatively young and the objectives are to increase sales and generate awareness we recommend that as much as you can afford is spent on marketing activity – setting figures on this is very difficult as your income is not guaranteed at this stage, but from forecasts seen you would be unlikely to achieve the profit levels required for the budget required for 'objective and task' methods. You have a well-developed working product which will need some money spending on it to ensure it is available for new phone models, but beyond that it would be best to spend your money on marketing activity.

Your small size does enable you to monitor and evaluate the marketing activity very closely as returns from promotional activity should be immediately obvious, for example. At present, the introduction of formalised measurement processes are unnecessary, but results must be monitored and appropriate actions taken.

3 Expanding your business

In order to expand sales for your organisation there are a number of alternative options you could consider. The potential strategies categorised by Ansoff are as follows:

		Products	
		Existing	New
Markets	Existing	**Market penetration** Aiming to increase or maintain market share. Acquiring more customers like the ones already served. Protecting the achieved position through consolidation.	**Market development** Offering existing products to new markets with the aim of increasing penetration of the market. This includes exploitation of new market channels.
	New	**Product development** Developing new products or services for existing customers to gain increased share of customer spend.	**Diversification** Either related – where the new product and market relate to the existing industry or resources and capabilities, or unrelated – where the new product and market is outside the current industry or capability and resource.

Risks increase from market penetration through market and product development to diversification.

3.1 The most appropriate growth strategies for Carmunicate

As I mentioned earlier in the report, the most appropriate strategies for you to use are market penetration and market development. You are a niche specialist with your current product, and lack the development budgets required to expand your product range so product development should not be a priority at present.

3.1.1 Market penetration

Through concentrating on the direct marketing channel and promotion through predominantly specialist media you will continue to attract enthusiastic, technologically aware consumers. Developing online sales through improved search engine marketing and limited online advertising will increase sales within your current market.

It is also important to utilise the existing database to promote the new product to previous customers – they may well have changed their cars or the in-car audio equipment they have and welcome the new product.

3.1.2 Market development

The potential to market the new product for the computer user market is an obvious market development opportunity. Utilising the specialist media for the computer user, and also promotion directly to organisations which have a large number of mobile phones and computer users can help you develop this market.

In addition to this, the development of new channels of distribution will provide opportunities for business growth.

The new product is ideally suited to be sold as an accessory by car manufacturers who provide appropriate connections in their new car models, and joint branding of the product for this application needs to be considered.

Managing to secure a distribution agreement through a national retailer should be regarded as a priority as this will increase awareness of the product massively and should allow large opportunities for growth.

As the UK is not unique in the size of the mobile phone market, overseas opportunities should be considered – the product does not need any adaptation for other markets, although there may be some differences in the range of phone models which are more popular.

4 Market segmentation

Understanding the customers who are interested in, and actually do, purchase your products is very important. In addition to this, categorising them into groups with similar characteristics to enable marketing activity to be related specifically to these groups makes marketing much more effective – this process is known as segmentation. The process of segmentation, targeting and positioning are as follows:

Segmentation

- o Identify segmentation variables and segment market
- o Develop profiles of resulting segments.

Market targeting

- o Evaluate the attractiveness of each segment
- o Select the target segment(s).

Product positioning

- o Identify positioning concepts for each target segment
- o Select, develop and signal the chosen positioning concept.

179

The possible bases for segmenting your market include:

o Demographic, for example sex, income level
o Geographic location
o Geodemographic grouping
o Planned usage – in car or computer
o Repeat purchasers
o Technology interest.

Paul Fifield outlines six steps for segmentation success:

o Identify your strengths from talking to your customers. Focus on these strengths – instead of diversifying into new markets when the existing one matures.
o Identify what your customers' different needs, wants and motivations are and how the market segments itself.
o Do not try to please everyone – decide which segments to make your own (and which to ignore), then differentiate to target that market.
o Don't overvalue data. Descriptive data is useful to target needs-based segments, but it does not equal good segmentation on its own.
o Try to identify the needs and wants your customers may not know they have. This will help you innovate in the future.
o Customers want value, not cheapness. 'Latent need' often masquerades as demand for the cheapest price. Resist, if the price is all that differentiates, the company will fail.

A profile of the typical Carmunicate customer is as follows:

o Interested in technology products
o Aged between 25 and 35 years
o Likely to change their mobile phone regularly
o Above average income levels.

5 International marketing mix decisions

Your product has international appeal as the popularity of mobile phones in almost universal, many of the cars with which your new product is compatible are sold around the world and, universally, computers have the appropriate input. You do need to be careful, however, to work within the resources you have available and not try to extend your international coverage too quickly as this might impact on the service you can offer to customers.

Before moving into international sales it is important to consider the international macro-environment situation – as already mentioned the two which have the main impact are the laws regarding driving with hand-held mobile phones and exchange rate fluctuations. In addition you will, of course, have to consider the language requirements for your website, packaging and instructions. An additional consideration is the extent to which your current patents can be applied in other countries – and the likelihood of copycat products.

For the marketing mix the following needs to be considered:

o *Product* – Ensure that it is compatible with the most popular mobile phones in each market, otherwise the product is unlikely to need modification.
o *Price* – As the product is relatively small and therefore cheap to transport, consideration should be given to a 'world' price to reduce any effects of grey trading. This price should

close enough when converted into local currencies to ensure all markets effectively pay the same. Consideration has to be taken of any legal requirements regarding price promotions such as introductory offers.

o *Promotion* – The obvious factor is the language, otherwise communication should be able to be consistent worldwide as the benefits remain the same and the customers most likely to buy could be classed as a global segment.

o *Place* – The interweb is obviously a channel which you can use worldwide, but you have to consider the cost and time involved in shipping products internationally from the UK. The appointment of agents or distributors to handle the product on either a regional or country basis would be the best way to manage your overseas sales. Your website could be used to generate the orders directly from customers, but local agents could ship the products. They should also be able to negotiate deals with retailers in their territories.

6 Conclusion

Although your resources are limited the product you have, particularly the new version, has a lot of potential if you create, implement and monitor your marketing plans. You can create appeals for specific customer groups and also have the opportunity for international expansion.

Mini-Case 3: 2008 Olympics in Beijing (June 2004, Question 1)

Check your answer

A good answer is likely to:

                                                   ☑

Link macro-environmental forces to the marketing plan ☐

Explain the macro–forces and their impacts ☐

Consider the ethical and social responsibility issues for the Beijing culture ☐

Explain the role of branding, brand extensions and links for sponsorship ☐

Discuss how the brand can be developed and communicated ☐

Explain the concept of service quality ☐

How service quality can be delivered in a service organisation ☐

Define the extended marketing mix elements for a service ☐

Recognise a role as author – External Marketing Consultant ☐

Use appropriate format – Report format requested ☐

*   *   *   *   *

REPORT

To: Olympic Organising Committee

From: Marketing Consultant

Date: XX/XX/XX

Re: Environmental forces, planning, branding and service

1 Introduction

As you have recognised, the 2008 Olympics present an opportunity to raise the profile of Beijing and China throughout the world.

Consideration has to be given to the impact of the 2008 Olympics from elements of the World environment, and also how the Olympics will impact the rest of the World. This will influence marketing decisions made.

Branding is a critical area for most organisations and the 2008 Olympics are no different. A brand is a name or symbol which identifies a product – successful brands identify products and distinguish them from other similar products. Therefore, for Beijing the brand needs to relate the identity of the 2008 Olympics with the city and country. For many organisation there is a corporate and product brand – a Mercedes (corporate) S-Class (product) being an example. For you the Olympics can be considered the corporate brand, Beijing 2008 being the product.

In addition to these factors, the delivery of an experience during the games themselves to the visitors is critical – this will be affected by the service which the visitors receive.

This report looks at these three areas to highlight some of the essential areas to ensure the 2008 Beijing Olympics are successful for all stakeholders.

2 The macroenvironment and the marketing plan

There are many environmental factors to consider for the development of the marketing plan for the games. Macro-environmental factors are those from the wider environment which will influence and affect the 2008 Olympics, but over which you as the Organising Committee have little influence. These factors are best considered using the mnemonic PESTEL – Political, Economic, Social, Technological, Environmental and Legal.

2.1 Political factors

There are many political factors worldwide which could affect the success of the 2008 Beijing Olympic Games. One of the main factors to consider is the impact of political unrest and conflict around the world, and the possible effect of wars which may arise. As an example, during the recent Iraq War people were less prepared to travel by air which would impact on the number of potential visitors to the games, and at worst may make them unviable at the time planned due to possible world unrest.

The Games themselves need to be considered as a potential target for terrorism due to world political positions.

A factor which is often required to be considered in the political environment is the possibility of political change in the country of the organisation which would have an impact – if the Beijing and Chinese political system changes, would this impact on the support level for the games?

2.2 Economic issues

Whilst the Olympic games are expected to raise US$600 million in sponsorship, the impact of the local economy in Beijing has to be considered. The creation of the facilities required for the games will be very expensive and the economy will have to pay for this, what if there is a change in the local economy which affects the ability to make the investment required.

On a wider issue, the sponsorship requires the world economy to be healthy as much of the sponsorship will come from global corporations such as Coca-Cola and Nike – if there is a downturn in the world economy before 2008 these organisations may decide to reduce their spend which will have an effect on the income for the games.

2.3 Social issues

World social issues will have an impact on the 2008 games – and also there is an opportunity to change social perceptions of Beijing and China generally.

Within Societal issues consideration needs to be given to world cultures and language in addition to the local requirements – part of the reason for the Olympics not having a permanent base is to gain cultural influence from different parts of the world, so the Beijing culture should show through in all marketing activity. However, language becomes a very critical issue as visitors will need to be able to understand what is going on and how to get around.

Global social issues therefore have to be considered, along with the impact they have on the communications before and during the games.

2.4 Technological issues

The Olympics are an event which utilises very sophisticated technological systems for communications – consideration has to be given for the reporting of the activities of the games through television in all its guises and the written reporting of events through newspapers magazines and the internet – the writers of this information will expect to have the latest technology available to them and the scale of requirements from the large numbers of journalists who will be at the games has to be considered, along with the requirements of the visitors, most of whom will be likely to expect mobile phone reception, for example.

The Olympics present an opportunity for Beijing to showcase its ability to provide high-technology solutions worldwide.

2.5 Environmental issues

The sheer scale of the Olympic event will have a major impact on the environment through the infrastructure required, the waste products which will be created during the event, and the potential impact on the natural environment of all the travel involved.

Consideration has to be given to use natural environmental issues to create a positive impression of Beijing as an environmentally aware place, considering how best to minimise any negative impacts on the local and wider environment through the use of environmentally friendly materials wherever possible.

2.6 Legal issues

Whilst the games will be held in China under Chinese law, consideration has to be taken of international laws which may affect the games. This gives Beijing a chance to show that it fully respects international law.

In conjunction with the above, consideration has to be given to the ethical and social responsibility issues which the Olympics may raise. These can be considered through the choice of sponsors for the event – for example, is it possible to ensure the sponsors chosen have good reputations for socially responsible practice. This can range from food suppliers using organic and fairly traded produce, sports clothing sponsors having good employment practices in their factories and so on.

3 The Beijing Olympic brand

Recent Olympic games have shown the commercial benefits which can be gained from building a brand around the event and linking this through brand extension. The brand and symbolism associated with it will play a vital role in the recognition of the Beijing 2008 Olympic games.

Objectives for the brand need to be established and all brand activity has to be related to these objectives. For yourselves, the brand needs to portray the games as being the 'People's Olympics' and show Beijing as a truly international city undergoing economic transformation. A brand imagery which displays this needs to be created – with people and probably the world as part of the symbol.

The brand will create a personality for the games – adding value to the event, creating a product the whole Chinese nation will buy into as representing themselves to the outside world and building a positive international profile for Beijing and China.

The brand created can be extended through licensing deals to sponsor partners – they can be permitted to use the brand on their own promotional materials depending upon the level of sponsorship agreed between the parties. For this to happen the brand has to add value for the sponsors – the communication of the values of the games should be something the sponsors will feel benefits their own brand. In addition, the brand can be extended into official merchandise, including clothing and other souvenirs to be sold globally.

As brands differentiate one product from another it is important to consider the brand imagery used by other Olympic games – for instance, the imagery should not be too similar to that used by Greece in 2004. A complication with this is the corporate Olympics brand with its five rings logo which will need to be incorporated within the Beijing brand for some applications.

An unfortunate side effect which has to be considered within the branding strategy is how to deal with organisations who may not be official partners but will want to create their own associations with the event – effectively creating competition. Strict guidelines need to be established to ensure the official symbols are used correctly and sufficiently protected by international copyright and trademark laws.

Overall, a personality needs to be created for the games which will attract investment from sponsors and other partners, whilst portraying an image which is in line with objectives set. The maximum amount of exposure possible for the chosen logo has to be obtained – the games are the most watched television event worldwide so people have to associate the brand imagery prior to the opening of the games. Choosing partners such as travel operators who will use the logo in materials a long time in advance of the games will help with this.

To ensure sponsors can utilise the brand effectively, colour schemes have to be considered – partners will want to use the Beijing logo along with their own, but the result will have to aesthetically pleasing for both parties, with synergistic benefits. Personalities – Chinese and from the rest of the world – can be used to enhance brand values for the games in the same way many of the potential sports clothing sponsors already use international sports personalities to promote their brands.

A final consideration for the brand needs to be that of the staff and volunteers working for the games – the imagery will need to make them want to work for the event, developing a relationship internally.

185

4 Service quality for the 2008 Olympic games

The Olympics can be regarded as a service rather than a product – they meet the criteria of a service in that they match the five main characteristics of a service:

○ *Lack of ownership* – As no goods change hands with services, there is no transfer of ownership, although a legal transaction does take place. The games involve an 'experience' for the customer, rather than gaining a possession.

○ *Intangibility* – The senses normally used in purchase decisions (touch, sight, smell, sound and taste) cannot experience a service before it has been purchased – the service itself is the provider of the experience which will be sensed – it is intangible and only delivered when the customer is committed to the experience.

Promotional material for services has to provide tangible cues to what the service may offer.

○ *Perishability* – Services, and certainly the Olympics, are manufactured at the same time they are consumed, often with the direct involvement of the consumer. This games event will happen just once, so customers have only that one chance to experience them as they cannot be repeated exactly.

This has implications for capacity maximisation and utilisation – the capacity has to be balanced between costs and requirements.

○ *Inseparability* – The service is linked directly to the provider, and often the customer – consumption taking place at the same time as production. The inseparability means that the customer will come into direct contact with Olympic staff – all of whom have to provide the service efficiently, whilst interacting with the customer.

In addition, it will be the case that visitors directly interact with other visitors during the games – this will affect the experience all other visitors, either good or bad.

○ *Heterogeneity* – Because the service is produced and consumed simultaneously, and because of the direct involvement of other visitors and staff it is difficult to standardise the experience for all customers. This is especially an issue when you will have a finite capacity and a labour-intensive service – the pressure can reduce the quality.

To overcome the issues of heterogeneity, procedures and staff training will take away some of the unpredictability.

4.1 Using the service quality model (Servqual)

Research undertaken by Parasuraman et al. highlighted five main dimensions by which customer service or service quality can be measured ('Servqual', as it is sometimes referred to). They are:

○ *Reliability* – consistency and dependability of performance
○ *Responsiveness* – the ability and readiness to provide service
○ *Assurance* – guaranteeing the security and effectiveness of the deliverable
○ *Empathy* – the ability to communicate with, understand and deal with customers in an appropriate manner
○ *Tangibles* – the physical evidence of the service.

Through the planning process and during the event you need to be able to measure and monitor service quality and its plans at frequent intervals.

The SERVQUAL model can be illustrated as follows:

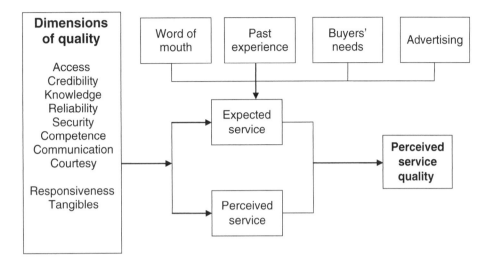

Factors which should be considered specifically for the event include access to the various sites which will be used, security measures, customer empathy, understanding and the responsiveness to requests through courteous and competent staff.

4.2 Service quality gaps

The 'Gap' model (Parasuraman et al. 1985) is a means of describing customer dissatisfaction in the context of service quality which can be used to ensure that service is delivered to a level where visitors are satisfied (or more) with the service they receive.

The model is illustrated as follows:

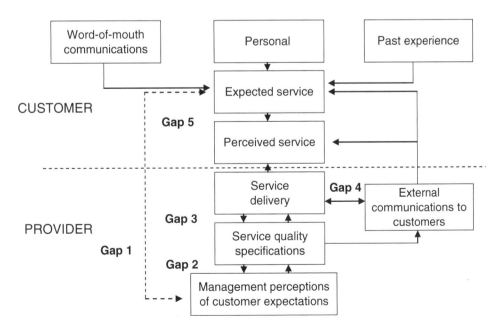

The five gaps being:

- Between customers' expectation and management's perceptions of those expectations, that is not knowing what visitors expect.
- Between management's perceptions of visitors' expectations and service quality specifications, that is the wrong service quality standards.
- Between service quality specifications and service delivery, that is the service performance gap.
- Between service delivery and external communications to visitors about service delivery, that is when promises do not match delivery.
- Between visitors' expectation and perceived service (the total of the other four gaps).

It is this last 'gap', which has the most significance. Using the 'Gap' model will keep a clear focus on the perceptions of the visitor, and these are paramount.

4.3 An extended marketing mix

These service considerations can be included within an extended marketing mix for the plan:

4.3.1 People
An internal marketing campaign emphasising the importance of service and supporting this through staff selection and training is vital. Consideration needs to be given to the volunteer status of many of the people involved in the games, and the satisfaction levels of staff have to be considered.

4.3.2 Process
Technology can be used to ensure the processes are as standardised as possible – this can include ticket issue, access to specific events. The processes put into place to support the service specifications are important and have to be consistent through suppliers involved in the process such as transport and other more integrated suppliers such as food and cleaning concessions.

4.3.3 Physical evidence
The use of the brand imagery as already discussed is vital for the physical evidence – it has to attract visitors to the games and also needs to be used consistently for the whole event on buildings, staff uniforms and all other physical contact points.

5 Conclusion

It may be an obvious truism, but the 2008 Beijing Olympics are a one-off event which provide only one chance to get it right. Careful planning of the event through consideration of the environmental factors which may affect it, the brand and its associations, and the service levels during the event are critical – along with measurement and assessment throughout the process.

Mini-Case 4: Moving Times

Check your answer

A good answer is likely to:

☑

Explain the micro-environment ☐

Outline the impact on the marketing plan of micro-environmental forces ☐

Identify and outline potential barriers to planning for Moving Times ☐

Explain the importance of customer relationships ☐

Outline how Moving Times can enhance their customer relationships ☐

Identify the basis on which competitive advantage can be created ☐

Relate to the context – A medium-sized service business ☐

Recognise a role as author – Recently appointed marketing Manager ☐

Use appropriate format – Report format requested ☐

*   *   *   *   *

REPORT

To: Commercial Manager – Moving Times

From: Marketing Manager

Date: XX/XX/XX

Re: Marketing within Moving Times

1 Introduction

Having now had time to look into how we operate at Moving Times from a marketing perspective here are my observations on the micro-environment, our situation as regards marketing planning, creating relationships with customers and developing competitive advantage.

2 Micro-environment issues

The micro-environment is made up of the groups or organisations who have a relationship with the organisation rather than impact on it. This, therefore is an area over which we have some influence. The micro-environment consists of internal and external groups of stakeholders.

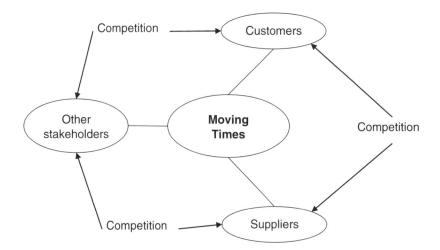

The micro-environment includes companies the organisation could potentially do business with in addition to those it currently deals with – for example customers and potential customers. It also includes competitors.

An alternative approach is to view this as five main areas which are described in the following sections.

2.1 Internal stakeholders

Collectively, the internal stakeholder group is made up of all levels of staff of an organisation. Because of this, they are a very powerful group, and marketing practices can play a part in developing and maintaining open communication through a planned programme of internal marketing.

Our internal stakeholders include the following groups:

- o *Board of Directors*
- o *Management*, both centrally and at branch level – because of their role and contact with the Board and other key stakeholders, managers hold considerable power in the organisation.
- o *Other employees*
- o *Trade Unions* – the representatives of these are our employees, who expect time off for associated duties, and can put pressure on management to meet the expectations of the staff.

When auditing the organisation from a marketing perspective we have to give consideration towards whether we have a marketing culture, which is the primary function to meet the needs, wants and expectations of customers. This has to include internal customers – internal and external. The elements which should be audited are managerial, competitive, financial and technical factors, probably by analysing these and grading each area.

The internal stakeholders are the people who will put the marketing plans into action, so it is important that they are understood, and that they understand what the plan is intended to achieve.

2.2 Competitors

In common with nearly all organisations, we have a large number of competitors and therefore a competitor analysis is essential. The marketing function has to have an up-to-date profile of all competitors which analyses their activities and behaviour.

The profile should include information on the marketing, managerial, staff and design capabilities of the competitors. With this information, kept up to date, it is less likely the organisation will be caught unaware by competitors' actions.

We need to consider the full range of competitors we have from the independent one-branch agency to the national chains. Marketing plans have to be designed to provide competitive advantage – if we do not know or understand what our competitors are doing we do not know how to offer advantage over them.

2.3 Suppliers

Supplier relationships are vital for success in an organisation, without consistency in supply customers will potentially suffer. The main suppliers we need to consider are the people who erect signs outside properties and the media we advertise through. Working with suppliers helps us in the production of successful plans.

2.4 Customers

Customers should be the centre of the business, they should be analysed, understood, their needs identified, their expectations are at the core of the marketing function. Through knowledge about customers it is possible to react to their requirements and remain competitive for them long term. Ultimately, without customers we do not have a business so they have to paramount in our planning process.

2.5 Other stakeholders

Stakeholders have an increasing influence on the way organisations do business. Pressure groups, for example, can change the way organisations have to work – as we have seen with the increasing regulation for the financial services you offer, and the general tightening of rules for estate agencies. Stakeholders can include customers, suppliers, shareholders, employees, financiers and the wider social community. Relationships have to be built with these groups to avoid any risk of collective or individual action.

These factors all indicate that our organisations relationship with a wide range of stakeholders is very important.

3 Barriers to marketing planning

There are many barriers that make marketing planning difficult to introduce effectively in organisations, Malcolm McDonald identifies ten barriers to marketing planning, some of which may be relevant to ourselves:

- ○ *Confusion between marketing tactics and strategy* – It is quite possible that the people involved in the process might be unclear about the distinctions between strategy (the way things will be done) and tactics (the actions involved in making the strategy happen).

- o *Isolating the marketing function from operations* – This is very likely to be the case for ourselves as we have not previously had a distinct marketing function.
- o *Confusion between the marketing function and the marketing concept* – As we did not have a marketing function this was not a major factor, however, now it exists it is important to ensure all staff understand they are part of marketing (the concept) and can help the function. It is also important people understand marketing is more than just promotion and advertising!
- o *Organisational barriers* – McDonald defines this as the tribal mentality, the failure to define strategic business units correctly. From what I have found out so far this is unlikely to be an issue as the branch and area responsibilities seem to be well understood.
- o *Lack of in-depth analysis* – Probably the case in the past, but a part of my job description to correct this.
- o *Confusion between process and output* – The gathering and possession of information is the foundation on which a marketing plan is built; however, it has to be used – providing intelligence.
- o *Lack of knowledge and skills* – Typically many people do not have the abilities and knowledge required to produce plans. It is intended to provide training to handle any difficulties in this area.
- o *Lack of a systematic approach to marketing planning* – you have acknowledged this to be the case previously.
- o *Failure to prioritise objectives* – Understanding what is most important to do and working on these areas first is important but difficult to get right.
- o *Hostile corporate cultures* – We need to ensure everyone understands what we are trying to achieve and help us deliver it.

4 Developing customer relationships

Although we may only deal with individual customers on what could be classed as a one-off basis – they are very unlikely to purchase off us every week! – it is still important to build relationships with them. There are two primary reasons for this:

- o Our customers are involved in very high value transactions through us and therefore have a right to expect high levels of service to go along with the value of the sale. As we deal in property of above average value, our customers are used to receiving high levels of service in other areas of their lives.
- o Word of mouth can be very important for generating custom, particularly in terms of getting people to use us to sell their properties.

The main determinant of our service is the people who work in our branches as these are the contact point between Moving Times and our customers. Research undertaken by Parasuraman et al. highlighted five main dimensions by which customer service, or service quality, can be measured ('Servqual', as it is sometimes referred to). They are as follows:

- o *Reliability* – The service we offer has to be reliable, this mainly involves doing what we promise, and making sure customers are aware that we are doing this.
- o *Responsiveness* – Ensuring that we respond in a timely manner to requests for assistance.
- o *Assurance* – Can our customers trust us to help with selling their property.

o *Empathy* – It is regularly said that moving house is the second most stressful event in peoples lives, and we are very involved in the process so we have to consider this in all our dealings with customers.

o *Tangibles* – The tangibles (or physical evidence) include the materials we produce on behalf of our customers. This includes such things as the standard of the fittings in our branches, the appearance of our staff, the quality of the paper on which we print details of the properties, the quality of the photographs and their reproduction and even goes as far as the style of language used in descriptions.

For the purposes of delivering customer service we need to consider the service quality for two elements:

o customers selling property through us
o customers buying property through us.

Whilst many of the requirements are similar for both groups, there are differences in requirements which we have to understand. The selling customers have put their faith in us to sell their property, and in most instances this is an exclusive arrangement. This is a large commitment from them, which they expect to be returned in terms of our effort in selling their property – they need to be informed about what we are doing, and we need to respect their wishes in terms of the way we handle the dealings. When a sale has been agreed they expect us to help them handle any issues they may have with the buyer.

The buying customers have more choice in some respects – they are not particularly concerned about which agency they buy through, their concern is the actual property. However, if we acknowledge their requirements and ensure the information they receive is related to the stated requirements they will be satisfied – although good staff will be able to point out if some of the expectations are unrealistic which can be the case. Again, when a sale has been agreed, the purchaser is likely to need assistance from us, and this is the stage at which we can offer our additional services. Although it may be sometime before it happens, if a purchaser has a good experience with us they are likely to consider us first when it comes to selling their home in the future. A final consideration is that we need to ensure our database is up to date as regards buyer requirements, and we have to respect any requests to be taken off mailing lists and so on.

5 Differentiation and competitive advantage

Competitive advantage is anything which can give an organisation an edge over its rivals in the products sold or services provided. Kotler (2005) defines it as 'an advantage over competitors gained by offering customers greater value, either through lower prices or by providing more benefits that justify higher prices'.

The nature of our business makes it difficult to offer lower prices to our purchasing customers (we would be unlikely to attract sellers as we undervalue their property) but could be applied to sellers' fees. The drawback here is that this may give a perception of lower quality, which would not fit the image we have of dealing with exclusive property. Therefore, I feel that following Kotler's definition we should provide more benefits to justify higher prices.

This can be backed up by the theory of Aaker (2001) who suggests that sustainable competitive advantage can be achieved through a framework of:

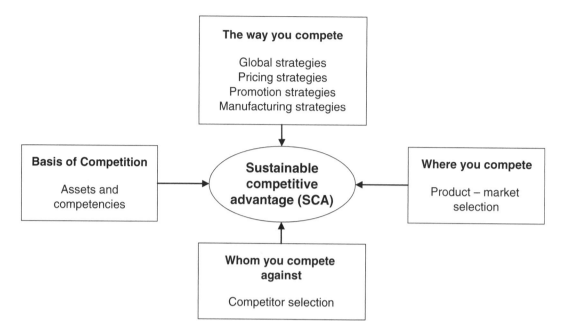

Further to this, Davidson (1997) suggests that organisations can gain competitive advantage in many ways, either based on one large advantage or a number of smaller advantages – basically being better than competitors in some way. The sources of advantage identified by Davidson are:

- *Superior product* – The product is objectively and measurably better than competitors' offerings; the idea of the best in class – ensuring that we offer the best quality of houses to our customers. This may involve rejecting some property which we are requested to sell. Additionally, we should consider that we have a service rather than a product so we have to offer superior service as discussed.
- *Perceived advantage* – The position and image of the product result in the customer perceiving that the product is better than the competition. Our physical evidence will help with the perceived advantage.
- *Global skills* – Davidson states these can include R&D, production, distribution and marketing skills of an organisation. Whilst not global, and some of these do not apply to us, the skills we can combine from our branch network will help us.
- *Low cost operator* – Setting out to achieve the lowest possible costs throughout the development, production, distribution and marketing process. We have to ensure our processes enable us to be extremely cost effective.
- *Superior competencies* – Encompass the processes and capabilities of the organisation. Having better online facilities than our competitors could be an example of this.
- *Superior assets* – The physical and intangible resources of the organisation such as capital, equipment and brands. Our branch network provides this at present.
- *Scale advantages* – Allow organisations to spread their fixed costs over a higher level of activity, yielding economies of scale. This is reflected in the comparative returns on investment discovered in the PIMS research. Again, we have scale advantages over smaller competitors, but lose out to the national chains.
- *Attitude advantages* – Attitudes reflect the culture and ability to act decisively in areas such as innovation, investment, response to competitive threats and long-term development of the market. We are small enough, with an appropriate management structure to be able to react quickly when necessary.

○ *Legal advantages* – Gained by use of patents and protection of copyright. Our compliance with all legal requirements for the financial services we offer is important here, particularly as our staff are trained for all identified future legislation.

○ *Superior relationships* – Encompass all forms of relationships with customers, distributors, competitors and suppliers and allow organisations to achieve with others what they cannot do on their own. They are used to share expertise, knowledge and risk. The links we have with solicitors helps us here.

The various advantages outlined above need to be strengthened and maintained as appropriate to increase our competitive advantage for the future.

6 Conclusion

We are in a great situation to move forward as an organisation through better understanding of our environment, overcoming any barriers which may exist to creating marketing plans, developing relationships with our customers and gaining competitive advantage.

PART B SUGGESTED ANSWERS

Answer 5
External environment monitoring, Information and communication technology

Check your answer

A good answer is likely to:

	☑
Define the external environment	☐
Explain why monitoring the environment is significant	☐
Relate the external environment to marketing plans	☐
Outline recent ICT developments for monitoring and planning	☐
Link the developments to changes in the planning process	☐
Relate the context to a not-for-profit organisation	☐
Recognise a role as author – Marketing consultant	☐
Use appropriate format – Report format requested	☐

* * * * *

REPORT

To: Marketing Director

From: Marketing Consultant

Date: XX/XX/XX

Re: The marketing environment and technology usage

1 Introduction

Marketing is about much more than just customers – it involves building relationships with customers, others in the company and external partners. To do this we have to understand the environmental forces which surround these relationships. The marketing environment is defined by Kotler (2005) as 'The actors and forces outside marketing that affect marketing management's abilities to build and maintain successful relationships with target customers.' Through monitoring of the environment, marketers can adapt their strategies to meet changing marketplace opportunities and threats.

2 The significance of monitoring the external environment

There are two factors which affect the strategies adopted by organisations: the external environment and the resource base enjoyed by the organisation. Relating the two together will allow you to develop marketing plans which are very effective. You need to monitor the environment in order to identify opportunities and threats which inform the situation analysis from which plans are built.

In addition to understanding the current situation, anticipating changes in external market drivers can enable effective planning based upon evolving consumer behaviour and competitor activity. Basically, environmental monitoring is a fundamental component of the marketing audit.

The areas which need to be considered are as follows:

2.1 Competition

Understanding the activities of competitors is very important – even though you offer a service which is not replicated by other charities when it comes to receiving donations the people that contribute to you are also potential donors to other charities. Understanding what others are doing and responding to competitive threats which may reduce your income is vital, and needs to be incorporated within your marketing plans.

2.2 Social factors

Social change involves changes in the nature, attitudes and habits of society. Social changes are continually happening, and trends which may affect you can be identified:

- ○ *Rising standards of living* – These may result in wider ownership of consumer and luxury goods, which may reduce the number of people who would shop in your stores which are seen as downmarket.
- ○ *Society's attitude to business* – Increasing social obligations and responsibilities are being heaped on to companies in many countries, not least with respect to ethical conduct (towards customers, employees, etc.) – this is an area from which you could benefit as you are not classified as a business by your customers.

Knowledge of these two factors will help with strategy development for your marketing plan.

Within the social environment demographic factors need to be considered for marketing activities – these include the age of the population, cultural factors such as religion and beliefs.

2.3 Legal factors

It is important to consider legal factors which may change and alter the way you do business – for example, the increasing restrictions on the use of data you may hold about donors through the data protection act has to be considered in your tactical activity.

2.4 Economic factors

The state of the economy affects all organisations, whether commercial and not. The rate of growth in the economy is a measure of the overall change in demand for goods and services. Growth is an indication of increases in demand – this will affect the levels of business you might expect to see in your shops. Also, the health of the economy will affect the amount of free income your donors have which will affect the amount of income you might receive.

2.5 Political factors

The implications of a change in government policy, irrespective of whether or not there is a change of government can be quite wide reaching. For example, when the national lottery was introduced (a political decision) the amount of direct giving to charities was reduced as people bought lottery tickets instead.

Government policy towards healthcare can have a direct influence on your operations as the support given through the National Health Service in your areas of expertise will influence the level of support you will receive from other areas and this needs to be considered for your marketing plans.

2.6 Technological factors

Although your services are not reliant on technology, the changes in the technological environment can have a major impact on your operations. Charity donations via the internet are increasing substantially as one example, and it is now possible to donate directly via mobile phones – your plans need to embrace this kind of technology to maximise opportunities. Indeed, one charity recently started using online auction sites to sell goods which have been donated via their shops.

Overall, you can see that the factors which make up the external environment have large impacts on your organisation, and need to be combined with your internal resources to produce very effective marketing plans.

3 Technological change and marketing planning

Information and Communications Technology (ICT) is now employed throughout the environmental monitoring and scanning process. In particular, you can apply this through improved market intelligence gathering. ICT has made it much easier and quicker to gain market intelligence; global communications are much easier, Internet sites provide large amounts of data which previously was time-consuming and costly to obtain, your shops can employ electronic communications-based reporting helping you to profile stock requirements better than ever before.

Marketing research techniques have been enhanced by ICT which provides better understanding of consumer and competitor behaviour – although the systems would be prohibitively expensive for you, electronic surveillance and observation of consumer behaviour through CCTV in shops can provide very useful data. Other commercial organisations who collect this data may be prepared to share it with you as part of their social responsibility programmes.

Customer/donor databases provide comprehensive data sets for planning and executing marketing activity – it is much easier than ever before to produce targeted promotion activity for individuals who have given you permission to contact them.

Overall ICT has led to modifications in the planning process, making it speedier, more sophisticated and allowing improved performance monitoring and control mechanisms.

4 Conclusion

As you can see from the above, when producing marketing plans it is essential to have as much information as possible about the current and future external environment situation so you can make plans to capitalise on the opportunities presented and minimise the risks. Fortunately, ICT has made the producing effective plans easier and more cost effective than previously.

Answer 6
Stakeholder relationships, extended marketing mix, international marketing

Check your answer

A good answer is likely to:

                                                        ☑

Define relationship marketing ☐

Explain the importance of relationship marketing and the stakeholders to have relationships with ☐

Consider the elements of an extended marketing mix for relationships ☐

Outline the differences when dealing with the above in an international context ☐

Relate answer to a not-for-profit organisation ☐

Recognise a role as author – Marketing Manager within organisation ☐

Use appropriate format – Report format requested ☐

*   *   *   *   *

REPORT

To: Marketing Director – Healthcare Charity

From: Marketing Manager

Date: XX/XX/XX

Re: Relationship marketing and the marketing mix

1 Introduction

Gronroos (2000) defined the purpose of relationship marketing as 'to establish, maintain and enhance long-term relationships with customers and other parties so that the objectives of both parties are met'.

Further, relationship marketing recognises the importance of the lifetime value of customers and that the key to successful long-term business success relies not just on getting new customers but, more importantly, on encouraging customer loyalty.

2 Developing and maintaining relationships

The concept of relationship marketing is not limited to building relationships with customers but can equally be applied to the other stakeholder groups with which we are associated. Building effective relationships with the various markets (six market model – Christopher et al.) will, in the longer term, enable us to more effectively meet our customers' needs and develop stronger relationships with stakeholders.

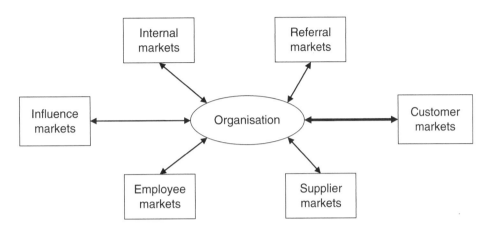

For ourselves, the key stakeholders are as follows:

o the customers (customer, supplier and referral markets) who visit our shops to purchase products, this group are part of the funding stream which helps us to support
o the recipients (customer markets) of the support we offer through our healthcare services
o the government (supplier markets) who provide us with lottery funding
o our staff and the volunteers (internal markets) who work for us
o the media (influence markets) who give us publicity
o the local community (employee and referral markets).

Relationship marketing is a concept which has always existed in business to business (although not necessarily referred to in this way), but has more recently come to prominence in the service sector (which we are in) due to the inseparability of the production and delivery of the service. This is especially true for us as a charity dealing with the recipients of the support we offer – we produce the support at the same time it is consumed, and the service level we offer is judged on that basis. Similarly, when we are dealing with donors (customers in our shops and when doing the various money collection activities we are involved in) we are delivering an inseparable experience from which there is no physical item transferred to take away and measure the quality of.

The relationship marketing ladder developed by Christopher et al. (1995) framework identifies a number of stages of relationship building. The objective of relationship marketing is to move people up the ladder from prospect through to advocate and to maintain this position.

The attributes of a product can be defined through the following diagram:

At the foot of the ladder, the *prospect* or target market is what classical marketing has tended to focus on turning into a *customer*. In relationship marketing the customer is someone who has transacted with us only once or occasionally. The next step is the *client* – someone who has regular transactions with us but who does not have a strong attitude about our organisation.

With the conversion to *supporter* the strength of the relationship becomes apparent – these people like to use us and maybe recommend us to others – they become *advocates* for an organisation.

The final step is where the stakeholder becomes a *partner*, and both parties work together to build the relationship and gain mutual benefit.

This ultimate stage is when the stakeholder (whether donor or recipient of support or other member of the six markets) becomes retained – that is they will automatically use us for the things we offer. This can include the media contacting us for our view of a situation which relates to the illnesses we support – if we can be their preferred contact we will gain additional publicity and exposure for very little effort.

3 An extended marketing mix for developing relationships

For the development and management of relationships it is essential that we have a product which people want to be and remain associated with – the core service around which we can establish and develop the relationships.

Philip Kotler defines a product as 'anything that can offered to a market for attention, acquisition, use or consumption that might satisfy a want or need. It includes physical objects, services, persons, places, organisations and ideas'.

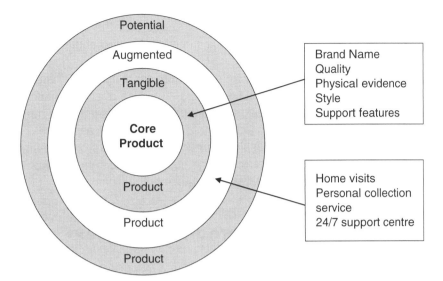

- The *core product* is the reason for the existence of our service – the basic features and benefits of our service support and the products sold through our shops.
- The *tangible product* or *actual product* relates to the support with the characteristics which make it a reality, and can be communicated to the recipients of the core product.
- The *augmented product* includes the features which make the services more desirable and differentiated – the features may not make the support perform any better, but add value long term.
- The *potential product* is what the support could become with evolution and development and through further added value and differentiation.

We can achieve the augmented product status by looking at the specific marketing mix elements beyond our core product:

- *Price*: we only charge a set amount for the items sold in our shops – these prices need to reflect the fact that we are a charity which gives people the perception that we offer good value for money. For donations we cannot set prices, but can suggest particular monthly donations from those donors who have moved up the loyalty ladder to become supporters.
- *Promotion*: we have to be careful to balance the amount we spend on promotion with the returns this will generate – through the establishment of relationship marketing we should build a database of stakeholders and use direct promotion to these parties which can be targeted and therefore more efficient, potentially moving towards key account management techniques. PR plays a key role in our promotion and well-managed relationships with the media can be very cost-effective.
- *Place*: where we have shops, and the channels through which we receive donations is very important. At present we do not use the Internet for donations and this is something, which we need to establish as people are becoming very open to this method of charity giving.
- *People*: our staff and volunteers are critical to our success as already mentioned – we need to have ongoing training for all staff to ensure they are providing excellent customer service. Our internal marketing needs to focus on efforts to move stakeholders up the loyalty ladder. A better feedback process needs to be established so we respond better to the ideas, which are generated by the staff and volunteers.

o *Process*: the processes have to be considered to make it easy for people to make donations and for the delivery of excellent support for the beneficiaries of our services. For relationship marketing the process needs to be personalised for those we want to improve our relationship with.

o *Physical evidence*: this needs to be considered for a number of areas. All staff need to present a uniform message to stakeholders – the use of simple uniforms with our name and logo discreetly featured needs to be a priority. All our vehicles need to be consistent with the image we wish to project to help maximise our exposure. For the shops, we need to project a clean, professional image, but we cannot be over-elaborate as this would not be maximising the return to the support recipients and would look wasteful to those we hope will become repeat donors.

4 Marketing activities in an international context

For the future if we intend to expand our operations overseas (which is easily possible as the healthcare we deliver is needed worldwide) there are many factors we need to consider.

Whilst the basic support service we offer could be transferred, the elements of the marketing mix have to be considered for standardisation or adaptation for the various markets. This becomes fundamental for the consideration of our fund-raising – the UK culture is very accepting of the 'charity shop' and it is a well-established feature of the high street, but this is not the case in all markets, and we would also have to consider the legal aspects of money collection methods for different countries; for instance, are door-to-door collections legal.

For promotion, we currently rely on the media to help us with promotion, again in other markets the types of media we use may not be as readily available, and the culture may make it harder to gain the free publicity which we currently enjoy and take advantage of.

Peoples attitudes and abilities towards working as volunteers can vary from culture to culture, so we would have to consider whether the UK model could be used in this area.

Through the use of technology, many of our processes should be able to be standardised, and as we develop our web- site we should be considering the facilities which we would require to enable it to work in other countries – languages and payments received in different currencies.

5 Conclusion

To develop relationships we have to consider the stakeholders and markets we serve, segmenting them into those we see as having potential and needing emphasis so we can increase the retention levels. Using the factors considered above, we should develop a relationship marketing plan which has a focus on the internal marketing needed to ensure all the organisation supports the relationship developments.

Answer 7
Segmentation, profiling and targeting

Check your answer

A good answer is likely to:

☑

Define marketing segmentation ☐

Explain factors influencing segmentation ☐

Evaluate the role of these factors for an FMCG product ☐

Define targeting ☐

Outline the evaluation process for target markets ☐

Recognise a role as author – Brand Manager within company ☐

Use appropriate format – Report format requested ☐

*   *   *   *   *

REPORT

To: Marketing Director

From: Brand Manager – Satellite Navigation Brand (SNB)

Date: XX/XX/XX

Re: Segmenting and targeting the market

1 Introduction

Many organisations use segmentation, targeting and positioning to create specific competitive positions for their chosen markets – to date we have not segmented our markets at brand level, even though our current segmentation models are at the heart of strategic marketing decision making.

Kotler (1999) define market segmentation as:

> *Dividing a market up into distinct groups of buyers with different needs, characteristics or behaviours, who might require separate products or marketing mixes.*

Segmentation provides us with many benefits, these include:

- o Enabling customers needs to be met more precisely
- o Increasing profits

- ○ Providing assistance for marketing planning as reactions can be more predictable, relative to groups
- ○ Identification of individuals who are likely to purchase
- ○ Increases knowledge about customers
- ○ Retain customers
- ○ Budgets can be allocated to segments for better control
- ○ Focused marketing activity

2 Segmenting the market for SNB

There are many factors on which we can segment our market. Two common forms of segmentation are *class* and **s***tatus*.

Class is a complex concept, including the ideas of:

- ○ *hierarchical distinction*: giving upper, middle, lower and working class – plus other similar distinctions
- ○ *occupations*: gives socio-economic status groups – white collar, manual, non-manual and so on.

These distinctions enable us to segment the population into groups which may have similar beliefs, attributes and values reflected in their behaviour. Class is an *objective* means of classifying people – implying an awareness of the class consciousness within the group.

Status, on the other hand, is a *subjective* criteria – a judgement on the social position of a person. There are three forms of status:

- ○ *Ascribed status* – related to birth through classifications such as gender or race the individual has little or no control over the status accorded by society.
- ○ *Achieved status* – achieved by individuals through such things as their occupation, place of residence and lifestyle.
- ○ *Desired status* – the social position a person wishes to attain: aspirational groups.

Other factors we can consider for segmentation for SNB include:

- ○ *Geographics* – the location in which people live: are people from certain geographical areas more likely to purchase the product?
- ○ *Demographics* – considering family size, age, income and so on: are these factors which affect purchase behaviour?
- ○ *Psychographic factors* – lifestyle factors related to class.
- ○ *Geodemographics* – based on the ACORN or PinPoint classifications
- ○ *Behaviour* – looking at the frequency of purchase or type of purchase occasion – how often and why are people buying SNB?
- ○ *Attitude* – considering which customers are technically competent as opposed to those who are 'timid'.
- ○ *Considering the benefits sought* – what the individuals aim to get from SNB – speed, quality, ease of use, cost and so on.
- ○ *Amateur vs. professional* – distinguishing between the domestic and business users from SNB.

3 Target market segments

Kotler (1999) defined *targeting* as:

> *The process of evaluating each market segment's attractiveness and selecting one or more segments to enter.*

This involves evaluating market opportunities against strategic fit with the organisation and is the second stage in the segmentation, targeting, positioning (STP) process. Positioning is defined by Kotler as:

> *Arranging for a product to occupy a clear, distinctive and desirable place relative to competing products in the minds of target consumers. Formulating competitive positioning for a product and a detailed marketing mix.*

Following our segmentation process we should develop profiles – creating 'pictures' of target segments based on a range of segmentation variables.

Targeting decision should be based on a systematic review of:

- o *Attractiveness* of the competing segments – based on criteria such as the potential to create a sustainable marketing position, the ability to satisfy the segment with current resources and structures, the 'fit' with the corporate mission, and consistency with organisational culture.
- o *Competitive capabilities* – this is the organisation's comparative ability to competitively address the needs of that segment. It should always be judged relative to the competition.

Three target market segments which I think we should consider for SNB are:

- o *Professional users* – The professional users are those drivers who use their vehicles for business, but make their own purchase decisions. Typically these people include sales representatives who travel throughout the country visiting customers. They can be segmented by class (typically B and C class), they seek similar benefits (ease of use and speed of response from the equipment along with readily installed updates) and there are some demographic similarities (many customers being in the 30–45 year age bracket and having families).
  This category of customers are likely to repeat purchase, and can be influential in sales to other customers, particularly their colleagues.
- o *Individual users* – These are people who are interested in technology (technically competent) and from higher levels of individual income, and are also predominantly male. Whilst some people with similar characteristics would not find justification for buying the product. The individual users we should target are likely to purchase

upgraded models as they come out – in product life cycle terms they would be classed as innovators.

○ *Businesses* – Whilst the professional users would purchase and use the product themselves (or make the decision to do so) there are many businesses who may provide for the product for their drivers – these would include delivery companies, ambulance operators and so on, for whom the accuracy of the data and the reliability of the equipment would be paramount.

For each of these three categories there are elements of the marketing mix which would need to change, even though the basic product can remain the same. Factors to consider for adaptation include:

○ *Promotion* – The channels to reach the different groups would be different – the individuals can be targeted through the new range of publications which give details of high-technology products. The professional users are the hardest to target as they read a variety of media – encouragement of word of mouth can be very useful here.

○ *Place* – The distribution channels need to be appropriate for each segment. The businesses would be best reached through personal selling and direct distribution. For the individuals online sales are the best channel, whilst traditional outlets are best for the professional users.

○ *Price* – Due to the potential to sell multiple units in one order we should consider volume discounts for businesses. People expect to pay less via the Internet than through shops so we need to reflect this in our pricing strategies.

4 Conclusion

Through the selection of appropriate segmentation variables, and the careful targeting of potential customer groups we can gain many benefits for the individual brand.

Answer 8
Innovation and new product development

Check your answer

A good answer is likely to:

☑

Describe the role of new products within an organisation ☐

Define innovation and approaches to it ☐

Outline the different types of innovation ☐

Explain why innovation has to be a continuous process ☐

Describe the new product development process ☐

Use examples throughout the answer ☐

Recognise that the new products are for an international market ☐

Recognise a role as author – working within the organisation ☐

Use appropriate format – Report format requested ☐

*   *   *   *   *

REPORT

To: Marketing Director

From: Marketing Manager

Date: XX/XX/XX

Re: Innovation and new product development for the French market

1 Introduction

We are in the early stages of our plan to develop a new product range specifically for the French market. These products are intended to be complementary to those we already produce and market domestically. Whilst being developed specifically with the French market in mind through later adaptation and development they may be suitable for other markets in the future.

2 The role of innovation within our organisation

Innovation has been defined as: 'The generation, acceptance and implementation of new ideas, processes, products or services'.

An innovation is the generation and implementation of an idea. An innovation can be anything – from the introduction of the Walkman by Sony, through a new parcel delivery service, to a truly genuine response to a customer's need. Innovation is in the eye of the receiver and therefore does not have to be novel to the producer. In addition, innovation does not have to be new – it may have existed for sometime (possibly in another application) before the receiver became aware of its existence.

Innovation is often linked to technological advances, but is not solely the result of this. It is often the result of an entrepreneur spotting opportunities created by changing market environments and exploiting them, using a combination of existing and new technology and techniques in a different context.

For example, in 2001 Hilton Hotels launched a new service for tired Executives at conferences. They launched a 'neck and shoulders massage' service, which caused some excitement at the first offering. This was an innovation in the hotel industry but Virgin had been offering this service on its first class flights for quite sometime. Innovation is not necessarily about high-technology products.

Innovation is frequently linked in marketing with product development – the concept that innovation and new products are inextricably linked. But this is to hide an important distinction. On one hand, an innovation may result in a new or modified product; on the other hand, innovations can also be made to processes used within an organisation to make them more efficient or more effective. So we need to bear in mind that innovation is about both:

o Developing and modifying products, and
o Developing and modifying processes.

2.1 Innovation and products

Innovation is important for the continuing existence of businesses. Seven types of products can be used to explain why we need to continually innovate, those which highlight this are:

o *Today's breadwinners* – Those products and services earning healthy profits and contributing positively to cash flow and profits.
o *Tomorrow's breadwinners* – Products in growth or other attractive markets and are expected to take over the breadwinning role when today's breadwinners fail.
o *Yesterday's breadwinners* – Products which have supported previously but are no longer contributing significant cash or profits.
o *Developments* – Products and services recently developed that may have some future but require further investments.

These categories highlight the need to continually innovate the product range to have a flow of developments into today's breadwinners. Other categories were as follows:

o *Sleepers*
o *Investments in managerial ego*
o *Failures.*

Further to this, the innovations can be of different types:

- New to the company, a minor innovation for the market – When Porsche introduced the Cayenne it was their first move away from sports cars, although the category it moved into (4x4) already existed, but there had never been such an overtly sporting 4x4 previously. This can also be categorised as continuous innovation.
- New to the company, no innovation to the market – Something the organisation has not done before, but a copycat product which offers no significant difference to current offerings – for example an electronics manufacturer introducing its first DVD player with the same features as those already manufactured.
- New to the company and a significant innovation for the market – Where the innovation is significantly different to pervious offerings – for example the introduction of flat pack furniture by IKEA. This type of innovation can be classified as discontinuous.

3 The new product development process

The new product development (NPD) process needs both the marketing and technology disciplines to work together. The technical capabilities of those working on the product will depend upon the organisation – these are expected to be professional in their outlook and approach.

It is important for marketers to work closely with technologists through the various stages of the NPD process. The higher the technology, usually the greater the demands on the skills of the marketer required to understand the features of the technology, therefore the benefits the product will offer, and contribute to the process. This is one reason that technologists, rather than marketers, tend to lead NPD in high-technology organisations and why these organisations are more likely to be technology-led.

The process I propose we follow for new product development is shown in the following diagram:

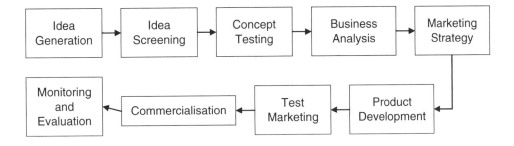

3.1 Idea generation

All new products start as ideas – sometimes something just comes from the imagination – the 'new to the world' type of product. The sources we can use for new product ideas are:

- *Research and Development* – This is the primary function of the department to generate and develop new product ideas.
- *Competitors* – The products produced by our current and potential competitors can influence the ideas we have or may have relative to new products. For our introduction to the French market it is important we look at the offerings of similar organisations in the country.

o *Customers* – Know what they want and may tell the organisation about their needs and wants – they should certainly be asked! Market research is vital for us for the new sales territory to establish customer attitudes, but we have to be careful that the research does not stifle.

o *Distributors and suppliers* – Resellers are close to the market and may know what customers want. In addition, suppliers may have their own product developments which can be incorporated into new products, again, this is a category who will be able to give us valuable information about the French market.

3.2 Idea screening

We need to evaluate ideas relative to appropriateness and potential. Factors can be weighted against given requirements. Screening criteria can include strategic fit, market size and growth, market access, profit potential, timing, synergy with existing products and capabilities.

3.3 Concept testing

This can be defined as: 'A printed or filmed representation of a product or service. It is simply a device to communicate the subject's benefits, strengths and reasons for being.'

3.4 Marketing strategy

We need to develop a marketing strategy for taking the product to market, describing the target market, the marketing mix (short and long term), and long-term sales and profit forecasts.

3.5 Business analysis

At this stage the product concept has to be evaluated in more detail, factors we should consider include:

o *History* – How have similar products fared previously.
o *Production* – How easily can the concept be produced, what have we made which is similar and so on. Financial aspects of production relative to predicted volumes are important.
o *Financial* – What are the cost implications for the new product: fixed and variable.
o *Competitors* – What is the likely reaction of market competitors, if it is an imitative product the effect of competitors changing their marketing mix elements have to be considered.

3.6 Product development

Full prototyping and development of the new product to ensure satisfactory performance.

3.7 Test marketing

Checking the customers reactions to the new product in a real environment, fine-tuning components and checking the marketing mix variables, generally carried out in specific geographical areas.

3.8 Commercialisation

Commercialisation of new products involves doing everything possible to ensure successful launch, leading to customer adoption and growth for the product.

4 Conclusion

Innovation is the lifeblood for organisations – it is the way they evolve to survive environments which change; however, it is risky and expensive. In many industries up to 95 per cent of new products fail, and a lot of expenditure is often undertaken before product developments are realised to be unviable. Car manufacturers can easily spend £1bn on development of a new model, and there have been examples where they have cancelled development late in the process meaning the expenditure has largely been committed with no reward.

Full business analysis is required at all stages, along with good knowledge of the environment and our own capabilities.

Answer 9
Distribution channels (place) and strategy

Check your answer

A good answer is likely to:

☑

Define marketing channels ☐

Outline appropriate channels for a holiday company ☐

Evaluate the criteria for deciding which is appropriate ☐

Identify appropriate criteria for making channel decisions ☐

Select a channel strategy for one possible channel ☐

Recognise a role as author – Marketing Manager within company ☐

Use appropriate format – Report format requested ☐

*   *   *   *   *

REPORT

To: Marketing Director

From: Marketing Manager

Date: XX/XX/XX

Re: Distribution Strategy

1 Introduction

Distribution channels are the routes used to get a product or service from the producer to the customer – this can involve the use of intermediaries or it can be done directly, in which case the physical location (place) may become important.

As our beach-orientated holidays targeted at families and staying in ready prepared tents is an established product, distribution channel decisions are a key element to consider for our marketing mix. Channels are an area in which our industry has seen large changes in recent years due to the increase in use of online holiday sites and the reduction in the dependence of the traditional high-street travel agents.

Essentially, even if we have the best holidays available, at very competitive prices and promotion to support them, if customers do not know where to go to buy them, or find the channel inconvenient compared to our competitors then we will not get the business the product deserves – hence the importance of a good distribution strategy.

2 Available distribution channels

It is important to consider our distribution channels – an innovative distribution chain can generate competitive advantage in a time when product offerings are becoming more homogenous, whilst the number of suppliers is increasing.

For our holidays the options we have available include:

2.1 High-street travel agent chains

We can continue to offer our holidays through travel agents as has been the case in the past. With this channel we generate a fixed level of business as the agents agree a minimum number of holidays each year, but we have to pay a commission to the agent for every holiday they sell. Using agents does not give us much control over the sale of the holiday, but has proved reliable in the past. This is a channel which is falling out of favour in line with many other high street operated services such as insurance companies and banks.

2.2 Online travel agents

These operate in a similar way to the high-street travel agents, but sell at lower prices to the end customers to reflect the lower costs of running their operations and the lower perceived levels of service offered. Whilst the high street is a shrinking market, this is a growing one.

2.3 Vertical integration

We could move into the travel agency business ourselves, either by purchasing an existing chain or setting up our own. This would mean that we would be gaining the commission ourselves which is currently paid to the agents, but our range offering is restricted to so would have to sell competitive products which may cause a conflict of interest. This would be a very costly, high-risk strategy, particularly at a time when agency business is declining.

2.4 Cooperative alliances

The range of independent holiday retailers who have formed cooperatives to increase their buying and advertising power have been a useful channel for us for selling our products. The advantages and disadvantages are similar for this channel to using travel agents, but the commissions we pay are lower, however, they do not place the guaranteed orders. We have more control over this channel than we would with the more traditional travel agents, and although they can be time-consuming we have good relationships with many of the individual outlets.

2.5 Direct sales

We could sell our holidays directly through mail brochures, national advertising in appropriate media supported by telephone call centres and we could sell directly via the Internet.

Using direct channels gives us full control over the distribution and pricing, but we would need to put systems and facilities in place to ensure we provide the levels of service which our customers would be likely to expect. As this is a growing channel for holidays it is one we need to consider seriously.

Overall we need to consider how many different channels we intend to use – are we going to remain restricted to the one channel of high-street retailers we have traditionally used, or do we want to maximise our opportunities by using a combination of channels.

The criteria we should use to make the decisions relate to:

- Access to and coverage of target market segments (TMS)
- Cost of operation (margins) and the expected return
- Control over brand policy
- Reputation for ourselves and the reputation of the intermediary
- The level of promotional support we can expect from the channel partner
- Staff knowledge and expertise within the intermediary channel.

3 Strategies for target segments

I recommend that we continue to use the existing high-street travel agents and cooperatives and introduce direct sales ourselves, initially using the Internet as a channel.

The reason for choosing to continue with the high-street travel agents is that despite the decline in this as a channel it still represents a significant proportion of the holiday business, and creates awareness of holiday options for people who may visit their local travel agency to collect brochures. We have good relationships with the head office staff of the agencies we currently deal with. In addition, this channel is very useful for providing feedback about customer requirements as they meet with potential holidaymakers well in advance of them actually using our services.

The joint promotions we have carried out with both the national and cooperative agencies have been effective in the past and need to be continued.

Having considered the option of working with the online travel agents I do not feel that this would be a good strategy for us – our prices would be undercut and service levels may drop. However, the Internet is a channel we cannot afford to ignore so I propose that we set up our own e-commerce website to service this market. We should invest in the appropriate website and support systems to service the online market – most of which we can do through outsource agencies to reduce our risk.

We will need to handle the relationship with existing travel agencies carefully when introducing this channel – they may be concerned that we will be taking business directly from them. By careful pricing and through off-line promotional activity we should be able to maintain the levels of business forecast for the agencies, whilst gaining additional business directly via the Internet.

4 Conclusion

Distribution channels are as critical for our business as they are for others. Due to changes in the market we need to respond and modify the strategy that has worked well in the past. Careful consideration and evaluation of the options and then managing relationships should enable to respond to the changes and maximise the opportunities available to us.

Answer 10
Product development, marketing mix (December 2005, Question 2)

Check your answer

A good answer is likely to:

	☑
Explain the Ansoff matrix	☐
Develop the requirements for a product development strategy	☐
Consider reactive and proactive product development	☐
Consider wider organization issues for product development	☐
Relate product development to the product life cycle	☐
Define branding strategies	☐
Explain the role of branding	☐
Relate brand positioning to the marketing mix	☐
Recognise a role as author – suggest consultant to FMCG company	☐
Use Report format	☐

* * * * *

REPORT

To: Marketing Director

From: Marketing Consultant

Date: XX/XX/XX

Re: Product Development and Branding

1 Introduction

In order to expand sales for your organisation there are a number of alternative options you could consider. Ansoff categorised these as follows:

		Products	
		Existing	New
Markets	Existing	Market Penetration	Product Development
	New	Market Development	Diversification

The potential strategies are explained:

Market penetration Aiming to increase or maintain market share. Acquiring more customers like the ones already served. Protecting the achieved position through consolidation **Product development** Developing new products or services for existing customers to gain increased share of customer spend	**Market development** Offering existing products to new markets with the aim of increasing penetration of the market. This includes exploitation of new market channels **Diversification** Either related – where the new product and market relate to the existing industry or resources and capabilities, or unrelated – where the new product and market is outside the current industry or capability and resource

Risks increase from market penetration through market and product development to diversification.

In common with many organisations, you have chosen a product development strategy. Product portfolios have to be updated to remain competitive, providing a balance of established and new products – the established ones generating funds for product development.

2 Product development strategies

Product development is important for attracting new customers and enabling organisations to reach new markets – but obviously requires large levels of investment – from Ansoff's strategies, second to diversification, product development takes the highest level of investment of resources. Financial analysis should be undertaken to determine how long it will take for the new product to break even.

Product development strategies can take two forms:

2.1 Replacement products

When products reach the decline stage of the product life cycle they need to be replaced – the PLC highlights the need for this continual update. Completely new products can replace those at the end of the PLC – for example, a car manufacturer such as Ford introducing a totally new model of the Focus (although in this instance it may utilise existing component such as engines).

2.2 Re-launched products

Manufacturers may also re-launch products through methods from new packaging, through to modifications to some product elements (the mid-life facelift which Ford may apply to the Focus). The different benefits of the product may be emphasised for each potential market that the organisation wishes to target.

In addition to these strategies, organisations may take either a reactive or proactive approach to product development.

2.3 Reactive approach

A reactive approach is typically the most economical and least risky approach to product development. Essentially it involves an organisation responding to the product developments of competitors rather than leading them. The first to market with a product type takes the risk of trying something new, and the reactive organisation can learn from any errors made by others, and can produce a product which is more specifically tailored to the needs of customers. Details in the design and engineering can be emphasised in promotion, rather than educating potential customers about the product in its entirety.

2.4 Proactive approach

When taking a proactive approach, an organisation sets out to be the first to market with a product type – beating the competition and being perceived (hopefully) as a leader and innovative company. A proactive approach carries higher risk levels as the organisation cannot benefit from research and development carried out by others – it has to commit heavily in this area. In addition, customer research has to be undertaken to find out if the product will be acceptable, who might buy it, and after launch it will research into market awareness which it has had to create. The company will have a culture of enterprise and encourage risk-taking amongst staff. Whist this type of new product development is expensive, time-consuming and risky the rewards are potentially high as being seen to be first to market establishes a reputation which the organisation benefits from – a good example of this is the dominance Apple have with the i-pod in the portable MP3 player market.

3 The role of branding

Kotler defines a brand as a 'name, term sign, symbol or design, or a combination of these intended to identify the goods or services of one seller or group of sellers and to differentiate them from those of competitors'. Successful brands are often linked with providers of good quality products or services, for example Ericsson, Coca-cola, Reebok, Adidas, Mercedes Benz.

Organisations use brands:

o to differentiate themselves from competitors and gain customer recognition
o to ease promotion – the brand helps to add substance to communication and promotions
o to integrate communication activities – sales promotion, personal selling and packaging can all convey similar messages through the brand values
o to help corporate image.

Typically a brand can deliver up to four levels of meaning:

o *Attributes*: The attributes associated with the brand – quality, reliability, value for money and so on.
o *Benefits*: The benefits the customer will get from the product or products – what is in it for them to buy that brand.
o *Values*: What the product says about the customers values – how will the product make the customer look in the eyes of others.
o *Personality*: The personality projected by the brand.

Brands exist primarily at two levels: company and product. To use the earlier example, Ford is a company brand, with Focus as the product brand.

3.1 Brand extensions

A benefit of branding is the ability to launch new products on the back of existing ones. Brand extensions occur when companies launch new products, under the same brand name, into the same broad market. For example, Mars extended their brand to boxed chocolates when they launched Celebrations. Typically, brand extensions are a less risky strategy than launching completely new products because customers will trust the brand. However, it is reported that five out of every ten brand extensions fail. This is not as high as the failure rate of new products (as high as nine out of ten) but obviously cause for concern.

3.2 Brand stretching

Traditionally brands tended to confine themselves to certain product areas. However, there are many examples of companies that are stretching their brands into unrelated areas, for example Virgin is selling cars and Coca-Cola has launched a new range of urban clothing. The success of these ventures will be influenced by the 'stretchability' of the brand. For example, the Virgin brand's core values appear to be transferable into a number of unrelated markets. However, if you think of Coca-Cola you think of a brown fizzy drink and it is difficult to see how these core values can be transferred into the clothing market.

Factors to consider when thinking about extending or stretching brands are:

- o Does the brand fit the new product class?
- o Does the brand add value to the offering in the new product class?
- o Will the extension enhance the brand name and image?
- o What effect will the new brand have on the image of the existing brand?

4 Marketing mix and product development

When developing a new product the complete marketing mix needs to be considered in relation to the organisations aims, its target customers and current perceptions of the brand. This means consideration of:

4.1 Product

What level of quality is to be produced – the inherent qualities of the product which customers will buy. This has implications for other areas of the mix.

4.2 Price

The price charged will have to reflect the costs of production, therefore a high-quality product will have to be charged at a higher level than a lower quality one would need. Price also creates a perception about a product in the mind of the customer so consideration needs to be taken of this.

4.3 Promotion

The product has to be promoted in a way which highlights the attributes of the product and creates a perception in the minds of potential customers to relate to the product and price. In addition, the promotion will probably be related to the brand of the company, but certainly relates to the product brand.

4.4 Place

The distribution channels to be used have to be suitable to reach the target customers, and in line with the image portrayed by the promotion, reflecting the price being charged and the product quality.

5 Conclusion

You are taking a risk by using a product development strategy, but this is a risk which if taken carefully can produce high returns. On the opposite side, if you do not develop new products your range will decline leaving you with an outdated product range and very few customers.

Answer 11
Ethics and social responsibility issues

Check your answer

A good answer is likely to:

        ☑

Define ethics and social responsibility   ☐

Outline ethical and social responsibility issues for a food retailer   ☐

Evaluate the impact of ethics and social responsibility   ☐

Outline the opportunities this may present   ☐

Identify appropriate changes to marketing activities   ☐

Recognise a role as author – Marketing Manager within company   ☐

Use appropriate format – Report format requested   ☐

*   *   *   *   *

REPORT

To: Chief Executive

From: Marketing Manager

Date: XX/XX/XX

Re: Ethics and Social Responsibility

1 Introduction

The subjects of business ethics and social responsibility are receiving a lot of exposure in the media at present, and we and some of our competitors are being accused of not ethical enough and not doing sufficient as regards social responsibility. There is also some confusion over the terms so I would like to define them:

    ○ *Ethics* – The moral values relating to the impacts of our activities. The institute of Business Ethics state that a code of ethics will start by setting out the values that underpin the code of conduct and will describe a company's obligation to its stake-holders. The code is addressed to anyone with an interest in the company's activities and the way it does business.

    o *Social responsibility* – Maximising the positive and minimising the negative effects on society of our activities; relates to the organisation as a whole. Corporate social responsibility is concerned with the ways in which an organisation exceeds the minimum obligations to stakeholders specified though regulation and corporate governance. The term 'Corporate Social Responsibility' is often used to include both the ethical stance and the issues of exceeding obligations.

To respond to the social environment it is important that we develop an appropriate framework of ethical behaviour. Our social responsibility issues can be classified into those relating to consumers, the community and the natural environment.

Adopting, and being seen to adopt, an ethical, socially responsible stance gives us an opportunity for repositioning of the retail brand. To do this we need to consider marketing's impact on: individual consumers, society as a whole, stakeholders and other businesses.

2 Ethical and social responsibility issues we face

There are many ethical and social responsibility issues which we face in the food retailing market. These include:

2.1 Ethical issues

Rather than just acting within the confines of the law, we need to act within code of moral principles. Some of the things we need to take account of are:

    o The way we deal with suppliers, both local and global. There has been much reported recently about retailers forcing suppliers to reduce prices and subsidise promotions to the extent that some suppliers have been forced out of business. Consumers do not see this as ethical and there is social pressure to adopt 'fair trade' policies.

    o Forcing small retailers out of business. It is suggested that organisations such as ours, through expansion, are causing smaller retailers to be unable to compete and putting them out of business and damaging livelihoods. This affects the attitude of customers, particularly towards our new smaller store programme.

    o Pollution caused by transporting products long distances. Many of our products are produced overseas and transported by highly polluting transport methods (air travel), which is being perceived as unethical, despite consumer demand for these products.

    o Reducing choice for disadvantaged (non-car owning) segments. Because we have many out-of-town stores, and are perceived to be putting smaller retailers out of business it is seen that we are reducing choice for those who do not have the ability to get to our stores.

2.2 Social responsibility issues

There are many social responsibility issues which may affect the views individual customers have of us. These can be related to four specific areas:

    o *Individual consumers*: it is suggested that we actually produce high prices for consumers due to the costs of distribution, the cost of advertising and promotion, and the generation of excessive margins.Marketers and businesses are accused of deceptive practices – using high-pressure selling techniques (something we need to consider particularly for our add-on services such as insurance and loans), the sale of shoddy and unsafe products, planned obsolescence in products and overall poor service.

o *Society as a whole*: Businesses are accused of creating false wants and materialism, too few social goods and cultural pollution (in particular as all high streets are beginning to look the same with the same retailers regardless of geographical location).

o *Environmental issues*: retail industries are seen to increase pollution and promote depletion of resources.

o *Other businesses*: producing unfair competition through price and promotion and increasing barriers to entry through the control we are seen to have over suppliers.

3 Responding to the issues

The above attitudes towards retail business' ethics and social responsibility issues mean that we need to consider how we manage our responses, and take advantage of the opportunities good ethics and social responsibility can create, provided they are not perceived as being cynical.

The responses are best considered by adapting the marketing mix to develop a strategic position and exploiting the marketing opportunity presented.

o *Price*: we need to ensure that we don't price below costs to force out competition – this is particularly important when opening new stores near existing, smaller outlets. In addition, and at the opposite end of our pricing spectrum we need to reduce excessive margins.

o *Product*: we need to introduce fair trade products wherever possible, particularly for our own brand items – this will help address the ethical issues and the social responsibility issues regarding sustainability. We should also introduce locally sourced products, particularly fresh produce, and also extend our range of organic produce which has environmental benefits.

o *Place*: reducing the opening of superstores in rural locations, whilst introducing free buses for disadvantaged customer segments will help to address the some of the issues of social responsibility.

o *Promotion*: we have to ensure clarity in all advertising of price promotions to ensure people understand what we are doing, and do not feel we are giving something with one hand and taking it back with another. Our community support promotions have to be considered carefully – some of the activity of our suppliers and competitors such as the sports equipment and computers for schools programmes have been criticised for not returning enough to society, or expecting children to eat the wrong type of food.

o *Physical evidence*: A current issue is the usage of plastic carrier bags, the introduction of biodegradable bags, and incentives to reuse bags can show evidence that we care about this issue. Parents will also appreciate us removing sweets from checkout positions where children often place them into trolleys without parental knowledge.

o *People*: Accusations have been made about employment practices in our industry so we have to be very clear in our equal opportunities and fair pay for staff policies. We also need to provide appropriate training and staffing levels to support service quality.

o *Processes*: It is important to review our process which affect our customers; as an example, having collected large amounts of data about customers through our loyalty scheme and EPOS we have to ensure all personal confidentially of data.

4 Conclusion

There are many ethical and social responsibility issues facing us at the moment, but through changing our strategies these present us with an opportunity to gain customer preference by exceeding expectations and the offers made by our competitors.

Answer 12
Devising marketing budgets, marketing plan evaluation and control (December 2005, Question 3)

Check your answer

A good answer is likely to:

☑

Describe how marketing budgets can be created ☐

Outline the advantages and disadvantages of alternative budget processes ☐

Illustrate potential problems with setting budgets ☐

Evaluate methods for controlling marketing plans ☐

– management

– financial

– efficiency

– strategic

Recognise a role as author – Marketing Manager within company ☐

Use appropriate format – Report format requested ☐

* * * * *

REPORT

To: Marketing Director

From: Marketing Manager

Date: XX/XX/XX

Re: Marketing Budgets and Control

1 Introduction

The strategic planning and budgeting processes are very closely linked. In real terms a budget enables execution and implement of a carefully laid plan in a controlled way – budgeting is probably the most common control mechanism of any planning process.

A marketing budget covers all the activities carried out by the marketing department and relates to the objectives – typically the budget will be agreed for a one-year period, with overall approval having been granted for longer-term project budgets, maybe up to five years.

As our organisation, in conjunction with all others, has limited resources we have to make the best use of those resources, making our marketing mix decisions based on business needs (opportunities and threats) and related to the resources and budget available.

2 Devising budgets

There are a number of methods which can be used to set budgets within the marketing function, two I wish to consider are Objective and Task, and Competitor Parity.

2.1 Objective and task

This is the most satisfactory method for budgeting. Objective and task looks at the objectives which are to be achieved and what resources are needed to carry them out. The marketing team need to clearly define the tasks that will be undertaken to achieve the objectives and specify clearly the resources required. Based upon this, budget may or may not be allocated. Also known as Zero Base, this type of budget works from the principle that all money spent is justified, and that if we do not need to spend money we will not do so.

For our restaurant chain it has advantages in that when each country business unit specifies their own objectives they can be required to cost out the achievement of those objectives and request appropriate funding for them. We can then evaluate the resources in relation to the potential returns from the objective and make a decision about whether to fund or not.

The major drawback of this method is that it can be very difficult to estimate the level of resource required with accuracy due to the changing needs of our market and the constantly changing opportunities and threats we face. We can also face difficulties within the organisation as this type of budgeting process can mean that our budget varies considerably from one year to the next which does not always fit well with how the finance department like to see things.

2.2 Competitor parity

Using competitor parity budgeting means matching our marketing spend to that of our competitors, maintaining position in relation to them. When compared to the largest international restaurant chains we have about half of their market size; in competitor parity budgeting we would set our marketing budget at about half that of theirs.

The advantage of this methodology is that we should be producing a marketing spend which helps us to maintain market position, and it should be quite easy to determine our budget. However, the disadvantage is that we would not have a budget which would allow us to make changes according to the marketplace, and we may struggle to determine what the competitors' budget will be for the forthcoming year.

Overall, this is probably the least customer-focused approach to take to budgeting.

(*Note*: Other methodologies could have been considered here. They include per cent of sales, per cent of forecast sales, 'All we can afford', incrementalist, etc.)

3 Evaluating and controlling marketing plans

Control is a way of making sure that what is supposed to happen, does happen. In marketing terms, control requires that objectives are set, and then evaluates the progress towards, and achievement of, those objectives. If the objectives are not met control means deciding what actions should be taken to correct the situation – and if any is necessary.

Marketing plans can be controlled in a variety of ways:

3.1 Management control

This control involves areas such as performance appraisals for the workforce of the organisation – are they achieving the results required of them, and are they working satisfactorily towards the marketing plan. We would have to consider for this how expectations may vary in the different countries in which we operate, and the different cultures and expectations this creates.

In addition to monitoring staff, management control involves benchmarking procedures against other organisations – either competitors, complimentary industries (which for us include other leisure providers) and those who provide best practice which we can learn from.

3.2 Financial control

Having established budgets, we need to ensure that we stick within them. Most organisations, and we are no exception, are good at calculating the financial results which indicate whether targets are being met. These include trend analysis – are we heading in the right direction? Financial controls can include comparison to previous periods, and to competitors where we can establish their financial information. Also, we can look at accounting ratios including liquidity, debt, activity, gearing and so on.

3.3 Efficiency control

This area would look at whether we are using our marketing assets efficiently – a major factor for us to consider would be: are we using our brand to full effect, particularly in relation to our international status.

3.4 Strategic control

When we have produced our strategic marketing plan and budget, strategic control means measuring the marketing activities against our performance against the objectives set. If, for example, we had an objective to open 10 new restaurants during the year this would be simple to measure at the end of the period or to check progress towards during the year. We can use strategic control to measure our market performance in relation to the plan we established for ourselves. These might include:

- o sales volumes and value
- o market share
- o advertising awareness
- o customer satisfaction and retention
- o any other objective we have set.

4 Conclusion

I hope you will see from the above that we can choose from many different methods when setting our marketing budget, but that each has advantages and disadvantages. Also, having set a budget, it then produces a specific tool with which we can form part of the control process for our strategic plan.

Answer 13
Marketing budget influences, budgets and mix elements, controlling the plan

Check your answer

A good answer is likely to:

☑

Define marketing budgeting ☐

Explain factors influencing the marketing budget ☐

Explain budgeting approaches ☐

Evaluate the alternative methods ☐

Explain the control techniques which can be used for a marketing plan ☐

Recognise a role as author – Marketing Manager within company ☐

Use appropriate format – Report format requested ☐

*   *   *   *   *

REPORT

To: Marketing Director

Finance Director

From: Marketing Manager

Date: XX/XX/XX

Re: Marketing Budget and control

1 Introduction

Our marketing budget covers all the activities which are carried out by the marketing function in the course of achieving their objectives. The budget is a control factor – it is used to show how much will, and can, be spent on the activity during a particular time period.

I am concerned that the marketing budget which has been set for the current period is not adequate to achieve the objectives.

2 Factors which have influenced the marketing budget

There are many factors which have influenced the budget which has been set, these include:

- *Power*: The power of the marketing function relative to other players in the organisation, in terms of structures and status. In the past, marketing has not been seen as very strong, but our role has moved from placing advertisements in the press to a more encompassing marketing role which requires larger expenditure.
- *Strategic contingencies*: Consideration of the importance with which the organisation has believed its market situation and customers to have to date have been embedded in decisions; however, we must now react more positively to the customers who are very aware of the market.
- *Process Control*: Which department and people have set the rules and agenda for the budgeting process.
- *Political influence*: Who controls the information and exerts control over what people think.
- *Bargaining and advocacy*: How good people are at building cases and doing deals to get resources – to date, I do not think we have been good enough in the marketing department at negotiating for our requirements.
- *Corporate culture*: Acceptability of resources claims and the historical frame of reference traditionally the sales department has been dominant in terms of budgets, but it should now be recognised that a well-funded marketing strategy can make the sales department much more efficient.

3 Setting budgets

For the future there are many methods which we can use to set our marketing budget. In turn these are:

3.1 Precedent

The budget is based on what has been spent previously and continues at that level. Obviously, this is a very easy way to set a budget, but takes no account of what might need to be done, and does not even allow for inflationary cost increases and is therefore not recommended.

3.2 Incrementalism

The budget relates to the previous year, but with an incremental increase. Similar comments apply to this as the precedent method.

3.3 Affordability

This means spending as much (or as little) as can be afforded based usually on a subjective decision. The major concern for this type of budget is that it does not take any account of what is happening in the marketplace, and it is quite likely that the power of other departments may mean that marketing does not get the budget it needs.

3.4 Maintaining parity with the competition

This involves spending the same as our competitors. There are two main problems with this – first is that there are very few competitors who are equal to us in terms of size and market representation, and secondly it is difficult to establish what their marketing budget is. Beyond these concerns is that matching the spend of competitors makes it very difficult to gain competitive advantage and change our market position. In addition, this is not a particularly customer-focused methodology.

3.5 Percentage of sales

Whether based on previous or forecast sales this method does not relate to the marketplace, and actually could mean that if sales reduced we would spend less on marketing at a time increasing the spend may reverse the decline. This is a very similar, and related, methodology to the precedent and incremental methods.

3.6 Objective and task

This methodology is based on identifying the objectives which are to be achieved and costing out the requirements to deliver them. This is the most logical way of arriving at a budget, but is also the most complicated as it can be difficult to forecast the costs of some activities accurately. As it reflects the outcomes desired and is related to market needs, this is the methodology which I think we should adopt for setting the marketing budget in the future.

I am prepared to cost out the activities which are required to meet the marketing objectives for this period and submit a budget proposal to you for your approval.

4 Controlling the marketing plan

There are many methods we can use to control the marketing plan, but as stated, having a budget is one of the primary methods for control – it allows the cost of marketing expenditure to be measured against the allocated finances.

There is more to controlling a plan, however, than just the costs involved. Other methods which should be used fall into four categories:

4.1 Management control

Appraisal of the performance against the plan and using benchmarking to measure our performance against other organisations. Throughout the plan we need to include the performance measures against which the plan can be judged.

4.2 Financial control

As an extension of the budget which would measure our expenditure we can use additional financial measures such as trend analysis, liquidity ratios, debt ratios, activity ratios and so on.

4.3 Efficiency control

This involves measurement of the value derived from marketing assets, and how efficiently we utilise them.

4.4 Strategic control

Strategic control involves measuring marketing activities against market performance – are we achieving targets in areas such as market growth and market share.

5 Conclusion

At present our marketing budget is insufficient to meet the objectives set for marketing due to a number of historic factors. By changing the basis on which we set our budget and relating it to market needs we can put our organisation in a position to deliver the results required. This can also be achieved by monitoring and controlling all stages of the marketing plan thoroughly.

Answer 14
Pricing and international distribution channels (December 2005, Question 4)

Check your answer

A good answer is likely to:

	☑
Describe different pricing frameworks	☐
Recognise the international nature of the business	☐
Evaluate the advantages and disadvantages of alternative tactical pricing approaches	☐
Evaluate the advantages and disadvantages of distribution channels	☐
Consider the actions required from the organisation to support the channels	☐
Recognise the business-to-business nature of the organisation	☐
Recognise a role as author – Marketing Manager within company	☐
Use Report format	☐

* * * * *

REPORT

To: Managing Director

From: Marketing Manager

Date: XX/XX/XX

Re: International Pricing and Distribution

1 Introduction

Pricing plays a vital role in the marketing mix for any organisation, but for us with our innovative product range it is absolutely vital that we get it right. The price we charge as one of the four mix elements will affect the perception of the other three elements for our customers – it will affect how they perceive the quality of the product, it will affect the channels of distribution available to us, and we will have to promote in the appropriate way for the price chosen. The perceptions created for existing products can be illustrated using the following framework:

		Price	
		High	Low
Quality	High	Premium Strategy	Good Value Strategy/ Penetration
	Low	Overcharging Strategy/ Exploitation	Economy Strategy

If our products reflected the properties of others we could determine the initial price from the factors above – product positioning against existing, competitive, products on the factors of quality and price.

2 Pricing approaches

For our innovative new products a decision about the way in which we will price the products. We are able to choose between *market skimming* and *market penetration*.

2.1 Market skimming pricing

With price skimming, prices are set high, attracting the least price-sensitive market segments. This gives:

o   high initial cash flow to offset the development costs
o   a quality brand image
o   a 'breathing space' with low volumes to sort production issues.

The potential drawback of price skimming is if the product does not meet the customer's expectations set by the high price – however, it is easier to reduce a price than to raise one.

2.2 Market penetration pricing

Penetration pricing involves setting initial prices low to sell in high volumes to gain market share in a short time – often necessary if high volumes are needed to break even.

A danger of penetration pricing is that the customer will perceive the product to be of low value, and prices can be difficult to raise. It does, however, make it difficult for competitors subsequently bringing out products to gain a foothold in the market.

When we establish the prices for the particular international markets segments we have various options. These include:

2.3 Price differentiation

This involves the use of different prices for different segments – for instance lower prices for less developed countries business, whilst charging more when a product is offered to a more developed nation. The outcome of this would be better levels of sales in the less developed country, with maximised revenue in others. The drawback, however, is that in today's global economy we may find that the products are grey traded from the less developed to the developed and we will not gain full advantage.

2.4 Quantity discounts

We could consider offering quantity discounts to either direct customers or intermediaries who order in large quantities. This would give us the benefit of economies of scale with each order. A drawback is that the intermediaries may not pass the discount on to their customers so we may not see the full volume which could be generated.

2.5 Cost-based pricing

Also referred to as cost-plus pricing, a standard factor is added to the cost of production of an item. The cost should include the total costs and an estimate of the expected sales units.

Cost-based pricing can be inaccurate because of the uncertainty of volumes to be sold, and also it takes no account of market conditions which can lead to prices too high and products not selling well, or prices too low and we might miss out on profit opportunities differential pricing could create.

A variation of cost based pricing is **break even** or **target profit** pricing – this is where we would aim for a price which will ensure we generate a particular level of profit.

2.6 Value- or market-based pricing

This pricing method uses buyers' perceptions of value, rather than the seller's costs to determine price decisions. With value-based pricing we have to consider the price during the design of products and set other elements of the marketing mix.

For value-based pricing, the value customers assign to different competitive offers becomes critical, although it can be very difficult. The measurement of perceived value requires research and experimentation.

3 Distribution and logistics

Marketing channels are the routes and intermediaries used by organisations to get their products to their end customers. A distribution channel is 'A set of interdependent organisations involved in the process of making a product or service available for use or consumption by the consumer or industrial user' – Kotler.

If the product is the 'core' of the marketing mix – what it is based on – then place enables the customer to be able to purchase – it reaches and services the customer.

Whilst direct distribution is possible and avoids the fact that using an intermediary means giving up some control over elements of the marketing mix, principally over to who and how the products are sold, intermediaries provide efficiency when making goods available to target markets.

We would sell to one intermediary who deals with a number of customers, rather than dealing with the larger number directly. Intermediaries typically sell on behalf of more than one manufacturer and are therefore able to offer a more complete range of products than we could on our own.

There are many possible types of intermediary, each of which works in a different way. In many instances an intermediary takes legal title to the goods, and is involved in the physical distribution of the goods, although this is not always the case.

The types of intermediary we should consider are as follows:

3.1 Distributors and dealers

These add value through the provision of services for end users such as inventory, credit terms and after-sales service. If using distributors we should aim for very close ties between ourselves and the distributors, allowing specialists skills to be developed and passed on to customers via improved service.

3.2 Franchises or licence agreements

A franchise or licence holder would be given a contract to supply and market a product or service in a particular territory. A franchise agreement would need to cover the way the product is marketed and sold and overall aspects of the business.

3.3 Agents and brokers

Agents and brokers would have legal authority to act on our behalf but, unlike distributors and franchisees, do not take legal title to goods and generally do not handle the product in any physical way, basically generating orders and passing them on to us. Agents and brokers make products more available to customers and may provide additional services.

I suggest that we should use a combination of distributors and agents according to the requirements of the different country cultures we intend to operate in. With distributors we have the advantage that they actually purchase the stock and therefore have an incentive to sell it on quickly and in volume. However, in some markets agents are a more usual way of doing business and we should respect this if necessary.

4 Channel support

Once we have selected our distribution channels they will need to be supported. The factors we should consider for this include:

- *Control* – How much control will be required of the channel. In some instances, we will have to consider whether the intermediary might try to copy our products and sell their own version rather than ours. Unfortunately this is common in some cultures.
- *Resources* – Whatever intermediary we choose, we will have to visit them regularly and provide support through promotion and potentially technical support which could take up a lot of our resources.
- *Buyer power* is something which we should consider. As a small company we may benefit from dealing with large intermediaries, but they might try to take advantage of our size and dictate unfavourable terms to us.
- *Inventory and warehousing* – We need to consider the levels of inventory which we need to carry, and also the logistics for getting this inventory to the intermediaries or end customers. This may involve us setting up warehouse facilities in some of the countries or regions in which we wish to operate in order to provide better service. Distributors would be helpful for this.
- Finally, we would have to consider our *order-processing facilities*. Intermediaries will want to have full information about their order status. For this we need to consider an extranet facility, and have to consider the physical distribution logistics.

5 Conclusion

Provided we handle the pricing and distribution issues carefully, we have a great opportunity with our innovative products to generate high levels of profits and to distribute them throughout the world.

Answer 15
The planning gap

Check your answer

A good answer is likely to:

	☑
Explain and illustrate the planning gap concept	☐
Discuss operational gaps and new strategies gaps	☐
Consider the implications for the marketing department of the gap	☐
Outline actions which can be taken to close both operational and new strategies gaps	☐
Relate the answer to a service organisation	☐
Recognise a role as author – Suggest external Marketing Consultant	☐
Use appropriate format – Report format requested	☐

*   *   *   *   *

REPORT

To: Marketing Manager

From: Marketing Consultant

Date: XX/XX/XX

Re: Addressing the shortfall in membership numbers

1 Introduction

You are in the unfortunate situation of not gaining as many health club members this year as had been targeted within your corporate plan, and further you have not met the same levels of membership as in previous years. This situation is referred to as a planning gap. McDonald (2002) states the following: 'Gap analysis states that if the corporate sales and financial objectives are greater than the current long-range forecasts, there is a gap which has to be filled.' This indicates that gap analysis is something which you as the marketing manager need to monitor and consider in terms of filling the gap should one occur.

2 The planning gap concept

Many organisations use objectives as a basis of forecasting the levels of performance of the business, then turn these into corporate goals – measuring success against these objectives is what highlights the gaps: the gap analysis.

For yourselves the current situation can be illustrated as:

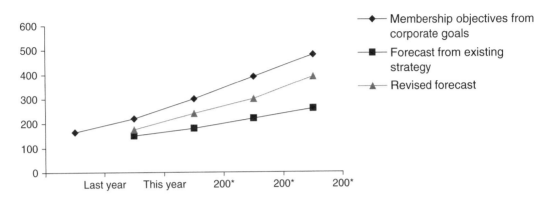

As you can see, there is a gap between your current membership levels and the objectives set in the corporate goals – effectively where you are now and where you want to be.

Fortunately, you have identified the gap at a stage when it is possible to take action to close it – the marketing department can see how much needs to be done to meet the corporate objectives.

Gaps can arise for a variety of reasons – the environment may change, for example, through the introduction of new competing products or a change in the economic situation affecting the ability of people to buy the current product.

The chart above shows the two levels of gaps which exist for yourselves. The forecast from existing strategy is what is likely to happen to your membership numbers if you were to continue with the strategies utilised in the past and take no other action. The revised forecast shows where you are likely to be given the initiatives which you already have put into place to counter the reduction in membership numbers. The difference between these two lines is known as the operational gap.

The second gap which is shown is the new strategies gap – the difference between the revised forecast and the corporate objectives. This is the gap which requires you to use new strategies to fill – these are discussed below.

Gap analysis has many implications for the marketing department – it highlights how much needs to be done, what steps need to be taken to fill the gaps.

A major implication of the gap is that it will highlight the situation with respect to the resources you need to provide within the health club – the corporate objectives as they currently stand would lead to an overcapacity situation which is not an efficient use of your resources, which can lead to difficulties for the marketing department in terms of budgets.

It is possible that the gaps exist because of poor forecasting or a change in the environment. The marketing department needs to consider whether the forecasts are realistic, and if not what action needs to be taken – this could be either positive if the forecasts are too low, or negative if they are too high. If the latter, it may be that the corporate objectives need to be lowered to a more realistic level.

Overall the planning gap highlights that actions need to be taken.

3 Closing the health clubs' gap

In general the methods for filling the gap relate to:

- considering more appropriate objectives
- productivity
- growth strategies.

As already discussed, there are two areas of the planning gap, and each needs different methods to close it.

3.1 Operations gap

The operations gap is filled through improvements to your productivity – it relates to the efficiency of the organisation. You need to look at the processes you use to gain members – are there enquiries which have not been followed up, for example. Improvements can be made through reducing costs, consideration of an improved sales mix, or by changing prices if possible.

If improved productivity is one method by which the expansion gap is to be filled, care must be taken not to take measures such as to reduce marketing costs – it may well be that an increase in marketing expenditure is required in the short term to boost membership numbers.

Another effective method is to increase market penetration via stimulating increased usage of the health club and increasing market share, getting people to switch membership from other local health clubs. Market penetration is less risky than other options and therefore should always be the first option. This can be achieved quite quickly by concentrating on loyalty schemes for existing members, encouraging customer retention and increasing communications such as sales promotion for limited periods for new joiners. It makes more sense in many cases to move along the horizontal axis for further growth before attempting to find new markets.

3.2 New strategies gap

A very radical, but realistic way to fill this gap is to reduce the corporate objectives.

Further strategies include those on the Ansoff matrix – market development, product development or differentiation – for example find new user groups, introduce new facilities or use the premises for other things than health. For yourselves this could mean rather than concentrating on annual membership subscriptions allowing people to pay for the facilities on a day-to-day usage basis. Other strategies would be to consider product development such as taking the facilities to other places – maybe even using a large vehicle to provide a mobile health club which could visit office parks at lunchtime. Finally, diversification, for example selling new product to new markets. This might mean converting part of your existing premises to a nightclub, for example.

A marketing audit should ensure that the method chosen to fill the gap is consistent with the company's capabilities and builds on its strengths.

4 Conclusion

Whilst in the short term you are experiencing a gap, the knowledge of its existence gives you the ability to rectify the situation before it causes major problems for your organisation – you can introduce changes and ensure your resources are correct for the levels of business to be expected.

Answer 16
The marketing planning process, analysis tools (December 2005, Question 5)

Check your answer

A good answer is likely to:

	☑
Describe the marketing planning process	☐
Explain how the marketing plan elements fit together	☐
Illustrate the links between plan stages	☐
Outline how marketing actions are monitored	☐
Explain the analysis tools used for marketing audits	☐
Evaluate the advantages and disadvantages of the *four* analysis tools	☐
Recognise a role as author – New Marketing Manager within company	☐
Use appropriate format – Memo format requested	☐

* * * * *

MEMO

To: Marketing and Sales Team

From: Marketing Manager

Date: XX/XX/XX

Re: Marketing Planning and Auditing

1 Corporate and marketing planning process

Our organisation produces a business plan each year, this corporate plan has a range of objectives which cross all the functions of the business, including marketing, and is created from the longer-term strategic plan for the organisation.

The marketing plan is produced from these strategic and corporate plans. We do this initially by market, then by product and then by region – this obviously requires a planning process.

The basic outline contents of a marketing plan are:

- ○ Where are we now – situation analysis
- ○ Where do we want to be – objectives
- ○ How are we going to get there – strategy and tactics
- ○ How do we ensure success – control

In more detail the areas we need to consider are discussed in the following sections.

2 Situational analysis

The current situation of our business and the market places we operate in. This involves an audit of our organisations strengths and weaknesses relative to our competitors, and also an evaluation of the opportunities and threats presented by the environment we operate in – a SWOT analysis.

We need to consider the activities of our competitors, both current and those we might face in the future.

Marketing research may be used at this stage to help us determine the environment situation. It can also help with the next stage in the process.

3 Objectives

We need to decide where we want to be – what are the objectives we have for market share? What opportunities are best for us to pursue?

This involves the process of segmentation and targeting – dividing the market into segments which have groups containing similar characteristics, and then choosing which of these segments provide a target market for our products.

All objectives should comply with the acronym SMART – they need to be Specific, Measurable, Aspirational, Relevant and Time bound.

4 Strategy

At the strategy stage we determine how we are going to deliver the objectives – how we will get to where we want to be.

The strategy delivers Positioning to the chosen target segments – making a proposition which will be attractive to the customers within the segment, which is sufficiently unique to be recognisable and different to other offerings available to them.

This is where we consider the 4Ps of the marketing mix – Product, Price, Promotion and Place (distribution channels). We determine a strategy for each of these areas – what products will we sell, at what price, how will they be promoted and where will they be sold.

5 Tactics and actions

Tactics and actions move the strategy into workable activities which can be built into the daily lives of those in the sales and marketing function (and elsewhere in the business) to deliver against the strategy. For example, if the strategy is to gain market share through price penetration the tactics and actions would involve the setting of the price and ensuring it is implemented throughout the distribution channels and would also involve some promotion related to the price activity.

6 Control

Throughout the period of the plan it is essential to measure and evaluate the results of the activities being undertaken. There are many ways in which this can be done (see below).

Control also involves taking any necessary corrective actions to get back on track towards the objectives if deviations are detected, or sometimes because the situation changes during the plan period.

7 Analysis tools

7.1 Porter's five forces

Porter's five forces is a model which looks at the competitive environment of an industry and is used to analyse a market's structure. It considers five forces that operate within a market or industry, which collectively impact on the degree of industry rivalry that exists:

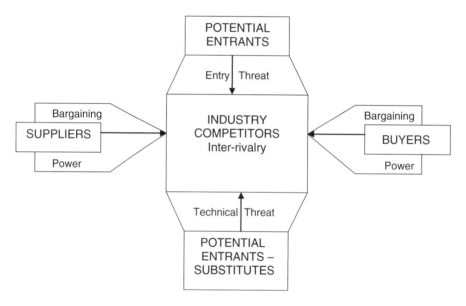

The five areas are:

o *Industry competitor rivalry* – The usual area considered for competition – the existing organisations with which our organisation competes. The level of intensity of rivalry may well be high if two or more organisations are fighting for the lead in a market that is experiencing rapid growth. Just considering this area would miss out on other competitor activity.

o *Threat of substitutes* – A substitute is an alternative product which performs the same function as an existing one, but without being exactly the same. New technology often allows companies to develop substitute rival products, which once the initial development costs have been recovered, can be offered at a cheaper price. Examples in the last 10–15 years include computers substituting typewriters, and hand-held Personal Digital Assistants (PDAs) substituting paper-based time management systems and digital cameras replacing film. The difficulty here is recognising what will become a substitute for something.

o *Threat of new entrants* – This threat depends on the barriers to entry in an industry. Barriers to entry can be categorised as:

  – scale economies necessary for profit
  – existing product differentiation requires expensive promotion

- switching costs discourage customers from seeking new suppliers
- existing firms have best access to distribution
- existing cost advantages.
- The threat of new entrants can be difficult to gauge because of the secrecy with which a new entrant may go about its activity prior to launch.

o *Power of suppliers* – An often-overlooked element in competitor analysis is the power of suppliers – where there are only a few suppliers in a market this power is likely to be high. In addition, if the supply of raw materials or products is controlled or scarce supplier power is typically high.
o *Power of buyers* – Where there are only a few buyers of products and supplies are plentiful, the power of buyers is likely to be high. A good example of this is the supermarket buyers in the UK. There are about half a dozen major UK supermarkets; as buyers they hold (and use) power over many thousands of small suppliers, including farmers.

8 Product life cycle

The product life cycle provides a useful background and basis for relating other portfolio analysis tools. The product life cycle highlights a range of important considerations:

o Products have a finite life and will eventually die.
o During their existence they will require different strategies to extend the life and generate profit.
o It highlights that the potential profit from each stage will vary considerably.

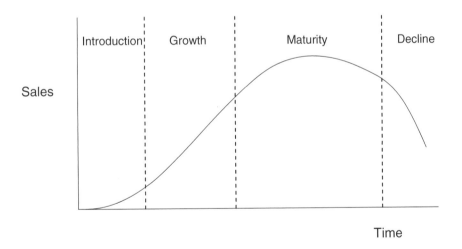

Whilst there are limitations to the uses of the Product Life Cycle as a marketing tool (principally through knowledge of where in the plc a product is, and the fact that it is the result of marketing activity not the cause) it is a very useful tool for helping plan the future of a product portfolio.

9 Boston consulting group growth share matrix (BCG)

The BCG matrix positions products on a simple 2 x 2 matrix according to the *market growth rate* and *relative market share*. The underlying principle is one of generation of cash within the business – market share being a measure of the ability to generate cash and market growth is the predictor of the need for cash.

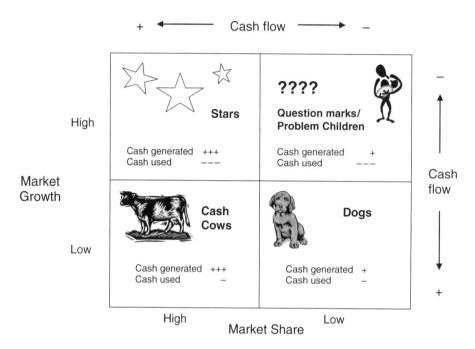

Relating the BCG matrix to the product life cycle, typically:

o Question marks are at the introductory stage, with high market growth and low share. They absorb cash to fund development and marketing.
o Stars are the future of the organisation with high market share and high market growth. They are at the growth and early maturity stage, balanced but still absorbing cash to sustain and develop market share.
o Cash cows are at the maturity stage, have high market share but slowing market growth. Marketing spend can be reduced leading to positive cash generation.
o Dogs are in the decline stage of the life cycle with low market share and low market growth. They can still generate cash in the short term.

The matrix highlights the need for introducing new products and the issue of relying on current cash cows. The tool is simple to use and communicate to others, but does have limitations in usage due to:

o Reliance on two dimensions make it overly simplistic whilst other factors affect cash generation.
o Definitions of markets, and measuring growth and shares can be very difficult and without these the position on the matrix cannot be determined.
o The matrix does not specifically include competition and competitive advantage.
o An assumption that slow growth markets are undesirable.
o The lack of ability to compare one opportunity with another.

The limitations of the BCG matrix can be overcome through the use of multi-factor matrices:

10 Gap analysis

By setting objectives based on forecasts, our organisation will be able to determine if the objective is realistic and achievable. Future performance predictions will be based upon past trends, current performance and future predictions to the end of the planning time frame.

A likely outcome of this approach is that there is a gap between performance and target objectives – marketing activities are used to fill this gap.

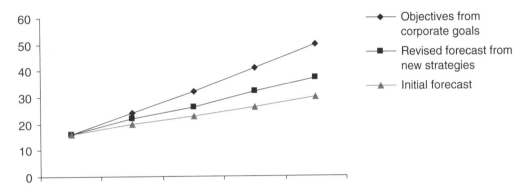

The gap between the forecast and the objectives is the 'performance gap' – marketing.

The problems with gap analysis are those which typically relate to forecasting accuracy – how well are we forecasting the future, and how realistic are our objectives.

Answer 17
Marketing plans and mix for online business

Check your answer

A good answer is likely to:

☑

Define the nature of the virtual marketplace ☐

Consider how a marketing plan for an online business would vary from an off-line one ☐

Outline the planning stages ☐

Consider the marketing mix for an online business ☐

Explain the differences between online and off-line marketing mixes ☐

Consider the service implications for an online business ☐

Recognise a role as author – Suggest external Marketing Consultant ☐

Use appropriate format – Report format requested ☐

*　*　*　*　*

REPORT

To: Marketing Manager

From: Marketing Consultant

Date: XX/XX/XX

Re: Marketing virtual products

1 Introduction

Thank you for inviting us to work with you on your new range of training programmes.

As you have recognised, there are considerable differences between the distribution of training courses via the Internet and the traditional delivery methods you have used previously.

2 Marketing plans for online business

A key factor to consider in the planning process for the new range of training programmes is that by selling and distributing them via the Internet they can be perceived as global products right from the very start – even if you currently have no plans to actively promote the courses outside your home market it will be possible for anyone who has Internet access, wherever they are in the world to access your information and they may wish to purchase the courses: you have to consider whether you wish them to actually be sold to people overseas, although you may have little choice. Effectively your courses will be 'born global'.

The technological developments of recent years, and increased use of the Internet has opened up new markets on scales which were not available in the past. Whilst most of the dot-com organisations that set up in the late 1990s failed sometime ago, those who have survived (such as Amazon) and those created more recently have developed their skills and activities and are able to deliver wider ranges of products to loyal customers.

Truly virtual organisations such as eBay use more traditional off-line marketing to support their online activity, and the online and off-line marketing plans needs to be integrated, whatever business model is used. The Internet offers an opportunity to get very close to customers who go online, and develop a one-to-one dialogue with them.

You have chosen to target a specific market segment for the new range of courses, using e-commerce as the channel to market. This alters the marketing planning process in some areas as compared with the plans required for more traditional distribution channels. These can be considered as follows:

2.1 Situation analysis

Research can be carried out via the Internet, in particular:

- o Competitor information can be more easily found for web-based competitors as it is available for all to see.
- o Customer research can be carried out by e-mail or web survey.
- o Information about international markets may be readily available

2.2 Objectives

As you are treating the online business separately from your existing business, the objectives can be independent.

2.3 Strategy

In itself the strategy is different – I have outlined the specific marketing mix areas in more detail below

2.4 Tactics and actions

The delivery of the online mix – whilst fundamentally different for an online business, this would be worked in similar way to off line businesses. The areas which would need special consideration include:

- o *Manpower* – Have you got the resources to offer back up customer service 24/7? Do you have the necessary skills?
- o *Money* – How much will you need to invest in back office services?
- o *Minutes* – What is the timeframe involved in developing your online facility and back-up services?

2.5 Control

You have to consider measurement – what metrics will be used to monitor online effectiveness? For example:

- Number of 'hits'.
- Number of new visitors registering.
- Number of visitors returning.
- Number of sales leads generated (some people will ring for more information regardless of what is on the website).
- Number of sales (via e-commerce).
- Value of sales (via e-commerce).
- Average time spent on the site.
- Awareness levels – pre- and post-campaign.

3 The marketing mix for the virtual marketplace

It has often been said that part of the reason why so many dot-com organisations failed was the fact that they lost sight of the basic business and marketing principles.

Now you have identified your target segment the marketing mix has to be designed. Even though the product you are looking at is a service to be delivered online (as close to a virtual product as is possible), the 7Ps of the traditional mix are still applicable:

3.1 Product

You have already created bespoke products for selling via the Internet, but can you use the internet channel to promote your traditional training courses? If so, will the current product range be suitable for offering online? Also, for future products you should consider whether the benefits offered translate to an online market.

3.2 Price

Some things you need to consider are:

- How much are customers prepared to pay for the online courses?
- How does this relate to the prices you are currently able to charge for traditional
- Will it cost more or less to sell products online?
- Looking across the mix, are distribution costs reduced or increased, and how much it is costing to offer customer service 24/7?

3.3 Place

You have chosen the Internet as a channel for the new products. In addition, you should consider whether continuing to use your existing channels, and improving communications to channel members to your website is appropriate.

3.4 Promotion

Promotion needs to be considered both online and off-line. For instance, the selection of appropriate electronic media is vital – search engines and directories, online advertising and so on. You also need to develop off-line promotion for the courses.

3.5 People

It is important to ensure staff have the necessary skills which may mean hiring additional people. Also, working patterns may have to be adjusted to respond to the 24-hour nature of the Internet, particularly when used globally and offering a full customer service response electronically?

3.6 Process

You have to be satisfied that appropriate processes are in place, both automated and manual, to support the new strategy.

3.7 Physical evidence

Off-line activity is needed to ensure maximum exposure for the URL, and imagery has to be consistent both online and off-line, with appropriate site design.

Finally, for customer service, the Internet requires customer support outside of normal trading hours. As is the case with off-line products, it is important to manage customer expectations – if a level of service is offered and promoted, it must be maintained.

Although service can be offered around the clock, there is a cost involved. It is worth spending time and money to monitor activity on your site to see if a personal service is required at all times. Expectations must be monitored, however, responding to changes as required.

Service is generally about compromise. Personal responses, either by phone or by e-mail, might be able to be extended by one or two hours outside traditional working hours, and this service is supplemented by an automated response outside of these times. The customer may be happy with an acknowledgement of their query, and a promise that it will be dealt with within a certain period of time – provided this promise is upheld. You have to consider, however, that if a customer is working through one of your programmes in their own time, they will not appreciate a long delay in replying to any queries they have.

4 Conclusion

There are many factors that have to be considered for a truly virtual product as yours is, but through the use of traditional good business and marketing practice, with consideration for the different channel to be used and customers likely to be attracted you should be very successful with your online training programmes.

Answer 18
Small business marketing plans and measurements

Check your answer

A good answer is likely to:

	☑
Define an SME	☐
Explain the constraints faced by SME's compared with larger organisation	☐
Consider the different objectives of the types of company	☐
Consider the different resource issues of small and large organisations	☐
Outline how marketing activities can be measured	☐
Explain how it would be possible to ensure the organisation applied the measures	☐
Recognise a role as author – Consultant to commercial manager company	☐
Use appropriate format – Report format requested	☐

* * * * *

REPORT

To: Managing Director

From: Commercial Manager

Date: XX/XX/XX

Re: Marketing Planning and Control within small businesses

1 Introduction

The UK government define a small-to-medium enterprise (SME) as one with less than 250 employees, a turnover of less than 50 million Euros per year and not part or wholly owned by an organisation larger than this. (NB: *this definition changes over time.*)

Your organisation actually fits within most definitions of a small business which is generally applied to organisations with less than 50 employees.

2 Constraints which face SMEs

In comparison with the large organisation you have moved from, there are a range of differences you are likely to notice within the SME – in all areas, but particularly when preparing marketing plans.

These differences start with the objectives which determine the marketing plan. Large companies are often interested in objectives such as product development, market leadership and growth in market share. However, you are likely to find within the smaller-sized organisation these objectives are not of concern; you are likely to concentrate more on the particular marketplace or niche market as your organisation is a small fish in a large pond – you have many competitors who are a similar size to you, but the industry is dominated by the larger organisations. This means that market share, and particularly market leadership is not a priority. The ability to grow the company and increase sales is much more important – in fact, for many of the smallest business survival is often the main objective. Typically, SMEs tend to be less strategic in their approach than large organisation, operating on more of a tactical approach – considering issues with a much shorter timescale.

The small size of your organisation has an obvious impact on the availability of resources – this is a major difference between large and small organisations. Both financial and human resources will be limited in an SME, with staff being required to, and having, the skills for multi-tasking. There is likely to be a limited amount of financial resources for research and other areas such as expansion. Obviously, all organisations, even the largest, have financial limits but it is likely that a large company will have more long-term plans and be financially viable.

The budget sizes within your organisation will be very small in comparison to larger companies. This is likely to have an impact on the marketing budgets, especially the communications budget. However, large organisations will often have the luxury of larger budgets for such communications in comparison to an SME. Indeed, often they will use communications agencies such as PR and/or advertising agencies, whereas SMEs view such services with scepticism, preferring to carry out activities in-house.

Whilst these areas may seem negative for the SME, there are many advantages, the principle one being flexibility. The size of the organisation means that it can respond much more quickly to changing environmental situations – there is a much shorter chain of command and decisions can be made more quickly. Also, processes tend to allow more variances within small organisations which can be a major benefit for customer service.

Many innovations originate from small organisations, often due to the freer thinking nature which you are likely to experience compared to the constraints of large corporation 'red tape' and formalised activity which rules the planning processes.

3 Evaluating marketing plans

A major difference between large and small organisations appears when the time comes to evaluate the plans. Whilst your organisation may not have as many processes as a larger one would, measurement and response to non-conformance can be much easier due to the lower number of people involved. The converse of this is that there are less people to do the monitoring, and they are probably occupied with other things.

Regardless of size, however, there are four main areas where control mechanisms should be considered within the marketing plan:

○ *Management control*: this includes areas such as performance appraisal for staff and the workforce, benchmarking procedures and so on, against other organisations – the size of your organisation makes this easy to view from an overall company perspective, the difficulty with benchmarking is getting data from equivalent-sized firms as they are not required to report information in the same way as larger ones and tend to be quite secretive.

○ *Financial control*: this includes financial controls which most companies are adept at calculating. It could include trend analysis, comparison, liquidity ratios, debt ratios, activity ratios and so on. In some small companies this information can be difficult to obtain as this data relates directly to the income of the owner of the business. However, I do know that your company will allow you access to the required information for you to work with the finance director to make appropriate measurements.

○ *Efficiency control*: here, this area considers the optimum value from marketing assets – measuring the value you are obtaining from things such as your brand can be quite difficult, but the good relationships you have with customers helps in this area.

○ *Strategic control*: the easiest method of control is to measure marketing activities against market performance or objectives set – these are where your small organisation provides many benefits over a larger one as you are personally responsible for implementing the activities and measuring them so there is no intermediary which could introduce error.

4 Conclusion

Whilst there are many differences you will experience within the small organisation compared with larger ones, you should find that there are at least as many advantages from the size as there are disadvantages.

Answer 19
Positioning, communications mix, plan evaluation (June 2004, Question 5)

Check your answer

A good answer is likely to:

☑

Explain the product life cycle and decline stage □

Define positioning strategies □

Use perception maps □

Consider segmentation and targeting issues □

Identify communication issues for repositioning □

Explain the role pricing plays in an organisation □

Consider communications mix elements □

Consider one measure of success □

Recognise a role as author – Brand manager □

Use Report format □

*   *   *   *   *

REPORT

To: Marketing Director

From: Brand Manager – Grapple

Date: XX/XX/XX

Re: Repositioning and communications

Note: this answer is not related to a particular product as would be required to answer the question correctly in an exam situation.

1 Introduction

As we discussed recently, our product 'Grapple' is in the decline stage of the product life cycle in its current form. The product life cycle is typically illustrated as:

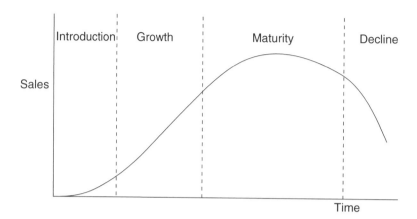

In the introduction stage, the company selling the product usually has the market to itself, with competitors entering the market during the growth stage. As the product reaches maturity customers are buying the product at the highest rate, but the market becomes very competitive. Eventually the product reaches decline – there are still many competitors, but customers reduce their buying of the product, typically because there are newer products available which have more appeal. Grapple has reached this stage.

2 Repositioning strategy

With Grapple having reached the decline stage in the product life cycle, we have two choices, one is to let the product die, and the other is, my preferred option, to reposition the product to attract new customers and rejuvenate the sales of it.

Products are perceived by customers and potential customers in particular ways. At present Grapple is perceived by customers as being old-fashioned and relevant for a particular segment of society, this can be illustrated on a perception map as follows:

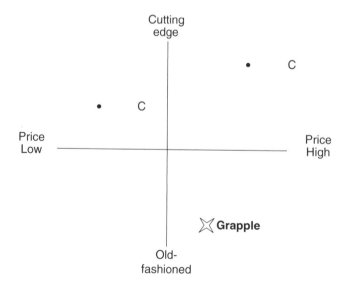

As we have a premium-priced product I intend to maintain this position, whilst changing the image from old-fashioned to cutting edge. With this change we should be able to target a younger customer age group (25–35 year old) for Grapple, but hopefully will not put off our current customers who are predominantly aged 50 and above. Our current customers are not concerned about buying 'cutting edge' products, preferring functionality over fashion. The reverse is typically the case for the new target market – they certainly want fashionable items, although they have to perform – as we know Grapple does.

This target market has been chosen for their high spending on Grapples competitors, they consume, on average, twice as many per year as our current customers.

To achieve this change we do not need to modify the actual product itself, but will need to repackage it, and make it available in outlets more frequently visited by the new target audience. The brand name we have is strong enough within the target audience, and does not have negative connotations for them. Compared to our two main competitors, A and B, we are perceived as having a product which is out of date.

3 Marketing communications mix

The main method we will have to use to reposition the product for the new target market is communication – it is essential that our target customers change their perception of our brand, recognising it for the values we wish for it, and those that currently do not purchase need to be made more aware of Grapple.

To achieve this I propose the following elements of a communications mix:

3.1 Advertising

Radio advertising should be predominant for the repositioning – our target audience are large radio listeners, and respond well to this media.

Internet – The target audience are very technologically aware, and a viral e-mail campaign with a well developed, interactive, website is essential to increase awareness.

We need to advertise the product via TV – this is expensive, but through careful selection of programmes during which to advertise, we can reach our target audience effectively.

In addition, we should have a campaign through printed media – there are many specialist magazines aimed at the target audience and we should use these to promote sales (see below).

Ambient media such as posters should also be used.

3.2 Sales promotion

In conjunction with the printed media we should use money off coupons to encourage trial of the product – primarily for the target audience – the advantage here is that we will be able to collect some information about the customers – even if it is only which magazines they got the voucher from. This should encourage switching to Grapple and our research shows that once they have tried the product, people will continue to use it.

3.3 Sponsorship and PR

We should establish a presence at summer festivals visited by the target audience – some of the music festivals and similar events, which we could consider sponsoring or having stalls at, to give samples and vouchers to encourage trial.

4 Evaluation of the marketing plan

When we put into place the repositioning strategy we need to evaluate the success of it – to do this I propose that we measure sales by distribution channel. The new target customers will most likely buy Grapple from different sources to our existing customers, therefore this measure will give us the best indication of who is buying out product without having to conduct expensive research into buying habits of individuals.

We can measure through the direct channel (Internet), through retailers we deal directly with, and through wholesale intermediaries. This method of measurement is relatively easy to do using our existing sales database. In addition, we can use our sales representatives to discuss with the various channels how they consider the sales to be going, and how happy they are without repositioning strategy.

Note – this is one measure as requested in the question – others could be measuring the sales through various other ways – by salesperson, by order size, by customer and so on. as appropriate for the chosen strategy. Marketing costs and profitability analysis would also be appropriate.

5 Conclusion

I hope you will agree that this repositioning is a good strategy for Grapple, and that it should move us from the decline stage of the product life cycle back to an equivalent to the start of the maturity stage, enabling at least five more years of successful sales for the product.

Answer 20
Marketing plans and business objectives (June 2004, Question 2)

Check your answer

A good answer is likely to:

	☑
Define marketing planning	☐
Outline the main components of the plan	☐
Discuss the importance of planning	☐
Discuss the synergistic planning process	☐
Recognise the links between marketing and wider business objectives	☐
Recognise the needs of a small company in the business-to-business environment	☐
Recognise your role as an external consultant	☐
Use Report format	☐

* * * * *

REPORT

To: Business Owner

From: Marketing Consultant

Date: XX/XX/XX

Re: Marketing Planning

1 Introduction

A marketing plan recognises that businesses cannot stand still, that they are operating in a dynamic environment with constantly evolving opportunities and threats. If as an organisation you do not keep up with these environmental changes, your competitors almost certainly will, and you will be left behind.

A marketing plan will help you to keep ahead of the competition and provides an outline of the marketing tasks which will be carried out during the period the plan covers. A well-constructed plan can be used with potential finance providers to show that the organisation has considered the environment in which it operates.

1.1 Marketing plan components

A marketing plan includes:

o Situation
o Objectives
o Strategy
o Tactics
o Actions
o Control.

This is often referred to by the acronym SOSTAC.

The initial stage in the production of a marketing plan is to understand the corporate objectives and mission of the business – the marketing plan should relate to these and form part of the process which delivers them.

2 The marketing plan includes

2.1 Situation

Understanding the current situation of the organisation and the environment in which it operates vital, the environmental analysis involving two areas:

o *Micro-environment* – Those factors which directly influence the organisation and over which the organisation has influence. Included in the micro-environment are suppliers, customers, shareholders, competitors, employees and local community.
o *Macro-environment* – Those factors which influence the organisation, but over which the organisation has little, if any, influence. The macro-environment includes social, legal, economic, political and technological influences.

Together the situational factors are used to produce a SWOT analysis – the **s**trengths and **w**eaknesses of the organisation relative to its competitors due to its internal situation and the **o**pportunities and **t**hreats presented to the organisation from the environment in which it operates.

This can be summarised as understanding 'where we are now?'

2.2 Objectives

Objectives include two areas – business objectives and marketing objectives. Business objectives relate to the overall organisation and cover all areas of the business – for example for a manufacturing organisation there will be objectives relating to product volumes and quality. Marketing objectives more specifically relate to marketing activities – the delivery of products and services to customers whilst making profits for the organisation.

Objectives should always be SMART – that means they should be:

o *Specific* – relating to a particular, individual area
o *Measurable* – there is something which can be measured to see if the objective has been met
o *Achievable (or Aspirational)* – they should be realistic, but stretch the organisation

> ◦ *Relevant* – appropriate for the organisation to carry out
> ◦ *Time bound* – delivered within a certain time period.

Objectives can be summarised as 'where we want to be'.

2.3 Strategy

Strategy defines the broad methodology which will get us to where we want to be.

Michael Porter defines three generic strategies that organisations can follow:

> ◦ *cost leadership* – being a lower cost provider than other organisations to enable pricing advantage
> ◦ *differentiation* – offering a product which is demonstrably different from others
> ◦ *focus* – targeting a particular segment of the market.

Ansoff offers four possibilities for strategy.

		Product	
		Existing	New
Market	Existing	Penetration	Product development
	New	Market development	Diversification

This highlights the basic areas in which an organisation can focus its strategies.

Within strategy an organisation will segment the potential market, choose which segments to target and position itself (using one of Porters' generic strategies) to best meet the needs of that segment.

2.4 Tactics and actions – Implementation

The marketing mix (7Ps) is used here to determine the activities the organisation will conduct during the plan period:

> ◦ *Product* – What product (or service) range is the organisation going to offer to customers.
> ◦ *Price* – What pricing strategy will be used.
> ◦ *Place* – How and where will the product be sold, what distribution channels will be used.
> ◦ *Promotion* – How will the product be promoted.
> ◦ *People* – What people skills will be needed to interact with customers.
> ◦ *Process* – What is the process used to ensure customer service.
> ◦ *Physical evidence* – What physical attributes beyond the product will support the activities.

The final three areas are particularly important when dealing with services rather than physical goods.

2.5 Monitoring and control

How will the marketing plan be monitored to ensure it is being carried out successfully, and that the plan was correct? This needs to be an ongoing and continual process throughout the plan period, and can often relate to the measurement as mentioned in Objectives.

For a small organisation such as yours it is recognised that there are limited resources for the marketing plan and in particular the development of the marketing mix.

3 The marketing plan related to business objectives

Business objectives are related to the overall vision and mission for the business, which you as the business owner have created. It relates to the marketing plans as illustrated below:

From this, it can be seen that corporate planning is at the top, with marketing planning below it. Also, alongside marketing plans there are operational, logistical and human resource management plans which relate to the other functional areas of the organisation.

The vision and mission drive the overall direction of the company and the functional areas work towards achieving corporate objectives.

Marketing strategy is concerned with three elements:

- ○ customers
- ○ competitors } Driven from the bottom upwards
- ○ internal corporate issues } Driven from the top downwards

4 Conclusion

Marketing plans provide an organisation with an understanding of the environment in which they operate and, provided they are kept up to date, enable the organisation to evolve in the best possible way for the changes that are going on around them, particularly relating to the needs of customers.

The production of a marketing plan shows potential funding bodies that the organisation understands its environment and how it will change to meet the changing needs of that environment.

Answer 21
Environmental audits, macro environmental issues, segmentation, targeting and positioning (June 2004, Question 3)

Check your answer

A good answer is likely to:

☑

Define the marketing environment	☐
Outline the main components of an environmental audit	☐
Micro and macro environment factors	☐
Explain how the environment impacts on organisations	☐
Ethical and social responsibility issues for a window company	☐
Define segmentation, targeting and positioning	☐
Relate STP to the organisation	☐
Recognise your role as an external consultant	☐
Use Report format	☐

*   *   *   *   *

REPORT

To: Business Owner

From: Marketing Management Consultant

Date: XX/XX/XX

Re: Marketing Audit

1 Introduction

Marketing plans have to be based on information and they are only as good as that information which is provided by the marketing audit. McDonald defines a marketing audit as a systematic, critical and unbiased review and appraisal of all the external and internal factors that have affected an organisations' performance over a time period. Essentially the audit answer the question 'where are we now?'

An audit of the marketing environment looks at the:

- ○ *Micro-environment* – Those factors which directly influence the organisation and over which the organisation has influence. Included in the micro-environment are suppliers, customers, shareholders, competitors, employees and local community.
- ○ *Macro-environment* – Those factors which influence the organisation, but over which the organisation has little, if any, influence. The macro-environment includes social, legal, economic, political and technological influences.

2 Micro-environment

In considering your micro-environment you need to consider:

- ○ *Customers* – Who are they, what do they buy off you, how often. I will look at customers in more detail later.
- ○ *Suppliers* – Those people who supply the materials you use to make the double glazing and window frames.
- ○ *Competitors* – Those other organisations who also sell double glazing and window frames.

For evaluation of the competitive environment in which you operate, Michael Porters' five forces model is very useful. It considers five forces that operate within a market or industry, which collectively impact on the degree of industry rivalry that exists:

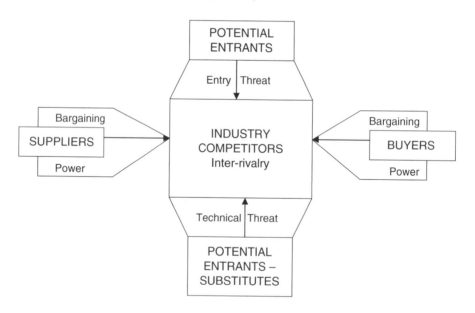

Looking at each of these five forces in turn.

2.1 Industry competitors inter-rivalry

The intensity of rivalry between companies in a market may well be high if two or more companies are fighting for the lead in a market that is experiencing rapid growth. It may also be high in a mature market where companies have to operate at or very near full capacity to cover their overheads which is probably the case for window companies.

2.2 Threat of substitutes

The fast development of new technology often allows companies to develop substitute rival products, which once the initial development costs have been recovered can be offered at a cheaper price.

2.3 Threat of new entrants

This depends on whether high or low barriers to entry exist, basically, how easy would it be for an organisation to set up in competition with you?

2.4 Power of suppliers

The power of suppliers is likely to be high if there are only a few suppliers in a market, and the supply of raw materials or products is controlled or scarce.

2.5 Power of buyers

The power of buyers is likely to be high if there are only a few buyers of products, and supplies are plentiful. For your industry, there are many suppliers producing plentiful supplies so buyers have power – the chance to easily shop around for a good deal.

3 Macroenvironment

In addition to the factors over which the organisation has influence, the audit has to cover the wider environmental factors. These are best defined through SLEPT:

3.1 Social

Social influences and implications are of utmost importance to the marketing environment. Social factors include such things as:

- *Demography* – age, sex, class and so on.
- *Society* – religion, culture, families and so on.
- *Culture* – language, religion, values and attitudes, education and so on.

3.2 Legal

An understanding of the legalisation in the marketing environment of the organisation is essential. More and more of our legislation is European or international, but this all has to be understood in marketing terms.

For your organisation, legal factors to consider include:

- Competitive activities
- Unfair trading
- Consumer protection
- Trade descriptions
- Health and safety
- Professional codes of conduct.

3.3 Economic

A key influence in any organisation is the economy, both nationally and internationally. Historical business cycles provide some indication about the future.

Factors, which influence the economic situation and have implication for your type of business include:

- o Inflation rates
- o Interest rates
- o Income levels
- o Employment levels
- o Consumer spending patterns.

3.4 Political

Politics influence many areas which have impact on marketers, these can include:

- o *taxation* – its effect on disposable income
- o *environmental protection* – green issues, recycling and so on.
- o employment laws
- o health and safety regulations.

3.5 Technological

The technological changes which have taken place over the last 20 years have had major implications for marketing, and will continue to do so. This can affect the way marketers do their job through areas such as the development of the Internet as a marketing tool. It can also have an effect on the products and services marketing works with – the decision to implement new technology can change an organisations cost base – marketing need to understand the impact this will have relative to pricing decision.

4 Impact of the audit

The audit enables the organisation to create a SWOT analysis – the strengths and weaknesses (factors relating to the organisations' competitive position) and the opportunities and threats (presented by the environment).

5 Ethical and social responsibility issues

There are many factors in the wider environment which you need to consider for your industry. In particular these include:

5.1 Ethical issues

The sales techniques used by double-glazing companies have been well documented and regularly criticised for being unethical which can have negative impacts on your organisation, making it harder to get business as some people probably actively resist talking to window companies, even if they want the product.

In addition to these, other ethical issues may include the materials used for the window frames – uPVC could be criticised as lacking environmental friendliness, whilst the use of hard wood could also be criticised. For the actual windows the use of recycled glass could be important.

5.2 Social responsibility issues

These may include your links to the local community and employees. Socially responsible policies would include sponsorship of charities and local works.

In addition, the way employees are treated would be important – for example having sales teams with full employee status contracts, and not expecting them to work purely unsocial hours.

6 Segmentation, targeting and positioning

Marketing should tailor products and messages to the culture in which the sale of the product or service is made. An important task is the segmentation of the society they are operating in to produce manageable units.

1.1 Two common forms of segmentation are class and status.

Class is a complex concept, including the ideas:

1.1.1 Hierarchical distinction – giving upper, middle, lower and working class – plus other similar distinctions

1.1.2 Occupations – which gives socio-economic status groups – white collar, manual, non-manual and so on.

These distinctions enable marketers to segment the population into groups which may have similar beliefs, attributes and values reflected in their behaviour – marketing messages can be sent which reflect the behaviour of the group.

Once possible segments have been identified, the final step at the segmentation stage is to compile profiles of customers in the main segments. These profiles are to test the likely effectiveness and success of the segments. A test might consider the following attributes of each segment:

1.2 Distinctive

1.3 Tangible

- o Viable
- o Accessible
- o Defendable

1.4 Selecting target segments

After identifying potential successful segments, the different segments need to be evaluated to see which segments the organisation should target.

269

This critical stage in the segmentation process matches the capabilities of the organisation to the opportunities available in the various segments. The 'targeting' decision is based on a systematic review of:

o *Attractiveness* of the competing segments
o *Competitive capabilities* – this is the organisation's comparative ability to competitively address the needs of that segment.

1.5 Positioning

Targeting the segment allows attractive segments to be identified and marketing mix strategy to be developed.

Positioning decisions are made once segments have been identified and target segments selected. The process of strategically positioning the products of an organisation involves the following steps:

o Selecting a strategic market position that is credible to the customers to pursue over the long term.
o Implementing the positioning strategy through products to support the position and branding policy.
o Communicating the position to the marketplace in such a way that it successfully differentiates the product in the mind of the customer.

7 Conclusion

Segmentation, targeting and positioning are a key part of marketing strategy, which should be informed by the marketing audit. Positioning is created through the elements of the marketing mix – the product is offered at the appropriate price through the appropriate channels and promoted in the correct way to appeal to the targeted segment.

Answer 22
Market penetration and development strategies, pricing decisions
(June 2004, Question 4)

Check your answer

A good answer is likely to:

	☑
Define marketing strategy	☐
Define market penetration strategy	☐
Define market development	☐
Operational factors for market penetration	☐
Explain the differences between market penetration and market development	☐
Explain the role pricing plays in an organisation	☐
Explain how pricing creates a market penetration strategy	☐
Recognise a role as author – Suggest an external consultant	☐
Relate factors to the recession mentioned in the question	☐
Use Report format	☐

* * * * *

REPORT

To: Managing Director

From: Marketing Consultant

Date: XX/XX/XX

Re: Marketing Audit

Note: this answer is not related to a particular organisation as would be required to answer the question correctly in an exam situation.

1 Introduction

Marketing strategy has been defined by Dibb, Simkin, Pride and Ferrell as a strategy indicating the specific targets and the types of competitive advantages that are to be exploited. You have chosen to expand your market share through a strategy of market penetration – one of the four options suggested by the Ansoff matrix:

Product

	Existing	New
Existing	Penetration	Product development
New	Market development	Diversification

Market (row label for Existing/New)

A market penetration strategy involves selling more of the products currently marketed to the type of customers who currently purchase them.

2 Achieving market penetration

Market penetration typically requires aggressive marketing, involving such factors as sales promotion, advertising and competitive pricing to increase market share – the fundamental outcome of market penetration.

Promotional activity is a key element of the marketing mix used to generate market penetration, increasing the amount of communication to generate awareness and sales of the products is essential. In addition, as customers are required to buy more products, customer loyalty schemes which increase customer retention and encourage repeat purchasing whilst building customer relationships are methods which will assist this strategy.

During a recession when the amount of products bought by customers is reducing, an organisation will have to take business from competitors to achieve market penetration. It can also be achieved by increasing consumption of products by customers – this is more common when business is increasing generally.

The basic options to pursue are:

○ encouraging existing customers to use more of the product, purchasing it more often
○ encouraging customers of competing products to switch to the product in place of their usual preference
○ encourage those who do not currently purchase the type of product being considered to make purchases.

As market penetration involves dealing with existing customers and existing products, it has the least risk of the four strategies outlined by Ansoff – however the potential for growth is limited. Competitor activity can make it difficult to achieve as, particularly in a recession, they may be reluctant to lose business and will react to the initial strategy.

3 Market development

In contrast, a market development strategy involves entering new markets or segments – this inherently involves increased risk over market development as the market or segment will not know as much about the product or supplier, and in some instances of market development may be overseas with further restricted knowledge.

It is usual that the organisation considering a market development strategy [will] research to learn about the markets and/or segments it is intending to enter – it w[ill] knowledge which is already understood by the competitors it will encounter in the ne[w]

To be successful with market development can include new distribution channels in order t[o] reach the new markets or segments, in addition it is quite likely to require increased promotional activity to ensure the new target customers are aware of the products being offered.

Market development can relate to changing the positioning of the product in the minds of customers which will open it up for new users.

4 Pricing for market penetration

To achieve market penetration a penetration pricing strategy is normally used – this involves reducing the price to a level at which customers will switch to the product from alternatives, increasing sales in a short time period.

Penetration pricing can be achieved through various methods:

- o promising to match, or undercut the prices of competitor products
- o offering a short-term price promotion which attracts customers
- o offering free 'extras' with the main product to effectively reduce the price – for example including a free printer with a computer.

Consideration has to be made of the communication required to ensure customers are aware of the pricing offers being made in order for it to be effective, and as previously mentioned, consideration has to be taken for potential competitor reaction to the initiative.

5 Conclusion

In times of recession, a market penetration strategy can be a very effective way to achieve increases in market shares – competitors may feel unable to match promotional and pricing strategies if they are facing reduced sales. Careful consideration of all the elements of the marketing mix can ensure it works quickly with the desired results.

ng
ınications

SYLLABUS INFORMATION – MARKETING COMMUNICATIONS

Aim

The Marketing Communications unit provides the skills and knowledge that enable marketers to manage marketing communications and brand support activities within organisations. It provides students with an understanding of the concepts and practice of promotional activity at an operational level. Although reference is made to relevant strategic issues in order to provide a relevant context for learning, the focus is primarily on creating applied co-ordinated promotional activities, campaign development and the management of relationships with a variety of stakeholders, particularly customers and members of marketing channels.

Learning outcomes

Students will be able to:

- o Explain the role of marketing communications and advise how personal influences might be used to develop promotional effectiveness.
- o Explain how the tools of the promotional mix can be co-ordinated in order to communicate effectively with customers and a range of stakeholders.
- o Devise a basic media plan based on specific campaign requirements using both off-line and online media.
- o Develop marketing communication and brand support activities based on an understanding of the salient characteristics of the target audience.
- o Explain the main elements, activities and linkages associated with the formulation and implementation of a marketing communications plan.
- o Recommend a suitable marketing communications budget.
- o Explain the importance of developing long-term relationships with customers, channel members, agencies and other stakeholders and transfer such knowledge to the development of marketing communication activities.
- o Suggest suitable methods to influence the relationships an organisation has with its customers, any marketing channel partners and other stakeholders, using marketing communications.
- o Use the vocabulary of the marketing communications industry and be able to communicate effectively with other marketing practitioners.

Indicative content and weighting

Element 1: Understanding customer dynamics (20 per cent)

1.1 Explain how individuals can influence the effectiveness of marketing communications through word-of-mouth communications, as opinion leaders, as opinion formers or in multi-step models.

1.2 Describe the main concepts associated with buyer information processing and explain how marketing communications might be used to change or reinforce attitudes, alter perceptions and develop knowledge and understanding about a brand.

1.3 Describe the main concepts associated with the purchase decision process, including source credibility, involvement, perceived risk and how they influence marketing communications.

1.4 Assess the principal differences between consumer and organisational markets and consider how they impact on marketing communications.

1.5 Summarise the importance for organisations of ethics and corporate responsibility, and their impact on brand reputation.

Element 2: Co-ordinated marketing communications (50 per cent)

2.1 Define and explain the roles of marketing communications to differentiate, remind or reassure, inform and persuade (DRIP).

2.2 Evaluate the effectiveness of each of the promotional tools using appropriate criteria such as cost, communication effectiveness, credibility and control.

2.3 Explain the meaning of the terms above-, through- and below-the-line.

2.4 Explain the role of each of the promotional tools within a co-ordinated marketing communications mix.

2.5 Evaluate the effectiveness of co-ordinated campaigns.

2.6 Identify primary and secondary media (online and off-line) and contrast their main characteristics.

2.7 Explain key media concepts (reach, frequency, duplication, GRPs, flighting) and describe the principal approaches used to measure media effectiveness.

2.8 Compare information and emotional-based advertising messages and explain the concept of likeability.

2.9 Outline the key characteristics associated with push, pull and profile strategies.

2.10 Describe the main characteristics of key accounts and explain the stages and issues associated with key account management.

2.11 Describe how co-ordinated marketing communications can be used to develop key account relationships.

2.12 Explain how marketing communications can be used to launch new products, support brands, maintain market share, develop retention levels encourage customer loyalty and support internal marketing within the organisation.

2.13 Draw and describe the main parts of a marketing communications planning framework and explain the principal linkages between the various elements.

2.14 Explain the main methods used to determine a marketing communications budget.

2.15 Discuss the main issues concerning the use of marketing communications in an international and global context, such as media availability, culture, religion, education and literacy.

2.16 Evaluate the effectiveness of marketing communications activities, tools, media and campaigns.

Element 3: Marketing channels (15 per cent)

3.1 Identify and explain how the promotional mix can be suitably configured for use in a range of marketing channels and business-to-business situations.

3.2 Explain, in terms of the impact on marketing communications within a relationship context, the structural concepts: interdependence, independence, disintermediation and reintermediation.

3.3 Explain the role of trust, commitment and satisfaction when developing marketing communication activities for use in the marketing channel and business-to-business contexts.

3.4 Identify the causes of conflict in trade channels and explain how marketing communications can be used to resolve such disagreements.

3.5 Explain how Internet- and digital-based technologies can been used to enhance marketing communications and relationships within channels and between business-to-business partners.

Element 4: Relationship management (15 per cent)

4.1 Compare the principles of transaction and relationship marketing.

4.2 Explain the characteristics of relationship marketing including the features, types, levels, development and implementation steps and communication issues.

4.3 Describe how marketing communications can be used to develop relationships with a range of stakeholders, based on an understanding of source credibility, trust and commitment.

4.4 Explain in broad terms the nature, structure, ownership and any key issues facing the marketing communications industry in any single country or region.

4.5 Describe how agencies manage their operations in order to meet client needs: pitching, briefing, structure, review, the role of account planners and managers, relationship management.

4.6 Explain how advertising agencies and marketing communication agencies use resources to meet the needs of clients with international and global requirements.

4.7 Describe in broad terms the regulatory and voluntary arrangements that are used to manage relationships between the public, customers, clients and agencies.

KEY CONCEPTS – REVISION CHECKLIST

These are the key concepts you should be aware of when you go into the exam. Be able to define or explain each concept, and to discuss key aspects of it. If you have revised this material then you should be able to cope with the theoretical aspects of the exam.

Syllabus element 1

Understanding customer dynamics

Word-of-mouth communication ☑

Viral marketing ☐

Opinion leaders ☐

Opinion formers ☑

Multi-step models ☑

B2B buyer decision-making model ☑

B2C buyer decision-making model ☑

Attitudes – components ☐

Attitudes – methods of changing ☑

Perception ☑

Source credibility ☑

Involvement ☑

Perceived risk ☑

B2B vs. B2C markets, and the impact on marketing communications. ☑

Ethics ☑

Corporate social responsibility ☑

Brand reputation ☑

Syllabus element 2

Coordinated marketing communications

Co-ordinated marketing communications ☑
The marketing communications mix ☑
Marketing communications roles (DRIP) ☑
The 'Four Cs Framework' ☑
Above the line ☑
Below the line ☑
Through the line ☑
Advertising ☑
Public relations ☑
Sales promotion ☑
Personal selling ☑
Direct marketing ☑
Evaluation of effectiveness of:
  o Campaigns
  o Individual tools

Media – online and off-line
Media types:
  o Print
  o Broadcast
  o Outdoor
  o Transport
  o Cinema
  o Ambient
  o New

Measuring media effectiveness
Media terms
  o Reach/coverage
  o Frequency
  o OTS
  o Duplication
  o Drip Burst
  o Flighting
  o GRPs
  o TVRs

☑ Message appeals
☑ Rational/informational messages
☑ Emotional messages
☑ Likeability
☑ Push strategy
☑ Pull strategy
☑ Profile strategy

☑ Brands
☑ Branding
☑ Product life cycle

Key account characteristics
☑ Key account management
☑ Key account stages

☑ Co-ordinated marketing
    communications for:
☑   o Product launch
☑   o Brand building
☑   o Maintaining market share
☑   o Customer retention
☑   o Internal marketing
☐ Intranets
☑

Marketing Communications Planning
☑   Framework (MCPF)
Budget methods
☑
☑ International marketing communications
☐ Standardisation
☐ Adaptation
☑ International marketing communications:
☑   issues to consider, e.g. media
☑   availability, literacy, culture, education,
☑   social roles

279

Syllabus element 3

Marketing channels

Marketing channels ☑	Channel conflict ☑
Marketing communications ☐	Marketing communications ☐
mix for channels/B2B	to resolve channel conflict

Interdependence ☐	Use of Internet and digital ☐
Independence ☐	technology for channels/B2B
Disintermediation ☐	Internet ☐
Reintermediation ☐	Extranet ☐
Channels and trust, ☐	Electronic data interchange (EDI) ☐
commitment and	
satisfaction	

Syllabus element 4

Relationship management

Transaction marketing: ☑	Current 'key issues' in marketing ☑
○ Definitions ☐	communications
○ Features ☐	Industry structure ☐
Relationship marketing: ☐	
○ Definitions ☐	Marketing communications ☐
○ Features ☐	industry regulation and control
Methods for building relationships ☐	Advertising Standards Authority ☐
CRM systems ☐	Marketing communications ☐
Target stakeholders ☐	agencies:
Stakeholders: ☐	○ Types ☐
○ Source credibility ☐	○ Pitching ☐
○ Trust ☐	○ Briefing ☐
○ Commitment ☐	○ Review ☐
	Role of:
	○ Account managers ☐
	○ Creative teams ☐
	○ Media buyers/planners ☐
	International agencies ☐

PART A MINI-CASES

Mini-Case 1: EasyPack (June 2005, Question 1)

Agency appointment process and criteria, Client brief and agency team roles, Above the line activities and consumer attitudes, Agency/client relationships.

Syllabus elements 1.2, 2.3, 4.5

EasyPack was one of the first furniture retailers to open large stores at out-of-town locations. Its initial success was founded on sales of flatpack kitchen and bedroom furniture, which it sold cheaply and discounted regularly. At the time it was a new retail concept whereby customers took home packs of furniture which they then assembled themselves. Trident, the name of the EasyPack kitchen brand, is still a strong brand name, although many people do not associate the name as part of EasyPack. However, despite the company's success, there were quality related problems typified by broken or missing parts. This association with poor quality has continued to tarnish the EasyPack brand. Recently EasyPack's sales performance has declined and last year turnover fell by approximately 10 per cent. It is still the market leader but the fall in market share from 11.6 to 8.4 per cent in a market which is actually showing signs of some growth, is of concern. More recent entrants to the market, Regents and ASF, are beginning to take market share from both ends of the market. Regents have strong design and quality attributes which are targeted at a niche market (of upwardly mobile professional people). Part of the strength of the ASF chain is its strong distribution and limited (flatpack) product range. Tougher competition combined with economic pressures and a series of strategy changes have served to confuse consumer's perception of EasyPack so that it is uncertain what the brand now offers customers. Home owners are taking increased interest in their homes as inflation remains low and the housing market booms. New television programmes aimed at people interested in home decoration and design for all types of houses, are attracting large audiences. As part of the boom a wave of new magazines have been launched to feed this market. The style of communications used by EasyPack is largely fast-paced, price-orientated and features happy family couples with their new furniture. Television is the main media, used to promote its sales promotion's activities. These are focused around the price-led sales at different times of the year (e.g. Winter sales) and various discount initiatives used to boost store traffic. It has been said that too much reliance was placed on the company's market leadership position and little was done to communicate the EasyPack offer. Indeed, much has been done to the product to correct the quality and missing parts problems but it is clear that these changes have not been communicated. Whilst the EasyPack approach to marketing communications has been reasonably innovative, it has been designed to maintain the company's downmarket positioning. Some competitors, however, have been quite radical, both in terms of the message and in terms of the variety of media used. Some have featured celebrities to bring personality into their brand-based advertising.

A new marketing team has been introduced and they plan to reverse the declining fortunes with a series of measures designed to change customer's attitudes towards the EasyPack brand. The company will continue its focus on bedroom and kitchen furniture, and instead of regular discounting, will move towards a value-for-money proposition. To accomplish this a range of other communication tools and media were considered. Rather than to just change brand attitudes, some members of the team believe that EasyPack should increase their below-the-line spend as this will help improve sales immediately and complement the value-for-money orientation.

(The above data has been based on a fictitious situation drawing on a variety of events and does not reflect the management practices of any particular organisation.)

Questions

Earlier this year, EasyPack decided that they needed to change their advertising agency. They invited three full-service agencies to pitch for the account. As a member of the new marketing team at EasyPack, prepare a report for your colleagues, which respond to the following questions:

a) Explain the sequence of events associated with the appointment of a new marketing communication agency and suggest the key criteria EasyPack should use when deciding which agency to appoint. (10 marks)

b) Briefly describe the role and content of a client brief and explain in note form the key tasks undertaken by account managers, creative teams and media planners. (10 marks)

c) Evaluate the extent to which above-the-line activities should dominate EasyPack's marketing communications in order to change customer attitudes. (20 marks)

d) Briefly discuss ways in which client–agency relationships might be developed. (10 marks)

(Total 50 marks)

Mini-Case 2: Car Recovery Services (June 2004, Question 1)

Rational vs. emotional messages; Changing attitudes; Customer magazines; Processes and procedures for a direct mail campaign

Syllabus elements 1.2, 2.8, 2.12

In the UK car recovery and breakdown market, the Royal Automobile Club (RAC) is regarded as the challenger brand with the Automobile Association (AA) as the undisputed market leader. In addition, Direct Line Rescue (DLR) has entered the market recently and taken a 10 per cent market share.

The perceived benefits of motor organisation membership have changed over the last 10 years. The provision of reassurance and driver support have become more important while there has been a decline in the importance of financial and economic factors. Motorists now tend to be more concerned about getting home quickly with or without their car than they are about the economic arguments between using motorist organisation membership and ad hoc services. In addition, customers in this market are no longer simply users of the vehicle breakdown services but expect a broad range of products and services, which the motoring organisations aim to satisfy in different ways.

Attitudes towards membership have changed for a number of reasons. Demographic factors are significant because the percentage of young and female drivers has increased at the expense of middle-aged male drivers. Motorists are now less willing to perform roadside repairs while cars are becoming more complex. The reliability of cars has increased but they are more challenging for drivers when they do go wrong. This is simply because of the nature of contemporary engine components (sealed units) and the need for specialist equipment to diagnose computer-related faults.

Traditionally, marketing communications messages in this market have been based on advertising and the development of brand values. Messages have been very product-focused, typified by messages featuring speed of recovery, 'get you home' services, helpfulness of staff and a range of ancillary products, such as car finance and legal and advisory services. During the 1990s, the promotional emphasis of the main motoring organisations changed from one that emphasised economic and tangible attributes to one that gave higher prominence to driver safety and reassurance. In addition to changes in the core messages used by the RAC and AA, greater emphasis has been placed on the other promotional tools, partly in response to the market entry and aggression of DLR.

In response to competitive pressures, profit margins declining on recovery services and private membership rising only slightly, the RAC has moved into Direct Response TV (DRTV) to support their ancillary services. One such campaign attempted to convey the idea that the RAC can help people afford their dream car, regardless of what it is, and secure the finance from a trusted brand to help them buy it. The adverts encouraged viewers to call a free phone number to apply for a loan and get an instant decision. Every successful loan applicant received free RAC Breakdown cover.

In addition, the RAC have developed their 36-page RAC Magazine as a means of communicating with their different markets. Of the several million copies mailed out three times a year everyone receives the standard 20 pages of content but in addition, there is also a 16-page insert that takes account of a person's life stage and their length of membership.

DLR is a very strong brand and lends itself to strong imagery and straightforward messages. It has been DLR's intention to develop a much closer relationship with their customers and they too have strategies that are designed to offer more than just vehicle breakdown services.

A recent campaign was designed to target customers of the RAC and AA and to reinforce their Rescue brand, which has nearly one million customers. Through their direct marketing agency they developed a series of mail packs, each containing a letter, envelope and insert, targeting different messages to existing AA and RAC members. These messages instructed recipients to 'Stop Paying Too Much' by switching to Direct Line. Direct Line's own car insurance customers received a third pack which said that 'First we save you money, then we save you'. This was intended to highlight the breakdown cover offer from £35 and to reassure people about the high level of service whilst prompting them to respond through bold calls to action and guaranteed low prices.

This mini-case has been prepared from a variety of sources. Some of the material has been changed for assessment purposes and does not reflect the current management practices.

Questions

As a member of the direct marketing agency which recently won the DLR account you are required to prepare answers to the following questions.

a) Explain the characteristics of rational and emotional-based messages and provide examples based on the Car Recovery market.   (10 marks)

b) Examine the ways in which marketing communications can be used to change motorists' attitudes towards vehicle recovery services.   (15 marks)

c) Evaluate the extent to which customer magazines can help develop relationships with customers.   (10 marks)

d) Recommend the key processes and procedures necessary to develop and implement an effective direct-mail campaign.   (15 marks)

(Total 50 marks)

Mini-Case 3: Burward's Night-Time Drink

Message appeals; opinion leaders, opinion formers and celebrity endorsement; international marketing communications; the co-ordinated marketing communications mix

Syllabus elements 1.2, 2.4, 2.8, 2.12, 2.15

Burward's has an enviable reputation as the first brand that the British public think of in relation to night-time non-alcoholic drinks. Made from natural ingredients, and sold as a powder in distinctively shaped jars, Burward's has been mixed with hot milk by generations of Britons to make a soothing drink before settling down to sleep. Burward's drinkers are fiercely loyal, and consumer research shows they have no doubt that it helps them to have a full and restful night's sleep. From its earliest days the drink has been associated in brand communications with its seemingly medicinal qualities – the message is that it will help you sleep better but without the use of prescription drugs.

Burward's was developed in the early 20th century and became firmly established as a British favourite during the Second World War when, mixed with milk powder, it became a quick and easy way to offer a warming, nutritional drink to both civilians and military personnel. It is one of a range of brands owned by ARW, a UK-based company with a diverse range of well-known household FMCG brands in a number of sectors. Burward's sales levels are fairly solid, contributing significant and consistent profits to ARW year on year.

On the face of it things are good for this popular brand, which holds 50 per cent of the night-time drinks market, 8 per cent more than its main competitor. But its main market is men and women aged over 55 and, though this demographic group is growing in the UK, the number of users of night-time drinks including Burward's is gradually declining, as fewer new users seem to be trying this product category. An additional threat comes from UK consumers' increasing willingness to migrate to supermarket own-brand labels for a wide range of FMCG products, meaning that Burward's cannot simply assume that its consumers will stay loyal to the brand indefinitely.

As newly appointed Brand Manager for Burward's you are keen to stem the slow decline of the drink, before sales lose critical mass and profits start to decline significantly. You have identified two main strategies.

First, you wish to broaden the appeal of the drink, reaching new demographic groups. You recognise that it is not just the over 55s who need a good night's sleep, and that there are opportunities to appeal to younger consumers who need help to unwind at the end of a stressful day at the office or looking after children. You have seen some recent external research which shows that over 70 per cent of adults admit to having sleeping difficulties sometimes.

Second, you are keen to take the drink into international markets. The need for a good night's sleep is universal, so that Burward's main proposition has potentially limitless appeal. Preliminary research has shown that there is scope to take the product first into Germany, the Netherlands and Scandinavia – markets in which ARW already has experience. If these prove successful then there could be other opportunities, for example elsewhere in Europe and in parts of Asia and Africa too.

The brand's marketing communications to date have typically focused on associations with relaxation and rest – calming images, shot in warm colours, of greying consumers cupping a mug of Burward's in their hands as they prepare to settle down for the night. Actors – always non-celebrities – in Burward's TV commercials, which are usually shown on weekday afternoons, advise viewers that Burward's calms them and helps them get a good night's sleep. Recent research, conducted by ARW's large in-house scientific team, offers some scientific support to the 'Burward's helps you sleep' core message and you are keen to look at ways that this evidence could be incorporated into your marketing communications. Some brand commentators have suggested that Burward's appeal is becoming similar to that of homeopathic, or 'complementary' medicines – with physiological benefits to users from traditional, non-pharmaceutical ingredients.

Because of its heritage, and its relatively conservative target market, the Burward's brand has not been known for its innovation. However some new ideas have recently been successfully trialled, including the introduction of single-use sachets for convenience, as have joint consumer promotions with a major supplier of milk in bottles and cartons to retailers. There is scope, you believe, to develop new brand associations, perhaps using celebrities or opinion formers.

The case is based upon a fictitious organisation and does not reflect the current marketing practices of any organisation.

Questions

You have been asked to prepare a report for ARW's Marketing Director on how to take the brand forward over the next two years. She has specifically asked you to address the following:

a) What is meant by using appropriate 'message appeals' (or 'communication appeals') in marketing communications, and what alternatives are there for this in relation to Burward's in the future?　　　　　　(10 marks)

b) Explain why opinion leaders and opinion formers are often used in marketing communications, and discuss how celebrity endorsement could benefit Burward's communications.　　(10 marks)

c) In the context of Burward's possible expansion into overseas sales, explain the terms 'adaptation' and 'standardisation' in relation to marketing communications. Briefly review what other factors businesses need to take into account when deciding on the their communications activities.　　　　　　(15 marks)

d) Select and justify an appropriate marketing communications mix for Burward's in the UK as it seeks to broaden its consumer appeal.　　　　　　(15 marks)

(Total 50 marks)

Mini-Case 4: Home Comforts

Consumer vs. organisational buying; Push, pull and profile communication strategies and a supporting marketing communications mix; Relationship marketing vs. transactional marketing; Internal marketing

Syllabus elements 1.4, 2.4, 2.9, 2.12, 3.1, 4.2

Home Comforts is a service business offering short-term furnished accommodation for business executives. The company was formed only two years ago and has operated on a fairly informal and unstructured basis. But demand is outstripping supply and Michael Peat, the founder, recognises that the business needs to develop a more planned approach if it is to take full advantage of this potentially huge market opportunity.

Many types of business regularly have senior staff temporarily located away from home, and the traditional solution has been to book hotel rooms for them. From his own board-level experience in the insurance industry, Peat recognised that many executives who need temporary accommodation would prefer to stay somewhere that felt more like a home; thus he saw a need for upmarket furnished apartments and houses in suitable areas to be available for short-term letting. Home Comforts itself rents each accommodation unit in its portfolio from owners, benefiting from low rents in exchange for taking long-term leases; profits then come from sub-letting the units for higher rents to Home Comforts' short-term customers.

Peat believes – and customer feedback bears this out – that using rented apartments costs corporate customers little more than using hotels but it offers far more style, comfort, privacy and security. Clients do not have to miss out on hotel-type services as Home Comforts offers cleaning, maintenance and laundry care through outsourcing. All accommodation is well equipped and has Internet access, essential for modern executives. It is located in areas with good restaurants, and details of reliable food delivery services are given to all occupants.

Analysis of occupants shows they are split roughly 50/50 between UK and overseas nationals, all working for companies with UK-based offices. It is the companies who book and pay for the accommodation for their employees, who are typically on secondments for anything between a week and six months. These companies tend to be large, often operating in the financial, media or consultancy sectors. There are also signs of growing demand from airlines, import/export companies and other businesses operating internationally.

Home Comforts has offices in three UK cities but Peat has plans to open another four over the next year. Peat has built the business up through personal contacts with board-level executives in the companies seeking staff accommodation, and through word-of-mouth recommendation, but a more formal approach is now needed to reach new target customers. As part of this approach you have been recruited for the new post of Marketing Manager, which includes responsibilities for sales operations. You recognise the importance of maintaining contacts with the corporate customers with whom Peat has already established connections, as well as finding and keeping new customers. HR and Purchasing departments are typically influential in negotiating staff accommodation and it is essential you establish good contacts with these departments in target businesses. You also plan to target relocation agents who provide services to companies when their employees are moving permanently to new locations – there is often a demand for short-term accommodation before staff complete their permanent move. Accommodation booking agents, working in the corporate market, are another key target.

You have some concerns about the business's haphazard approach to internal communications. At present there are seventeen permanent Home Comforts staff and this will more than double with Peat's expansion plans. There are no structured internal communications – though news spreads fast through e-mails and phone calls. Peat is friendly and approachable and visits each office at least once a month so he has chance to chat to staff then, but employees at each office have little knowledge of clients of the other offices and there is no attempt to formalise who knows what about the business. There is no company Intranet, but there is at least an Internet site though it is fairly rudimentary – good contacts, personable staff and well-presented printed literature on each accommodation unit have been largely sufficient to see the business through this far. Both you and Peat recognise that more needs to be done for the future. You are also conscious that Home Comforts will have to start to focus more on building relationships with customers, as the business grows and the emphasis on Peat's' existing contact network inevitably decreases. This is even more important as competitors eye this lucrative market – a number of rival operations have set up recently.

Questions

You have been asked to present a report to Michael Peat on various aspects of Home Comforts' marketing communications. In particular, Peat has asked you to address the following:

a) What are the main differences between consumer and organisational buying and what effect do these differences have on business-to-business communication? (10 marks)

b) What are meant by push, pull and profile strategies? How could these strategies be used by Home Comforts? Briefly recommend a suitable co-ordinated marketing communications mix to support these strategies. (15 marks)

c) Describe the characteristics of relationship marketing, contrasting it with transactional marketing. How can relationship marketing be used by Home Comforts in the future? (15 marks)

d) Give reasons why you believe there is a need to develop a more planned approach to internal marketing. Briefly explain the benefits of internal marketing and explain *three* suitable communication methods that Home Comforts could use. (10 marks)

(Total 50 marks)

PART B QUESTIONS

Question 5

Direct marketing and advertising contrasted; Evaluation of the promotional mix; Word-of-mouth communication. (Dec'03, Question 2)

Syllabus elements 1.1, 2.2, 2.5, 2.16

As a newly appointed Marketing Manager at an organisation that produces a brand of energy drinks, you Marketing Director has asked you to prepare notes for her use at a forthcoming meeting with their current advertising agency. She is concerned that there is too much promotional activity targeted at brand development and too little at encouraging product purchase. Prepare your notes in answer to the following issues:

a) Using appropriate criteria, compare and contrast the effectiveness of the following two promotional tools: direct marketing and advertising. (10 marks)

b) Explain how the promotional mix might be best evaluated in order to maximise its effectiveness in achieving the stated objectives. (10 marks)

c) Recommend ways in which word-of-mouth communications might be encouraged as part of the promotional effort. (5 marks)

(Total 25 marks)

Question 6

Outdoor vs. print media; Sales promotion techniques; Relationship marketing vs. transaction marketing of services offered by such airlines. However, low-price competitors continue to grow (Dec.'03, Question 3)

Syllabus elements 2.4, 2.6, 4.1

The national airline, in a country of your choice, wishes to continue targeting full fare business travellers, who prefer the full range as new travellers enter the market.

The Marketing Communications Manager for the national airline has asked you to research and prepare a report in order to help reverse their current disappointing operating performance.

Your report should answer the following issues:

a) Discuss the advantages and disadvantages of both outdoor and print media. (10 marks)

b) Explain how four different sales promotion techniques work. (5 marks)

c) Make recommendations concerning the adoption of a relationship marketing approach, based upon a comparison with transaction marketing. (10 marks)

(Total 25 marks)

Question 7

Business-to-business communications mix and roles; New media and digital technologies; Key account management (June 2004, Question 2)

Syllabus elements 1.4, 2.1, 2.6, 2.11, 3.1, 3.5

The organisation you work for manufactures robotic equipment, which is used by other organisations as part of their production and assembly facilities. Having recently attended a conference on the impact of technology on marketing communications, you wish to share some ideas with colleagues, for improving the effectiveness of your organisation's marketing communications. In preparation for this meeting, prepare notes on the following topics.

a) Evaluate the business-to-business (B2B) marketing communication mix and explain the main roles that promotional activities need to undertake.   (10 marks)

b) Explain how the use of new media and associated digital technologies can assist the use of personal selling activities in the B2B sector.   (10 marks)

c) Recommend ways in which key account management might assist the development of relationships in the organisation.   (5 marks)

(Total 25 marks)

Question 8

Channel conflict; Key account management; Transaction vs. relationship marketing, and the benefits of CRM systems (Dec. 2004, Question 3)

Syllabus elements 2.10, 2.12, 3.4, 4.1, 4.2

Gregory FME are a medium-sized manufacturer of farm machinery and equipment. In the past they have used geographically based distributors to reach their customers. Channel relationships have generally been sound but recently some distributors have begun to voice their concern about some of the manufacturer's new product ranges and promotional policies. As a marketing consultant employed by Gregory, you have been asked to respond to the following questions.

a) Discuss the possible causes of conflict in marketing channels and explain how marketing communications can be used to resolve disagreements.   (10 marks)

b) Describe the main characteristics of key accounts and explain the stages and issues that Gregory FME should be aware of with key account management.   (5 marks)

c) Explain the key characteristics associated with both transaction and relationship marketing and determine the benefits Gregory FME might experience following the adoption of a customer relationship management (CRM) system.   (10 marks)

(Total 25 marks)

Question 9

Independence and interdependence; Direct marketing, and its impact on customers. (Dec. 2004, Question 2)

Syllabus elements 2.4, 2.12, 3.2

The organisation you work for imports ethnic knitwear products from Eastern Europe and distributes them via selected retailers and wholesalers in a country of your choice. The company intends moving towards a direct marketing strategy, based primarily on use of the Internet. You have been asked to review and report on the following prior to a strategy being developed.

a) In the context of the knitwear organisation, compare the following two distribution channel concepts: interdependence and independence. (5 marks)

b) Evaluate how the marketing communications mix might change as a result of adopting a direct marketing strategy. (10 marks)

c) Consider how the move to direct marketing might impact on end-user customers. (10 marks)

(Total 25 marks)

Question 10

Business-to-business CRM systems; New media and digital technologies (June'05, Question 2)

Syllabus elements 1.4, 2.12, 3.1, 3.5, 4.1, 4.2

The organisation you work for, Liftright, manufactures and services hydraulic lifting and earth-moving equipment. Having recently attended a conference on customer relationship marketing (CRM), you wish to share some ideas with colleagues, for improving the effectiveness of your organisation's marketing communications and customer relationships.

In preparation for this meeting, prepare notes on the following topics:

a) Explain how CRM systems might assist the development of a customer orientation within Liftright. (10 marks)

b) Evaluate the potential problems that Liftright might experience when implementing a CRM system. (10 marks)

c) Briefly identify *three* issues that would need to be addressed when Liftright introduces new media and associated digital technologies. (5 marks)

(Total 25 marks)

Question 11

Sales promotion and advertising compared; the B2B purchase decision process and relevant promotional tools; B2B sales promotions (June '05, Question 4)

Syllabus elements 1.4, 2.2, 2.4, 2.12, 3.1

As marketing manager for a medium-sized specialist printing company, you are concerned that the number of leads converted into orders by the salesforce is falling. It has been suggested that the use of sales promotions might be useful in improving the number of leads that are converted into sales. As a result you are preparing notes in advance of a meeting with a prospective sales promotion agency.

a) Using appropriate criteria, compare and contrast the effectiveness of the following TWO promotional tools: sales promotion and advertising. (10 marks)

b) Explain how the promotional tools could be used through the different stages of the business-to-business (B2B) purchase decision process. (10 marks)

c) Describe *three* different methods of B2B sales promotions and show how they might assist the printer's salesforce. (5 marks)

(Total 25 marks)

Question 12

Budgets; Agency remuneration; Campaign evaluation (Dec. 2005, Question 3)

Syllabus elements 2.5, 2.14, 2.16, 4.5

The advertising agency for which you work as an account executive has recently gained a substantial number of new accounts. You have been asked to prepare a short report advising them about the following topics:

a) Discuss *three* different ways in which organisations might develop a suitable marketing communications budget. Recommend and justify a particular method. (10 marks)

b) Identify and explain the different methods by which the agency might be rewarded (paid) for its work on their clients' behalf. (5 marks)

c) Evaluate *four* methods the agency might use to determine the effectiveness of an advertising campaign. (10 marks)

(Total 25 marks)

Question 13

Account management and client briefs; Relationship marketing (Specimen paper, Question 5)

Syllabus elements 4.2, 4.5

The PEN company, an established manufacturer and distributor of personal electronic products, seeks an agency to help launch their new personal organiser. The advertising agency for whom you work has just been invited to pitch for PEN's international account following a successful credentials presentation. As the potential Account Manager for this client, you are required to organise a documentation pack that will be given to the client at the pitch. You are required to prepare the following:

a) An explanation of the role of the Account Manager and the nature and characteristics of the Client Brief. (15 marks)

b) An evaluation of the importance of adopting a relationship marketing approach with clients. (10 marks)

(Total 25 marks)

Question 14

Customer retention; Disintermediation and reintermediation; A marketing communications mix for the launch of new services

Syllabus elements 2.4, 2.12, 3.2, 4.1, 4.2

You are the marketing manager for TransChannel, a ferry operator running freight and passenger ships between the UK and Europe. Your firms sells tickets through travel agents and also accepts bookings directly from travellers via the company's website. The market is highly competitive, with competition from other ferry operators and the Channel Tunnel.

TransChannel is about to launch a new service using high-speed vessels which will reduce existing journey times by more than a third. The firm will also start operating on several new routes.

A new member has joined your team and she has asked you to explain several things. Prepare notes for a meeting with her covering the following:

a) What is meant by the phrase 'customer retention'? Suggest four practical steps companies can take to increase their rates of customer retention. (10 marks)

b) The words 'disintermediation' and 'reintermediation' are being used increasingly in marketing communications. With reference to the travel industry explain these terms and briefly indicate some issues that companies might need to address if considering running a disintermediated operation alongside traditional means of distribution. (5 marks)

c) Suggest and justify a suitable co-ordinated marketing communications mix to launch TransChannel's new services. (10 marks)

(Total 25 marks)

293

Question 15

Cinema and broadcast media compared; Cost per thousand; a recommended media mix

Syllabus elements 2.6, 2.7

You work for a city council that is introducing a congestion charge (a charge for vehicles to enter the centre of a the city, with the aim of reducing traffic levels).

The move is to be publicised via a local advertising campaign. As Marketing Manager for the city, write a memo to your marketing team on aspects of media selection.

The memo should cover the following:

a) Identify the advantages and disadvantages of cinema and broadcast media.   (10 marks)

b) Explain the concept of 'cost per thousand' and indicate how it might help in making choices about media to use for the campaign.   (5 marks)

c) Make and justify recommendation concerning the media mix the council might use for its advertising.   (10 marks)

(Total 25 marks)

Question 16

Perceived risk; Source credibility; Ethics and regulation (Charity sector)

Syllabus elements 1.3, 1.5, 4.7

You work for War-Relief, a UK-based charity, operating internationally, which supports civilians and/or their families affected by death and injury arising from war and terrorism. A new fund-raising print and poster advertising campaign is planned and you are exploring a number of creative ideas. These include inviting celebrities who have previously expressed an interest in War-Relief's work to endorse it publicly.

Prepare a report to the Fund-raising Director of the charity which covers the following:

a) Explain the concept of perceived risk and illustrate how the charity's marketing communications can be used to reduce it.   (10 marks)

b) What is source credibility, and how can it be used to the charity's advantage in its planned campaign?   (5 marks)

c) One senior employee of the charity has suggested using graphic images of victims of violence in fund-raising campaigns to shock the public into supporting the charity. Discuss some of the ethical and regulatory issues this suggestion throws up.   (10 marks)

(Total 25 marks)

Question 17

Communications industry and current issues; Corporate social responsibility; Evaluation of public relations and sales promotion

Syllabus elements 1.5, 4.4, 2.16

Kiddipops is a popular brand of children's breakfast cereal owned by an international company. You are the brand manager.

A colleague has joined you on secondment from one of the company's overseas offices and has asked you several questions about marketing communications in the UK (or a country of your choice). Prepare notes for a meeting with him which covers the following issues.

a) Describe the structure of your country's marketing communications industry. Identify two current issues the industry is facing. (10 marks)

b) Explain what is meant by the term 'corporate social responsibility' (CSR). What benefits are there to businesses of acting with social responsibility? Illustrate your answers with examples. (10 marks)

c) How can the effectiveness of the following two activities be evaluated: sales promotions and public relations? (5 marks)

(Total 25 marks)

Question 18

Product life cycle and the promotional mix; Sales promotional and public relations compared; Involvement

Syllabus elements 1.3, 2.2, 2.12

You are the Brand Manager for a popular washing powder. A new assistant has joined you and has asked several questions. Write a memo to him that covers the following issues.

a) Explain how the tools of the promotional mix might be best used over the life of a product. (10 marks)

b) Using appropriate criteria compare and contrast the effectiveness of the following two promotional tools: sale promotions and public relations. (10 marks)

c) What is meant by the term 'involvement' in relation to marketing communications and briefly describe what impact it has on promotional activity. (5 marks)

(Total 25 marks)

Question 19

The roles of marketing communications; Planning an advertising campaign; Key media terms

Syllabus elements 2.1, 2.7, 2.12

As part of a personal development programme, you have been seconded from your full-time marketing job in industry to provide advice on marketing communications to a charity (of your choice). The charity's Operations Director is thinking of running a fund-raising advertising campaign and has asked you for information on various aspects of marketing communications. Prepare a report for her which covers the following topics.

a) Explain the differing roles of marketing communications, applicable to the charity sector.

(10 marks)

b) Identify the main steps in planning an advertising campaign.

(10 marks)

c) Explain the following four terms in connection with advertising campaign: reach, frequency, drip and burst.

(5 marks)

(25 marks in total)

Question 20

Direct marketing and public relations compared; Marketing communications planning process; Likeability

Syllabus elements 2.2, 2.8, 2.13

You are the newly appointed Marketing Communications Manager working at the Head Office of Fit for Life, a national firm of health and fitness clubs. Each of the 25 clubs around the country offers fully equipped gymnasiums, swimming pools and exercise classes for all ages and abilities.

You are aware that there have been problems in the past with the business's use of marketing communications including a poorly received advertising campaign in local and national media. Also, it has become clear that the planning process for the organisation's range of marketing communications activities has been rather haphazard. Prepare notes for a meeting with the rest of your marketing team to cover the following:

a) Using appropriate criteria compare and contrast the effectiveness of the following two promotional tools: direct marketing and public relations.

(10 marks)

b) Outline a suitable marketing communications planning process for Fit for Life, and include an explanation of how the planning stages relate to one another.

(10 marks)

c) In relation to the poorly received advertising campaign explain the concept of 'likeability' in marketing communications.

(5 marks)

(Total 25 marks)

Question 21

Distribution channels: Marketing communications uses and mix; Trust, commitment and satisfaction; Digital technologies and relationships

Syllabus elements 3.1, 3.3, 3.5, 4.3

You are the newly appointed Marketing Manager for an insurance company that sells policies that cover a wide range of risks, including commercial and private properties, small boats and agricultural machinery. The companies' policies are sold only via insurance brokers who act as intermediaries between your company and the policyholders – there are no sales direct to the public by your firm. The Managing Director believes that the firm should place more emphasis on channel relationships and has asked you to report to her on the following:

a) What are the main uses of marketing communications between distribution channel members? Briefly explain and justify which TWO tools of the promotional mix you consider to be the most useful for companies to use with intermediaries such as insurance brokers.

(10 marks)

b) Evaluate the importance of trust, commitment and satisfaction in channel relationships.

(5 marks)

c) Suggest ways that digital technologies could be used to help build relationships with distribution channels. Briefly comment on the extent to which these methods can be relied on for relationship building.

(10 marks)

(Total 25 marks)

Question 22

Personal selling vs. advertising; Global advertising agencies; Marketing communications industry regulation

Syllabus elements 2.2, 4.6, 4.7

Village Opportunities is a UK company selling holiday village accommodation in luxury chalets in rural locations in Britain. Buyers may purchase outright, or can buy weeks in timeshare arrangements. On-site salespeople sell the properties/timeshare weeks to buyers who call by appointment, with interest created by Village Opportunities' advertising in glossy magazines and Sunday supplements.

As Marketing Director for the company you have been asked to present a report to the Managing Director on various aspects of the firm's communications. Amongst other things he is concerned about claims made by competitors' advertising. He has asked you to cover the following:

a) Explain how the UK marketing communications industry is regulated (or the communications industry in a country of your choice).
(10 marks)

b) Using appropriate criteria compare and contrast the effectiveness of the following two promotional tools: advertising and personal selling.
(10 marks)

c) The company is considering advertising in selected European markets. Explain the different types of advertising agency that are available to companies seeking to advertise overseas.
(5 marks)

(Total 25 marks)

PART A SUGGESTED ANSWERS

Mini-Case 1: EasyPack (June 2005, Question 1)

Check your answer

A good answer is likely to:

☑

Explain the sequence of events and give selection criteria in Part a. ☐

In Part b describe the client brief, and consider all three job roles. ☐

In Part c explain or define 'above the line' and 'attitudes' ☐

Use an evaluative approach in Part c, i.e. discuss and consider how much above-the-line ☐
activities can help, and compare their merits against the relevant below the line
methods.

Include discussion of the importance of agency–client relationships in Part d. ☐

Relate your answer to a flat-pack retailer, in the circumstances described ☐

Use Report format. ☐

* * * * *

REPORT

To: Marketing Communications Team

From: Marketing Communications Manager

Date: XX/XX/XX

Re: EasyPack's Marketing Communications

1 Introduction

I am pleased to be working with you to start reversing the decline of EasyPack's fortunes.
Increased competition has adversely affected the business in recent years but the market is
growing and better product and service quality, coupled with new approaches to our marketing
communications, mean that there are plenty of opportunities to turn things round. Finding a new
advertising agency is an important part of this process and I want to address this, as well as
some other issues, in this Report.

2 The agency appointment process and selection criteria

You will be aware that three agencies have been invited to pitch for EasyPack's advertising business. It may be helpful to explain where pitching falls in the selection process.

2.1 Appointment process

- o *Search*: the start point is to find possible agencies to pitch. There are several possible sources including classified telephone listings, advertisements in marketing magazines, and listings in industry directories such as the Marketing Manager's Yearbook and the Advertising Agency Register. One of the most reliable sources is likely to be recommendation from others who have used an agency's services.
- o *Credentials presentation*: many potential clients ask agencies to give some initial information such as a summary of past work, a current client list, team members' profiles, company structure and history. This helps to screen out obviously unsuitable agencies at an early stage.
- o *Briefing*: once a shortlist of, perhaps, three or four agencies has been drawn up the client gives them a briefing document. This sets out details of the business task that the client wants the agency to undertake. More details are given in the next section of this report.
- o *Pitching*: the agency is given time – generally several weeks – to prepare their suggestions for how the task should be tackled. The agency then pitches for the business by presenting their creative and media proposals to the client. This is the agency's chance to demonstrate their abilities, and usually the full agency team that would be working on the account is involved with the pitch.
- o *Selection*: this is the time when the client makes a decision as to which agency they are going to use; a formal contract will then be drawn up between the client and the successful agency. Inevitably some agencies will not be selected but, as they have put much time and effort into preparing their pitch, it is ethical practice for clients to give unsuccessful agencies constructive feedback on why they were not selected.

2.2 Selection criteria

I suggest we use the following criteria to help us judge which agency would be most suitable:

- o *Understanding of our business*: the agency needs to understand how the retail furniture market works, our place in it and the strengths and weaknesses of the competition.
- o *Client conflicts*: we need to ensure that they are not working for our competitors as this could present ethical and practical problems. We can check this at the credentials presentation.
- o *Creative ability*: we have been 'reasonably innovative' in the past but our competitors have been 'quite radical'. The agency needs to come up with fresh, well-executed ideas that will make a real impact in crowded market. We must be impressed with their ideas – this is a critical criterion.
- o *Size and resources*: the agency must have all the skills we require, and in the appropriate depth. Research, production and media planning and buying are important capabilities.
- o *Ability to work with other agencies*: we are considering using below-the-line activity as well as above the line. Some full-service advertising agencies offer below-the-line services too, if they do not offer these, a proven track record of constructive working with other agencies will be needed.

- ○ *Location*: the ability to meet easily from time to time is important, though electronic communications, such as videoconferencing, mean this is less important than it once was.
- ○ *Fees and costs*: we need to agree a fair price for their services and an appropriate remuneration basis. I suggest we include a performance-related element in the package.
- ○ *Relationships*: very importantly, we must get on with the agency team members. We will be working closely with them so having the right chemistry is important.

3 The client brief

A briefing document is given to a shortlisted agency before the pitch stage of the agency selection process. The role of the brief is to give the agency all the information it needs to devise proposals for a campaign. It also advises the agency what is required from them, for example proposals for a multi-media campaign to meet certain time and budget criteria, to be presented to the client on a particular date. Many agencies have their own template for a Brief to ensure that no key information is missed but the following key information is likely to be included in each briefing document:

- ○ *Client information*: name, address, contact names and details.
- ○ *Client background*: ownership, areas of business, time in business, brands owned, corporate image.
- ○ *Product/service information*: the product/service to be promoted; its key features, benefits and unique selling propositions (USPs); packaging and presentation; pricing.
- ○ *Target audience*: who the product/service is aimed at, and how it is to be used by them.
- ○ *The market for the product/service*: size, life cycle stage, distribution, competition.
- ○ *Campaign objectives*: these need to be devised using SMART (specific, measurable, agreed, realistic, time-bound) principles; the objectives might relate to sales, awareness, attitudes and so on.
- ○ *Media*: previous campaigns and media used; media preferences (if any).
- ○ *Budget*: final costs will need to include creative work, production and media spend.
- ○ *Timescales*: both when the campaign is to start and its duration.
- ○ *Other requirements*: for example, mandatory inclusions.

There are several key members of the agency team.

- ○ *Account manager*: he or she is the vital link between the agency and the client. They relay client requirements, comments and other feedback to the other agency personnel to ensure that the client's needs are met; equally they represent the agency when talking to the client, presenting their ideas, suggestions and so on. They will be the point of day-to-day contact between the two parties and are vital in building a strong agency–client relationship. They will attend joint meetings and write up Contact Reports of the discussions.
- ○ *Creative teams*: these are the people who come up with, and develop, the ideas to meet the client's brief. Typically, creative teams will comprise both copywriters – responsible for the words – and art directors who look after the graphics and design work. The team's abilities lie in capturing an often-complex proposition into a simple, appealing and understandable message.
- ○ *Media planners*: they decide on the appropriate media to use to meet creative requirements and to reach the identified target audience. They will have access to a range of statistical data on audience size and composition for different traditional and new media, and on their costs. They will also devise media schedules to meet reach and frequency targets. They work closely with the media buyers who negotiate the best rates for their clients.

4 Above-the-line activities and customer attitudes

The phrase 'above-the-line' activity refers to advertising activity, and contrasts with 'below-the-line' activity which relates to other element of the marketing communications mix. (Direct marketing is sometimes referred to as 'through-the-line' activity.) The term 'above the line' originated from the way that agency remuneration appeared in accounts when paid commission by the media for advertising space bought.

Above-the-line activity has many uses and benefits:

o It is excellent at creating awareness. The large reach of TV advertising, as we have been using, means that almost all our target audience know about our offering.
o It is excellent at creating brand associations. This has been a weakness to date with little connection made between EasyPack and the well-known Trident brand. EasyPack has also neglected to create consumer recognition of quality and value for money which are now core parts of our proposition.
o It has complemented below-the-line activity by creating awareness of our sales promotion offers.

Below-the-line activity can be a valuable stimulus to increasing instore traffic – some marketing staff have commented that 'this will increase sales immediately'. Sales promotions attract people who are seeking the added value the sales promotion offers. And personalised direct marketing activity can prompt responses by appealing to targeted consumers, giving them reasons to visit our stores. These activities can be complemented by the personal selling activities of well-trained instore sales staff who can answer shoppers' questions and provide reassurance when needed. But sales promotions, in particular, have several disadvantages. Continued reliance on these detracts from the brand's image – there are overtones of 'cheapness' – an image we want to move away from, and of desperation to get business at any price. Discounts are also costly, and do not necessarily change long-term shopping patterns – they just incentivise people to 'buy now while it's cheap'.

Our objective for the future should be to change consumer attitudes to EasyPack. Attitudes can be described as the expression of an individual's feeling towards a product, service or organisation. Attitudes can be positive or negative and comprise three elements:

o *Cognitive* – what people know or understand about the product;
o *Affective* – what they feel about it;
o *Conative* – what they intend to do about it.

Our below-the-line activity has been good at influencing the conative aspects of behaviour – getting consumers to take action. But our long-term proposition should be about influencing:

o the cognitive aspects, so that people understand about our quality and reliability, and our value-for-money proposition; and
o the affective aspects, so they feel positive about, and confident in, our products, like them and feel proud to own them.

Attention is needed to changing consumer attitudes and we could pick from several ways to do this including:

o correcting misunderstanding, for example, about quality;
o building credibility, perhaps by gaining endorsements from popular home furnishing programmes and magazines;
o changing beliefs in competitor products, exploiting their weaknesses;

o creating new brand associations, for example, with images of style and comfort, maybe using celebrities;

o introducing new attributes, such as better instore facilities

o reviewing our brand name – are consumers confused by both the EasyPack and Trident names?

Whatever strategy we pursue it is essential that it is communicated effectively, and above-the-line activity is certain to play a key part in this process. Below-the-line activity can be used to encourage interest but should not be allowed to detract from our new branding.

5 Developing client – agency relationships

We will be working closely alongside the appointed agency so it is important that we have a good relationship with them. Good relationships mean that both sides will feel comfortable working together and this is likely to mean better outcomes, i.e. better campaigns. Energy will not be lost in disputes and infighting; instead everyone can concentrate on the task in hand. Here are some suggestions for developing strong relationships:

o *Treat the agency team as part of our marketing team*: the agency effectively becomes an extension of our own team. Treat them well, share information and make them feel valued.

o *Communicate*: every relationship depends upon communication. Share information, discuss problems, talk regularly, meet at agreed intervals.

o *Trust them*: we expect them to act professionally (and they expect us to). Trust them with important information, and trust that they will do their job well.

o *Explain how we work*: let them know our systems, processes, sign-off procedures and so on, so they are not left wondering, for example, why things are taking longer than expected.

o *Undertake regular reviews*: agency and client will meet at least monthly to discuss operational issues, but we should also meet, say, every quarter for a more strategic review. We should use this occasion to review how the agency/client relationship is working so that corrective action can be taken if needed.

o *Have a good contract in place*: a well-written agreed contract reduces the scope for misunderstanding. In particular a fair remuneration system needs to have been agreed.

o *Get to know each other personally*: work at developing personal relationships, talk about more than just work, and meet from time to time for social events.

6 Conclusion

This is an exciting time for EasyPack. Let us work together to make the most of it. Please let me know if any of the above is unclear.

Mini-Case 2: Car Recovery Market (June 2004, Question 1)

Check your answer

A good answer is likely to:

 ☑

In Part a, explain the characteristics of the different message types, i.e. typical features. ☐

In Part a, use examples based on information in the case (other relevant examples could also be used). ☐

Define 'attitude' and briefly explain its components. ☐

Suggest several ways to change attitudes using marketing communications. ☐

Take an evaluative approach to part c, i.e. assessing how far customer magazines can be useful for relationship building. ☐

Look at both the development *and* implementation of a mailing campaign. ☐

Build the answer around the car recovery services market. ☐

Use Report format (bearing in mind you work for an external agency). ☐

*   *   *   *   *

REPORT

To: DLR Marketing Director

From: Agency Account Manager

Date: XX/XX/XX

Re: Car Recovery Marketing Communications

1 Introduction

DLR has made a strong entry into the Car recovery market. Our agency intends to help DLR accelerate its growth in market share. With this in mind this report sets out some thoughts on key aspects of marketing communications for the future.

2 Characteristics of rational and emotional messages

Marketing communications messages can be categorised in two main ways – they can appeal to the target audience's rational thought processes, or they can appeal to their emotional side. These choices can be viewed as representing two ends of a spectrum – messages can also be composed which are part rational and part emotional.

Rational messages will tend to have the following characteristics:

- o They will tend to be information based. The emphasis will be on facts so that buyers can make decisions based on informed choices.
- o There will be a focus on product features, or the rational benefits of having those features such as time or money-saving.
- o The messages will tend to be constructed in a structured, ordered, logical way.
- o This form of message is usually used for complex decision-making when products are complicated and/or there is a lot at stake in terms of money, reputation and so on. Rational marketing communication messages are commonly used in business-to-business markets.

Marketing communication messages traditionally used in the Car recovery market have been very rational. They have been product focused, emphasising speed of service or the variety of services available including finance and legal services. Target consumers have ended up with a range of facts and information from which to compare alterative service offerings.

Emotional messages are oriented towards individuals' feelings. They attempt to engage with people, not by appealing to their logic, but by developing an emotional link between the product/service and the consumer. This can be very powerful. Appeals can be directed at a wide range of emotions including humour, fear, shock, pleasure and comfort.

In the 1990s the car recovery firms' messages turned towards more emotional appeals with an emphasis on driver safety and reassurance. They wanted to show that people could *feel* secure if they had a recovery service. Emotional messages can also appeal to individuals' aspirations: one RAC campaign showed how people can afford their 'dream' car – they could satisfy an emotional desire.

The recent Direct Line campaign with the strapline 'First we save you money, then we save you' had a combined appeal. The rational message was about the low cost of the service; but saving money has an emotional appeal too – people love a bargain. The promise to 'save you' is also an emotional appeal to individuals' security needs.

3 Changing attitudes towards recovery services

Attitudes can be defined as the expression of an individual's feeling towards a product, service or organisation. Attitudes may be positive or negative and, once formed, tend to be hard to change.

Attitudes comprise three components, as follows:

- o *Cognitive*: this is about what people understand or know about a product or service. This knowledge will be largely information based, for example, that a particular recovery service has the largest fleet of vehicles or the quickest response times.
- o *Affective*: this is how people feel about the subject. It may be a simple 'like' or 'dislike', or it may go deeper – 'it makes me feel secure' or 'they're good fun'.
- o *Conative*: this is about people's behaviour; how they intend to act based on their knowledge and feelings. A good DRTV campaign may make target consumers feel disposed to pick up the phone or go online to get more information or subscribe.

The above three components have been characterised as 'Learn, Feel, Do'.

A marketing communications campaign aimed at changing individuals' attitudes could target any of the above components or a combination of them. There are a number of techniques that can be used to attempt to persuade people to change attitudes; some of these are listed below.

- ○ *Correct misunderstanding*: it may be that potential buyers have a mistaken impression of one or more aspects of the service – that it is too expensive or slow, for example. This misunderstanding may be revealed by research. A campaign could be created to correct this view.
- ○ *Building credibility*: it may help to create more trust in the service. Emphasising size, strength or heritage may help. Or obtaining endorsement from a motoring magazine, TV programme or opinion leader could be beneficial.
- ○ *Changing consumer priorities*: maybe consumer are too focused on one aspect of the service, for example price, without realising the range of benefits it buys. A campaign could aim to shift consumers' focus onto these.
- ○ *Introduce new attributes*: the addition of new 'free' services might attract new buyers. Some car recovery services have now introduced a text message service, for example, to tell stranded motorists when the recovery vehicle is due to arrive.
- ○ *Change beliefs about competitors*: this is a very competitive market and each competitor has weaknesses. It is perfectly fair to run a campaign that compares DLR's areas of advantage against competitors' weaknesses.
- ○ *Introduce new brand associations*: again, celebrities could be used to build positive associations between the popular figure and the DLR brand. A different tack was taken by one car recovery brand which claimed they were the 'Fourth Emergency Service' – a direct association with the three essential emergency services.
- ○ *Change the service*: in some cases it may be necessary to radically alter the product or service itself (as Volkswagen did with Skoda cars when they bought the brand). Of course, any changes need to well communicated if the change is to yield any benefit.

To get these messages across to target consumers it may be necessary to find new ways to communicate them. A move from TV advertising to direct marketing creates a more direct appeal to individuals which may have more impact and relevance to them. Traditional TV is excellent at creating awareness and building brand values, thus developing cognitive and affective aspects of attitude which may be enough to prompt people to buy. But DRTV, and other direct mechanisms, are directed at influencing the conative aspect of attitude.

4 Customer magazines

Customer magazines have grown substantially in importance over the past decade as businesses have recognised that they are valuable in building relationships with customers. Good customer relationships are important to any business – customer who buy again and again provide a secure means of income, and often refer new buyers to the business. They also help keep costs down as retention costs are usually lower than the costs of acquiring new customers.

Magazines typically offer a number of articles likely to appeal to the target readership, as well as news, competitions, offers and celebrity features. They offer businesses a number of advantages for relationship building:

- ○ *Tailored content*: as we have seen with the RAC, different content can be offered to different segments of the membership. This means the content will be more relevant to the recipient than a general magazine's, strengthening the bond between customer and organisation.

- o *Added value*: magazines are usually offered free to selected customers; they are therefore getting added value from their membership which enhances their view of the benefits received.
- o *Extended life*: magazines can be kept, taken anywhere (maybe on a car journey or holiday) and articles even cut out and kept. This keeps the organisation in the customers' eye for longer than a newspaper advertisement, or even a direct mail letter, is likely to do. This ongoing stimulus helps to remind the customer about the business – valuable to keep the relationship going.
- o *Receptivity to messages*: customers, by definition, already have some form of relationship with the organisation. They are more willing to read and absorb messages received from a known organisation than from one that, for example, mails them out of the blue. They are therefore more likely to respond to offers and other invitations, helping to deepen the relationship.

Magazines, though, cannot be the sole method of relationship building. Not everyone has the time or inclination to read magazines so other means may be needed to engage with these customers. Magazines are also expensive to produce and distribute. It might only be financially justifiable to target higher value customers, with different communication methods needed for other segments. Businesses also need to research whether customers would prefer to see the money spent on magazines used in other ways, for example, to reduce membership costs or enhance other benefits.

5 Processes and procedures for a direct-mail campaign

Running an effective direct-mail campaign is a complex process. Based on our extensive experience, I thought it might be helpful to outline the steps to both develop and implement the campaign.

5.1 Development stage

- o *Planning* – The process starts with campaign planning. Target recipients will be identified, maybe from your company's own database or maybe from bought-in lists. (Prior interrogation of databases may be conducted, using sophisticated software, to identify suitable targets). The communications message needs to be agreed, as do campaign dates, budgets and availability of any other resources. If the mailing forms part of an integrated campaign then the other promotional activity needs to be identified and planned alongside.
- o *Design of creatives* – Both the artwork and copy needs to have a real impact on target individuals so that it gets noticed and read. Designing good material is critical, drawing on our skilled individuals using dedicated computer hardware and software. Proofs will need to be prepared and agreed materials signed off at the appropriate level of authority within DLR. Different versions of materials may be needed for different target segments.
- o *Arrange response-handling and fulfilment* – A campaign is intended to generate responses from recipients: this may be a phone call, the return of a reply slip or an online enquiry. Appropriate facilities need to be put in place to handle each possible reply mechanism, and to prepare for a range of responses. Call handlers will need scripts to deal with responses. A dedicated response handling service may be used.
- o *Print and Insert* – After designing, signed off material can then be printed and inserted using specialist machinery.

5.2 Implementation stage

○ *Mailing* – Mailing packs can then be posted. Discounted postage costs are usually available for bulk mailing, especially when pre-sorted by postcode.

○ *Handling of responses* – This should have been planned prior to implementation, so systems should slip into operation. Close liaison is required between response handlers and the organisation in case of any problems.

○ *Fulfilment* – This is where the respondent receives whatever they have requested – more information, membership application etc. Requests should be fulfilled quickly and accurately.

○ *Control Processes* – Every operation should have secure control processes in place. These have two functions. First, they enable activity to be monitored and corrective action taken if necessary. If, for example, response levels are higher than expected, additional resources need to be put into dealing with them. Secondly, data gathered during implementation becomes an input to planning the next campaign. This will enable better assessment of future responses rates, fulfilment packs needed and so on.

○ *Evaluation* – At the end of the campaign it should be evaluated. What did it cost? How much business did it generate? What was the cost per response, and cost per £ of business written? This enables evaluation of the effectiveness of the campaign and comparison with alternative media and promotional mechanisms.

6 Conclusion

I hope you have found these comments helpful. We look forward to working with you on future direct marketing campaigns.

Mini-Case 3: Burward's Night-Time Drink

Check your answer

A good answer is likely to:

☑

Define and/or explain 'message appeals', 'opinion formers', opinion leaders' 'celebrity endorsement', 'adaptation' and 'standardisation' and 'co-ordinated marketing communications mix'. ☐

Recognise that each part of the question asks the student to do two things (including 'select and justify' in Part d). ☐

Allocate more time to Parts c and d. ☐

Answer in the context of the situation faced by Burward's night-time drink. ☐

Use a Report format. ☐

* * * * *

REPORT

To: Marketing Director

From: Burward's Brand Manager

Date: XX/XX/XX

Re: Burward's Communications for the next two years

1 Introduction

Burward's has been a tremendously successful brand for decades and I am keen that we maintain this situation. However, we cannot be complacent and need to address the threats coming from a declining market and from supermarket own-brand products. With this in mind I have set out some thoughts on how we should be taking the brand forward over the next couple of years.

2 Message appeals and our options

'Message appeals' are about what basis we use to build our messages to consumers on. There are two basic choices – to use an emotional approach, or to use a rational one; we can also use a combination of the two. Both rational and emotional approaches can be effective in building brands.

Rational messages tend to be more product-oriented, focusing on its key features and attributes. These messages are usually information-based and appeal to the logical, reasoning side of consumers' thought processes. Rational messages are often used where there is 'high involvement', that is where a purchase has high relevance to an individual's needs and where there is high-perceived risk of one type or another. In these situations individuals are more likely to undertake an extensive information search as part of the buying process. Rational messages are commonly used in business-to-business marketing where buying decisions are often complex and open to scrutiny. But they are common in business-to-consumer situations too – credit card companies will stress low interest rates or product flexibility; Bird's Eye frozen foods stress the lack of additives in their products; and each Ronseal DIY product famously 'does exactly what it says on the tin'.

Emotion-based messages appeal to the heart rather than the head. Many different emotional approaches can be taken to attract our attention to, and liking for, the brand. Possible emotional platforms include humour, love, sex, fear, anger, comfort, excitement, fun, hope, security, patriotism and many more – the list is virtually endless.

Burward's messages so far have tended to emphasise emotional associations of the product. The calming images and warm colours stress the feelings of comfort, warmth and relaxation that we all like to feel before we settle down for the night. We want our audience to associate these positive feelings with using Burward's. There is a rational element to the message – that Burward's helps you sleep well – but no attempt is made to give this message extra credibility by using research or serious endorsement. One option is to continue with similar messages for the future but if we want to halt the slide in sales we should consider new options.

The new research showing that there is a scientific basis to our 'Burward's helps you sleep' message could be the basis for a rational-based campaign. For the first time we can make evidence-based claims for our brand's effectiveness. This is likely to appeal to any of the large numbers of people who suffer from sleep difficulties, but who are looking for something that is *proven* to be able to help sufferers.

Alternatively we could create an emotional message appeal. If we are planning to reach a younger market then the ability to enjoy life to the full is an attractive message. Communications could focus on people having fun or being fulfilled because they have had a good night's sleep after drinking Burward's.

Focusing on Burward's as a form of homeopathic remedy could be a message that sits somewhere between emotional and rational. On the rational side many people have an unshakable belief that homeopathic medicines work, believing these as effective as proven, tested pharmaceutical drugs. But homeopathy also has an emotional side – feeling good by using natural ingredients that 'in tune with' our body; there is no need for 'nasty' laboratory-created medicines.

I recommend that we undertake consumer research to identify what message appeals would be most effective with target consumers.

3 Opinion leaders, opinion formers and celebrity endorsement

Marketing communications can be given more impact by using opinion leaders and opinion formers to convey the message.

Opinion formers are experts in a relevant field; they are people who would be expected to have through knowledge of the subject area. Their opinions are generally well respected so their endorsement of a product or service gives high credibility to the message and helps reduce perceived risk. An example would be a motoring journalist recommending a particular model of car.

Opinion leaders are not necessarily experts in a field but they are people who are socially attractive to others and who are looked up to. Again, their opinions tend to be respected, adding credibility to a message and reducing perceived risk. A new upmarket restaurant might invite local business leaders and professionals to its opening night; the restaurant owners know that people in the diners' social network are likely to respect their opinion of the restaurant.

Opinion leaders and formers can be used to deliver messages directly. Burward's advisements, for example, could be given extra credibility by having a medically qualified person confirming the brand's sleep-enhancing benefits. Opinion formers and leaders are also very influential in word-of-mouth communications, helping to create awareness, shape attitudes and motivate purchase. A recommendation by the family general practitioner, or from a friend who is a parent and who is no longer stressed out by sleeplessness, can carry great weight.

Celebrity endorsement is a variation on the opinion leader/former theme. Here the aim is to create positive associations between the brand and someone who is well known to, and liked by, members of our target audience. Thus a top footballer may be an opinion former for a brand of boots, and also an opinion leader as a fashion icon.

Celebrity endorsement could be used by Burward's. This would have several benefits:

- It adds credibility to our message.
- It helps our message to stand out against competing communications.
- Provided we find a celebrity with the right attributes it will help to build positive brand associations for Burward's.

Celebrities could reinforce both rational and emotional message appeals. If the rational approach is preferred we can find well-known names who are respected in fact-based fields, such as TV presenters on science or medical programmes; they could endorse the research-based findings we have obtained. Alternatively we can find a celebrity who has a more general consumer appeal and show him/her drinking Burward's to relax, or enjoying life after a good night's sleep. Care would have to be taken to choose a celebrity who has appeal across the diverse consumer markets we want to target in the future.

4 Expansion into overseas markets

When an organisation chooses to promote its products in more than one country it must choose whether to adopt a policy of 'standardisation' or of 'adaptation' in relation to its marketing communications. Standardisation means that the basic marketing communications messages are undifferentiated between the different overseas markets the brand is targeting. Thus the presentation of the brand (e.g. packaging), the underlying brand values, and execution of the brand communications (e.g. advertisements) are all the same across the world. This offers many advantages:

- In an age of international travel and international media, consumers are often exposed to messages from outside their home country. Standardisation ensures that consumers get the same message wherever they are, which ensures consistency of understanding of the brand.
- It is not easy to develop strong communication ideas; if good ideas are found, why not used them as widely as possible?
- Standardisation avoids the duplication of effort which comes from designing a different campaign in each market. This saves direct costs as well as management time.

One danger of adopting a standardised approach is that references which associate the brand too much with one culture or another are stripped out, leaving communications that are bland and uninteresting.

Adaptation of communications means that messages are adapted for different markets. At its most extreme it means that a completely different communication strategy is used in every country in which the brand is sold. Adaptation is appropriate where:

o   Cultural differences between markets means that messages in one would not be appropriate in another, or that messages would have more appeal if expressed in a local context.
o   The positioning adopted for a product has already been adopted by a competitor in a particular market.
o   There are significant differences in other element of the marketing mix, especially in the product/service.

Communications can fall between these two extremes with, for example, a centrally created communications theme adopted overseas but with some adaptation for local tastes.

Burward's underlying message – that it helps you sleep better – is likely to have universal appeal; to this extent the message could be used across the world. Further, the contexts in which the product is likely to be used in northern Europe will be very similar to the UK which gives considerable scope for standardisation of messages. If, though, we want to take our product to Asia or Africa, then cultural differences mean that adaptation of our communications will be essential to reflect use in typical homes there.

There are a number of other factors companies need to consider when planning overseas communications:

o   *Language*: a) Which one to use? b) Obtaining appropriate translation – simple word-for-word translation is often inappropriate. c) Care must also be taken with correct use of body language.
o   *Advertising culture*: some cultures' 'advertising literacy' is more sophisticated than others; subtle messages that would work in one country may be lost on others.
o   *Culture and tradition*: these will influence both how designs, images, colours and so on are interpreted in different countries, and also how products are shown as being used in different places.
o   *Media availability*: there are international differences in the availability of media accepting advertising; some countries do not have commercial TV channels; others have a plethora of satellite cannels to choose from. We also need to take into account target consumers' ability to access the media we use, including whether they prefer local or national media.
o   *Legal restrictions*: we must make sure we do not breach any local laws. In particular any medical claims about Burward's could be closely scrutinised if there are laws concerning the promotion of medicines.
o   *The competitive position*: we need to understand who our competitors are and what their messages are, to ensure we differentiate ourselves.

5 A co-ordinated marketing communications mix for the UK

The marketing communications mix can be defined as a range of marketing communications tools which can be used individually or together, in a co-ordinated way, to achieve pre-determined objectives. The five tools are advertising, sales promotion, public relations, personal selling and direct marketing. Co-ordination is important to maximise both the effectiveness and efficiency of the communication campaign. It ensures that the tools are used in ways that support and complement each other; consumers receive consistent messages and this consistency reinforces the impact of the communications.

There is scope for Burward's to target a number of different audiences, and a different marketing communications mix will be appropriate for each sector.

5.1 Business to consumer

An important task for Burward's over the next two years is to build brand awareness amongst new target consumer segments. In addition we must develop whichever brand associations will be most effective and also ensure that buyers will recognise the product easily in-store. A well-constructed advertising campaign can help with all these tasks, provided we choose the appropriate media for our messages and target audience. Advertising can reach large audiences so is good for building awareness; strong visual cues can create lasting brand associations; and visual media also help develop pack recognition.

To persuade new users to adopt the product in the long term we need to get them to try it in the first place. Sales promotion will, therefore, be an important part of our strategy. Free samples and trial sizes need to be widely available. Discount or 'try-it-for-free' coupons will also encourage people to trial Burward's. Sachets could be pasted onto our advertisement pages in selected magazines.

There is plenty of scope for PR activity to boost awareness and create positive associations with our brand. The media are often keen to cover 'vox pop' surveys on subjects close to readers'/viewers'/listeners' hearts – sleep is a subject everyone cares about, so an interesting or quirky survey finding is sure to grab attention. We could also underline the serious side of our brand by publishing advice (in hard copy or on the Internet) for people having sleep difficulties. Much of our PR activity can be linked in with endorsement by our chosen celebrity.

Coupon responses can be used to gather customer information, and we can collect details from people visiting our website for sleep advice. It is also possible to buy lists of people who fit our target profiles. All these activities can be used to build a database from which to generate direct marketing activity. This could be via direct mail, or via e-mail (subject to legal requirements). Direct marketing enables us to create personalised communications and, in turn, to build long-term relationship with users.

5.2 Business to business

There is no point in having widespread consumer recognition and acceptance if they are unable to buy the product. Ensuring there is continued widespread availability of Burward's is critical. Personal selling is likely to be the most important tool here. Our sales team need to continue to develop and maintain strong relationships with retailers' buying teams to ensure that our products are stocked. They also need to persuade stores to accept appropriate point-of-sale promotional material to allocate extra shelf space and to accept discount vouchers etc. Retailers will need to be convinced that our consumer-focused 'pull' communications will mean a sales uplift and increased profits for them.

Personal selling activity should be supported by the other tools in the marketing mix; advertising and PR coverage in retail and marketing trade magazines could be effective here.

Finally, we should start targeting sectors such as hotels and long-haul airlines – places where people are looking to get a good night's sleep. Sachets of Burward's should be in every hotel room, for example. Again, personal selling supported by advertising and PR would be required. Direct marketing activity to smaller hotels and chains would leave our sales team free to concentrate on the major targets. Sales promotions in the form of free samples may be required to persuade these businesses to trial Burward's with their guests.

6 Conclusion

I believe this is an exciting time for Burward's; there is scope to develop the brand in several different directions. While I am keen to develop these ideas further it is important to remember that they must be implemented in a planned, controlled and co-ordinated way so that consumers are not confused, also ensuring we do not jeopardise our existing loyal customer base.

Mini-Case 4: Home Comforts

Check your answer

A good answer is likely to:

☑

Recognise there are two tasks in Part a – the differences and the impacts. ☐

Recognise that there are three tasks in Part b. ☐

Will explain or define 'push', 'pull', 'profile', 'relationship marketing', 'transactional marketing' and 'internal marketing'. ☐

Recognise there are three tasks in Part d. ☐

Answer from the perspective of a Marketing Manager in an organisation providing rented accommodation to executives. ☐

Use a Report format. ☐

*   *   *   *   *

REPORT

To: Michael Peat.

From: Marketing Manager

Date: XX/XX/XX

Marketing Communications for Home Comforts

1 Introduction

Home Comforts is at a critical point in its development. The informal, unplanned approach has seen the business through well to this point, but increasing competition means that we cannot rest on our laurels if we want to take advantage of the business opportunities available. The appropriate use of marketing communications could be very influential in enabling us to take the business forward from here, and this report looks at various aspects of these communications.

2 Business-to-business (B2B) vs. Business-to-consumer (B2C) buying

2.1 Differences between B2B and B2C buying

There are many differences between B2B buying and B2C buying. These can be summarised as follows:

- *Fewer buyers*: the size of the B2B market is smaller than for B2C. There are millions of consumers of, say, tins of beans but there are far fewer businesses, and even fewer who have a need for, and can afford, the facilities we offer.
- *Larger orders*: businesses tend to order goods or service in larger quantities than consumers do. They buy in bulk, or order services on behalf of several employees at once. This means that order values tend to be much larger too.
- *Complex decision-making unit (DMU)*: the consumer DMU tends to be fairly small and uncomplicated. Often one person plays all DMU member roles. In B2B there may be many people involved with the buying decision. In our case this could include an executive (the user), a booking agent (the buyer), the company MD (the decider), the Purchasing Department (gatekeeper and influencer), a Head Office department head (the initiator).
- *Product/service complexity*: business purchases tend to be more complex, with bespoke requirements for each order. This may extend to complex contract terms for payments, delivery of products, additional services and so on.
- *Process complexity and timescale*: the complexity of the DMU and product/service tends to make the whole buying process more complex, with more exchange of communication between interested parties. This tends to make the whole process last longer.
- *Use of company money*: this means the buyer is likely to be accountable to others for how he/she spends the company's cash.

2.2 Impacts on communications

The above have several communication impacts.

- Because of the various level of complexity, and the buyer's accountability, the customer needs good *information* to make an appropriate decision. This means that B2B communications tend to use rational rather than emotional messages. Our communications, then, must give plenty of *information* about properties, services available, contract terms and so on.
- Customised communications are essential. An advertisement, or even a brochure, is unlikely to be able to answer all of a customer's questions, or to recognise how the process/service needs to be tailored to individual company needs; this is why personal selling tends to be the dominant communications method in B2B markets.
- Communications need to be aimed at each DMU member; each will play a different part in the process and will have different requirements which communications must respond to.

3 Push, pull and profile strategies and a marketing communications mix

3.1 Push, pull and profile

These terms describe the different ways in which we can use our communications. I will look at each separately.

- o *Pull communications*: these are communications aimed at end-user customers, in our case the companies that require accommodation for their executives. This will give them the information to make an informed buying decision, and will explain how they can find out more or how to book. Our communications will need to recognise the requirements of different DMU members. We can also use these communications to differentiate ourselves from competitors, for example, by branding and stressing our points of competitive advantage such as favourable locations. Also, these pull communications can persuade customers to use us, either through the customer focus and polite persuasiveness of our staff or, where appropriate, through the offering of booking incentives.
- o *Push communications*: these are targeted at intermediaries – the people who stand between us and the customers. Push communications are always B2B, whereas pull communications can be B2B or B2C (though ours are only B2B). Accommodation booking agents and relocation agents are our most important intermediaries at present. Whilst they will be interested in finding out about attractive, appropriately priced accommodation to offer to *their* corporate customers, they will be looking for other things too: ease of administration and competitive commission will be important factors.
- o *Profile communications*: these do not focus on the product or service itself, but on the company. As such, these communications tend to target a wide range of stakeholders. The aim is to build up the 'profile' of the business; this creates awareness and a positive attitude, so that stakeholders will think favourably of the organisation. For example, newspaper coverage of the success of the business to date could lead more companies to seek out our services, and could also create favourable impressions with potential lenders or investors if we need to raise more capital for expansion.

I recommend that Home Comforts uses all these approaches in its communications. We clearly cannot afford to ignore either end-user businesses or intermediaries in our quest for bookings, particularly as competition increases. Profile communications provide a means of support for the push and pull communications, with positive messages about the business reaching customers and intermediaries, as well as building positive relations with other key stakeholders such as the media, financiers and suppliers of outsourced services.

3.2 A suitable marketing communications mix

With the above in mind I have set out below brief thoughts on the marketing communications mix that we could adopt to meet the various communications tasks.

The marketing communications mix is a range of marketing communications tools which can be used individually or together, in a co-ordinated way, to achieve pre-determined objectives. Co-ordination is important to maximise both the effectiveness and efficiency of the communication campaign.

- o *Advertising*: there is a role here, to reach both end-user customers and intermediaries. Good targeting will be important and we should research which publications DMU members use. The Financial Times, business pages of national daily newspapers and trade publications for the hotel and travel industry are likely to be relevant.

317

Messages will be information-based, stressing the advantages of our accommodation versus hotels.

o *Personal selling*: this will be very important to us. The small sales team should be tasked with targeting intermediaries; we should also try to reach purchasing departments of business that we have identified as being likely targets. The sales team can provide relevant information and build relationships with target personnel. It is important to remember that in our business *all* staff are, effectively, salespeople. Anyone who answers the phone to a customer needs to be friendly, efficient, informative etc., thus creating the right impression of our service offering.

o *Direct marketing*: this too will be very important. Given the number of businesses who, potentially, could use our service, and the variety of DMU members within those businesses, direct marketing – probably direct mail – could be a valuable tool. This, however, needs to be very carefully targeted to ensure it is used effectively. Over time e-mail can become an effective tool too, for those businesses who opt in to receiving information that way.

o *Public relations*: PR activity will help build our profile amongst financial backers and suppliers of outsourced services, as well as making us more generally known in the marketplace. A media contact plan needs to be developed. I suggest we also consider sponsorship of events likely to be attended by target end-users and intermediaries, e.g. arts and sports events.

o *Sales promotions*: given the quality of our offering we need to be careful not to offer sales promotions that devalue the image of our business. However it may be appropriate to offer incentives to intermediaries to start to promote our service, or, perhaps, as part of a customer retention scheme.

I should add that developing our Internet site is a critical development, enabling us to reach audiences worldwide. We can provide comprehensive information about each property, with still and video images, and use it to give booking facilities for end-users and intermediaries. It can also help our profile communications by giving company information, sponsorship details and so on.

4 The need for relationship marketing

Gronroos[1] has said that the purpose of relationship marketing 'is to identify and establish, maintain and enhance, and when necessary terminate relationships with customer [and other parties] so that the objectives regarding economic and other variables of all parties are met. This is achieved through a mutual exchange and fulfilment of promises'.

The concept of relationship marketing can be contrasted with that of transactional marketing; the principles are set out in the table below:

Transactional Marketing	Relationship Marketing
Focus on a single sale	Focus on an ongoing relationship
Focus on product features	Focus on meeting customer needs
One-off communication	Ongoing communication
Short-term activity	Long-term relationship
Focus on 'selling'	Focus on service, pre-, during- and post-sale
Limited commitment to meeting expectations	Strong commitment to meeting expectations
Quality – need for the product only	Quality – applies to every aspect of the business

[1] Service Management and Marketing (2004), John Wiley & Sons.

The aim of relationship marketing, then, is to build a long-term relationship with customers so that they buy from us not just once, but each time they have a need for our type of service. Not only does this mean repeat business but it is also likely to lead to word-of-mouth recommendation between business contacts – effectively promoting our accommodation service at no cost to us.

Customers will only want to have a relationship with an organisation if they believe it delivers quality and value. This means that every aspect of our proposition must reflect the quality of our service, and that every staff member must be committed to delivering quality. Only by constantly delivering to customer expectations can we develop the trust that is the foundation of a relationship. With this trust comes a commitment to work together to meet our mutual needs.

We need to use relationship-building techniques in several areas of our business in the future.

o *Customers*: we already have many satisfied customers, and we know that positive word-of-mouth referrals are leading to business for us. But we cannot take these business sources for granted, particularly as competition increases. Developing and maintaining these relationships must become a focus of our activity. Identifying and ensuring we meet these customers' needs is critical.

o *Intermediaries*: these present a way into many new customers. We need to develop relationships with key individuals within these intermediary businesses. The aim is to become the preferred supplier to them and to maintain that position. We also want them to be strong advocates of Home Comforts. Again, ensuring we do not disappoint them will be vital, to avoid damaging the relationship.

o *Other stakeholders*: the Six Markets Framework[2] identifies the six key stakeholder groups with whom businesses need to have good relations.

Figure 1 The six markets framework

We have already mentioned customers and influence markets (i.e. intermediaries and word-of-mouth referrals). The other groups would include:

o *Suppliers* – customers will judge us by the quality of service they receive from the outsourced service suppliers. We must, therefore, work in close co-operation with them.

o *Lenders* – (i.e. suppliers of capital) are also every important to enable us to fund existing and new leases – we need to retain their confidence.

[2] 'Relationship Marketing' – Christopher, Payne & Ballantyne. Elsevier Butterworth-Heinemann (2004).

Influence markets could include the media. Positive coverage can only help improve other relationships; negative stories could drive customers to seek new suppliers of accommodation services.

We aim to recruit several new staff members over the next year. Positive media reporting, together with good relationships with well-chosen recruitment agencies, will help us to reach staff of the calibre we need.

The final key market is the internal one, which I will consider in the next section.

5 Internal marketing

Internal marketing has been defined as 'the application of marketing internally, with pro-grammes of communication and guidance targeted at internal audiences to develop respon-siveness and a unified sense of purpose among employees.'[3]

I believe there is a need to adopt a more planned approach to internal marketing at Home Comforts for a number of reasons.

- *Expansion*: our informal approach to date has worked satisfactorily, but with the opening of several new offices and a large increase in staff we will not be able to rely on everyone getting the right messages at the right time.
- *Co-ordination*: with our own growth, and the rise of competition, it is important that we adopt a co-ordinated approach, with consistent presentation of the Home Comforts brand. Everyone needs to work to the same business agenda, and to deliver consistent quality standards.
- *Business opportunities*: by failing to take a more structured approach to internal com-munications we may be losing business opportunities. Prospective customers doing business with us in one location may have operations near another of our locations, but without sharing information effectively we may not capitalise on this.

Implementing a proper internal marketing programme will have several benefits:

- *Improved performance*: all staff will have an increased understanding of the business – its operations, plans, performance and so on. This will enable them to deal with enquiries more effectively, and to recognise opportunities and threats. There should also be increased efficiency – for example, by learning from other parts of the business and avoiding duplicate activity.
- *Brand consistency*: by standardising and sharing operational information we present a more co-ordinated and consistent image to our customers. They are likely to judge the performance of all offices by their experience of just one, so we need to get everyone working together to the same company objectives, plans, processes etc. achieve this.
- *Motivation*: better-informed staff tend to be more motivated. They do not feel ill equipped to do their job, and know where to go for more information. Good internal communications also help create more of a 'team' atmosphere, encouraging mutual support and co-operation and, again, improving motivation.

---

[3] 'Marketing Concepts and Strategies', Dibb, Simkin, Pride & Ferrell. (Houghton Mifflin (2001)

Some suitable methods for internal communication include:

- o *Intranet*: this gives everyone in the business access to relevant information whenever they need it. Plans, company news, property details, customer information, staff contacts, supplier details and so on can all be included, and ensures everyone has consistent information. Knowledge sharing should be encouraged on the Intranet.
- o *Team meetings*: these are a good opportunity for interactive communication within each office – staff not only hear information from management but can also ask questions, share information and put forward ideas.
- o *Conferences*: staff are dispersed across the country, but it would be valuable to bring them all together, say once per year. As well as an opportunity to learn from each other and share information, this helps to build internal relationships, developing motivation and teamwork.

PART B SUGGESTED ANSWERS

Answer 5
Direct marketing and advertising contrasted; Evaluation of the promotional mix; Word-of-mouth communication. (Dec. 2003, Question 2)

Check your answer

A good answer is likely to:

☑

Define or explain 'advertising' and 'direct marketing' ☐

Use appropriate criteria to compare these two tools; the 'Four Cs Framework' is recommended. ☐

Consider evaluation of all the elements of the promotional mix that might be relevant. ☐

Make recommendations in Part c. ☐

Answer from the perspective of an energy drinks brand, where there appears to be insufficient promotional attention paid to product purchase. ☐

Lay out the answer in 'Notes' format. ☐

* * * * *

NOTES

For: Meeting between Marketing Director and Advertising Agency

By: Marketing Manager

Date: XX/XX/XX

Re: Promotional activity for our 'Energiser' drinks brand

1 Introduction

I understand you are meeting with our advertising agency with a view to reviewing current promotional activity. Whilst much effort to date has gone into brand development there is scope to increase promotional efforts to encourage product purchase. With this in mind I have drafted the following notes.

2 Comparison of direct marketing and advertising

Advertising has been defined as 'a paid form of non-formal communication that is transmitted through mass media'.[4] Brassington and Pettitt define direct marketing (building on the American Direct Marketing Association's definition) as 'an interactive system of marketing which uses one or more advertising media to effect a measurable response at any location, forming a basis for creating and further developing an ongoing direct relationship between an organisation and its customers.'[5]

In order to compare these tools it would be helpful to use the criteria of the 'Four Cs Framework'.

2.1 Communication

As the above definition indicates advertising is a mass medium, aiming to reach large numbers of people. It is impossible for these mass-targeted messages to be different for each recipient so the message is standardised. Good direct marketing takes the very opposite approach – creating personalised messages developed around known information on target recipients. Direct marketing will aim to trigger an immediate response in its targets; whilst some advertising does too, its effect is often longer term, by helping to build brand association over time. This has been the focus of our promotions to date but we need to now get consumers to turn those positive brand associations into buying actions.

2.2 Credibility

Many advertisements are ignored by consumers; sometimes they are distrusted too. But there have been many admired campaigns developed by our competitors – many of the large-scale Pepsi and Coke campaigns with expensive sets and major stars have had high resonance; the quirky 'You've been Tango'ed' advertisements were also popular in the UK amongst a youth audience. Many people have a low opinion of direct marketing – especially junk mail. But well-targeted, relevant direct communications can be valued by recipients.

2.3 Costs

Advertising can be very expensive in absolute terms, especially big consumer campaigns that include TV activity. Costs arise from creative development, production and media buying. However, large numbers of people see these campaigns so the cost per contact can be very low. The costs of direct marketing campaigns depends greatly on the type of activity and the media used. A typical direct-mail pack costs around 50p per delivered item; and cheaper methods such as text messaging and e-mailing are now available.

---

[4] 'Marketing Communications'. Hughes & Fill. Elsevier Butterworth-Heinemann (2005).
[5] 'Principles of Marketing' (2003) Pearson Education Ltd.

2.4 Control

Direct mail can – and should – be very tightly targeted; advertising is less precise but we can still choose media that are preferred by our target audiences, for example cinema, music and sports magazines, and TV programmes popular with youth. We can end, or re-work, a direct marketing campaign at any time. Advertising is less flexible as long lead times and high production costs make it unsuitable for sudden changes.

3 Evaluation of the promotional mix

Evaluation of our use of the promotional tools is a very important aspect of promotional activity. Evaluation is about assessing the effectiveness of the activity. We do this to identify whether we have used our limited budget effectively and efficiently; this information then guides future decision-making and allocation of resources.

3.1 Advertising and brand building

So far our activity has focused largely on brand building, creating awareness and building brand associations and values. These can identify what percentage of consumers have heard of our brand. We can monitor this over time – using tracking studies – to see how this measure changes with our promotional activity. Recognition and recall survey research can also be used to identify how memorable our advertising has been, and whether target consumers have understood and remembered the key messages.

We can also identify what attitudes consumers have to the brand. Again this could be done using quantitative techniques but we can also use qualitative methods such as focus groups and depth interviews to understand more about people's opinions.

3.2 Direct marketing

Direct marketing offers the benefit of being able to measure directly the response rates to a campaign, whether it is click-through from an e-mail, reply to a text message or some other form of response to a letter. In turn, we can measure how many responses lead to actual sales: a comparison of costs and sales leads us to the 'cost per sale' which we can use to compare different campaigns.

3.3 Public relations

Effectiveness can, again, be measured quantitatively. We can count the number of media our brand was mentioned in, the reach of these media, the space/airtime obtained, whether favourable or not, and the Advertising Value Equivalent (AVE) – how much the equivalent amount of advertising would have cost.

3.4 Sales promotions

If we wish to change promotional focus to persuading consumers to purchase, then sales promotions may be very effective. We can conduct consumer audits to count sales volumes before, during and after promotional periods. If the promotion includes coupons or vouchers then we can count the number redeemed and, if they are coded, identify where they were obtained.

3.5 Personal selling

This is not relevant for consumer sales, but we do need to target retailers to ensure they are prepared for a rising demand because of a consumer campaign. Retail audits will allow us to see how much stock retailers are taking and shelf space allocated.

Many campaigns use several tools in a co-ordinated way so it is not always possible to separate out the effect of individual tools, for example a consumer may have been reminded about our drink via both PR and advertising. Thus some measures need to be applied to a campaign as a whole. In particular, if we want to boost sales, then measuring sales volumes is an essential task. We can break these figures down by, for example, region or distributor, to see where we are being most effective. Ultimately, any campaign must be evaluated by reference to the SMART objectives that were initially set for it, whether sales volumes or any other measure.

4 Word-of-mouth communications

Word-of-mouth (WOM) communications – when consumers tell others about their experience – are very valuable to any marketer; they are fast, inexpensive and have high credibility. I therefore recommend we use WOM in the following ways.

Word of mouth can be initiated because of interest in the product itself. Giving free samples encourages people to talk about their free drink to friends; maybe using it as a novel mixer with an alcoholic drink would create interest. We can also incentivise influential professionals – bar people for example – to recommend the drink to customers.

Word of mouth can also be initiated because of interest in the message, rather than the product. Unusual or amusing promotions gets people talking about it; perhaps a TV advertisement that everyone finds funny or 'building wraps' that cover vast areas in promotional messages. This technique extends to viral marketing where amusing (or, sometimes, indecent) marketing messages are circulated via e-mail. Sponsorships are another great way to get people to mention the product. Red Bull, who specialise in prompting WOM in all sorts of ways, sponsor adrenaline sports around the world. These sports have particular appeal in the youth/ young adult market which they are targeting; the drink's name is constantly mentioned by people attending or participating in these events.

Answer 6
Outdoor vs. print media; Sales promotion techniques; Relationship marketing vs. transaction marketing. (Dec.'03, Question 3)

Check your answer

A good answer is likely to:

☑

Look at both some advantages and disadvantages, of both outdoor and print media – four things in total. ☐

Consider four sales promotion techniques and look at how they work, not just describe them. ☐

Explain or define 'relationship marketing' and 'transaction marketing' ☐

Make some recommendations in Part c. ☐

Answer in the context of a national airline facing growing competition. ☐

Use Report format. ☐

* * * * *

REPORT

To: Marketing Communications Manager

From: Marketing Communications Assistant

Date: XX/XX/XX

Re: UK Airways Communications

1 Introduction

You are aware that the low-cost airlines are continuing to make inroads into our sales. This Report sets out information on how we can use marketing communications to improve our trading position.

2 The advantages and disadvantages of outdoor and print media

Media – sometimes called communication channels – are the methods we select to deliver messages to our target audiences. Examples of advertising media include print, broadcast, outdoor, cinema and ambient (or non-traditional) media. New media, such as the Internet and e-mail, are growing in importance.

2.1 Outdoor media

Outdoor media includes hoardings and posters, and are categorised by the Outdoor Advertising Association as either 'Roadside', 'Transport' or 'Retail/Point of Sale/Leisure'. Sizes range from small pavement-side flyers to building wraps covering whole buildings.

Outdoor advertising has several advantages. They are as follows:

- o It has high reach and frequency. Tens of thousands potential sites mean that campaigns can reach large sections of our target audiences, and these people are likely to see the advertisements more than once as they travel around.
- o It can be location-specific. We can place outdoor material where it is most likely to be seen by our targets, for example around transport hubs or along routes used by business commuters.
- o It can be high impact. Bold wording, eye-catching images and strong colours (such as Easyjet's bright orange) mean that good advertisements will be noticed. Some sites allow movement and 3D effects, which also attract attention.
- o Is relatively low cost compared to, say, TV advertising.

Disadvantages of outdoor advertising include:

- o It is generally seen by people on the move, which means that it is not particularly suitable for detailed messages.
- o There is a lot of outdoor 'clutter' with competing messages all around. Careful site selection is important.
- o It is hard to isolate the impact of our poster advertising for evaluation purposes against other forms of advertising.

2.2 Print media

Print advertising can be found in newspaper and magazines. Pros of using print media include:

- o It is a permanent record. Unlike posters, people can, for example, cut out and keep information on routes and fares for later reference.
- o We can target very specifically. For example, we can use the financial pages of newspapers to reach business travellers; tabloid newspapers and the regional press may be best for the leisure market; and we can use trade magazines to reach travel agents.
- o People are more likely to have time to take in and re-read, if necessary, more detailed messages.

But print media:

- o Suffers from clutter too, with many publications full of messages competing for attention, including those from rival airlines.
- o Have a short lifespan – Newspapers, in particular, are routinely discarded so we will need high impact treatments and repetition to make sure our messages get through.
- o Magazines typically have long lead times – They are not a good medium to advertise short-term promotional offers to fill unexpectedly empty seats.

3 Promotional techniques we could use

Sales promotions are tactical initiatives, integrated into a strategic framework, to prompt action by offering additional value to buyers. They are a persuasive tool and are sometimes termed 'sales accelerators'.

Technique we could use include:

- o *Frequent Flyer Schemes*. These incentivise flyers to remain loyal to our airline, rather than switching to lower cost operators. Flyers earn 'points' or 'miles' each time they travel with us. By flying regularly, these accumulate into worthwhile rewards – maybe free flights, or discounted goods and hotel accommodation. These schemes also enable us to gather information on flyers to improve our marketing activity.
- o *Discounted fares*. There are certain times of the year when bookings are lower on certain routes. We could discount prices at these times to attract more customers. These would bring our fares closer to our competitors, whilst continuing to offer the same full range of services our customers prefer.
- o *Intermediary incentive Schemes*. We still depend on intermediaries for a large proportion of our business, including high-street travel agents and online booking sites. We should introduce incentive schemes to motivate staff/sites to promote our routes rather than competitors'. Incentives could include enhanced commission, bonuses for reaching certain sales thresholds or free flights for achieving agreed targets.
- o *Buy-One-Get-One-Free (BOGOFs)*. BOGOFS are a form of two-for-one discount; but they also encourage flyers to take a partner/spouse/colleague on flights when they may not have otherwise done so. This introduces new customers to the superior benefits of our airline. An alternative form of BOGOF has been much promoted by United Airlines in recent years – buy one full-fare transatlantic ticket and get two free economy ones to anywhere – this encourages business travellers, for example, to use United for business travel to obtain the free economy tickets for leisure use.

4 Relationship marketing vs. transactional marketing

Gronroos (1994) said that relationship marketing (RM) is 'to establish maintain and enhance relationships with customers and other parties at a profit so that objectives of the parties involved are met. This is done by mutual exchange and fulfilment of promises'. This contrasts with transactional marketing where, instead of focusing on communication with *customers* and meeting their various needs, the focus is on simply making the sale. Whilst getting sales *is* vital, relationship marketing recognises this is better achieved through satisfying customers and getting them to re-buy or recommend. In relation to our business I have the following comments and recommendations:

- o *Customer Contact*. An important feature of RM is the need for ongoing customer contact. Communication does not stop at the sale, but becomes part of a continued process of two-way dialogue. Our airline should develop a communication programme which keeps us regularly in touch with our target customers, intermediaries etc., and encourages them to give us information, comments etc.
- o *Timescale*. By definition, transactionally focused businesses take a short-term view of customer relationships. In developing our programme we must recognise that our communications may last for years and span pre-, during- and post-sale communication. Our commitment of resources to meet the programme must be seen as an investment to build the business long term.

○ *Quality*. Transactionally focused businesses only need to do enough to create passable products that will satisfy short-term needs. To build relationships, everyone in the business must pull together to deliver ongoing quality and service both to internal and external customers. This will require a commitment to quality across every part of the business, impacting recruitment, training, recognition, rewards and so on. Consistent delivery of quality services will help build the trust and commitment of customers, which are essential to good relationships.

○ *Features vs. Value*. Short-term orientation means that the sales focus is on features of the product/service. We need to shift the focus to identifying and delivering in relation to what customers think is most important – in other words to delivering value. Different segments will have different views of what is 'value' but our communications and delivery must focus on these elements, which will reduce the attention given to competitors' low prices.

○ *Meeting customer expectations*. Relationship-focused businesses recognise that to build trust they must not disappoint customers (and other key audiences). We need a research programme to identify customer expectations to ensure we can meet them. Where we are exceeding expectations we should promote this message. We must also not promote what we cannot deliver – our communications must help to manage expectations.

5 Conclusion

I believe using marketing communications in the ways I have outlined can make a major contribution to improving our business operations. I hope you will agree to implementation of the recommendations made and look forward to discussing these more fully.

Answer 7
Business-to-business communications mix and roles; New media and digital technologies; Key account management (June'04, Question 2)

Check your answer

A good answer is likely to:

    ☑

Recognise two tasks in Part a.   ☐

Include evaluation of the mix elements, i.e. discuss their relative importance.   ☐

See the word 'role' as a cue to talk about the 'DRIP' elements (differentiate, remind and reassure, inform and persuade).   ☐

Explain or define 'new media' and 'personal selling'.   ☐

Show how new media *helps the sales team*; don't just discuss characteristics of the new media.   ☐

Explain or define 'key account management' and relate it to relationship building.   ☐

Answer from the perspective of a manufacturer of robotics equipment.   ☐

Lay out the answer in the form of a 'Notes'.   ☐

*   *   *   *   *

NOTES

For: Meeting with Marketing Colleagues

By: Marketing Communications Manager

Date: XX/XX/XX

Re: Improving the Effectiveness of Marketing communications in UK Robotics Ltd.

1 Introduction

I have recently attended a conference on marketing communications technology, and think there is much we can do to improve our use of these communications. I would like to share some thoughts with you on this today.

1.1 The business-to-business (B2B) marketing communications mix and the role of the activities

The marketing communications mix is the range of communications tools available for us to use to communicate with our stakeholders. The range comprises advertising, sales promotions, public relations, direct marketing and personal selling. It is important that the tools are used in a co-ordinated way to maximise their impact. I will evaluate each tool separately.

- o *Personal selling*: in B2B markets like ours, personal selling is usually the most important tool. Robotic equipment is very complex and each customer has unique requirements. A salesperson is able to identify each prospect's needs and to give tailored information and advice throughout the sales process from the initial enquiry to providing after-sales service. Salespeople can also use their persuasive and negotiating skills to secure deals, and build relationships with customers in the longer term. Personal selling is expensive though, and is not suitable for reaching large numbers of prospects.
- o *Direct marketing*: this is a valuable support tool for the sales team. Whilst the number of buyers of robotic equipment is limited, there are more potential customers than our sales team can reach. Direct marketing can be used to target named individuals in businesses, which are potential users of our equipment; this activity can generate sales leads to follow-up. Direct marketing can also be used to reach minor members of the decision-making units of target businesses, and helps maintain relationships with customers between sales calls.

Advertising and PR will probably play a lesser, but nevertheless important, role than the above tools.

- o *Advertising*: information-based advertising in carefully chosen business publications and trade directories will help broaden awareness of UK Robotics, so that we, at least, can get onto the list of potential suppliers for firms needing robotic equipment.
- o *PR*: can fulfil a similar role. Positive media coverage has a similar effect to advertising. In addition it can boost the firm's image and credibility by gaining third-party endorsement for what we do.

Sales promotions are likely to play only a limited role in our activity. Every sale will be negotiated separately. Large orders may warrant discounts and we may offer 'free' additional service such as training or other support. But on the whole customers expect to buy a package of products and services to meet exacting requirements and are less likely to be swayed by 'special deals'.

These tools will perform the following roles:

- o *To differentiate us from competitors*: to secure sales we must offer better value than competing firms. Salespeople will stress the advantages of our products and aftercare. Third-party endorsement in the media will indicate areas where we are superior.
- o *Remind and reassure*: regular, low-key advertising will keep us constantly in the eye of potential buyers. Direct marketing will help remind both prospects and existing customers of our services. The sales team's messages and our corporate literature, must reassure buyers, to minimise their perceived risk of our complex products.
- o *Inform*: buying robotics requires a very rational business process. Communications will be geared towards providing technical information, as well as information on pricing, technical support, training and so on, so buyers can make informed choices.
- o *Persuade*: communications may try to get people to take action, such as requesting information or buying a product. Salespeople often use persuasive techniques; incentives offered by sale promotions can also be very persuasive.

2 New media and digital technologies

New media comprises the digital technologies that enable us to communicate electronically with prospects and customers. Personal selling is an interpersonal communication method, involving face-to-face activities between representatives of two or more organisations, with the ultimate aim of securing or retaining business. New media can assist personal selling activities in several ways.

- o *The Internet*: this is one of our 'shop windows'. Organisations anywhere in the world can find out about us there, or seek more information about our products and associated services. Enquiries become 'leads' for our salespeople to follow up, reducing the amount of prospecting they have to do. Enquirers can give online information about their needs, so that the salesperson can better tailor their responses to customer's specific needs. Prospects and customers can often find answers to more straightforward questions on the website, giving them quick answers and avoiding using salespeople's time unnecessarily.
- o *Extranet*: we do not currently offer this facility but we should consider doing so. This is an Internet-based system offering access to general and bespoke information about our products and services to selected customers, suppliers, and distributors. They could access, for example, training manuals, detailed production specifications or details of the progress of their order. Offering this facility to selected customers underlines their importance to us, helping to build the sales relationship. There may also be a lock-in effect as customers learn to rely on our system and don't want the disruption of moving to competitors. Again, the system can also release the salesperson from dealing with routine enquiries.
- o *E-mail*: this has become a prime means of personalised correspondence between our sales team and their customers. It is convenient for customers and enables them to get quick answers from salespeople. A permanent record is created, often useful if customers want to refer back to technical information.
- o *Remote office technology*: our salespeople are often away from the office. Technology that gives them access to the Internet and e-mails remotely means that they always have up-to-date information and can respond to customer needs quickly and accurately. Personal organisers, linked to head office diary systems, mean that meetings can be arranged easily too.

3 Key account management and relationship building

Key account management (KAM) is about organisations offering enhanced resources to selected customers, for example those who give us most business. Allocating enhanced resources is a sign of commitment on our part to a customer. It also indicates that we trust them not to abuse these resources. Both trust and commitment are pre-requisites to relationship building.

There are a number of ways I would like to recommend that KAM be used to build relationships:

- o Developing trust: as well as showing we trust our key customers they must be able to trust us. That means delivering on promises, keeping them informed and dealing quickly and fairly with any problems.
- o *Technical support*: we can offer the extranet facility, help with training and R&D and enhanced after-sales support;
- o *Financial support*: key accounts appreciate, for example, more favourable credit terms or marketing support for their own communications activity.
- o *Service levels*: again the extranet can help here. We can also offer fast call-outs to deal with problems, a dedicated help-desk facility and quicker delivery times.
- o *Risk reduction*: offering, for example, initial free trial periods, superior guarantees and preventative maintenance contracts.

Having shared these thoughts with you, I would appreciate your views on what I have had to say.

**Answer 8
Channel conflict; Key account management; Transaction vs. relationship marketing, and the benefits of CRM systems.
(Dec.'04, Question 3)**

Check your answer

A good answer is likely to:

☑

In Part a explain 'conflict' and its importance, discuss its causes and discuss the value ☐
of marketing communications in resolving it.

Explain or define 'key accounts' and list the typical stages such an account goes through. ☐

Explain or define 'relationship marketing', 'transactional marketing', and 'CRM systems'. ☐

Identify potential benefits to Gregory FME of CRM systems. ☐

Answer from the perspective of a B2B agricultural machinery manufacturer. ☐

Lay out the answer in a suitable format (bear in mind you are a consultant). ☐

* * * * *

REPORT

To: Marketing Director

From: Marketing Consultant

Date: XX/XX/XX

Re: Gregory FME's Channel Relationships

1 Introduction

Thank you for your instruction to review Gregory FME's channel relationships. I am pleased to set out below my thoughts on some key aspects of these relationships and on the role of marketing communications in building and maintaining them.

2 Channel conflict and resolution of disagreements

Members of marketing channels normally need to work together to achieve their respective goals – the channel members are interdependent, so must co-operate. Channel conflicts occur when there is a breakdown in this pattern of co-operation, impairing the efficient operation of the channel.

2.1 Causes of conflict

There can be many causes of channel conflict; the most likely are:

o *Incompatible goals*. each channel member has different goals and sometimes different members' goals are incompatible. This problem may underlie many of the other causes of conflict and could, ultimately, make the channel relationship unsustainable.

o *Conflict over roles*. each channel member plays a different role, for example a wholesaler breaks bulk and develops assortments, while a retailer provides a means for products to reach end-users. Each channel member has expectations of how the others will perform their roles; failure to meet these expectations can cause conflict.

o *Disagreement over policy issues*. In this situation there are disagreements about strategic or operational decisions made by a channel member. Often these disagreements relate to areas such as profit margins or territories and may be triggered by differing objectives. In Gregory FME's case some channel members are upset about the firm's product ranges and promotional policies.

o *Different perceptions of reality*. this is about differing interpretations of the same thing.

o *Some organisations*. say traditional intermediaries – may see the Internet as a threat to their existence. Brand owners on the other hand, may see it as an exciting new way of building relationships with buyers. Each party is viewing the same thing from a different perspective.

o *Decision domain conflict*: this is disagreement over who has the right to make decisions. A retailer may argue that they are closer to the consumer and should control pricing and promotion; the manufacturer may argue that it is *their* brand and they should make these decisions.

2.2 Communications and conflict resolution

Communications can help resolve disagreements in many ways:

o Correcting misunderstanding: it may be that one or both parties misunderstand the other's position. Communication can ensure this is corrected.

o Lack of communication can be interpreted as a sign of not caring about the channel relationship. Equally, reinstatement of communications can demonstrate a willingness to repair relationships.

o Communications can help to build trust, for example, through sharing sensitive information. Trust is essential to strong relationships, so demonstrating this can help to mend fences.

o Reviewing communication policies: it may be that it is the communications themselves that have been the cause of the problem – their frequency, tone, speed or source, for example. This issue should be explored and steps taken to review the communications to eliminate the problem.

o Using *personal* communications: written communications can be viewed as impersonal. A visit, say from a salesperson or a senior manager, can demonstrate that a customer is valued; relationships can be developed, problem areas discussed and actions agreed in an amicable way.

3 Key accounts and the stages of key account relationships

Key account management is a specialist technique suppliers use in connection with personal selling. The technique targets strategically important customers and offers them additional support.

3.1 Characteristics of key accounts

The most common characteristic of key accounts and why they are strategically important is because they generate large business volumes for the supplier. But there may be other reasons – perhaps they offer a route into a new market; or, by paying them attention, it prevents one of the supplier's competitors from getting a foothold. Some of Gregory FME's customers may merit Key Account status – perhaps the main agricultural machinery trade retailers.

Key accounts will typically benefit from:

- o higher levels of technical support (e.g. training and access to specialist knowledge):
- o more personalised attention, from dedicated Key Account Managers;
- o improved financial terms, for example low-interest loans, extended credit periods, or shared marketing costs;
- o superior service, such as extranet facilities or just-in-time delivery;
- o risk reduction opportunities such as free demonstrations and improved guarantees.

3.2 Stages of KAM

A key account relationship may move through six stages:

- o *Pre-KAM*: when potential key accounts are being assessed; data on prospects is gathered by the supplier.
- o *Early-KAM*: tentative early relationship building, where trust is built and mutual understanding increased.
- o *Mid-KAM*: trust is well established; contacts operate at several levels between the two businesses.
- o *Partnership KAM*: a collaborative arrangement where there is a sole supplier relationship and joint problem-solving is undertaken.
- o *Synergistic KAM*: where the two organisations effectively form one, with joint board meetings and so on.
- o *Uncoupling KAM*: where both parties recognise that there is no further benefit in the relationship and separate amicably.

4 Relationship marketing

Gronroos[6] has said that the purpose of relationship marketing 'is to identify and establish, maintain and enhance, and when necessary terminate relationships with customer [and other parties] so that the objectives regarding economic and other variables of all parties are met. This is achieved through a mutual exchange and fulfilment of promises'.

---

[6] Service Management and Marketing (2004), John Wiley & Sons.

4.1 Transaction vs. relationship marketing

The concept of relationship marketing can be contrasted with that of transactional marketing where the focus is on simply making the next sale; the principles are set out in the table below:

Transactional Marketing	Relationship Marketing
Focus on a single sale	Focus on an ongoing relationship
Focus on product features	Focus on meeting customer needs
One-off communication	Ongoing communication
Short-term activity	Long-term relationship
Focus on 'selling'	Focus on service, pre-, during- and post-sale
Limited commitment to meeting expectations	Strong commitment to meeting expectations
Quality – need for the product only	Quality – applies to every aspect of the business.

Relationship marketing, then, aims to develop long-term relationships with customers built on a foundations of quality, service and customer satisfaction. Attention to individual needs is important which is where a CRM system can help. This can be defined as 'a computer database for collecting, storing, analysing and using information on customers to help build relationships with them.' A system can store details of:

o past transactions: value, frequency, product specifications and so on;
o details of named contacts, their positions, e-mail address and so on;
o past communications with these contacts including mailings sent and Visit Reports.

4.2 Benefits to Gregory FME

Creating such a system would offer Gregory FME many benefits:

o Gregory FME's staff would have immediate access (via computer) to information on every aspect of a customer's relationship; this means they can respond more quickly and accurately to customer needs, offering a more individual and valuable service.
o Potential key accounts could be identified more easily, and superior service offered.
o Improved service levels and personalised attention is likely to strengthen relationships with customers, thus improving retention levels.
o The improved service is also more likely to lead customers to recommending Gregory FME to their own contacts, so the business grows through referrals.
o Greater customer retention and more referrals means less marketing effort needs to be put into customer acquisition. This is likely to mean cost-savings.
o Stronger customer relationships means better mutual understanding; this is likely to lead to cost-savings as the two organisations collaborate on problem-solving, and adapt to each other's systems and processes.

Answer 9
Distribution channels – interdependence and independence direct marketing. (Dec. 2004, Question 2)

Check your answer

A good answer is likely to:

☑

Define and/or explain interdependence and independence, as well as identifying some points of comparison. ☐

Demonstrate understanding of the marketing mix, and mention all the tools of the mix. ☐

Be focused on the Internet as the direct marketing method this business will primarily use. ☐

Recognise this is a B2C organisation selling knitwear. ☐

Use Report format. ☐

* * * * *

REPORT

To: Managing Director

From: Marketing Director

Date: XX/XX/XX

Re: Distribution Channel strategy

1 Introduction

In view of our proposed move away from distribution of our knitwear via intermediaries towards a direct selling approach, this report sets out my views on various aspects of communications, to ensure we have thought through the relevant issues.

2 Independence and interdependence

Businesses can either distribute independently or interdependently. Interdependence means that we rely on others for our products to reach end-user customers – and the intermediaries rely on us for suitable products for them to sell; independence means that we go straight to end users without relying on intermediaries. In our case we are currently using wholesalers and retailers within our distribution chain, i.e. they and we are interdependent. Interdependence requires collaboration and co-operation between channel members. Trust and commitment are vital aspects of this arrangement; these factors enable good relationships to be established and maintained. However our strategy is to move to a position of independence, offering our products direct to users, mainly via the Internet.

Some advantages of interdependence include sharing risk (e.g. we do not have to hold all stocks) and having a wide range of outlets to reach diverse markets. Independence means that the responsibility for effective marketing communications activity falls wholly on us, but we are able to obtain retail rather than wholesale prices for our goods.

3 Impact on the marketing communications mix

The marketing communications mix can be defined as a range of marketing communications tools which can be used individually or together, in a co-ordinated way, to achieve pre-determined objectives. The five tools are advertising, sales promotion, public relations, personal selling and direct marketing.

To date, we have relied on both a push and a pull communications strategy.

3.1 Push strategy

A push strategy requires communications to go to intermediaries, persuading them to stock and advocate our products. The most important tool of the mix for this is personal selling, with our small sales team calling on, and building relations with, retailers and wholesalers. Clearly this need will disappear if we are to stop using intermediaries. Our personal selling activity to date has been supported by the use of other tools – occasional advertising and PR activity in trade magazines, and direct mail letters to appropriate intermediary DMU members. Sales promotion activity has been limited to occasional discounting to encourage intermediaries to take our surplus stocks. Again, these activities will become unnecessary.

3.2 Pull strategy

Pull communications will become the focus of our activity in the future. These are communications directed at end-user customers. Our only pull activity to date has been occasional advertisements in women's magazines and Sunday newspaper supplements to create awareness and brand recognition within our retailers' stores.

Direct marketing will become our main promotional tool. Our product will be offered via our website and customers will be able to order them direct from us. Information will be collected about buyers and we can use this for future communications. Information can also be collected about people who visit our site but do not buy, to keep them informed in the future about the company. We will need a good database but we must, however, take care to comply with the terms of 2003 Privacy and Electronic Communications Regulations regarding permission-based marketing, and also the Data Protection Act 1998.

Other online activity will be needed. We should investigate the use of banner advertisements on relevant websites, links from complementary sites and appearance on relevant search engine responses. We also need to encourage customers to use word-of-mouth communication – this is easy for them to do via e-mails but we need to incentivise them through some forms of sale promotion. The use of viral marketing, where interesting or amusing messages we create are passed from one e-mail user to another, should also be considered.

The role of our off-line communications will change. Their main role will be to drive traffic to our website. Advertising will have to prominently feature the web address and will be particularly important as we migrate to the direct route, so that loyal in-store buyers can continue to buy our brand. PR activity will also be needed to raise awareness of the brand and of where customers can buy it. Face-to-face personal selling will no longer be appropriate but, assuming we want to give customers the option to contact us by phone as well as via the Internet/e-mail, good interpersonal skills will be needed by call centre staff.

Whilst our primary direct marketing method will be online, we should also consider making paper-based communication an option. Some people may prefer to browse our products through a mail order catalogue; others may not have Internet access so need a paper catalogue. We should consider the costs and benefits of this option.

4 Impact on end-user customers

Moving to a direct approach will offer many advantages to our customers.

- They will be able to shop whenever and wherever they want. Our site will be available 24 hours per day and buyers will not need to be located near a store to choose and order products. We can also reach customers from abroad but, if we want this business, we need to ensure we are capable of fulfilling overseas orders and dealing with the extra costs and risks these might entail.
- Customer will also benefit from lower prices. Our distribution costs should fall dramatically, as we no longer have to pay intermediaries or move stock around the country. At least some of these cost-savings can be passed on to customers. Postage costs will be incurred but these should not outweigh the other savings.
- The customer buying experience will change dramatically. An attraction of our traditional distribution methods has been that shoppers can visit stores, browse our range, feel the quality and comfort, and try garments on for size. Browsing will be a very different experience online, so we need to design a website that makes the process as user-friendly as possible. Customers will no longer be able to feel or try on clothing; this means that we should expect returns if items do not fit or do not meet expectations for other reasons. We need to make the handling of returns as streamlined as possible to keep costs low and to make the buying process as low risk as possible for customers.
- Risk is an important issue to address in our communications. Customers will be asked to pay money upfront for garments they have not seen or worn – there will be high degrees of perceived performance, financial and social risk. Our communications need to reassure customers about these risks.

5 Conclusion

The proposed move to a direct strategy offer both opportunities and challenges. I look forward to discussing the points in the report with you in the near future.

Answer 10
Business-to-business CRM systems, New Media and Digital Technologies (June 2005, Question 2)

Check your answer

A good answer is likely to:

	☑
Define and/or explain 'CRM systems' and 'customer orientation'.	☐
Relate the above two concepts to each other.	☐
Recognise some problems of change management in Part b.	☐
Identify three issues in Part c, and relate them to the introduction of new media and digital technologies, not specifically the CRM systems.	☐
Recognise this is a B2B situation (the manufacture and service of heavy machinery).	☐
Use Notes format.	☐

* * * * *

NOTES

For: Meeting with Marketing colleagues

By: Marketing Manager

Date: XX/XX/XX

Re: Use of Customer Relationship Marketing within Liftright

1 Introduction

It is increasingly important for us to have good relationships with our customers. Large order sizes mean that every extra sale makes a big difference to our bottom line. And increasing foreign competition from low-cost manufacturers means that we are at increased risk of losing sales. At this meeting I would like to discuss how we can use Customer Relationship Marketing (CRM) systems to develop our business.

2 CRM systems and customer orientation

Gronroos[7] has said that the purpose of relationship marketing 'is to identify and establish, maintain and enhance, and when necessary terminate relationships with customer [and other parties] so that the objectives regarding economic and other variables of all parties are met. This is achieved

---

[7] Service Management and Marketing (2004), John Wiley & Sons.

through a mutual exchange and fulfilment of promises'. In other words relationship marketing is about finding and keeping profitable customers, by meeting their needs and expectations.

When businesses are trading in complex products like ours it is in their interests to build strong long-term relationships. They learn to understand each other's needs and to adapt their offerings accordingly. Risk – both financial and functional – is reduced for both businesses. As customer numbers grow, efficient systems help manage these relationships better. A CRM system can be defined as 'a computer database for collecting, storing, analysing and using information on customers to help build relationships with them'.

We can use a CRM system to store three main types of data:

- o Personal details, for example names of contacts, their job titles and address and phone information. Given the complexity of organisational decision-making units (DMU), there may be several people from one organisation on our database.
- o Transactions details, such as value, frequency, product type and specification.
- o Communications history, including what letters and literature were sent when, and appointments made.

A good CRM system will enable us to be far more customer focused i.e. to have a 'customer orientation'. This means that everything the business does stems from the desire to identify and satisfy the customer's needs. If we fail to put customers at the heart of what we do we are less likely to be satisfying them, and much less likely to be able to build relationships with them.

The information on the CRM system enables us to do several things.

First, it enables us to better understand our customers as a group. We can identify different segments – perhaps broken down by geographical location or product type – and trends in their needs or dislikes. This general information can inform product development and general marketing communication activity.

Secondly, the CRM system enables us to better understand individual customers. All the information about each customer is available for immediate access. We know their needs, buying patterns and contact history. By having this personalised information, relating to the company or DMU-member – we can tailor what we say and do to their requirements – in other words, adopt a customer orientation. In our case, having information on our CRM systems means that:

- o We know which products customers have so that we can ensure only appropriate service updates and technical information is sent.
- o We can ensure information is sent at the right time – for example when servicing is due.
- o Everyone in our organisation has access to the same information, which ensures consistency of service. Thus, whether it is sales staff accessing information in the field via their laptops, or service desk staff on the telephones, everyone has the correct and up-to-date information.
- o The right DMU members receive the right information through the right communication channel at the right time – ensuring our communications are specific to their needs.

3 Implementation problems

There are several potential problems that we might face when implementing a CRM system.

- o *Resistance to change.* The new system means two major internal changes – a move to a more customer oriented, relationship-based approach; and the development of new processes to operate an efficient system. Both of these could meet with resistance from staff. Staff may feel they have done a very good job up till now and feel 'accused' of not being sufficiently customer focused. A new system means new processes and procedures, and people often prefer the comfort of known, existing systems. We need to work hard to identify potential sources of resistance and to overcome them in a positive way. Identifying 'change champions' within the organisation would be a constructive early step. Careful attention needs to be paid to internal marketing and training issues.

○ *Technology-led systems.* The new system will be there to support a new *marketing* approach. Sometimes new CRM systems fail because the design, construction and implementation are led by IT technicians rather than by marketers. Whilst both IT and marketing need to work closely together on the project, we need to ensure that it is ultimately *customer needs* that drive it.

○ *Disruption to customers.* Creating a new system means taking up some staff's time to develop it. It will mean putting in place new data-gathering processes, and changing the way we currently do many things. There is a real risk in all this that service to existing and potential customers becomes disrupted. We must pay attention to maintaining service levels whilst developing the system.

○ *Managing expectations.* A new system will deliver real benefits, but they may take time to come in – the system may have to be implemented in phases and staff will take time to learn to get the best from it. We need to manage staff expectations that the system will not necessarily deliver benefits overnight; we also need to ensure that unreal expectations of enhanced service delivery are not created in customers' minds.

4 Issues in relation to new media and digital technology

An area where our business can improve is in the use of digital technologies. An effective Intranet can ensure our staff have better access to information to provide an efficient service. The Internet can make our products and services visible to many more potential buyers. And the development of a extranet facilities for key customers (and suppliers) can be an excellent way to demonstrate and enhance relationships. However, there are three important issues we need to address:

○ Again, fear of change will be an important issue. Many of our staff have been with us a long time and are not particularly computer literate. We need to carefully introduce them to the benefits of the different digital technologies, and to give them thorough training so they can use the technologies with confidence. They also need access to ongoing internal 'helpdesk' support to deal with queries.

○ Customer orientation: if we are to be a customer-oriented business then we must develop facilities that our customer will find useful. For the development of the website and extranet, we should undertake customer research to see what facilities they would like – this research itself shows customers they are valued and helps with relationship building. Equally, we must ask staff about what they want from an Intranet.

○ Maintenance: failing to provide up-to-date information can have a negative effect on customer and other web-users. Whilst the launch of extranet and other facilities is important, we must also ensure that systems are in place to keep all information on all platforms regularly updated. Failure to do so means that the system will lose credibility.

5 Conclusion

The development of new technologies presents exciting opportunities for communication and relationship building. However, we need to be alert to the challenges such technologies present. I look forward to working with you to implement these proposals.

Answer 11
Sales promotion and advertising compared; the B2B purchase decision process and relevant tools; B2B sales promotions. (June 2005, Question 4)

Check your answer

A good answer is likely to:

                                                    ☑

Define and/or explain sales promotion and advertising. ☐

Select an appropriate set of criteria; the 4Cs Framework is recommended. ☐

Compare and contrast the criteria; do not just list or do a table of tick-boxes. ☐

Use the B2B, not B2C, purchase decision process, and relate the answer to use of the *promotional tools*. ☐

Discuss three relevant types of B2B sales promotion and relate these to supporting the salesforce. ☐

Relate you answer to a medium-sized printing company with low conversion rates for leads. ☐

Use Notes format. ☐

*   *   *   *   *

NOTES

For: Meeting with Sales Promotion Co.

By: Marketing Manager

Date: XX/XX/XX

Re: Improving lead conversion rates

1 Introduction

Our company needs to address the problem of low conversion rates for leads. Improving conversion rates means higher sales, but we need to consider whether we need to undertake increased sales promotion activity to help our salesforce achieve the desired conversion rates.

2 Sales promotion and advertising compared

Fill[8] has described sales promotions as 'a range of tactical marketing techniques designed within a strategic marketing framework to add value to a product or service in order to achieve specific sales and marketing objectives'. He described advertising as 'a paid form of non-formal communication that is transmitted through mass media'. The 'Four Cs Framework' is a helpful model to enable comparison of these two elements of the promotional mix.

2.1 Communications

By definition advertising uses mass media, which means that a standardised message can reach a wide audience, for example all the businesses who need our specialist services. Tailoring of the message does not come until our salesforce becomes involved. Similarly, sales promotions – such as bulk order discounts – are often undifferentiated amongst all those who may be attracted to buy and who see information on offers in advertisements or flyers. Advertising is not a particularly interactive medium – the information is often just physically or mentally stored until needed later. However sales promotions are a persuasive tool – they are sometimes termed 'sales accelerators' because they incentivise people to act to obtain the added value on offer.

2.2 Credibility

Advertising has limited credibility. Advertisements are inevitably one-sided, putting the company's best face forward. The target audience is often left thinking 'But what haven't they told us?' though this effect can be reduced as we build trust with our customers and develop a positive reputation generally. Sales promotions are also sometimes treated with suspicion – 'Is there a catch?'. There is also a risk that too many sales promotions, or promotions of the wrong sort, devalue our brand image – they sometimes suggest desperation to get business.

2.3 Costs

The absolute costs of advertising can be high – particularly for businesses using broadcast media or high-circulation print media. Costs are not as great for the local print media and selected specialist business publications that we use but, given the relatively small numbers of potential customers, the cost per contact (i.e. absolute cost divided by total readership of our target audience) can be quite high. There is also a real problem that numerous people will miss or ignore our message so that wastage is high. Sales promotions can be costly: there are the costs of the extra value and also the associated promotional costs, for example literature. We can, however control the impact of these costs by limiting offers to our higher margin services.

2.4 Control

We can be selective in which audiences we target with both our sale promotions and advertising by careful selection of media used to publicise our message. If we want, sales promotions can be restricted to selected customers or prospects, and personalised using direct mail. We need to take care to put limits on the promotions, for example their duration and value to ensure

---

[8] 'Marketing Communications' (2005). Elsevier Butterworth-Heinemann.

we do not compromise the business. Advertising can be stopped at by time, subject to lead times of the media used.

3 The business-to-business (B2B) Purchase Decision process

The B2B Purchase Decisions process consists of six steps, and the different promotional tools can help at various stages.

3.1 Need or problem recognition

This is when the target decision-making unit (DMU) members identify a difference between their business's current state and desired state. External cues can prompt this recognition – for example target businesses may become aware of a new printing service available, through our advertising, appropriately targeted direct marketing, a salesforce member's visit, or a piece of editorial in a trade magazine.

3.2 Need description/product specification

DMU members will need to decide on the business's exact requirements – this may take the form of a formal product specification. Company promotional literature can act as a prompt for criteria to specify; and a salesperson's advice can also help to narrow down requirements.

3.3 Supplier search

The business then needs to identify which businesses can meet their need. It is essential that our business is considered by the relevant DMU members at this stage. They may seek suppliers though trade directories or classified listing publications – ensuring we have entries, and maybe advertising, in these is essential. Being well known, though PR and sales contacts will also help. Word-of-mouth recommendation is important so having good relationships with customers is important. Reaching DMU members through direct marketing will also help.

3.4 Evaluation of proposals and supplier selection

The salesperson will play a key role here by ensuring that the proposal we put forward will meet customer needs, based on the salespersons' knowledge. We hope our proposal will stand up on its own but extra influence can be exercised through the salesperson's persuasive skills, or the added incentive of some kind of sales promotional offer. This might be time-limited to persuade quick action, cutting out competitors.

3.5 Purchase order/contract specification

Our sales team can, again, help here to ensure this is correctly worded and meets both parties' needs.

3.6 Performance evaluation

Here the buyer will be assessing the service against their expectations. Promotional literature, the content of advertisements and direct marketing material, and salesforce statements will all have contributed to these expectations so we must ensure we do not over-promise before the sale. Proactive customer service, through salesforce calls and relevant, targeted direct mail – for example information about after-care services – can all help to improve customer satisfaction at this stage.

4 Sales promotion methods

Our immediate need is to assist our salesforce to convert leads into sales. The following methods could help.

4.1 Bulk-order discounts

These incentivise customers to place large orders in return for benefiting from reduced prices. These would help our sale force by making our services look more attractive for bigger orders. We could price the discounts to undercut the competitors who we know our prospects are using, thus giving our salespeople a reason to make a sales call/visit.

4.2 Buy one get one free

To incentivise business customers to try us for the first time we could offer them two jobs for the price of one, for example making the smaller job free. We could restrict this offer to non-customers who our salesforce have identified as good prospects and place an upper financial limit on it to ensure that the cost is kept reasonable. This offer might act as a loss leader – we make little or no profit in the short term but use it to build longer-term relationships.

4.3 Free merchandise

Many of our customer use the items we print to put on display or give to *their* customers, for example promotional and information literature. We could offer free merchandise to assist these customers, for example display racks or leaflet dispensers. This would help improve the professionalism of customers' promotional efforts.

These methods would offer many benefits to the salesforce including:

- o incentivising prospects to try our business;
- o helping to build relationships with customers by offering added value and service;
- o reducing perceived financial risk for customers by them giving more for their money.

Answer 12
Budgets, Agency remuneration, Campaign evaluation (Dec. 2005, Question 3)

Check your answer

A good answer is likely to:

☑

Define and/or explain 'budgets'. ☐

Have three relevant methods in Part a; two in b; four in c. ☐

Give a recommendation and justification in Part a. ☐

Discuss the techniques for Part a, i.e. consider pros and cons. ☐

Explain the need to determine effectiveness in Part c, i.e. indicate how useful they are. ☐

Evaluate the four methods in part c. ☐

Recognise your role as Account Executive in a successful advertising agency. ☐

Use Report format. ☐

*   *   *   *   *

REPORT

To: A. Client

From: Account Exec.

Date: XX/XX/XX

Re: Successful Communications Campaigns

1 Introduction

As your Account Executive I thought it might be helpful to give you some information on subjects that our clients often ask about at the start of our relationship. I hope this information will enable us to jointly deliver effective future campaigns.

2 Marketing communications budgets

The communications budget is the amount we plan to spend on marketing communications in a particular period. There are many ways to set budgets; here are three that might be most appropriate for your business:

2.1 Percentage of sales methods

This links the communications budget to the business' sales levels. For example, if sales are £1 million, and the percentage figure is 5, then the communications budget would be £50 000. The 'sales' figure used may be historical, based on last year's sales, or projected, using a forecast. The percentage used typically varies with the market sector and the level of competition. Business-to-business markets usually have lower percentages than highly competitive FMCG markets. One advantage of this method is its simplicity of calculation. Further, the percentage figure can be set at a level that is likely to be affordable – important for any method selected. The big disadvantage is that it can mean the tail is wagging the dog. If, for example, sales fall this means a consequent fall in the communications budget, when just the opposite may be needed. Also, there is no specific link to business objectives.

2.2 'Objective and task' method

This is a three-step process: determine the communications objectives; identify what communications tasks are needed to achieve them; determine the cost of those tasks. The sum of these costs is the required budget. Because the overall budget starts with a series of separate figures this is sometimes called a 'bottom–up' approach (as opposed to a 'top–down' one). This method is clearly linked to communication objectives, and requires careful evaluation of campaign needs which is good business practice. However, there may be a temptation to over-estimate costs to ensure objectives are met, and the final total budget may be unrealistic, needing to be reduced to be affordable.

2.3 Matching the competition

If the organisation's messages are to be heard amongst competitors' clutter it may be appropriate to aim to match their spending on communications. However this method takes no account of affordability, or whether you and they have matching objectives. It may also be difficult to obtain up-to-date data on competitor spend, particularly for below-the-line activity. A more sophisticated variant of this method is using 'share of voice' where advertising spending is linked to market share.

The appropriate method for your business will require individual discussion. However, in general, I would recommend the 'Objective and task' method as it is the best way to ensure that your campaign objectives are achieved.

3 Agency remuneration

This will already have been discussed during the pitching process. However it may be helpful to outline a couple of key methods we use:

3.1 Agency commission

Many advertising agencies receive commission from the media with whom the advertising is placed, rather than from clients (this payment method gave rise to the phrase 'above the line' for advertising activity, to distinguish it in accounts from 'below-the–line' activity paid for directly by clients). The percentage – 12 per cent in our case – is applied to the cost of the print space or broadcast airtime purchased.

3.2 Payment by results

Some of our clients prefer to operate on a 'payment by results' basis. Here our remuneration, or at least part of it, is linked to the effectiveness of the activity we undertake. This performance-related method can offer additional incentives to agencies to create effective campaigns, and penalises under-performance. It is essential to set clear and measurable objectives if this method is used. It must also be fair; for example an agency must not be penalised if a salesforce is ineffective in following up leads generated from an effective advertising campaign.

4 Campaign evaluation methods

Finally, I want to turn to effective methods for evaluating the campaigns we produce. It is essential to judge effectiveness of campaigns so that we can assess whether our money was well spent, and learn for the future. We use the following methods:

- ○ *Objectives* – The most important effectiveness criterion is whether the campaign met its objectives. These need to be carefully thought through during initial planning, perhaps based on research findings. All objectives must be SMART (specific, measurable, agreed, realistic and timed). Poor objectives setting is likely to lead to an ineffective campaign and wasted money.
- ○ *Pre-testing* – Before a campaign is launched we test unfinished creative materials on a sample of our target audience, usually in focus groups. The aim is to ensure that they understand the communication and 'get' the message. Their views on both the copy (the text) and the visual elements (illustration and design) will be considered. This is a valuable early check of effectiveness, allowing the advertisements to be reworked if necessary, but does not guarantee that the group's views represent the wider market.
- ○ Recognition and recall test are often used as a form of post-testing. In the former, members of the target audience are asked if they recognise an advertisement and, if so, how much they can remember about it, testing their ability to process information from the communication. In recall tests, which may be 'prompted' or 'spontaneous', respondents are asked to remember which advertisements they have seen recently. This helps identify how much impact a particular campaign has had.

   ○ *Enquiry tests* – These measure the number of responses to an advertisement, for example requests for more information or for a follow-up visit from a salesperson. This is a simple measure but, to be most effective, advertisements in different media need to be coded to identify which source the enquirer used. This method is only relevant where the aim of the advertisement is to prompt an immediate response – but many advertisement are aimed at creating awareness or brand-building where this test is not relevant.

5 Conclusion

I hope this information will prove of use to you and look forward to discussing these issues in more detail at out next meeting.

Answer 13
Account management and client briefs; Relationship marketing
(Specimen paper, Question 5)

Check your answer

A good answer is likely to:

☑

Fully explain about the account manager's role. ☐

Look at the 'nature' and 'characteristics' of the Client Brief, i.e. what it is and what it comprises. ☐

Explain or define 'relationship marketing'. ☐

Evaluate the importance of relationship marketing, i.e. consider how important it is and why. ☐

Answer from the perspective of an agency Account Manager, pitching for business with a distributor of personal electronic products. Note that the question mentions international business. ☐

Lay out the answer in the form of a 'Document Pack'. ☐

* * * * *

DOCUMENT PACK

For: Marketing Team, PEN company

From: Account Manager, Ace-UK Advertising agency

Date: XX/XX/XX

Re: Ace-UK, and how we can Help Successfully Launch the new Personal Organiser

Document 1: The Account Manager's role and the client brief

This document sets out information on my role as Account Manager, and on the brief we would invite you to submit to give us information on the task that you wish to use our services for.

1.1 The Account Manager

The Account Manager plays a critical role in the relationship between an agency and its client, acting as the main link between the two.

The Account Manager needs to thoroughly understand the client's needs, through discussion, review of documentation, evaluation of research and so on. The Account Manager's principal jobs are to then relay relevant information to people within the agency to ensure that they deliver to customer requirements, and to keep the client informed about progress. The Account Manager is thus an intermediary or bridge between the two parties, constantly liasing between them. Within the agency itself the Account Manager plays a co-ordinating role, pulling together the efforts of the rest of the agency staff. In a large agency this might include the Creative, Media, Research and Production teams. An Account Manager will also contribute to development of the campaign through assisting with planning, idea generation, research and so on.

The Account Manager will be the day-to-day point of contact between the client and the agency. He or she will typically report to the Account Director who takes less of a 'hands-on' approach but who monitors progress and gives guidance. Meetings between the agency and the client will usually be written up by the Account Manager in a Contact Report, with a copy provided for each party.

1.2 The client brief

To enable us to come up with firm proposals to successfully launch a new product it is necessary to thoroughly understand the circumstances of the launch, for example the nature of the product and the market it is aimed at. This information is contained within a 'brief'. The brief is a written document provided by the client, though it is usually also discussed at a joint meeting to ensure it is thoroughly understood.

Most agencies have their own proforma for a brief. Ours has the following headings (I have included some notes on the types of information that should be included under each heading):

- o *Client information*: name, address, contact names and details.
- o *Client background*: ownership, areas of business, time in business, brands owned, corporate image.
- o *Product/service information*: the product/service to be promoted; its key features, benefits and unique selling propositions (USPs); packaging and presentation; pricing.
- o *Target audience*: who is the product/service aimed at (we ask clients to be as specific as possible here); how it is to be used by them.
- o *The market for the product/service* – size, life cycle stage, distribution, competition.
- o *Campaign objectives*: the more SMART (specific, measurable, agreed, realistic, time-bound), the better; the objectives might relate to sales, awareness, attitudes and so on.
- o *Media*: previous campaigns and media used, media preferences (if any).
- o *Budget*: final costs will need to include creative work, production and media spend.
- o *Timescales*: both when the campaign is to start and its duration.
- o *Other requirements*: for example, mandatory inclusions.

A good brief gives the agency all the information it needs to create a campaign, and also sets out what is expected from the agency i.e. to deliver to certain budgets, timescales and objectives.

Document 2: Relationship marketing

Gronroos[9] has said that the purpose of relationship marketing 'is to identify and establish, maintain and enhance, and when necessary terminate relationships with customer [and other parties] so that the objectives regarding economic and other variables of all parties are met. This is achieved through a mutual exchange and fulfilment of promises'. In other words relationship marketing is about finding and keeping profitable customers, by meeting their needs and expectations.

---

[9] Service Management and Marketing (2004), John Wiley & Sons.

At Ace-UK agency we believe that having good relationships with our clients is fundamental to achieving both parties' objectives. In relation to the campaign being developed we effectively need to become part of your company's marketing team and, just as within any effective team, we are keen to benefit from shared ideas and information and to work in co-operative way.

Relationship marketing can be contrasted with transactional marketing. With the latter the focus of marketing activity is on simply achieving 'the sale' (or, in the context of agency work, getting the contract to create a single campaign). No attempt is made to turn this short-term focus into a longer-term relationship. The focus of delivery is simply 'doing the job', probably to the minimum specification to get by, so that effort can quickly be turned to finding the *next* sale. There is little attention paid to quality and customer service; indeed, quality only has to be delivered by the people directly responsible for the service or product – scant attention is paid to quality delivery by, for example, reception, back office or after-sales staff.

With relationship marketing, however, the focus is on achieving long-term relationships built on delivering real value to our clients; what constitutes that value is determined by them, as every client has different needs. Customer satisfaction is critical and it means that everyone in our business has to focus on delivering quality, whether to internal or external customers. Only by delivering to customer expectations can trust be developed, which is a foundation for mutual commitment and long-term relationships.

Having strong relationships with customers should be important to all businesses. From our point of view it means that customers provide an ongoing source of income and profits. We can spend time and money working on existing accounts rather than trying to chase new business – finding new customers is notoriously more expensive than looking after existing ones. We also hope that, if we do a good job for you, you will recommend us to your own business contacts so that our business will grow by word-of-mouth referrals. From the client's perspective, a relationships orientation means that the agency is focused on delivering exactly what *you* want, meeting *your* needs. And by working with you in the long term we get to know your organisation, your markets and your products better so that we can continually improve our service. Thus as you grow your international markets for the personal organiser we can be there to support you all the way. Thus, by building good relationships, as Gronroos says, the objectives of all parties are met.

Answer 14
Customer retention; Disintermediation and reintermediation;
A marketing communications mix for the launch of new services

Check your answer

A good answer is likely to:

 ☑

Define or explain 'customer retention' and say why it is important. ☐

Identify four methods of customer retention (be practical rather than theoretical) ☐

In Part b define the two words, relating it and the rest of the answer to the travel industry. ☐

Explain the term 'co-ordinated marketing communications mix' ☐

Justify as well as suggest a co-ordinated marketing communications mix. ☐

Answer in the context of a ferry operator. ☐

Use Notes format. ☐

*   *   *   *   *

NOTES

For: Meeting with Marketing Communications Assistant

By: Marketing Communications Manager

Date: XX/XX/XX

Re: TransChannel's Marketing Communications

1 Introduction

TransChannel operates in a highly competitive and fast-changing market. The issues to be discussed are all very relevant to our current operations.

2 Customer retention and retention methods

Customer retention is about keeping, or retaining, customers. It means that after they have bought from our firm they buy from us again next time they have a similar need, rather than using competitors. Our customers are freight operators, and also business and leisure passengers; we want them to use us every time they want to cross to Europe.

Retaining customers is very important for any business, for several reasons:

- o Returning customers provide a steady source of continuing income for the business. This offers direct financially benefits, and also makes planning easier.
- o Seeking new customer is expensive, particularly in terms of marketing communications costs. The more we can retain existing customers, the more we can reduce these acquisition costs.
- o Retained customers tend to be happy customers, which means they are likely to recommend us to other firms/individuals. Word-of-mouth communications is a very effective form of endorsement.
- o Loyal customers tend to spend more money as the relationship develops; their trust grows and they learn more about the company's services.

Retention rates measure the percentage of customers who are buying from us again. We aim constantly to increase retention rates. Here are four ways that companies can increase retention rates:

- o *Develop and use a customer database.* a database can tell us who has bought before and who has not. We can use it to 'profile' our customer (i.e. find out their characteristics) so that we can try to find more, similar customers. We can also use it to manage communication programmes – see next.
- o *Introduce a customer communication programme.* a managed programme of communications can help to build relationships with customers. Ongoing communication keeps our name in front of them regularly so that they do not forget about our services. We can use the programme to keep them informed about new services and to offer them discounts and deals.
- o *Develop a loyalty programme.* a loyalty scheme rewards regular users of our services. They accumulate points each time they travel with us; over time these points can be turned into free trips or vouchers to spend on board. These schemes incentivise people to use us each time they travel to Europe.
- o *Emphasise the importance of customer service to all staff.* every member of staff, whether on land or on board, can influence the customer's perception of our service. Training is needed to underline the importance of retention, and to remind staff of the quality of service customers expect.

3 Disintermediation and reintermediation

The term 'disintermediation' relates to a move by a company to remove intermediaries from their distribution channel and sell direct to the public. Technology has made disintermediation easier, so that people can book tickets by phone or over the Internet directly with the travel operator, rather than having to go to a high-street travel agent. We offer this option.

'Reintermediation' refers to the development of new forms of intermediary to replace the traditional ones. Reintermediation is found on the Internet where web-only businesses operate sites that bring together suppliers of flights, hotels etc. and consumers seeking these services in an online exchange. They are effectively brokers of travel services.

A company thinking of disintermediation needs to consider:

○ *The effect on intermediaries*: if the company is running an operation in parallel to an intermediated operation the intermediaries may be upset; they stand to lose business and some may refuse to continue promoting the company's services.
○ *Customer enquiries*: the company will need an efficient method of handling enquiries. Customers of the disintermediated channel will no longer be able to direct their questions to intermediaries.
○ *Service promotion*: intermediaries helped the company in promoting its services and advocating it to customers. New marketing communications will be needed to promote the new direct booking service.

4 A co-ordinated marketing communications mix for a launch

The marketing communications mix can be defined as a range of marketing communications tools which can be used individually or together, in a co-ordinated way, to achieve predetermined objectives. The five tools are advertising, sales promotion, public relations, personal selling and direct marketing. Co-ordination means that the tools support and complement each other, and do not offer conflicting messages.

The new ferry services will be available for booking both through intermediaries and directly. This means that a launch campaign needs to target both travel agents and travellers themselves.

Each element of the mix will be considered separately.

4.1 Advertising

Creating awareness of our services amongst the travelling public will be a critical first step: buyers can then choose whether to book online or use an agent. Advertising is an excellent promotional tool for creating awareness. If used appropriately it can reach large numbers of people; repetition of the ads in selected media, in a co-ordinated way, will help the message to sink in. Media should be selected that will be seen by our target audience – we should identify their characteristics from research.

We should also target large freight operators. They are big users of cross-channel services and the changes can offer them real benefits. Again, we should identify appropriate freight trade magazines.

As well as targeting users we should also target the travel trade. Intermediaries need to know about the forthcoming services so that they are able to handle customer enquiries and make bookings.

4.2 Personal selling

This will be an appropriate promotional tool to use with the travel trade. Our sales team must target intermediary contacts and make them fully aware of the new services.

4.3 Direct marketing

This is an appropriate method to use in both intermediary and customer markets.

From our database we can identify past customers – both business and consumer. We can target them with direct mail giving information on the new routes, schedules and journey times. We can also buy in lists of potentially relevant targets, for example owners of second homes on the Continent and export businesses.

Direct marketing can be used to support our personal selling activity in the intermediary market. This can reach small agent's offices that we will not have time to visit personally.

4.4 Public relations

Press releases on the launch of the services should go to travel trade, consumer and business publications – the new high-speed service should be particularly newsworthy. Corporate hospitality can be offered too – offering onboard entertainment and shore-based activity to selected customers, intermediaries, opinion leaders and opinion formers.

4.5 Sales promotions

If publicised effectively, for example in our advertising, these are a good way to grab the public's attention. Discounts for early bookings will get the service off to a good start and encourage word-of-mouth communication.

Answer 15
Cinema and broadcast media compared; Cost per thousand;
A recommended media mix

Check your answer

A good answer is likely to:

	☑
Define 'media'.	☐
List the advantages and disadvantages of cinema and broadcast media, i.e. four things.	☐
Both define cost per thousand and show how it can help in decision-making.	☐
Make specific recommendations in Part c and justify them.	☐
Use memo format.	☐
Answer from the perspective of a council employee in the situation described.	☐

* * * * *

MEMO

To: Marketing Team

From: Marketing Manager

Date: XX/XX/XX

Re: Media Selection for Forthcoming Congestion Charge Campaign

1 Introduction

You will be aware of the forthcoming introduction of the congestion charge, to be publicised by an advertising campaign. It is essential that we select the right media for the campaign – media are the channels of communications that we use to deliver our advertising message – so that as many people as possible in our target audience understand our message. With this in mind I have put together some notes on selected key media topics.

2 The advantages and disadvantages of cinema and broadcast media

Broadcast media can be divided into two main categories – television and radio.

Television is a very flexible format which combines visual and aural stimuli – this appeal to different senses can engage powerfully with its audience. TV advertising can be targeted increasingly precisely. With a huge range of satellite and cable channels now available, advertisements can reach clearly defined segments. Local commercial programming makes it ideal for getting messages across to the city's population and incoming commuters. There is plenty of scope for local advertising on radio too with many commercial stations. It would be an ideal medium for reaching parts of our target audience who listen to the radio as they commute to work.

A big disadvantage of TV advertising is the amount of 'clutter' or competing messages. Advertisements need to be able to stand out from the surrounding advertisements and programming. Radio advertisements suffer from this too; in addition people are usually doing other things when listening to the radio so the message needs frequent repetition to gain audience attention. Another disadvantage of TV advertising is the cost: production costs and airtime are expensive, although the large reach of TV can make the cost per contact very low. Production and airtime costs for radio are much lower.

Cinema advertising has several advantages. There is a captive audience, without the distractions that surround TV viewers at home – meals, phone calls, crying children and so on. A single message is therefore likely to have greater impact.

Also, there are excellent opportunities for targeting. We can choose which films to show advertisement during, based on the characteristics of the anticipated audience. We can also be very selective about which cinemas show our advertisements, making it easy to target the local population with our congestion charge message.

However, the reach (per cent of target audience covered) for cinema advertising will be much lower than for TV activity. The costs of showing advertisements is relatively low but there are still the associated production costs – though these can be kept low by, for example, using still images only.

3 Cost per thousand

Cost per thousand (CPT) is a method of comparing the efficiency of different advertising media, or media vehicles. It is sometimes known as 'Cost per Mille' (CPM).

Cost per thousand is calculated by dividing the cost of a unit of space or airtime by the size of the audience a particular publication or programme reaches; this figure is then multiplied by 1000 to reach the CPT. For example if a page in a newspaper costs £40 000 and the paper is read by two million people then the CPT is £40 000 divided by 2 000 000, times by 1000 = £20.00 per thousand readers.

This calculation helps marketers to select media by giving data for comparing options on a like-for-like basis, in terms of audience numbers. Comparisons can be made between two vehicles in the same media category – for example two national newspapers; or media in different categories – for example local newspaper and radio. We can use CPT to compare alternative local media for our advertising campaign.

Though CPT measures the efficiency of the media it does not take account of qualitative factors, for example the characteristics of the media's different audiences or their likely levels of receptiveness to a particular message. Also, care needs to be taken in comparing like with like – for example, is it fairer to compare a full-page newspaper advertisement against a 30-second TV slot or a 45-second one?

4 A recommended media mix

I would welcome your suggestions for an effective mix of media to reach our target audience. Here are my own thoughts to start the discussion off.

Our campaign will need to achieve both reach and frequency targets. The former relates to what percentage of our target audience will be exposed to the message at least once. Frequency is about the number of times that they will see it. We want as many city drivers as possible to hear about the congestion charge. However, people are unlikely to fully absorb the message from a single exposure so we need to make sure they hear or see it more than once. A co-ordinated media mix is recommended so that our audience is exposed to the message in different ways, each message complementing and reinforcing the others.

Suggested media are:

- *Outdoor and Transport*. Posters are effective at getting simple messages across to local audiences. These can be positioned on commuter routes and other areas of large traffic volumes. Sizes could vary from a typical 48-sheet site down to single sheet at bus shelters. Advertising can also be displayed on panels on taxis and buses. Drivers would have a relatively brief exposure to each message but would see it on many occasions. We should also consider advertising on the reverse of local car parking tickets.
- *Local Radio*. Many people listen to local commercial radio – at home or driving to work, school or the shops. This is an ideal way to reach them. Messages would need to be short and simple as complex messages cannot be easily absorbed this way – clutter and other distractions can obscure what is heard. We would also need to buy many slots over several weeks to ensure that the message is fully absorbed. However, production costs and airtime are relatively cheap, making this a practical and affordable option.
- *Newspapers*. There are many options here, ranging from paid-for daily city newspapers to free-sheets distributed weekly to local homes. CPT calculations would help in evaluating the alternatives, though we would also need to factor in user characteristics such as the percentage of readers that are city drivers. Newspapers have the advantage of our being able to include more detail in the advertisement, and of people being able to re-read the message to fully understand it.
- *Cinema*. The advantages of cinema advertising have already been stated. Adult audiences could be targeted in local cinemas; I suggest, given limited council budgets, that production is kept very simple. I do not recommend we use TV advertising. Airtime costs would be high, particularly if we intend to repeat our message frequently, and I am not convinced it would particularly increase the reach of our message.

I have mentioned that the media mix should be used in a co-ordinated way. I would add that the advertising itself should be part of a wider co-ordinated campaign using public relations, and direct mail to large employers, supported by web information.

5 Conclusion

I hope this assists you with your media planning. I look forward to receiving your comments and alternative suggestions.

Answer 16
Perceived risk; Source credibility; Ethics and regulation (Charity sector)

Check your answer

A good answer is likely to:

☑

Define or explain 'perceived risk' and its importance in marketing communications. ☐

Define or explain 'source credibility', and discuss its relevance to a charity. ☐

Briefly explain the concepts of ethics and regulation of communications. ☐

Identify at least four regulatory and/or ethical issues the suggested campaign raises. ☐

Relate your answer to a charity. ☐

Use Report format. ☐

* * * * *

REPORT

To: Fund-Raising Director

From: Marketing Communications Manager

Date: XX/XX/XX

Re: Proposed New Fund-Raising Advertising Campaign

1 Introduction

Fund-raising is a fundamental aspect of War-Relief's activities. I am currently developing ideas for a new fund-raising advertising campaign and have set out below some thoughts on key aspects of this communications activity.

2 Perceived risk

Perceived risk is an important consideration for communications campaigns in any sector, including charities. The concept concerns how much donors (or, in the case of FMCG markets, buyers) believe is at stake when making a gift of money or time. It is the amount of risk the donors *perceive* that counts; they may overestimate the risk but it is this perception, rather than the reality, that will influence their action. It is therefore important for marketing communications to reduce the levels of perceived risk and to correct any misunderstanding about risk levels that donor may have. There are six categories of perceived risk – I will explain each one and its impact for our communications.

- ○ *Financial risk*. this concerns how much money is at stake. Obviously donors decide how much they want to give but they must feel that this is not an open-ended commitment. We must reassure them that standing orders can be cancelled at any time, and that they won't constantly be pestered for more. They also need to know their money won't be wasted, which leads to . . .
- ○ *Performance risk*. we must prove that we do what we say. Case studies can illustrate the benefits of our activity; eyewitness accounts from credible sources can vouch for what we do; in some instances we can arrange letters of thanks from families or communities we have helped.
- ○ *Ego risk*. this is about how people feel about themselves as a result of their donation. We want people to feel good, that they have made difference. Personalising the message by stressing just what can be bought with *their* £10 helps here. We also need to stress that we are helping victims, not taking sides and prolonging conflict.
- ○ *Social risk*. this is about what others might think of donors. We want donors to feel proud to associate themselves with War-Relief. Positive publicity about our activities always helps here. People can proclaim their support for us by wearing lapel badges or using car stickers.
- ○ *Time risk*. this is about how much time is at stake for donors. We need to make it quick and easy for them to give. Collection boxes are obviously convenient; but we need to have an efficient system for telephone donations or online giving. Corporate donors' needs also need to be considered.
- ○ *Physical risk*. this is about concerns over personal safety. Volunteers such as collectors need to be given advice on health and safety aspects of their role. With regard to more general personal security, financial donors must be reassured that any personal or financial information they give us won't be misused in any way.

3 The value of source credibility

We want all our communications to be believed and trusted. An important part of the way that people process messages is by assessing the source of the message. The more objective and authoritative the source of the message – in other words how much 'source credibility' it has – the more the message is likely to be accepted by the target audience.

If an organisation puts out any form of message in its advertising there may always be some readers/viewers who are sceptical about what is said. They expect an advertiser to be biased in its own organisation's favour – in our case, they would expect us to stress our effectiveness and efficiency. But this message can be given more weight if it comes from someone who is expected to be more independent and impartial, such as an opinion former or an opinion leader. Celebrities – a type of opinion leader – would be seen to have nothing to gain by exaggerating War-Relief's good work. And, as these celebrities are already liked by the public, we would hope that the public's liking would be transferred, by association, to War-Relief. Harnessing the support of celebrities, and others with high credibility, and making them an explicit part of our campaign, is likely to have a positive effect on future fund-raising.

4 Ethical and regulatory considerations

The marketing communications industry is largely self-regulated. The public have the right to take complaints to the Advertising Standards Authority (ASA) who apply rules laid down in various Codes. The CAP Code sets out the principle that advertising must be 'legal, decent, honest and truthful' and must be prepared with a sense of responsibility to consumers and society. It has been suggested that we use graphic images in our advertising but there is a real risk that some members of the public would feel these breach the 'decency' and 'sense of responsibility' rules, and these would give rise to complaints to the ASA. The ASA has a Copy Advice Committee and I suggest we consult them before running any potential controversial campaign.

'Ethics' concern what moral principles an individual or organisation operates to. One difficulty with ethics is that everyone has different views about what is ethical and where ethical boundaries can be drawn.

Using a campaign to shock people into action may be seen by some as crossing an ethical boundary. Whilst some members of the public may be moved by the graphic images, others may find them offensive, unnecessary and in bad taste. There is a risk that we alienate the public, rather than gaining more support.

There is a particular ethical issue about using poster advertising. We cannot discriminate about who views posters – children may see them, as well as sensitive adults. Many people would argue that it is wrong to impose hard-hitting images on passers-by who have not chosen to view them. A similar argument applies to press advertising although we can be rather more selective in who sees this.

There are also ethical considerations around whether this is the right way to use the charity's money. Most donors will have given their money expecting it to be used directly to help our good causes. Using money on administration and marketing is often viewed poorly by donors; this could be even more of a problem if the campaign was controversial. We would have to be very confident of our business case if we plan to proceed with this form of campaign.

On the other hand, an argument in favour of a hard-hitting campaign is that it is necessary, to gain attention and support. The public are increasingly afflicted by 'compassion fatigue' and there is an argument that extraordinary action is needed to get people to notice a worthy cause.

I look forward to discussing all these issues with you in more detail at our next meeting.

Answer 17
Communications industry and current issues; Corporate social responsibility; Evaluation of public relations and sales promotion

Check your answer

A good answer is likely to:

 ☑

Describe the five main parties in the UK marketing communications industry and identify two issues affecting the industry. ☐

Define Corporate Social Responsibility, and give at least three examples of companies that practice it. ☐

Explain evaluation and its importance, before relating it to the two stated promotional tools. ☐

Answer from the perspective of a children's breakfast cereal manufacturer. ☐

Lay out the answer in Notes format. ☐

*   *   *   *   *

NOTES

For: Meeting with [overseas colleague]

By: KiddiPops Brand Manager

Date: XX/XX/XX

Re: Kiddipops and UK marketing Communications

1 Introduction

Thank you for your questions about the marketing communications environment in which Kiddipops operates. I hope you will find the following answers useful.

2 The UK communications industry

The UK marketing communications industry consists of five main parties:

- ○ *The businesses who want to communicate*: these are the companies, brands or organisations that want to get a message across to target audiences. Often these businesses use the services of . . .
- ○ *Marketing communications agencies*: agencies undertake activity on behalf of their clients (the businesses above). There are many types of agencies whose services include advertising, sales promotions, public relations, new media work, sponsorship, research and many other specialisms.

    o *The media*: these are the channels through which certain forms of communication take place. Newspapers, TV and radio stations, and website owners are key examples.

    o *Regulators*: these are the organisations that oversee conduct of communications activity to ensure that it is legal, decent, honest and truthful. The leading body is the Advertising Standards Authority which is answerable to Ofcom (the Office of Communications) and the Office of Fair Trading, depending on the medium used.

    o *Trade bodies*: a wide range of organisations represent, advise or support sections of the industry. The CIM, the Advertising Association and The Chartered Institute of Public Relations are just three examples.

The communications industry is fast moving and new issues arise all the time. Here are two important ones:

2.1 Advertising and children

In the past the UK has had a fairly relaxed attitude to advertising aimed at children. Only three other EU countries have had similarly liberal laws (France, Ireland and the Netherlands). This means that any products targeted at children could be advertised during programmes they normally watch, including toys, food and drinks. However there are increasing concerns in the UK about childhood obesity and Ofcom has introduced rules to ban advertising of foods high in fat, salt and sugar to children under 1b. They have also banned the use of celebrities and 'characters' in advertisements for these foods. Opponents say the ban is unfair and programme-makers say that the lost advertising revenue will mean less children's programming. Clearly, KiddiPops is studying how the new regulations affect the advertising of its products.

2.2 Uncoupling of the consumer decision-making process

Traditionally, for most goods, the 'information search' and 'purchase decision' stages of the consumer decision process occurred in the same place – in a shop. With the growth of the Internet this process is becoming decoupled. For example, people are going to shops to view and handle a product, then going home and ordering it from the cheapest supplier on the Internet. This trend has many impacts. Traditional distribution channels are feeling aggrieved; but attempts to reward high-street retailers for their value-adding service has upset Internet sellers. Some manufacturers and service suppliers are turning to disintermediation; and everyone is having to re-think how information is supplied to consumers. The situation continues to evolve.

3 Corporate social responsibility (CSR) and its benefits

CSR is concerned with the extent to which companies recognise their obligations to a wide range of stakeholders. Every business recognises it has responsibilities to its owners, but socially responsible organisations also recognise responsibilities to employees, customers, suppliers and society as a whole, to name just a few stakeholder groups.

Business in the Community (BITC) publish an annual survey of UK companies' social responsibility – the Corporate Responsibility Index. Participating companies are assessed on a range of factors under several categories including:

    o *Community*: example areas included the impact of operations on the local area, social inclusion and employee volunteering.

    o *Environment*: including issues around energy efficiency, waste management and the sustainable use of natural resources.

o *Marketplace*: this includes ethical business conduct, product safety and fair treatment of supply chain members.

o *Workplace*: this includes attention to health and safety issues, employee training and employee communication.

Corporate social responsibility is more than a passing fad. Consumers, and society as a whole, have higher expectations of businesses, and are interested not only in *what* is produced but *how* it is done. There is much greater transparency, with companies' social responsibility reporting highly visible – or sometimes noticeably absent – on their websites and in Annual Reports.

There are many benefits to businesses in acting responsibility.

o *Reputation*: responsible activities enhance a business's reputation. Reputations are built over time and are deep-rooted. A positive reputation means that the business is widely liked which will probably lead to increased willingness of consumers to buy from them, and of suppliers, distributors and so on to work with them. Marks and Spencer has recently widely advertised its winning of the BITC award for top UK business for social responsibility.

o *Differentiation*: socially responsible companies stand out from others and can use their stance as a specific point of differentiation. Innocent (drinks), Green & Black's (choco- late) and Bodyshop (health and beauty products) are all strong examples.

o *Retention*: socially responsible companies tend to be nicer places to work. Staff are happier and stay longer, which cuts recruitment costs and helps business continuity.

o *Shareholder value*: businesses that act responsibly have been shown often to be more profitable than less responsible businesses. Both Green & Black's and Bodyshop, mentioned above, have been the subject of recent acquisitions because their stance had made them into strong, attractive brands.

4 Evaluation of public relations and sales promotions

When planning any promotional activity it is essential to include evaluation as part of the process. Evaluation assesses the benefits of the activity, which can be compared against the costs to see if the investment of time and money in the promotion was well spent. This information becomes an input for future decision-making about promotional activity. Evaluation needs to include an assessment of both the efficiency and effectiveness of what was done, and needs to be related to the initial objectives set for the activity.

KiddiPops undertakes a range of sale promotion activities, so evaluation takes many forms:

o *Consumer audits*: researchers monitor consumers' spending patterns and identify changes, which may result from a sales promotional campaign.

o *Coupon and voucher redemptions*: the number of coupon or vouchers redeemed can be counted. These can be source-coded to identify which sources (e.g. magazine adver- tisements) led to the widest take-up of the offer;

o *Competitions, mail-in premiums and so on*: again, these can be counted, their value lies in creating brand interest and in generating database information.

o *Sales volumes*: sale promotions may lead to a direct uplift in sales which is measured. This needs to be weighed against the longer-term impact, for example if consumers stop buying after the promotion as they use up home stocks.

Public relations activity can also be measured in several ways:

- ○ *Press coverage* (following a press release, or sponsorship activity, for example): the number of media vehicles (individuals newspapers, radio stations, etc.) in which KiddiPops is mentioned can be counted. Press coverage can be counted in 'column centimetres'; and broadcast coverage in 'Airtime' (in seconds); these can be categorised into positive, neutral or negative coverage. The equivalent cost of advertising space – the advertising value equivalent or AVE – can be calculated.
- ○ *Sales*: PR may sometimes lead to an increase in sales (or, with negative publicity, a decrease). This can be measured.
- ○ *Responses*: sometimes PR is intended to generate responses, for example publicising the availability of an information pack on KiddiPops' nutritional value.
- ○ *Brand building*: the effect of PR is often longer term, helping to build brand values in target consumers. Attitudes to brands can be measured over time, though it may be hard to isolate the effects of a single activity such as PR.

Answer 18
Product life cycle and the promotional mix; Sales promotional and public relations compared; Involvement

Check your answer

A good answer is likely to:

☑

Explain what the product life cycle is. ☐

In Part a consider tools for both the consumer and intermediary markets. ☐

Use appropriate criteria in Part b – the 'Four Cs Framework' is recommended. ☐

Define 'sales promotions' and 'public relations'. ☐

Define 'involvement' and relate this theoretical concept to marketing communications operations. ☐

Use the context of a washing powder manufacturer. ☐

Use memo format. ☐

* * * * *

MEMO

To: Marketing Assistant

From: Brand Manager

Date: XX/XX/XX

Re: Marketing Communications and the Washing Powder Market

1 Introduction

Thank you for your questions about the use of marketing communications. The washing powder industry is highly competitive with a wide choice of brands and product types for consumers to choose. Using marketing communications appropriately is therefore very important and I hope this memo will help your understanding.

2 The product life cycle and marketing communications

The product life cycle describes the pattern of growth, maturity and decline that a product experiences from launch to withdrawal. It is often used generically but the pattern for a new product category may be very different from the cycle of a variant to an existing washing powder brand. The following description, then, is a general one and would need to be adapted for individual situations.

There are four main phases to the life cycle, and different tools of the promotional mix are best used in different phases. (The promotional mix is the range of marketing communications tools which can be used individually or together, in a co-ordinated way, to achieve predetermined objectives.)

2.1 Introduction phase

The main objectives at this early stage are to create awareness of the product and of its features, benefits and brand values. Advertising is a valuable tool as it can reach large audiences. A product launch is often an attractive opportunity to use PR because of media interest in things that are 'new'. Sales promotion is valuable too, encouraging trial through the use of vouchers and free samples.

There can be no successful consumer launch without trade support. Personal selling will be critical to get the retail industry on board, and this activity will need to take place prior to consumer launch to ensure stocks are in place. Personal selling may be supported by advertising and PR.

2.2 Growth phase

The growth phase is typified by stronger sales than at launch and by the introduction of similar product by competitors. The communication emphasis shifts, therefore, to differentiating the product and to emphasising its different positioning and brand values. Advertising remains key in the consumer market, maybe supported by PR. Sales promotions may be targeted at segments who have not yet tried the product.

Retaining the confidence of the retail sector remains essential. Personal selling, keeping retailers informed of promotional activity, remains valuable here.

2.3 Maturity phase

Many markets, including washing powders, are stuck in this phase. Sales have peaked with little room for growth in individual markets. Communications emphasis is on retaining interest in the product/brand and hanging on to, or attempting to grow, market share.

Product variants may be launched – new formats and formulations of washing powders for example – starting their own launch cycle. In the absence of new product developments sales promotions help to maintain interest, through offers, competitions, premiums and so on. These also help encourage loyalty and entice consumers to switch from competitors. Occasional advertising will be used to keep the product at the front of consumers' minds. Direct marketing may help to reach selected segments and to form stronger relationships between the brand and target consumers – many have registered with us to receive offers, advice and so on.

PR and sponsorship activity will also help to maintain brand interest and remind consumers of brand values.

The retail trade remains important. Personal contact will be ongoing. Trade promotions may help encourage retailers to take larger stocks and allocate more shelf space.

2.4 Decline

In this phase, sales fall away as interest develops in alternatives. There will be little incentive to invest in expensive promotions in a declining market. However they may be used selectively, perhaps advertising to reach enduring segments, or sales promotions to shift surplus stocks.

3 Sales promotions and public relations (PR) compared

The Chartered Institute of Public Relations defines PR as 'the deliberate, planned and sustained effort to institute and maintain mutual understanding between an organisation and its publics'. Fill[10] has described sales promotions as 'a range of tactical marketing techniques designed within a strategic marketing framework to add value to a product or service in order to achieve specific sales and marketing objectives'.

The 'Four Cs Framework' provides a useful set of criteria to compare these two promotional tools.

- ○ *Communication* – PR has the ability to reach a large audience. Media coverage of brand activity, including sponsorships (such as our sponsorship of tennis players and tournaments) can be seen by large numbers of consumers. However, the message is undifferentiated for each person and does not invite interaction. General sales promotions activity also tends to be undifferentiated – discounts and premiums are available to everyone. But store loyalty cards have given more opportunities for individual targeting of offers, and sale promotions do invite consumers to interact with the brand to a limited extent.
- ○ *Credibility* – PR activity tends to be highly credible. Endorsement by a journalist or association with a respected third party, such as a sports personality, adds a degree of perceived trustworthiness to the brand. Sales promotions do not benefit from this effect. A certain level of promotional activity is expected in the FMCG (fast-moving consumer goods) market, but too much can damage a brand's standing.
- ○ *Costs* – The cost of public relations activity can vary enormously. The simple electronic issue of press releases is very inexpensive, but sponsorships or corporate hospitality can be very costly. When calculated against the potential audience for PR activity though, the cost per contact becomes low. Total costs for sale promotions vary with the type of activity too, though they will tend to be low per consumer. However, sales promotions may incur investment costs, such as supporting advertising.
- ○ *Control* – Sales promotions can usually be carefully controlled. Budgets can be pre-agreed, and the campaign can be ended when goals have been met. Public relations activity is much less controllable: the company has no direct control over the extent and tone of media coverage, and problems with sponsored organisations or individuals can impact negatively on the brand.

4 Involvement

The term 'involvement' relates to the degree of personal relevance and importance a buying decision has for a consumer. Purchases can be categorised in two basic ways:

- ○ *High involvement*: these are important purchases where there is usually a high degree of perceived risk – for example, there may be a lot of money at stake or one's status and

---

[10] 'Marketing Communications' (2005). Elsevier Butterworth-Heinemann.

credibility is on the line. Examples might be buying a car or expensive home entertainment centre, or a large business purchase. Time and effort will usually be expended before these purchases, researching the market and comparing alternatives.

o *Low involvement*: these tend to be routine purchases where little risk is involved. Little, if any, time is spent weighing alternatives or understanding product features, with decisions guided more by habit. Washing powders would fall into this category as would many other FMCG products.

Where high involvement purchases are involved, marketing communications will have an emphasis on information provision. This information can come from many sources including product literature and packaging, websites, opinion formers and advertising. Attention needs to be paid to maximising the message's credibility.

In low involvement purchases the sub-conscious mind is more important than conscious thought. Branding is therefore important, so that consumers' feeling for the brand come from the associations that have been made with it. Branding messages tend to be short and uncomplicated and require frequent repetition to lodge securely in consumers' minds.

Answer 19
The roles of marketing communications; Planning an advertising campaign; Key media terms

Check your answer

A good answer is likely to:

☑

Recognise that the word 'roles' is a prompt for using the mnemonic DRIP.   ☐

Takes a logical step-by-step approach to advertising campaign planning.   ☐

Explains all four terms in Part c.   ☐

Answer in the context of a charity, not goods or services.   ☐

Use report format.   ☐

*   *   *   *   *

REPORT

To: Operations Director, Water-Aid

From: Marketing Communications Adviser

Date: XX/XX/XX

Re: Water-Aid's Marketing Communications

1 Introduction

I am delighted to be working with Water-Aid and assisting with your efforts to raise funds to provide access to clean water in communities throughout the developing world. I understand you are considering running an advertising campaign. With this in mind, I have put together some ideas that are relevant to marketing communications activity.

2 The roles of marketing communications

The ways that marketing communications can be used can be categorised in many ways. However a useful mnemonic to use is DRIP which stands for Differentiate, Remind and Reassure, Inform and Persuade. I will consider each in turn.

- ○ *Differentiate* – in the charity and other sectors you are competing for people's money. Your communications need to make your charity stand out from others and to make it instantly recognisable in communications. Many techniques could be used: distinctive branding with a striking logo and consistent use of design; association with particularly things or people, for example a celebrity; and verbal or visual reminders of the work you do which is unique.

o *Remind or reassure* – with so many competing demands on them it is easy for individuals to forget about your charity. Regular communications help to remind them of its existence and activities, so that it will be remembered when they are considering making a charitable donation. Your communications also need to reassure: people want to know that their hard-earned money really will be used to help the Water-Aid cause and would not be misused or consumed in disproportionately large expenses. Reassurance can be given both before and after donations have been made – the latter so that people do not suffer from the equivalent of 'post-purchase dissonance'.

o *Inform* – communications messages must advise the target audience what their money will be used for, for example where it is spent and on what? People are unlikely to want to donate, particularly significant sums, if they do not know about the cause. They also need information on how to give, for example via a website or using standing order. Corporate donors, who may involve employees in fund-raising activity, will need information for staff too.

o *Persuade* – ultimately, we want our communications to encourage people to take action. Usually this is about making a donation but, alternatively, we may want them to seek more information to start with, or to give time or goods. Persuasive communications must give people good reasons for taking action, and they may be incentivised with a plea of urgency. It needs to be easy for people to act – offering a choice of ways to give and, for example, enclosing pre-addressed envelopes for postal replies.

3 Advertising campaign planning

An advertising campaign comprises a discrete series of advertisements aimed at achieving particular objectives. The campaign may use a variety of messages and media. There are several steps to creating a successful campaign.

o *Decide campaign responsibilities.* You need to decide whether to undertake the activity in-house, or whether to outsource it to an agency. For a charity this will largely depend on resources – do you have sufficient skills within the organisation, and do you have sufficient financial resources to pay an agency (note, some agencies will do charity work for a reduced fee, or even none).

o *Define the target audience.* Who do you want to reach, for example new donors or existing donors? And are you aiming for a national campaign, or only certain geographical or other segments?

o *Set campaign objectives.* This is very important and it will guide the rest of the campaign planning. Your proposed campaign relates to fund-raising, but charities also undertake issue-based advertising, or promotion of the services they offer. Whatever the objectives, they need to be expressed in SMART terms (specific, measurable, agreed, realistic and time-bound).

o *Budget-setting.* A budget for the campaign needs to be agreed. This needs to cover any agency or other development costs, production costs (photography for example) and media costs which are likely to be the largest element.

o *Media selection and planning.* The choice of advertising media will need to be made. Broadcast media, especially TV, may be too expensive; print may be preferred. It may be possible to find an organisation willing to sponsor the cost of media, in return for a small mention in the final creative.

o *Creative development and testing.* The basic message, or series of messages, need to be agreed, and creative ideas developed. Copy will need to be written and artwork designed to suit the selected media. The creatives should be tested at various stages to check they will be understood and have the necessary impact, although the charity's limited budget may severely limit the amount of testing possible.

- ○ *Scheduling and implementation.* The campaign needs to be scheduled across the selected media, and artwork provided in time to meet their copy deadlines. Plans needs to have been made to handle responses to the campaign and these need to start operating.
- ○ *Campaign evaluation.* At the end of the campaign you need to ask, Did it achieve the desired objectives? What worked, and what did not? A positive outcome can be used to justify charity spending on marketing. *Any* outcome gives information to help with planning future campaigns.

4 Key media terms

The following terms are often used in connection with advertising campaigns:

- ○ *Reach*: this is the number of people in the target audience who will be exposed to the advertisement at least once. For example, if an advertiser is targeting the 10 million UK males aged 20–40, and three million of them watch a TV programme during which the advertisement is shown, then there is a reach figure of 30 per cent. Reach does not mean all three million noticed the advertisement, or absorbed its message, just that they were exposed to it. Another word for reach is 'coverage'.
- ○ *Frequency*: this is the number of times that people in the target audience will be exposed to the advertisement. Generally, an advertisement needs to be seen several times to communicate its message effectively. Given limited budgets, there is a trade-off between reach and frequency – do you aim for reaching 100 per cent of the target audience by advertising in all suitable media, or do you aim to drive the message home by repetition to a smaller number of people?
- ○ *Burst and drip*: these are alternative approaches to a campaign. The former relates to a short period of intense advertising activity, perhaps supporting the launch of a new phase of charity activity. A drip campaign uses less intense activity over a longer period, reminding the target audience regularly of the charity's message.

5 Conclusion

This report shows that the creation of an effective advertising campaign is a complex process with many things to consider. I would be pleased to offer you more advice.

Answer 20
Direct marketing and public relations compared; Marketing communications planning process; Likeability

Check your answer

A good answer is likely to:

        ☑

Select relevant criteria for Part a; the '4Cs Framework' is recommended. ☐

Explain or define direct marketing and public relations. ☐

In Part b, set out a process AND explains the links between its stages. ☐

Define/explain 'likeability', relating it to why an advertising campaign may have been poorly received. ☐

Relate your answer to a national chain of health and fitness clubs. ☐

Use Notes format. ☐

*   *   *   *   *

NOTES

For: Meeting with Marketing Communications Team

By: Marketing Communications Manager

Date: XX/XX/XX

Re: Fit for Life's Communications

1 Introduction

Having spent time looking into the past use of marketing communications at Fit for Life I am keen that we learn from past activities and make best use of our resources and opportunities in the future. I hope the following thoughts will be helpful for forthcoming communications activity.

2 Public relations and direct marketing

The Chartered Institute of Public Relations defines PR as 'the deliberate, planned and sustained effort to institute and maintain mutual understanding between an organisation and its publics'. Brassington and Pettitt define direct marketing (building on the American Direct

Marketing Association's definition) as 'an interactive system of marketing which uses one or more advertising media to effect a measurable response at any location, forming a basis for creating and further developing an ongoing direct relationship between an organisation and its customers.'[11] Both of these communication tools could be used by Fit for Life as part of an integrated compaign. I would like to compare them using four criteria.

- o *Communication*: both methods have the ability to reach quite large target audiences, but careful targeting will limit the number of people for whom we use direct marketing. Media stories and sponsorship activity, both part of PR, can reach a wide audience but not as much as, say, advertising. Direct marketing messages will be personalised to the recipient and based on our understanding of their circumstances; PR usually entails messages intended for a wider audience, non-specific to individuals. As per the earlier definition, direct marketing is an interactive tool, aimed at prompting a response.
- o *Credibility*: if direct marketing is well targeted it should be relevant – it is mis-targeted 'junk mail' that has low credibility. However the messages are recognised as being generated by our own firm so they will not have as high a degree of credibility as PR can achieve: if we are able to generate positive independent media coverage then this is likely to have very high credibility with our audience as the message comes from a third party.
- o *Costs*: direct-mail packs require printing, inserting and posting, all of which costs money. However, by using in-house facilities, and pre-sorting mail into postcodes, costs can be contained. If we can use other methods such as e-mail and text messaging, subject to recipients' permission, then both absolute costs and costs per recipient can fall dramatically. No matter how good our targeting, though, our message will be wasted on some recipients. Many people will miss or ignore our PR messages too but activities aimed at raising our profile such as issuing press releases and undertaking local community activity can be very inexpensive while still gaining coverage and goodwill.
- o *Control*: PR can be hard to control. A carping journalist or an aggrieved customer can generate coverage that is hard to contain. With direct marketing, though, we can wholly control the message and its timing. Direct marketing also has the advantage of being easy to measure in terms of response rates, sales made and so on.

3 Marketing communications planning

It makes sense to use a proven, logical process for planning our communications activity. This ensures that all necessary inputs are considered and makes best use of time and effort. In turn, this should give the best outcomes. I recommend we use the 'Marketing Communications Planning Framework'.[12]

[11] 'Principles of Marketing' (2003) Pearson Education Ltd.
[12] From 'Marketing Communications' by G. Hughes & C. Fill. Elsevier Butterworth-Heinemann, 2005.

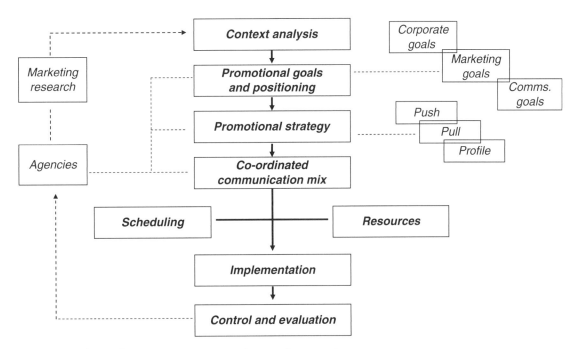

Figure 2 The marketing communications planning framework

The planning process starts with a Context Analysis. There are five contexts – Business, Customer, Internal, External and Stakeholder and these ensure we consider all the main factors likely to impact our communications. Only when we fully understand the Fit for Life's ·operating environment can we set appropriate communications goals or objectives (which need to be Specific, Measurable, Agreed, Realistic and Time-bound) and decide on an appropriate positioning, for example one not adopted by competitors. These objectives will also reflect Fit for Life's corporate goals, and the Marketing Department's overall aims.

Only when we have decided on our goals we can then decide on our strategy, in other words the method used to achieve the objectives. Here the choice is between push (intermediary-targeted communications), pull (end-user targeted communications) and profile (stakeholder communications about the organisation). Having determined strategy we can select an appropriate co-ordinated Marketing Communications mix. Knowing the strategy first is important as some communication tools are better suited to some tasks, for example PR for a profile strategy; advertising for consumer targeting and personal selling for business targeting.

Deciding the mix will then enable us to identify budgets and timescales – though these will also be *inputs* into the planning process. Once we know what we want to say and what tools we will be using, we can proceed to implementation – but planning should never end there. We must monitor how things are progressing and take corrective action if they are going off track. This information becomes part of the input to the start of the next planning cycle.

I should mention that Market Research and the use of agencies may play important roles at various stages.

This then is my recommended plan and I should stress that it should not be a series of separate, disjointed stages but a smooth, co-ordinated process.

4 The importance of likeability in advertising

Likeability is an important concept in advertising because research has shown that there is a strong correlation between how much people like an advertisement and whether or not they go on to buy the product or service advertised. If Fit for Life's advertising has failed in the past it may be because, for some reason, the advertisements were not liked by the target audience.

The term 'like' needs clarifying: it goes beyond being simply pleasant or fun. It also encompasses the message being meaningful, relevant, credible, useful or stimulating. For example, we may not 'like' (in terms of finding 'nice') a hard-hitting advertisement for a children's charity about child abuse; but at a deeper level it may have 'likeability' because the well-constructed message strikes a chord in us, prompting us to take action such as donating to the charity.

It may be that our firm's past advertising was not liked by our audience. Perhaps its images or words: 'turned off' our target audience. Or perhaps they just didn't find it relevant or interesting. We should learn from this by trying to find out why the campaign lacked likeability. We should also test any new advertising to check that it does have likeability.

5 Conclusion

I hope this information has been useful. I look forward to working with you to deliver successful campaigns in the future.

Answer 21
Distribution channels: Marketing communications uses and mix; Trust, commitment and satisfaction; Digital technologies and relationships

Check your answer

A good answer is likely to:

☑

Identify several uses for marketing communications, probably using a framework such as 'DRIP'. ☐

Include a justification for your choice of tools in the second part of a. ☐

Consider the importance of all three terms in Part b. ☐

Suggest a range of digital technologies in Part c and relate your answer to relationship building. ☐

Recognise that lasting business relationships are seldom solely dependent on technology. ☐

Relate directly to an insurance company. ☐

Use report format. ☐

*　*　*　*　*

REPORT

To: Managing Director

From: Marketing Manager

Date: XX/XX/XX

Re: Channel Relationships and Marketing Communications

1 Introduction

Good channel relationships are essential for our business. Our intermediaries, the insurance brokers, offer our sole route to market and we need to make sure they are happy to continue to promote us in a competitive marketplace. This report will focus on key aspects of managing these channel relationships.

2 Marketing communications between channel members

2.1 The uses of marketing communications

Marketing communications play many roles in channel relationships. A key point to note is that good communications are two-way – we need to communicate with intermediaries and they need to communicate with us. It may be helpful to use the mnemonic 'DRIP' to outline the roles of communications.

- o *Differentiate*: our communications need to explain how we differ from competitors, for example on superior service or lower premiums. This gives brokers reasons to use us. Equally many brokers will be looking to convince us that they offer the best opportunities to distribute our products, and that they should receive preferential service.
- o *Remind or reassure*: we need constantly to keep our products in broker's minds so they do not forget about them. Communications help with this process, reminding brokers about product features and benefits, our service etc. Reassurance is critical in the insurance market: positive information on our financial strength, excellent claims payment record and speed of service are all factors that will reassure brokers. Meanwhile brokers will want to remind us about their particular needs and to reassure us that they are offering their clients a good service and are recommending us when appropriate.
- o *Information*: insurance is a complex subject so brokers need plenty of information about the terms and conditions of our policies, claims procedures, payment methods and so on. Supplying timely, accurate information to our brokers will help develop their trust in our company. Information from brokers can be very valuable to us, telling us about competitor activity, changing buyer needs and any administration problems we need to address.
- o *Persuade*: our marketing communications aim to persuade brokers to recommend our products to their clients and to allocate scarce resources to them, for example training time, literature shelf space and promotional budgets. For tangible products communications would also aim to persuade intermediaries to hold stock. Intermediaries will try to persuade us to give them preferential terms, such as faster service or financial support for promotions.

2.2 Marketing communications tools

I will briefly outline the two main marketing communications tools that we should use with intermediaries:

- o *Personal Selling*: this involves face-to-face visits between representatives of our company and brokers. Given the complexity of financial products, a salesperson is able to discuss these in detail with brokers and identify the most suitable polices for their clients' needs. A salesperson can also be persuasive, encouraging intermediaries to advocate our products and allocate resources. As we want long-term relationships with our brokers a further valuable sales role is to build those relationships.
- o *Direct marketing*: this helps to keep our firm in touch with brokers between sales visits. The written nature of direct mail, in particular, means that detailed information can be sent to brokers to retain. Direct marketing also enables our marketing messages to reach brokers who we do not currently have time to visit in person.

3 The importance of trust, commitment and satisfaction

In any relationship – business and personal – trust plays a key role. If you do not trust someone, or an organisation, you are unlikely to want to continue dealing with them/it unless you have to. Initially trust may simply be based on recommendation or reputation, but over time it develops into a deeper, interpersonal bond, becoming the foundation of a relationship and a commitment to working together. In turn, this becomes a basis for mutual support and co-operation. Brokers undertake to recommend our products in suitable circumstances; we undertake to provide information, administrative support and remuneration (commission). A feature of co-operative arrangements is that the firms jointly problem-solve, finding acceptable solutions to challenges, such as non-standard customer needs.

Trust and commitment, then, are critical to relationships, but they can be broken. In particular, if one party feels let down, it is likely to damage their trust in the other party. This is why satisfaction is also important in channel relationships. Our firm must commit to delivering the service levels the broker expects, to meeting promises and to offering personal support and attention. If the broker become dissatisfied with our performance this is likely to damage both their trust in us and their commitment to us – and hence our mutual relationship.

Trust, commitment and satisfaction are also important in relation to conflict in distribution channels. The greater the amount of trust, commitment and satisfaction the less likely it is that channel conflict will arise, and if it does arise, then the stronger the relationship the more likely it is that a mutually satisfactory solution can be found.

4 Technology and relationship building

Digital technologies can be used in several ways to support our broker relationships.

- o *The Internet*: we can use the Internet to give basic details of the policies we offer, for members of the public to access. If they then input their postcode we can direct them to their nearest broker who offers our products. Thus, we are supporting our brokers, helping to build relationships with them. Failing to offer our products via the Internet, but only via brokers, is another form of support. It implies that we value the broker's advice to clients and that we will not take away their livelihoods.
- o *Extranets*: an extranet facility offers selected business contacts, such as intermediaries, the facility to access information online relevant to their relationship with us. It could be product details, information on the progress of a claim, or the latest commission statement. Extranets are fast and secure, and eliminate the need for much paper. Offering selected brokers access to an extranet implies they are special to us which helps enhance the relationship. There is also a degree of lock-in with an extranet: brokers come to rely on the information it provides, and would find a time cost, and maybe a technical cost, in switching to alternative insurers.
- o *The Intranet*: this is an internal facility offering staff access to information relevant to them, from the company's five-year strategic plan to today's restaurant menu. The Intranet can also give information on individual clients (maybe on password protected pages) and on general information such as product details and service standards. This ensures that staff have information to hand whenever they need it, so that they can handle enquiries from brokers quickly and effectively.
- o *E-mail*: this provides an efficient means of day-to-day contact between our firm and brokers. It is paperless, and means that broker queries can be dealt with quickly, leaving a permanent record. Emails are generally personalised which helps builds one-to-one relationships with brokers.

It would be a mistake, however, to think that digital technologies can be relied on to build broker relationships. Accurate and efficient electronic information *is* essential, and *some* businesses can operate solely electronically – eBay traders and Internet commodity brokers, for example – but business relationships stem primarily from personal service: the friendly salesperson, the sympathetic call centre operator or helpful respondent to an e-mail enquiry. Failure to design systems that are efficient and user-friendly can certainly damage broker relationships. But we must also pay attention to recruiting, and training the right staff and recognising and rewarding them appropriately, if we want brokers to keep recommending us.

Answer 22
Personal selling vs. advertising; Global advertising agencies; Marketing communications industry regulation

Check your answer

A good answer is likely to:

☑

Consider both the statutory *and* voluntary aspects of control of the communications industry in their chosen country. ☐

Use appropriate criteria in Part b – the 'Four Cs Framework' is recommended. ☐

Explain reasoning in Part b; simply saying 'high', 'medium' or 'low' is insufficient. ☐

Consider the three main types of overseas agency operations in Part c. ☐

Relate the answer to a property sales business. ☐

Use Report format. ☐

* * * * *

REPORT

To: Managing Director

From: Marketing Manager

Date: XX/XX/XX

Re: Village Opportunities' Marketing Communications

1 Introduction

Marketing communications play a key role in both our business and our competitors. We need to be alert to the threat that their communications present and also to the opportunities to maximise our use of communications both at home and overseas. With this in mind I have drafted a Report which covers three areas.

2 The regulation of marketing communications in the UK

The UK marketing communications industry is subject to both statutory and voluntary controls. Examples of the former include:

○ The Property Misdescriptions Act 1991, banning the making of false statements about a property.
○ The Data Protection Act 1998 which regulates how data is used, for example in direct marketing.

o The Privacy and Electronic Communication Regulations 2003 which, amongst other things, bans the use of spam ('junk' e-mail).

Issues relating to the latter two items above are dealt with by the Information Commissioner.

However, much control activity is handled on a voluntary basis. Voluntary arrangements give more flexibility than statute so that 'rules' can be adapted for different situations or can evolve as society changes.

The lead organisation is the Advertising Standards Authority (ASA) which looks after traditional advertising (e.g. on TV or outdoors) but whose remit also includes direct marketing and sales promotions. The ASA is a non-governmental body, funded by the marketing communications industry. A few years ago it took on responsibility for overseeing the conduct of broadcast advertising, to add to its previous responsibilities for non-broadcast material. Rules for good practice are set down in the British Code of Advertising, Sales Promotion and Direct Marketing (The CAP Code), with the Office of Fair Trading (OFT) acting as legal backstop. Broadcast rules are laid down in the Radio and TV Advertising Codes, with the Office of Communications (Ofcom) as legal backstop.

The ASA has three main functions:

o Research and monitoring: Every year it spot checks thousands of advertisements to check that they are adhering to the Codes.
o Pre-publication advice: Advertisers can seek guidance from the ASA about proposed advertisement to ensure they will not contravene the rules.
o Resolving complaints: The ASA receives thousands of complaints each year from the public, consumer groups and organisations (like us) who feel that our competitors have acted inappropriately.

There are a number of sanctions the ASA can apply including requesting amendment or withdrawal of offending advertisements and refusing to allow advertisers to have further advertising space. In extreme instances cases can be referred to Ofcom or the OFT for legal action.

There are a number of other industry bodies and many of these have their own rules. For example the Chartered Institute of Marketing and The Chartered Institute of Public Relations both have codes of conduct. The Direct Marketing Association operates a number of preferences services which consumers can register with to ensure they do not receive unwanted marketing communications.

3 Advertising and personal selling compared

Advertising and personal selling are two very different tools of the marketing communications mix. Fill[13] has described advertising as a 'paid form of non-formal communication that is transmitted through mass media'. Personal selling comprises face-to-face meetings between the representatives of an organisation and potential or current customers with the aim of persuading the latter to make a purchase. A helpful set of criteria by which to compare these tools is Fill's 'Four Cs Framework'.

o *Communication*: as the definition above makes clear, advertising is a mass medium with an undifferentiated message targeted at a mass audience. It is not suitable for delivering personalised messages. There is relatively little interaction via advertising although it

[13] 'Marketing Communications (2005) Elsevier Butterworth-Heinemann.

may provoke individuals to take action, such as contacting us to find out about our properties. Personal selling is the opposite of advertising in many respects. It cannot be used to reach large audiences, but involves highly personalised, and interactive dialogue on a one-to-one or one-to-few basis.

o *Credibility*: the credibility of a salesperson will depend on the reputation of the organisation he or she represents, his/her own interpersonal skills and, in some situations, his/her qualifications and experience. A good salesperson should *earn* a prospect's trust. People can be a little sceptical about advertising. They expect it to be one-sided and, particularly, with a complex product such as ours, may wonder what is hidden in the small print which the advertisements are not saying.

o *Costs*: advertising can be expensive, particular if we use full-colour advertisements in glossy publications as we do to reach our target audiences. However, when you divide this cost by the number of readers it appears very small. Many of them, though, will miss seeing the advertisement or it would not be relevant to them. Personal selling is expensive: salaries, commissions, on-costs such as pensions and national insurance, office space and so on all make it costly; on top of this there are the initial recruitment and training costs. As a salesperson can speak to relatively few people, the cost per contact is also high; but the salesperson will be speaking to interested parties – the message is of direct interest so wastage is low.

o *Control*: advertising can be selectively targeted, for example by advertising in appropriate magazines, but our message will never be relevant to every reader. We can seek to pull an advertisement whenever we need – but long lead times may mean that this is not immediate. Salespeople can target their efforts well, provided the prospecting process has been effective. Good training should mean the salesperson is 'on message' but occasionally a company can found itself tarred by a rogue sales employee. It is easy to measure the effectiveness of a salesperson by comparison to sale targets. Advertising is less easy, though if the objective is lead generation this is easy to measure.

It can be seen that advertising and personal selling have very different properties. They are complementary and this makes them valuable to use in co-ordinated marketing communications activity as we currently do.

4 Choice of overseas advertising agency

We have three main choices when it comes to selecting the type of advertising agency to handle any overseas campaign we mount.

o *Multinational agencies*: these are agencies that operate in several countries, perhaps with a UK head office and a number of overseas offices. The UK office would handle liaison between this country and the overseas operation. This makes finding and communicating with an overseas office very straightforward from our point of view, but we would need to make sure the multinational has operations in the countries we are interested in.

o *Independent networks*: these comprise independent agencies in overseas countries who group together to form an alliance. While each one may not directly own an operation in other countries they have strong links with partner firms, with whom they are used to working, so can handle the communications and co-ordination with them. The home country agency often acts as 'lead agency' in this respect. Nevertheless, from a client's perspective, there is a risk that the overseas business feels too remote from our own needs.

    ○ *Local independents*: these are firms wholly based in one country. They have the advantages of having local knowledge and reputation. The challenge to clients comes in finding and choosing an appropriate agency. Also, using an independent in one country many be fine, but if we plan to expand into several countries then managing a multiplicity of relationships becomes complex and time-consuming.

5 Conclusion

I hope this report supplies you with the information you require. Using marketing communications effectively is critical to our business's success and I look forward to continuing to do so.

marketing
management
in practice

SYLLABUS

Aims and objectives

The Marketing Management in Practice unit practices students in developing and implementing marketing plans at an operational level in organisations. A key part of this unit is working within a team to develop the plan and managing teams implementing the plan by undertaking marketing activities and projects. Its aim is to assist students in integrating and applying knowledge from all the units at the Professional Diploma level, particularly as part of a team. This unit also forms the summative assessment for the Professional Diploma level.

Learning outcomes

Students will be able to:

o Explain the roles and structure of the marketing function and the nature of relationships with other functions within various types of organisation.
o Plan and undertake or commission marketing research for an operational marketing plan or business decision.
o Interpret qualitative and quantitative data and present appropriate and coherent recommendations that lead to effective marketing and business decisions.
o Develop marketing objectives and plans at an operational level appropriate to the organisation's internal and external environments.
o Develop an effective plan for a campaign and supporting customers and members of a marketing channel.
o Use appropriate management techniques to plan and control marketing activities and projects.
o Use appropriate techniques to develop, manage and motivate a team so that it performs effectively and delivers required results.
o Define measures for, and evaluate the performance of, marketing plans, activities and projects and make recommendations for improvements.

Indicative content and weighting

Element 1: Managing people and teams (30 per cent)

o Describe the functions, roles of marketing managers and typical marketing jobs and the nature of relationships with other functions in organisations operating in a range of different industries and contexts.
o Develop and maintain effective relationships with people in other functions and disciplines within the organisation.
o Identify and explain the key challenges of managing marketing teams in a multi-national or multicultural context.
o Explain how you would use the techniques available for selecting, building, developing and motivating marketing teams to improve performance.
o Allocate and lead the work of marketing teams, agreeing objectives and work plans with teams and individuals.

o Respond to poor performance within a marketing team by minimising conflict, supporting team members, overcoming problems and maintaining discipline.

o Explain the sources and nature of change affecting organisations and the techniques available for managing change.

o Evaluate individual and team performance against objectives or targets and provide constructive feedback on their performance.

Element 2: Managing marketing projects (10 per cent)

o Describe the main stages of a project and the roles of people involved at each stage.

o Describe the main characteristics of successful and less successful projects and identify the main reasons for success or failure.

o Explain the importance of, and techniques for, establishing the project's scope, definition and goals.

o Use the main techniques available for planning, scheduling, resourcing and controlling activities on a project.

o Explain the importance of preparing budgets and techniques for controlling progress throughout a project to ensure it is completed on time and within budget.

o Explain the main techniques for evaluating the effectiveness of a project on its completion.

Element 3: Managing knowledge and delivering marketing research projects (20 per cent)

o Explain the concept, and give examples, of the application of information and knowledge management, highlighting the role of marketing and employees within the organisation.

o Design a research project aimed at providing information as part of a marketing audit or for marketing and business decisions.

o Manage a marketing research project by gathering relevant information on time and within the agreed budget.

o Make arrangements to record, store and, if appropriate, update information in the MkIS, a database created for the purpose or another system.

o Analyse and interpret information and present, as a written report or oral presentation, appropriate conclusions or recommendations that inform the marketing and business decisions for which the research was undertaken.

o Review and evaluate the effectiveness of the activities and the role of the individual and team in this process.

Element 4: Developing and implementing marketing plans (20 per cent)

o Develop an operational marketing plan, selecting an appropriate marketing mix for an organisation operating in any context such as FMCG, business-to-business (supply chain), large or capital project-based services, voluntary and not-for-profit, or sales support (e.g. SMEs).

o Use the main techniques available for planning, scheduling and resourcing activities within the plan.

o Identify appropriate measures for evaluating and controlling the marketing plan.

o Review and evaluate the effectiveness of planning activities and the role of the individual and team in this process.

Element 5: Delivering communications and customer service programmes (20 per cent)

- o Plan the design, development, execution and evaluation of communications campaigns by a team of marketers, including external agencies and suppliers.
- o Use appropriate marketing communications to develop relationships or communicate with a range of stakeholders
- o Manage and monitor the provision of effective customer service.
- o Use marketing communications to provide support for members of a marketing channel.
- o Use marketing communications techniques for an internal marketing plan to support management of change within an organisation.
- o Review and evaluate the effectiveness of communications activities and the role of the individual and team in this process.

KEY CONCEPTS – REVISION CHECKLIST

These are the key concepts you should be aware of when you go into the exam. Be able to define or explain each concept, and to discuss key aspects of it. If you have revised this material the you should be able to cope with the theoretical aspects of the exam.

Syllabus element 1

Managing people and teams

☑

Roles of marketing ☐
Marketing management process ☐
Internal marketing ☐
Building relationships ☐
Building marketing teams ☐
Effective teams ☐
Job analysis ☐
Job descriptions ☐
Person specification ☐
Recruitment ☐
Selection ☐
Team development ☐
Team effectiveness ☐
Motivation ☐

☑

Managing marketing teams
– objective setting ☐
– work plans ☐
– improving performance ☐
– appraisals ☐
– training ☐
Managing change
– people and change ☐
– implementing change ☐

Syllabus element 2

Managing marketing projects

☑

Project definition ☐
Project scope ☐
Project stages ☐
Project teams ☐
Project roles ☐

☑

Project plans ☐
Project control ☐
Budgets ☐
Gantt charts ☐
Critical path analysis ☐

Syllabus element 3

Managing knowledge and delivering marketing research projects

☑
☐
Based on the Marketing Research and Information module

Syllabus element 4

Developing and implementing marketing plans

☑
☐
Based on the Marketing Planning module

Syllabus element 5

Delivering communications and customer service programmes

☑
☐
Based on the Marketing Communications module

PART A MINI-CASES

Mini-Case 1: Pinnacle Pictures (December 2004)

Location

Pinnacle Pictures has been in business for 10 years operating from a single centre on a local regional basis.

Core business

Overnight and postal photographic processing, that is developing and printing of films.

Customers leave their films at selected high-street agents around the region. The films are collected by van in the late afternoon. The films are processed overnight and completed pictures are delivered early the next day for collection by the customer. Customers can also elect to post their films in prepaid envelopes, and prints are returned by post (this offers better value for money to the customer but obviously takes longer).

Business profile

Pinnacle Pictures has gained regional dominance by offering a value-for-money service with quality processing and reliable deliveries. With some fifty staff the company has become profitable with a turnover of £5 000 000.

Digital photography and the changing business of photographic development mean that instant photographs are much more accessible now to the general public. The expensive-to-use instant Polaroid camera has been replaced by relatively cheap digital cameras. With these, images can be downloaded onto a computer, printed out on inexpensive colour printers or sent to friends via e-mail or on disc. Pictures can also be posted on a website easily to form an online photograph album; this can be accessed by friends and family or business contacts around the world.

Digital cameras have become part of the digital technology revolution and are often regarded as a necessary computer accessory, like the digital scanner, or are 'bundled' with new computers by the big chains of stores. In addition, many old-style photographs and other pictures can be scanned by people, enabling them to e-mail the images to their friends or to be stored digitally on computer or disc. Many of the highest quality photographic images are still obtained using traditional photography (e.g. fashion photography). However, the press and public relations (PR) companies often use the highest quality digital cameras due to the convenience and necessity for speedy transfer from sometimes remote locations.

The challenge

Pinnacle Pictures must rise to this challenge. Photographs appear to be following music down the digital path, where online downloads such as MP3 files are challenging more tangible products like CDs and the already obsolete vinyl record. 'Wet film' processing technology will increasingly be replaced with digital technologies needing new skills, new people, new production processes and new marketing strategies: a management of change situation.

Your role

You have been appointed as Marketing Manager to participate in the development of the digital business including the development of Internet-based business.

The management of Pinnacle Pictures have also decided that a good website is critical to the development of the business. Given that this e-commerce activity will be core to the future company strategy it has been decided to recruit a webmaster to develop and maintain the Pinnacle Pictures website. Your advice will be required.

A most important capital city international art gallery has completed a digital photography programme and now has an archive of over 2000 major pictures in high-quality digital format. Visitors to the art gallery can now have postcards and reproductions produced 'online' within minutes replacing the previous restricted range produced by traditional photography and printing. The gallery wishes to make its heritage available on a more regional basis and has approached Pinnacle Pictures with a proposal that they might license these digital images. Your input will be needed.

Appendix 1

Section one

Background notes on the market for Pinnacle Pictures. The market can be segmented by a number of variables, which include:

- *Cost and quality of service*: professional photographers use expensive laboratories that are able to provide the highest standards and specialised services. At the other extreme low-cost providers provide a very inexpensive service with sound basic processing and very few 'extras'. Pinnacle Pictures at present occupies a middle segment providing high-quality services for the amateur enthusiast and for other more demanding customers (see Appendix 2 for outline of services offered).
- *Type of photographer*: professional photographers (at present not a target for Pinnacle Pictures), serious amateur photographic enthusiasts, hobbyists such as bird watchers who take pictures as part of their hobby and general domestic customers (photographs of holidays, parties, family occasions such as birthdays, etc.).
- *Type of media*: film (various types and sizes), digital (various types of storage media and Internet file downloads).
- *Range of services demanded*: basic prints, enlargements and special services (see Appendix 2).

Competition

- *Specialist laboratories* – these dominate the top end of the market for professional photography.
- *'No frills' basic providers* – these dominate the lower end of the market where cheapness is the issue.
- *Other middle market players*
- *Home processing* – previously with chemical 'wet' processing, only the most dedicated amateur would set up a home laboratory/dark room. Now most PCs with a colour printer can become a home digital photograph 'laboratory'. However, the quality of low-cost colour printers is limited and with high costs of ink cartridges and photographic quality paper, home printing is an expensive process.

Service issues

○ *Processing time* – a key issue with many customers wanting to see their images as soon as possible. This has led to many high-street outlets building 'mini laboratories' onsite to process films within one hour. Many outlets have now also incorporated computer terminals to allow customers to download files from their digital cameras for local printing at the high-street outlet or for onwards transmission to a central processing facility.

○ *Print quality* – home-produced prints may have a restricted life, particularly if printed on poor paper. Some of the one-hour processing equipment also produces lower quality reproduction with little account made of film type. Pinnacle Pictures printing technology gives prints with an expected life of over 100 years of good quality

○ *Access* – with the increasing popularity of 'broadband' access within the domestic market giving fast internet downloads and uploads, the cost and time of transmitting large files from home to a central processing laboratory have been greatly reduced. Thus people do not need to go to a high-street outlet to send their files for processing. Online business is now a clear possibility.

Section two: Archive sources of high-quality digital images

Certain types of organisations have been producing digital image archives:

○ Newspapers and magazines use them to preserve and have immediate access to their library of images.

○ Museums and art galleries use them for research purposes and to provide international access to their collections.

Appendix 2

Pinnacle Pictures: outline of existing services and products

Film processing

○ Standard colour processing
○ Enlargements up to 30" × 40" (762 × 1016 mm)
○ Slide services
○ Black and white processing.

Digital services

○ Digital image processing with high-quality 'professional' prints
○ Traditional photographic prints to digital image files
○ Media conversion (e.g. Cine film to video, video to DVD, etc.)
○ 'Online photograph albums' (Internet access to pictures for family and friends) either from digital images or by converting traditional photographs to digital format.

Special services

Restoration (e.g. blemishes can be removed from old prints before re-printing) of photographic gifts (customers own image incorporated into the product) include:

- Baseball caps
- Ceramic mugs
- Jigsaw puzzles
- Mouse mats
- Sweatshirts, and so on.

(Material has been taken from industry sources. Pinnacle Pictures is a fictitious company for assessment purposes only.)

Part A (Compulsory)

Question 1

Marketing planning, recruitment, selection and induction

Syllabus elements 1.4, 4.1

a) Outline a marketing plan to develop a profitable regional business for the art gallery opportunity (incorporated in your role). This should include partnership arrangements with local organisations such as art galleries, museums and theatres for the art images.   (30 marks)

b) What issues and actions do Pinnacle Pictures' management need to consider in the selection, appointment and induction of a webmaster into the organisation?   (20 marks)

(Total 50 Marks)

Part B (Answer *two* questions only)

Question 2

Information needs and sources to support an online business operation

Syllabus elements 3.1, 3.2

The online digital business will be a radical departure for Pinnacle Pictures from its traditional overnight developing and printing business via high-street agents.

a) What information will the company require for the development of the online digital business?
(15 Marks)

b) How might it be obtained?   (10 Marks)

(Total 25 Marks)

Question 3

Marketing communications activities

Syllabus elements 5.1–5.6

Outline the integrated marketing communications activities required to promote the online digital image processing service. (25 Marks)

Question 4

Change issues confronting the company and how they might be managed effectively

Syllabus element 1.7

Pinnacle Pictures will have to extend its operations to include the addition of computer-based digital processes. What are the management of change issues confronting the company and how might these be dealt with effectively? (25 Marks)

Question 5

Project management

Syllabus elements 2.1, 2.2, 2.3, 2.4

Pinnacle's new website will be launched at a major photographic exhibition in six months' time. What project management tools and actions would you recommend to ensure that all necessary activities were undertaken to ensure a trouble-free exhibition launch? (25 Marks)

Mini-Case 2: WRBSA – Supporting Businesses

West Rochshire Business Support Association (WRBSA) is a member-owned body, which supports businesses of all sizes throughout the West Rochshire region. WRBSA is a non-profit making organisation which receives income from membership subscriptions and grant support from local, national and supra-national government bodies which is awarded to assist enterprises of various sizes. The membership companies are from all sectors – business to business, business to consumer and not-for-profit organisations. Membership is currently about 4000 businesses, accounting for approximately 15 000 employees – much of the membership is small one person or family-run businesses, but it includes a few of the larger employers from the region who have over 500 employees.

Established in 1950 as a lunch club for business owners in the county town, WRBSA is still seen by some members of the business community as a club which favours those who are closest to it, even though the support offered is available to any member organisation.

Members can benefit from a variety of services, but the main resource used is the facility to establish the availability of financial support to expand business through various methods. The support is available in the form of grants towards equipment, both production and IT, and marketing support for both research and promotion, in particular online marketing developments. The grants are not available uniformly to all businesses – they have to meet the criteria specified by the awarding body which can range from a European Union department to a local government funding group, and the criteria can vary according to geographic location, size of organisation and type of business carried out.

In addition to this service the members benefit from events held by WRBSA, which aim to assist businesses – these include training programmes and networking events. Many of the training programmes are available to non-member organisations but members get discounts on the cost for these courses. Networking events include both lunches and dinners – generally with guest speakers. Members also receive a monthly newsletter with business success stories and advice, in which they can also advertise at competitive rates.

Membership has been declining over recent years, with a steady flow of new members being outweighed by those who are leaving; however, no effort has been made to investigate why members do not renew their subscriptions.

Your role

You have been appointed Marketing and Membership Services Development Manager – a new position for the organisation.

The challenge

WRBSA needs to retain the existing members, increase membership numbers and also would see a larger proportion of its membership using the services it offers. Take up of grants is usually high, but the number of member organisations who attend courses and network events is very low, and it is typically the same people who turn up regularly.

New incentives to encourage participation are required, as are incentives for businesses to join the association.

Competition

There are a large number of organisations which offer business support, ranging from Government departments and agencies through local Chambers of Commerce to commercial organisations including banks and accountants who offer some of the services provided by WRBSA.

Competition for training comes from a wide variety of sources, typically local colleges and private training companies who can be either national or local.

In addition, there are many networking organisations including a number who organise events within the West Rochshire area.

Appendix 1

WRBSA services offered

o   access to a database of funding available for various projects
o   assistance with application for funding
o   general business advice
o   training courses in business and IT skills
o   networking events – lunches, dinners, social events
o   monthly newsletter to members
o   website with secure area for member only access
o   representing local businesses to local and national government and lobbying when necessary.

Membership fees

o   the membership fees are related to the number of employees the member company has

o   1–5 employees – £125 per year
o   5–10 employees – £150 per year
o   10–20 employees – £175 per year
o   Over 20 employees – £200 per year

WRBSA facilities

WRBSA have just moved into purpose built new premises which are owned by the Association. They have been designed with future expansion in mind and as such, in addition to office accommodation, include:

o   Two meeting/training rooms with full multimedia features
o   An IT training suite with 10 student PCs and one for a tutor, all networked with full Internet connectivity
o   On site catering facilities to be used by catering companies supporting events held in the building.

Appendix 2

Job description

The Marketing and Membership Services Development Manager reports to the Membership Director. Specific duties include:

- o Development of a three-year marketing programme for WRBSA
- o Responsibility for all marketing communication activities for WRBSA, including the newsletter
- o Marketing research into member requirements and satisfaction levels
- o Creation of an online database of members
- o Creation of online communication programme to members
- o Development of new services for the membership to encourage participation from a greater percentage of member organisations
- o Recruitment and development of two part-time (job share) marketing assistants.

Appendix 3

Notes from initial meetings held within WRBSA

Membership objectives:

- o Maintain current levels of micro-business membership (organisations with up to 10 employees).
- o Increase membership of organisations with more than 20 employees by 20 per cent over next two years.
- o Increase numbers of member organisations participating in events by 40 per cent over two years.

Event targets:

- o In addition to training programmes, hold one member event per week.
- o Four days training to be held per week (some sessions are one day, the longest courses are four days).
- o New types of events to be introduced to meet targets for increased participation at events.

An online database of member organisations which can be used by the members to be available within nine months.

Marketing assistants to be in place within three months.

Part A (Compulsory)

Question 1

Marketing research programme, marketing activity plan, selection and recruitment

Syllabus elements 1.4, 3.2, 4.1

a) Outline a research programme which will help ensure that WRBSA objectives and activities are better focused on the real needs of its members. (20 marks)

b) Produce a marketing action plan for the next 12 months which will meet the objectives for membership and events, and provide the required database. (20 marks)

c) How would you select and induct the two new marketing assistants? (10 marks)

(Total 50 marks)

Part B (Answer *two* questions only)

Question 2

Project planning

Syllabus elements 2.1, 2.2, 2.3

A launch event is planned for the new premises in three months' time (to allow everything to have settled down following the move). It is your responsibility to organise and run the event.

a) How would you ensure your plan for and run the event successfully? (10 marks)

b) Which are the key groups you need to involve in the planning of the event? (5 marks)

c) Outline the most important publics expected to attend the launch event? (10 marks)

(Total 25 marks)

Question 3

Change management; e-communications

Syllabus elements 1.7, 5.1, 5.2, 5.5

How can WRBSA convert the majority of their communication (newsletters, event promotion, availability of new grant information, etc.) to members to electronic format whilst ensuring that members perceive higher levels of service and information? (25 marks)

Question 4

Researching customer requirements and satisfaction

Syllabus elements 3.2, 3.3, 3.4

a) Training programmes form a large part of the income WRBSA receive each year. How can WRBSA ensure that the programmes offered are appropriate to the needs of the business community in West Rochshire to protect this income which is vital for providing member benefits. (15 marks)

b) Produce a form which would enable WRBSA to determine if the training programmes meet the needs of the delegates. This should be the form which delegates complete at the end of the training. (10 marks)

(Total 25 marks)

Question 5

Team development and customer satisfaction

Syllabus elements 1.3, 1.4, 1.6, 1.8, 5.3, 5.6

Within WRBSA there are many people who communicate directly with member organisations.

a) What team development techniques could be used to bring together these people to ensure a consistent message is given to the members? (15 marks)

b) How might a staff motivation be improved to ensure customers always receive the best possible advice? (10 marks)

(Total 25 marks)

Mini-Case 3: JJ Motorbikes (December 2005)

Business was going well for JJ Motorbikes, founded five years ago by John Jones. 'JJ', as he was known, had been the world champion in the 'Super Bikes' class 10 years previously, setting up JJ Motorbikes on retirement from active motorcycle racing, five years ago.

A successful business was developed by converting an old car showroom, but the business has now outgrown the present facilities and a new 'Bike City' complex is being constructed. It is being built adjacent to the main motorway on the edge of the city, about 2 miles (3 kilometres) from the present site. Building work is now underway and the new facilities will be ready to open in June 2006.

Key aspects of the business formula

With 'JJ' a well-known personality in the biking community, JJ Motorbikes has become not only a place to buy motorbikes but for 'bikers' to meet and chat. The area outside the service centre has a small coffee machine and bikers meet fellow riders to chat and then browse in the accessory shop. They do not always buy, but overall, the accessory shop is one of the major profit centres in the business. 'JJ' remembers buying his first second-hand motorbike when he was young and did not have much money; therefore he has kept part of the show room for affordable, second-hand motorbikes (with a 'JJ' guarantee). The young entry bikers of today become the big spending enthusiasts in a few years, and so the relationship becomes established with JJ Motorbikes. Not only does the business have a selection of the newest and most exciting performance bikes, but also a full range of smaller motorbikes for the commuter, who wants to cut both travel time and costs. All customers appreciate the small display of classic motorbikes. The display changes each month, motorbikes being loaned by individual enthusiasts, museums and manufacturers.

These experiences have been built into the plan for the new JJ Motorbikes. The new site was selected for easy motorway access and has ample parking. The facilities will include:

- o motorbike showroom
- o accessories and clothing shop
- o the 'Pit Stop' café
- o used bike showroom at rear
- o service centre
- o reception area
- o classic bike display area.

JJ Motorbikes is a fictitious company for assessment purposes only. This case study has been based on various industry sources and press reports.

Appendix 1

Your role

You are the new marketing executive.

JJ Motorbikes has not employed a full-time marketing person before. The sales manager was previously responsible for marketing communications. With the expansion of the business, the decision has been made to appoint you as 'Communications and Marketing Executive.'

A budget of £100 000 has been allocated for communications during the launch period and a further £15 000 is available for internal communications and frontline staff training in customer care.

JJ Motorbikes

Summary outline job description for marketing executive

Reports to: Sales and Marketing Director

Collaborates with: Sales Manager

Responsibilities

- external communications, including advertising, PR and implementation of the corporate 'house style'
- internal communications, including the company staff newsletter
- to develop initiatives to strengthen customer relationships, with the objective of increasing profitable sales
- to conduct market research as required
- to develop information systems for the continued profitable development of the business
- to work with the Sales Manager (who also reports to the Sales and Marketing Director), to ensure the proper integration of marketing with the day-to-day sales activities
- to work with the Sales Manager in the development of appropriate sales promotion activities
- to manage marketing projects as required.

Appendix 2

JJ Motorbikes' Marketing and Sales Director's outline fact file

The Sales and Marketing Director (to whom you report) has prepared this brief fact file to give you some background and context to the business.

Although JJ Motorbikes only operates from a single outlet, it has achieved domination of the regional market.

JJ Motorbikes has a portfolio of some major leading bike brands, including Ducati, Honda, Harley Davidson and Kawasaki.

The 'JJ' product range includes the following types of bikes:

- *Scooters* – Small, light engines with a low top speed, an ideal economical, yet stylish, town run-around
- *Small motorbikes* – Small to medium engines with higher top speeds, ideal market entry for the younger biker or for longer distance commuting
- *Sports motorbikes* – Powerful bikes with high performance for the enthusiast; built for performance rather than comfort
- *Touring motorbikes* – Larger bikes built for comfort as much as performance (stereo sound, global positioning system, etc.)

With increasing concern for safety, gaining a motorcycle driving licence has become more difficult. To meet this challenge, JJ Motorbikes has set up a 'Bike Academy', linked with a local racetrack for 'off-road' tuition. The off-road space has proved popular, and one year ago the company started an advanced course for enthusiasts and racers.

The present website is basic and contains only contact information.

Segmentation of the market

Below are some of the segmentation issues. Part of your initial activities will be to refine JJ Motorbikes' segmentation strategy in order to better serve key defined segments and develop profitable business (especially in expanding market segments).

Enthusiasts

o Young people who have just reached the age to ride a motorbike and want to purchase their first one (they have limited spending power but are the future high-spending enthusiasts).
o Single people or newly married with no children, mainly in their 20s, with high disposable incomes. Married with children and limited disposable incomes, may have to give up biking due to financial constraints.
o Older people (35–55) whose children have left home, with high disposable incomes; often returning to biking ('born-again' bikers).
o The number of female bikers is increasing.

Utility riders

o People who are seeking to exploit the convenience of a bike for commuting in the age of heavy traffic, threat of congestion charges (for taking cars into city centres), parking charges and fuel costs. The advantages are convenience and lower travel costs.

Selected macro- and micro-environment issues

o Increasing pressures and legislation regarding safety and environmental (green) issues.
o Increasing costs of car ownership, including taxation, fuel and parking charges.
o Increasing acceptability of motorbikes as a convenient city 'run-around' means of transport.
o Increasing motorbike ownership by women.
o Increasing technical sophistication of motorbikes makes quality servicing by professional technicians in well-equipped workshops important. This is critical to maintain engine emission standards and safety performance built into modern bikes.
o Increasing political pressures – limited car access to city centres with 'congestion charging' and parking limitations. These favour bike users.
o Selected competition issues:

  o from other similar outlets.
  o local independent trainers (who do not have JJ Motorbikes' 'off-road' facilities).
  o specialists in motorcycle clothing, helmets and accessories. International chains are increasing their presence in city centre locations. The recent opening of a Damerell's outlet (accessories-only shop) is a threat to local clothing and accessories businesses.

o increasingly, people are test-riding at their regional centre, then purchasing via the Internet to gain lowest possible prices.

o some car servicing centres have noted the opportunity and added motorbike servicing to their portfolio of services. Servicing is profitable not only for the service elements but for parts needed (e.g. tyres for a sports bike can be over £250 a pair and need replacing after some 4000 miles).

JJ Motorbikes have been considering the introduction of a loyalty card (the 'JJ' card). The racetrack where JJ Motorbikes have their training centre is interested in collaborating on this (e.g. reduced prices and preferential race day booking for 'JJ' cardholders). More local business partners would be desirable.

Part A (Compulsory)

Question 1

Segmentation, targeting, positioning and marketing plans

Syllabus elements 4.1, 4.2, 5.2, 5.3

a) Review the segmentation variables that are relevant to JJ Motorbikes' present situation, and propose what segments represent profitable opportunities for the business.   (10 marks)

b) Outline a marketing plan for Bike City for the next two years (the full 7Ps service extended marketing mix should be used).   (30 marks)

c) Harley Davidson and other brands have found the female motorbike enthusiast a developing segment in some countries. Suggest marketing initiatives to attract and retain female motorbike enthusiasts as profitable JJ customers.   (10 marks)

(Total 50 marks)

Part B (Answer *two* questions only)

Question 2

Marketing communications activities for revenue generation

Syllabus elements 5.1, 5.2, 5.3

With the expansion of JJ Motorbikes, the income needed for profitable operation is increasing. Select and analyse the marketing communications that could help achieve this, including the generation of additional revenue from the existing client base.   (25 marks)

Question 3

Change management and marketing orientation

Syllabus elements 1.1, 1.2, 1.7

What management actions can JJ take to change the organisation from a product-focused philosophy to a marketing orientation? (25 marks)

Question 4

Information to support website development decision, project management

Syllabus elements 2.1, 2.2, 2.4, 3.1, 3.2, 3.3

The present website is only basic. A decision has been taken to completely re-launch it, to link in with the opening of the new facility. You have been assigned this project.

a) What information is needed before making a decision to launch the website? (10 marks)

b) Outline project management theory that is relevant to this situation. (15 marks)

(Total 25 marks)

Question 5

Customer satisfaction and relationships

Syllabus elements 4.2, 5.2, 5.3, 5.6

The maintenance and repair shop for the bikes is not only an important profit stream for JJ Motorbikes, but also important in customer retention. What issues should the company consider, to develop and maintain customer satisfaction with service quality in the maintenance and repair services? (25 marks)

Mini-Case 4: The Engineers' Store

The Engineers' Store is a distributor of mechanical components to the engineering industry with nine branches spread around the country. Started over 50 years ago the business has grown from a small one-man operation to its current size, employing 85 people with a large customer base. The business is currently owned by Managing Director James Evans, the son of the founder, who is actively involved in the day-to-day running of the business.

The business has a very good reputation in each area where it is located, stock levels are maintained at very high levels ensuring good availability of products for customers, and all customer facing staff have good levels of product knowledge to be able to assist with unusual requests. The Engineers' Store is in a very competitive industry, with a range of competitors from large nationals with up to 150 branches through to small, single outlet companies, generally established by people who previously worked for a larger company.

Customers visit the branches of The Engineers' Store to order and collect goods, or they telephone orders though which are delivered by the company's own fleet of vans. Each branch has a salesperson who regularly visits customers to discuss requirements, solve technical issues and build relationships for long-term business.

Customers are typically engineering businesses who purchase components required to keep their own machines working, and also to incorporate in the products they manufacture.

The Engineers' store has one main advantage over many of the smaller organisations in having direct access to the best products directly from manufacturers through authorised distributor status – this is rarely given to the small companies by the better respected manufacturers, and in recent years many of them have been reducing the number of distributors they sell through. Maintaining the relationships with the manufacturers is something James Evans has worked hard at to retain his advantage.

Your role

You are the recently appointed Marketing and Relationship Manager for the Engineers' Store.

Appendix 1

Excerpt of job description – Marketing and Relationship Manager, the Engineers' Store

The Marketing and Relationship Manager reports directly to the Managing Director, and the responsibilities include:

- Development and implementation of a national marketing plan for the Engineers' Store
- Marketing communications and PR for the company nationally and to support each branch locally
- Development of product range through building relationships with existing and new suppliers
- Investigating opportunities for expansion through research into geographical areas currently not covered – either through organic growth or acquisition
- Development of a consistent brand image for all branches
- Development of support materials for presentations to customers by the salesforce
- Creation of an extranet to enable existing customers to purchase online
- Production of a newsletter to send to customers on a quarterly basis.

Appendix 2

Notes made during initial discussions in new job

The Engineers' Store has a reputation for being old-fashioned and conservative in the way it does business – this is seen as a positive by most existing customers.

Many customers enjoy visiting the branches to discuss requirements, and generally have a chat – if they arrive at the right time they even get a free drink!

The product range stocked is vast, but there are items in stock which are very old – probably up to 20 years old which is longer than the recommendations made by the manufacturers. It is these products, however, which the larger competitors do not usually have available quickly and therefore provide competitive advantage for the Engineers' Store.

There is no uniform corporate identity – the signs at each branch are different, there is no consistency across other materials including stationery, and delivery vehicles are functional rather than promotional.

Premises are not as smart as some competitors, but the nature of the products customers bring in to demonstrate what they need (old, dirty and oil covered components) means keeping the customer areas clean can be difficult.

Promotional literature tends to be provided by the manufacturers, with little or no space for personalisation.

Manufacturer product quality has increased meaning products last longer and need less replacement.

Many parts are made specifically for customers by the component manufacturers and these are only available through authorised distributors.

Most products which are not in stock can be obtained on a next day delivery from the manufacturers, although there can be a carriage charge incurred for this. In the worst case, however, very unusual products can take up to six months to be delivered, so close liaison is required with customers and suppliers.

The Engineers' Store is predominantly a product-oriented organisation, with some elements of a sales orientation, in an industry where price is the most commonly used promotional tool when selling to customers.

When stores have been opened they have been staffed by a manager who has moved from a previous store, and new recruits to the company.

Part A (Compulsory)

Question 1

Information needs, data collection, marketing plan, environmental analysis

Syllabus elements 3.1, 3.2, 3.3, 4.1, 4.2

a) Outline the information which would be needed by the Engineers' Store to expand its business into new geographic areas and new product ranges and also the procedures which would be used to collect it. (25 marks)

b) Outline a marketing plan which would be appropriate for the development of the existing branches of the Engineers' Store, including a *brief* environmental and SWOT analysis.

(25 marks)

(Total 50 marks)

Part B (Answer *two* questions only)

Question 2

Marketing communications activities; evaluation of effectiveness

Syllabus elements 5.2, 5.3, 5.6

a) Outline the marketing communications activities which you would undertake to create a uniform image for the Engineers' Store to maintain its status with current customers and attract others from competitors. (15 marks)

b) How would you evaluate the effectiveness of the communication activities? (10 marks)

(Total 25 marks)

Question 3

Recruitment, training and team building

Syllabus elements 1.4, 1.5

The opening of a new branch would involve the Engineers' Store in the recruitment and training of staff. How would you select, train and team build the staff of a new branch?

(25 marks)

Question 4

Project management, and associated problems

Syllabus elements 2.1–2.6

The development of a consistent brand image for all visible elements of the Engineers' Store is a significant project. Using appropriate management tools, outline the stages of this process, and consider the difficulties which may be encountered and how to overcome them.

(25 marks)

Question 5

Training programme for changing business emphasis

Syllabus elements 1.4, 1.6, 1.7, 1.8

Management and staff at the Engineers' Store are very good at communicating with customers, but at times they are not particularly focused on business. Outline the objectives and programme for a half-day training workshop to ensure the focus moves to developing business whilst maintaining relationships.

(25 marks)

SUGGESTED ANSWERS

PART A

Mini-Case 1: Pinnacle Pictures (December 2004)

Answer 1 (Compulsory)

Marketing planning, recruitment, selection and induction

Check your answer

A good answer is likely to:

	☑
	☐
Produce an outline marketing plan – Suggest use SOSTAC	☐
Include the potential art gallery business in the plan	☐
Consider environmental audit and marketing mix	☐
Outline the recruitment process for appointment of a webmaster	☐
Explain the recruitment process for this role	☐
Use an appropriate format – Suggest a report	☐

* * * * *

REPORT

To: Senior Management

From: Marketing Manager

Date: XX/XX/XXXX

Subject: Regional Art Gallery Business

1 Introduction

We have been presented with a new business opportunity from the international art gallery to create 'reproductions' of their pictures on an as demanded basis and by their customers on a licence basis. This opportunity relates to elements of our core business – digital image processing – and also gives us the opportunity to build relationships with a new business partner.

Below is an outline marketing plan for this venture, and on a related subject, the considerations for the appointment of a webmaster. Whilst we have a need for this person in general terms, there is also a requirement if we pursue the art gallery opportunity.

411

2 The marketing plan

2.1 Situational analysis

Strengths	**Weaknesses**
o 10 years experience	o Current weak website
o High-quality printing technology utilised	o Dependence on local 'wet film' business
o Ability to handle latest media	o Lack of people skills for digital processes
o Overall high quality and service – 100-year print life	
Opportunities	**Threats**
o Offering 'wet film' processing to professional photographers	o 'Home' processing of digital photographs
o Digital image archiving	o Increasing availability of 'no frills' basic providers of printing
o Expansion of online services	o Reduction in technology prices
o Online service providing international expansion capability	

The major threat to our business is the reducing prices of the technology products required to produce good quality images. At the same time as the equipment required to produce digital prints is getting cheaper, the quality of printing it is capable of is getting higher which means we have to find ways to develop competitive advantage.

Competition

Our competition comes from many sources, using Porter's five forces we can see the following:

Threat of new entrants
The barriers to entry are being lowered due to the reduction in price of equipment, e.g. many supermarkets now have in store processing enabling customers to request prints when they enter the store and collect them when they finish shopping

Power of suppliers
The suppliers of equipment have the capability to vertically integrate and open outlets of their own. As there are many industry competitors and restricted numbers of suppliers (for printers and paper), the suppliers have power

Industry rivalry
Pinnacle Pictures fall in the middle ground, below the specialist processors, but above the basic 'no frills' providers who are increasing in numbers

Power of buyers
Buyers – particularly high-street agents – have the ability to vertically integrate and carry out the printing process themselves. The same comment applies to individuals who can buy home printing equipment

Threat of substitutes
Home processing is a major threat to our business as equipment becomes more common and cost-effective

2.2 Objectives

- o Develop a profitable regional business based around the opportunity with the international art gallery.
- o Create partnerships with other local organisations such as journals, museums, art galleries and theories.
- o Develop our website presence to offer our services and the digital image archives online.

2.3 Segmentation and targeting

Segments	Variable requirements
Photographers	Quality – professional, high
o professional	– general domestic, low
o amateur	Service requirements – speed of return, etc.
o general domestic	
PR agencies	High quality, fast response
Newspapers and magazines	Lower quality, speed not urgent
Art galleries, Museums, Theatres	High quality, instant print capability
Potential customers	Needs further investigation

- o Positioning for the above should be done accordingly.

  - o For example, a separate brand may be appropriate for the professional photographer to emphasise the quality of the printing.

2.4 Marketing mix – Strategies

Product
- o Licensed online database of high-quality art gallery images
- o On site printing and payment facility for the gallery
- o Regional availability

Price
- o Premium pricing to reflect the quality of print, 'instant' service and art gallery situation
- o Differentiate pricing according to location type/online or offline payment

Place
- o Using art galleries as distribution channel
- o Current high-street agents
- o Internet/website distribution and payment

Promotion
- o Online promotion for wider promotion of the image database
- o Point-of-sale materials for on-site printing facilities in art gallery

o Point of sale and partner promotion materials for promotion through current high-street agents
o Joint PR campaign with art gallery to promote to the public
o Direct promotion to other art galleries and museums relating to the service which can be offered

People

o As a service our people are vital to provide the required service levels to customers
o Full training will be required in the changed processes from 'wet film' to digital
o Support services for website users will be needed

Process

o Online payment facility will need to be developed
o Equipment required for processing has to be up to date and reliable, with automated links to online processing
o Speed of response from processes is critical

Physical evidence

o For on-site printing at the art gallery the appearance of equipment is critical
o Staff uniforms for those on site at galleries would enhance physical evidence
o For online sales the website appearance and reliability is important physical evidence and needs to be correct
o The physical materials sent to online customers has to reflect a premium image

2.5 Budget

o Full costing needs to be carried out for the above marketing mix. In particular the costs of the technology development for the online services need to be factored, including the development of our website including the recruitment costs for the webmaster and staff training.
o Promotional aspects for development of partnership arrangements with our local art galleries, museums and theatre should be included in the budget.
o The budget should be based on 'objective and task' principles – that is how much do we need to spend to ensure success.

2.6 Implementation and control

o A project team with myself as project manager should be established to implement the plan.
o Throughout the plan consideration needs to be given to how we will measure success.
o This could include the expected returns from sales through the art galleries, online services and so on.
o Targets for numbers of galleries and museums should be set.
o The balanced scorecard approach to measurement would be ideal:

o Innovation and learning – training of staff, staff development
o Internal perspective – new processes to provide customer satisfaction
o Customer perspective – market share, customer satisfaction
o Financial perspective – return on investment, profitability and so on.

3 Recruiting a webmaster

We have identified that a good website is critical to the development of our business, and as such we need a webmaster to develop and maintain the Pinnacle Pictures website.

There are four main areas we need to consider to ensure success with the website and webmaster recruitment.

3.1 Selection

We need to consider what we want the webmaster to do – it is not as simple as to 'create a website'. The format of the site and its capabilities mean that we need to select a candidate with appropriate website development skills. In addition to this, the successful candidate will be appropriate to our organisation as they will be working with people from all departments in the creation and maintenance of the website.

An initial decision to be made is whether to handle the recruitment ourselves or appoint an agency – this would be my preferred method as they should help us to identify the characteristics and skills we require in the webmaster, and should also know where to look. As this is a new venture for us our lack of experience would make it hard to be sure we made the correct decisions as regards candidate specification.

Some of the points we need to include are:

Job description
- o To develop a website for Pinnacle Pictures.
- o Location – head office.
- o Report to – Marketing manager.
- o Experience as a webmaster for a similar size project.

Personal specifications
- o Creativity is essential in the recruit to produce an attractive site.
- o Ability to be adaptable to any changes in the future relating to new business opportunities to the organisation.
- o Needs to be willing to learn new technologies and have good communication skills to relate with customers and all levels of staff.
- o Be prepared to be flexible about working hours.

Even though I suggest we use a recruitment company to help us with the selection, we need to be involved in the interview process to ensure that the person selected has a cultural 'fit' with Pinnacle Pictures.

3.2 Induction programme

When our webmaster has been appointed and commenced work with us they need to have an induction programme which should be fully organised prior to their start date. As it is unlikely we will find a candidate with experience of our industry training will be required to ensure a full understanding. Areas we need to consider are:

- o Human Resources procedures – setting up all required HR data including computer access, payroll data and so on.

415

○ Understanding the business – time spend in each area understanding the processes we currently use, and those we want to incorporate within the online trading facility.

○ Understanding our customers – where possible we should introduce the webmaster to the business-to-business customers who may use our online facilities. This should include the high-street agents and art galleries.

The induction process may take up to one month to ensure the recruit is fully familiar with requirements

3.3 Training needs

Identification of additional training needs – whilst we hopefully will appoint a webmaster with all relevant technical skills, due to the variety of programming skills needed we may need to consider using outside courses to ensure he or she is fully capable of delivering the technical requirements we have.

3.4 Motivation and conflict

This person is being introduced into the organisation to bring new skills. It is important that they are kept motivated. We need to consider this from two elements – the webmaster will initially create the website and then maintain and develop it. As these are different skills we need someone who is adaptable and flexible enough to be happy working on both areas – they also need to gain personal reward for both elements. Secondly, given the change within Pinnacle Pictures it is probable that the webmaster will encounter resistance to change and some conflict – potentially from those people who have spent their lives using the skills required for wet film development rather than sitting at computers.

People will feel threatened by the new role in the organisation – it may be seen to be taking over from their role, therefore getting full buy in from staff will require involving them in the process and developing an understanding of the changing nature of our business.

4 Conclusion

We have a great opportunity to develop a new business through licensing with the international art gallery – and it is an opportunity which we can expand to other business partners in the future. If handled correctly it will provide a profitable business for many years to come.

Combined with this opportunity is the requirement to appoint and train a webmaster to develop a website for our business to fully exploit the changes that are taking place within our industry and markets.

PART B

Answer 2
Information needs and sources to support an online business operation

Check your answer

A good answer is likely to:

☑

In the introduction, create the need for the information and research to support the online digital business; justify your reasoning. ☐

In Part a, list and justify the types of internal/external information that would be needed to support the decision. Give reasons to justify why this information is required. ☐

In Part b, explain how this information can be obtained, identifying specific sources where possible. ☐

Adopt the role of the new marketing manager for Pinnacle Pictures. ☐

Use Report format. ☐

*   *   *   *   *

REPORT

To: Managing Director

From: Marketing Manager

Date: XX/XX/XX

Re: Information Needs and Sources for Online Digital Business

1 Introduction

The launch of the online digital business represents an exciting development for Pinnacle Pictures and an opportunity to capitalise on the rapid growth in digital photography and imaging. The move is also potentially very risky, both in terms of the market and in the technology used to create and deliver the product. To minimise or respond to the risks, we need accessible and up-to-date information, about a range of factors and a variety of sources. This information helps us identify weaknesses we may have to overcome or to respond to threats from competitors.

This report describes our information requirements, identifying internal and external sources.

2 Information requirements

For the online digital business to be successful, we need relevant information to help identify opportunities and threats (using external information) and information about our organisational strength and weaknesses (using internal information).

2.1 External information

2.1.1 Customers

This includes both our current customers and those we have the potential to serve.

We must understand what they buy, how much they spend, where they buy and how often. We need to segment customers into groups and determine which we should target. This will require demographic data, information on photo print spending patterns, market forecasts and growth patterns, information on specific customer needs and the particular benefits sought from an online service.

Armed with this information, we can identify segment sizes (volume and revenue), forecast future growth prospects and assess likely profit potential, enabling decisions concerning customer targeting and positioning.

We must also recognise that as our focus shifts away from traditional film, we may leave some of our loyal customers behind. We need to analyse the impact of this and see whether we can migrate existing customers to our digital services.

We already have top-level segment information (professional, pro-amateurs, home users, etc.) but we need to expand the depth of this both quantitatively and qualitatively for accurate targeting and positioning and subsequently for marketing mix decisions relevant to the online digital service.

A further vitally important aspect is for us to understand the website facilities, features and usability issues from the perspective of the target customer. If we get these elements wrong, visitors will not use the service.

2.1.2 Competitors

We need to identify and then segment competitors in terms of their size, capacity, service capabilities, quality and products offered. This will involve defining precisely who our competitors are – without doing this it will become very costly and inefficient to gather competitor information. At present, we have only top-level information on:

- o Specialist laboratories
- o No frills providers
- o Middle market
- o Home processing.

To fully define the competition, we should refer the mission and objectives and also link competitor identification to customer targeting and positioning. We can then collect more detailed information about individual competitors.

We need to investigate the competitor websites, to collect usability information, ideally using real customers to understand what competitors do well and where the gaps are.

2.1.3 Channels of distribution

As a traditional film processor, we have an effective network of retail collection points with agents who might play a role in the digital business model, acting as final stage photo printers. We also have the direct-mail order channel to consider.

We require both qualitative and quantitative information regarding existing and possible future channels in terms of:

○ Number of retail agents, their locations, space available for installation of production print machines.
○ Sales turnover and growth data for each agent, including our profit/agent data for comparison.
○ Willingness of each retail agent to work with us by embracing the new business model.
○ Understanding of the future needs of the agents; there expectations regarding margins and incentives, leasing, dealer training and so on.
○ How we recruit additional agents to cover the geographic gaps – most of our agents are located in our local region; we wish to expand or retail coverage geographically.
○ Data to help determine the most effective distribution approach for future growth: wholly owned, third party agent, franchise.
○ Specific information about the features and facilities of the new website in terms of what retail agents require to support them.

2.1.4 Wider environment

The key requirement is to monitor relevant changes in technology that have an impact on the business (opportunity or threat). The impact might arise from:

○ Changes in the technology used by the customer, for example the trend towards camera phones, not dedicated digital cameras.
○ Changes in the available production technology we might use. For example – a move from inks and toners to direct laser etching on special papers.
○ Changes in web technology, enabling us to deliver faster, more efficient or more flexible products and services. Example – development of electronic purse or other risk-free web- or phone-based payment systems.

The socio-cultural and ecological environments are also important and will require on-going monitoring.

2.2 Internal environment

Information will be required from all areas including marketing. Information, for example, to answer the following questions:

○ Do we have the right people, skills and experience for the online digital operation?
○ Do we have the brand strength and reputation to appear credible; how do we develop this, especially beyond our current geographic region and customer base?
○ Do we have sufficient customer and partner loyalty to support us?
○ Do we have an appropriate internal structure, processes and systems? How might we develop this? Is the culture supportive?
○ Can we develop an appropriate information system to support strategic and operational decisions?

3 Sources of the information

3.1 Internal – secondary (desk) research

Internal secondary sources include departmental records and sales/accounting and transaction data that would help with the acquisition of customer behavioural information, details of retail agent sales performance and so on. We can also gain some understanding of customer and retail agent attitudes and opinions from feedback and complaints forms, sales visit to partner reports. We also hold basic competitor information in the sales department.

We will address internal audit (strengths and weaknesses) requirements using internal data, departmental audits and reports and meeting minutes as well as operational and production data.

Internal marketing intelligence sources are also important – the information that our staff gathers from reading, talking to customers, suppliers and competitors. This form of information gathering can also help address the need for wider environmental data.

A weakness in this information currently is that it relates mainly to our traditional film development business model, our current customers and competitors. Much of this data will be of little relevance to the new online digital business model.

3.2 External – secondary (desk) research

Market, customer and competitor data can be obtained from trade associations, production equipment/photographic equipment manufacturers and the consumer photographic and trade press. The BBC and other media websites, including newspaper sites are useful in building the information we need.

Published research and market reports can be purchased, providing market, customer and competitor information as well as forecasts and future trends. Mintel, Key Note, Euromonitor and other syndicated research providers are resources for purchased research.

Online forums and blog sites are a potentially powerful way of gaining consumer insight.

Competitor information can be sourced from annual reports UK Companies House and Kompass Directory. Local and regional business library serves are also helpful as annual reports, market reports, directories and CD-ROM are accessible free of charge.

3.3 External – primary (field) research

This will require an ad hoc programme of research to be undertaken with specific information objectives, usually by employing a marketing research agency.

3.3.1 Qualitative research

Discussion groups and one-to-one individual depth interviews, focused on customers or retail agents, are invaluable for insight into the attitudes, opinions and motivations that drive behaviour, as well as competitor information; this would help us develop the service to meet needs and preferences.

Competitor perceptions can also be gained from consumers and agents using this approach.

3.3.2 Observational research

Electronic means, such as web browser and mouse click stream analysis, and use of Internet cookies as well as use of human observers viewing consumers using our website or competitor websites.

Mystery shopping employed to measure our service performance and that of competitors – responsiveness, accuracy of order, delivery reliability, print quality and so on.

3.3.3 Quantitative research

Use of surveys and questionnaires, whether delivered face-to-face (in retail agent locations) or sent by post, e-mail or web survey forms, can be used to measure specific attitudes and behaviours. These techniques would help to confirm qualitative research findings: what they buy, where, when, how much they spend and so on.

4 Concluding remarks

In order to capitalise on the information that we collect, we will need to create a marketing information system (MKIS) and maintain this with relevant and current information on the key information areas listed above. Such a system will improve accessibility to information for decision, both during formal planning processes and also for decisions that might arise at any time due to competitor actions, customer demands or environmental change.

Answer 3
Marketing communications activities

Check your answer

A good answer is likely to:

    ☑

Identify a range of activities, covering both internal and external communications. ☐

Suggest outline objectives for these communication activities. ☐

Relate your answer to the launch of an online digital image processing service (i.e. not just a traditional photo-processing service). ☐

Recognise that there are different target audiences for the communications. ☐

Use an appropriate format, e.g. a report. ☐

*   *   *   *   *

REPORT

To: Marketing Director

From: Marketing Manager

Date: XX/XX/XX

Re: Promotion of Online Digital Image Processing Service

1 Introduction

The decline of the traditional film processing market presents a threat to Pinnacle but, at the same time, the growth in digital photography presents great opportunities. I am confident that Pinnacle can capitalise on the online processing market but to do so requires a strong communications programme. The aims of the programme would be to:

- ○ Create awareness of our online digital image processing;
- ○ To reassure potential users about its speed and quality.

In designing the programme it is important to recognise that there are several market segments that we need to address:

- ○ home users who want their family snaps quickly and easily;
- ○ the more serious private user – amateur photographers and hobbyists;
- ○ business users, for example PR companies;
- ○ institutions such as galleries and museums.

These markets could be further segmented into those who have used Pinnacle before and those who have not. Different communication methods will need to be used for these different segments.

2 Marketing communications activities

A range of activities is suggested to reach the different markets. It is essential that these are 'integrated', in other words that they complement and support each other and do not provide conflicting messages that confuse consumers and detract from the Pinnacle brand. Activity to promote the online processing must also be integrated with promotional activity for other services.

2.1 Advertising

Advertising is an effective way to reach large numbers of people and create awareness of Pinnacle's service. To date Pinnacle's activities have been largely regionally focused but online processing means that images can be sent from anywhere. However, as we do not have an unlimited advertising budget we need to keep our advertising tightly focused, for example advertising in specialist photography or wildlife magazines to reach the hobbyist, and general interest consumer magazines for the family market.

2.2 Direct marketing

Over the years, Pinnacle has processed films for hundreds of thousands of households. Their address information will be held on our database, which we can use as the basis for a direct mailshot introducing our new service – many of these people will have moved on to digital cameras now.

2.3 Relationship marketing

Online customers will be e-mailing us their photographs. We can collect their e-mail details, and use this to keep customers informed about Pinnacle's services and to make promotional offers from time to time. (However, it is essential that we gain consumers' permission before we send them marketing e-mails, in accordance with the Privacy and Electronic Communications Regulations 2003.) The aim of relationship marketing is to retain customers – very important given the large number of alternative providers of digital processing services. We should also investigate the introduction of a frequent user scheme, offering discounts on processing or free extra services. This would incentivise consumers, both the casual user and the hobbyist, to return to us.

2.4 Sales promotions

Reference has already been made to making promotional offers as part of our relationship marketing programme. Offers could be extended to wider audience at selected times, for example outside peak holiday periods to encourage use of our facilities. These could be promoted via advertising and direct marketing schemes. We must attempt to capture a slice of the huge 'holiday snaps' market – we should start by forming alliances with holiday companies who could include details of our services in their brochures. They could also provide links to our website from theirs, in return for using images of their holidays on our own site. A further idea is to distribute promotional flyers, perhaps with a discount voucher attached, at events where many photos are likely to be taken – carnivals, air shows, pop concerts, garden festivals and so on.

2.5 Public relations

Publicity should be sought for the launch of our online service. On its own the launch is unlikely to be of significant media interest other than to the photographic processing trade press so we should link it to some other activity, for example. a photo competition in a general interest magazine, or some interesting or amusing survey results on a photography-related issue.

2.6 Museums and galleries; public relations companies

Again, the introduction of online services means that museums and galleries anywhere could use our services to produce pictures ordered by customers. This is a specialist market which should probably be approached, initially, by a direct marketing letter to named senior marketers within each institution. I suggest this letter is followed up by a telephone call from one of our team; a personal visit may subsequently be needed.

Similarly, public relations businesses may best be approached via letter and then phone call. They will often be up against tight deadlines so will be looking for quick delivery which may restrict us to a more local market to which prints can easily be couriered.

Both these markets will require reassurance about the print quality and other aspects of the service – personal discussion is likely to be essential.

2.7 Internet

Our website will be the point of entry to our services for all consumers, and it is essential that the website address is prominently displayed in all advertising and promotional material. The site must be highly user-friendly making it easy for people to send us their digital images. The opportunity should be taken to offer other services to consumers, for example the making of photographic gifts such as sweatshirts and ceramic mugs. We can offer other features on the site, encouraging people to visit or re-visit it, for example tips on taking good photographs, or a 'Best Photo' competition based on a theme that regularly changes. Links to the websites of museums and galleries for whom we offer printing services should also be included.

2.8 Internal markets

It is important that staff understand and are positive about the launch of any new service; this is particularly so for customer-facing staff (whether dealing with the public personally, by phone or by e-mail). Briefings should be given to staff well in advance with supporting written information in hard copy and/or on the Pinnacle intranet. Staff should have every opportunity to ask questions so that they are clear about what is on offer. Internal newsletters, posters and desk-drops can all be used to build interest up to the launch day.

2.9 Dealer relationships

Online processing relies wholly on direct links between consumers and Pinnacle, posing a threat to dealers. Care needs to be taken to maintain our dealer relationships, on whom we still rely for traditional and non-Internet business. This requires the skills of our sales team.

3 Conclusion

This report has outlined a range of activities to promote our new online digital image processing service. We are well known in the industry so, provided we promote our new service successfully using the methods described in an integrated way, there is no reason why we cannot be successful in this market.

Please contact me if you have any queries.

Answer 4
Change issues confronting the company and how they might be managed effectively

Check your answer

A good answer is likely to:

☑

Recognise the reasons for change. ☐

Outline the implications for change within Pinnacle Pictures. ☐

Apply relevant management change theory. ☐

Consider where there may be resistance to change. ☐

Suggest actions for managing the resistance. ☐

Use an appropriate format, e.g. a report. ☐

* * * * *

REPORT

To: Senior Management

From: Marketing Manager

Date: XX/XX/XXXX

Subject: Managing the change to digital processes

1 Introduction

The environment in which we operate is undergoing massive change at present with technology being the main driver – the move from wet film processing to computer based digital processes. We have recognised the need to respond to these changes through the development of our own digital processes and online business but this can bring issues within the business which need to be addressed.

2 Managing the change

Having been in business for five years, predominantly dealing with wet film processing, we now need to create a business which will be largely digital-based – this will mean a lot of change for the company and its employees. I believe we do have all the right ingredients for a successful and sustainable change:

- o a compelling reason to change – the environment is changing and our current business will disappear;
- o a clear vision of the future – we know the way the photography business is moving and the other opportunities presented (e.g. art gallery licensing);
- o a coherent plan for getting there.

Given that we have these three factors we have to ensure the change happens, and this will involve overcoming resistance which we may find from some of the staff.

People will resist change for a variety of reasons, primarily the fear of the unknown. Also, we have staff whose expertise is in the areas of wet film processing and the skills for digital processing can be quite different so they may be concerned about job security. Bacal argues that people go through four stages in their attempts to cope with change:

- o *Denial* – they deny that the change is happening, or that it will continue. We have to ensure that people realise we have to change, and that we intend to do so. This will require communication to the staff about the changes in the market – most of them should be aware of this because of their own adoption of digital cameras in place of film. We can reassure people, however, that we are not totally dropping the wet film processing, just that we cannot rely on it long term.
- o *Anger and resistance* – when it is accepted that the change is going to happen, or it has happened, people can become angry and resistant. At this stage, our leadership of the change is vital to ensure people move on from this stage. Supporting people through the change, and ensuring top-quality training is given becomes very important.
- o *Exploration and acceptance* – people develop an understanding of the change and are prepared to look further and accept it – there is more participation in the change process and we can utilise the staff to contribute additional ideas for implementation of the change.
- o *Commitment* – people work towards making the change succeed, they have adapted to the change and they want the organisation to be effective. We have to offer continual support and training at this stage as it may take some time for everything to work properly, and people to become as skilled at the new requirements as they are with their current situations.

A step-by-step model for the change we have to go though should include:

- o Ensure there is a receptive climate towards the proposed change – internal marketing will help here, communicating the opportunities which the change in the organisation will create.
- o Identify the champion to promote the change – this is a key element to consider. Whilst I am very happy to be the champion, I think it important to be part of a team. As I am a relative newcomer to the organisation it is important that there are others who also are seen to support the change – from all levels of the organisation.
- o Assess the competencies and capabilities of the team to see if there are any gaps to fill through training – it is quite likely that the team will not have much experience of managing change so we may need to use specialist training, or outside facilitators, to help us with the process.
- o Market the change to the target audience – this involves us creating a vision of the new organisation and conveying the vision to all staff through internal marketing. As an initial suggestion, I think that we should hold an event which all staff should attend to explain the changes proposed, and the benefits the staff will gain from the change. This event

should be fun and informal, and to minimise any negative impact on the business we may need to hold it outside working hours, possibly at a weekend.

○ Develop the plan, including a budget – as we have previously discussed, we need to have a plan for the change. In addition to the marketing plan, the change team need to develop a specific change plan which will detail the requirements for staff training, new equipment requirements, alterations to premises to accommodate the changes, possible new appointments to fill any skills gaps which cannot be sorted through training (the webmaster is one of these) and so on.

○ Anticipate the arguments against the change and produce positive responses to them.

Lewin proposed a simple three-step process for change:

Unfreeze – Transition – Refreeze

This involves making people recognise that they have to do things differently, changing the status quo (unfreeze). An extreme example, which I do not propose we follow, of unfreezing is to make every job in the organisation redundant so people have to reapply for the new positions. For our situation, it is more appropriate to show people the figures which highlight the trend away from wet film to digital processes.

The change process itself is the transition – getting people doing the new roles which are required of them. This is the part which the change team have to do.

The third stage – refreeze – involves making the new processes the normal way of doing business. We have to make the digital processes the familiar way of working that the existing processes are. In other words, the new way we will work will seem the right way to people, and the way we currently work would be wrong.

3 Conclusion

Change is vital for us, both in terms of moving our processes from wet film to digital and the new opportunities afforded by areas such as licensing from art galleries. Provided we manage the change well-through planning, communication and thoughtful, successful implementation – we can build a business which is very strong and ready for the future.

Answer 5
Project management

Check your answer

A good answer is likely to:

☑

Recognise the objectives for attending the exhibition. ☐

Outline project management tools to use. ☐

Consider the requirements for a successful exhibition. ☐

Illustrate using appropriate project management tool – e.g. Gantt chart, critical path analysis. ☐

Outline the expected budget for the exhibition. ☐

Use an appropriate format, e.g. an approval request. ☐

* * * * *

WEBSITE LAUNCH PLAN APPROVAL REQUEST

To: Senior Management

From: Marketing Manager

Date: XX/XX/XXXX

We have scheduled a launch for our new website at the National Photographic Exhibition which takes place six months from now. In order to achieve this date, and for it to be a successful exhibition for us we have to ensure we have to plan our activities over the next three months very carefully.

There are two areas we have to consider:

- ○ The website has to be ready to go live without any issues by the date of the exhibition.

- ○ We have to ensure our participation at the exhibition itself is successful.

Our objective for attending the exhibition is to create awareness of our website with as many potential customers as possible. This means that we have to ensure visitors to the exhibition visit our stand to find out for themselves and also, as there is a large amount of media attention surrounding the exhibition, we need to ensure good coverage for ourselves in the media.

The main issues we therefore have to consider are:

Website	Exhibition

Creation
Testing
Robust hosting
e-commerce enabled and tested
	Staffing requirements
	Stand
	   o visual appearance
	   o physical requirements
	Support materials
	   o literature
	   o on-stand web demonstration
	Promotion surrounding the event

Effectively, the delivery of a fully working website and a successful exhibition launch for it are our objectives, with a successful launch meaning that 90 per cent of attendees to the exhibition visit our stand and receive information about our website, and that we are positively reported in 75 per cent of the media coverage of the exhibition.

This is a project, so we should follow project planning guidelines:

Agree precise specification for the project

This has already been agreed through the support you have provided to my website design and creation programme and the launch of the website at the National Photographic Exhibition.

Plan the project

The timescale – this is now fixed at the six months between now and the exhibition date.

The project team – I propose that the core team consists of myself, the Commercial Director, our new webmaster and a representative from HR.

An activity plan, including resource requirements and budgets – see below.

Communicate the project plan to the project team

This is a role I will take on subject to your approval of this plan.

Agree and delegate project actions

This is an essential objective to achieve at the first meeting of the core project team.

Manage, motivate, inform, encourage, enable the project team

As project leader I feel that this is my role.

Check, measure, review project progress; adjust project plans, and inform the project team and others

The activity plan includes the timescales and budget measures to enable progress to be checked and monitored.

Complete project

Review and report on project performance; give praise and thanks to the project team. Again, I see this as my role.

Activity Plan

The activity plan for this project is as follows:

Activity	Month						Exhibition	Post exhib.
	1	2	3	4	5	6		
Website development	▓	▓						
Website testing			▓	▓				
Appoint website host			▓					
e-commerce trials					▓	▓		
Agree exhibition stand size	▓							
Design exhibition stand		▓						
Design exhibition support materials		▓						
Stand production			▓	▓				
Support material production				▓				
Exhibition staff selection			▓					
Staff training				▓				
Press release writing			▓					
Invite media to exhibition				▓				
Distribute press release					▓			
Dummy exhibition stand set up						▓		
Host media event							▓	
Collect visitor information							▓	
Thank staff and suppliers								▓
Input visitor data into database							▓	
Post-exhibition mailing to visitors								▓
Second press release								▓
Monitor results								▓

Budget

The proposed budget for the exhibition is:

Activity	Cost
Stand space	10 000
Exhibition stand	15 000
Literature	2 000
Staff costs*	2 800
Staff training	1 500
PR	2 500
Media event	4 250
Mailing	1 000
Project team dinner	500
Miscellaneous	1 000
Total	**40 550**

*Travel and accommodation during exhibition, exhibition uniforms.

This exhibition presents an opportunity to create awareness for our website on a large scale in a very short space of time. The exhibition and surrounding media coverage will create awareness with a large portion of our target customers at a relatively low cost. When combined with the additional communication plans we have agreed this should ensure a successful launch for our online services.

I look forward to receiving your approval of this proposal.

SUGGESTED ANSWERS

PART A

Mini-Case 2: WRBSA – Supporting Businesses

Answer 1 (Compulsory)

Check your answer

A good answer is likely to:

☑

Provide a rationale, research objectives, methodology, sampling and timescales for the research, linked to WRBSA and the mini-case material. ☐

Adopt the role of the marketing and membership services manager. ☐

Use key sections from a research proposal or information user specification to produce an outline research programme. ☐

Outline the actions required to achieve the objectives (note this does not require an environmental analysis, just the strategy, tactics and control elements). ☐

Consider the recruitment and induction requirements for the two new marketing assistants. ☐

Reflect the role of a new marketing and membership services manager. ☐

Use an appropriate format – report style. ☐

* * * * *

REPORT

To:

From:

Date: XX/XX/XXXX

Subject:

Part (a) Marketing research programme

West Rochshire Business Support Association

1 Background and rationale

Although we have a current membership representing 4000 businesses and 15 000 employees, only a relatively small number regularly take part in our activities and we have been suffering from an overall decline in our membership for a number of years. Although we do receive new membership applications every month, the number is less than the attrition rate.

There is a growing concern within the paid professional staff and management that our activities and events no longer meet the needs of members and so we fail to retain them for more than a year or two. Despite these concerns, until now we have not attempted to investigate this problem.

The purpose of this research programme is to investigate the reasons why WRBSA is failing to retain and grow the membership. The findings and conclusions drawn from the research will be used to revise our organisation's aims and objectives and to design and implement a reflective programme of activities, events and services that will meet the needs of the current membership and act as the basis for marketing and promotional activities having the objective of meeting the membership retention and growth targets that have been set.

2 Research objectives

The following research objectives will be addressed:

To understand the attitudes and perceptions of the members with respect to the activities, events and services provided by WRBSA; more specifically:

- To define the reasons why members join.
- To evaluate the attractiveness of the programme of events and activities currently provided for the members.
- To evaluate the attractiveness of the various member services available: funding database; application assistance; business advice service; training products; newsletter; website; meeting and conference facilities.
- To measure satisfaction levels with respect to events, activities and services that have been attended or used by members.
- To measure satisfaction levels with respect to WRBSA management, member communications and levels of customer care.
- To understand the reasons why members decide not to renew their membership; more specifically:
- To identify the reasons why lapsed member originally joined.
- To identify the reasons for leaving.
- To describe the level of attendance and types of activity pursued during the period of membership.
- To explore lapsed member perceptions of the WRBSA brand.
- To identify organisations that lapsed members have joined since leaving WRBSA.

To explore ideas regarding objectives, activities and events that will provide for the needs of the membership and will assist in recruitment and retention, more specifically:

- To define and prioritise needs and requirements with respect to their WRBSA membership.
- To generate and explore ideas for activities, events and services of value to the membership.
- To explore member's attitudes and perceptions of the WRBSA brand.

433

3 Research methodology

The following programme of research is proposed for this project:

3.1 Secondary research

3.1.1 Internal records

This will focus on the following internal records: membership forms, feedback and complaints forms, committee meeting minutes and past AGM presentations and will have the objective of capturing information that reflects member's opinions and ideas regarding the objectives and activities of the WRBSA.

The phase will also examine the aims and current objectives of the organisation with a view to reviewing these on completion of the research.

3.1.2 External sources

We will identify and collect information from other (competing) membership organisations in the Rochshire area and beyond. The objective will be to identify the objectives, activities and events held by these organisations in order to generate ideas for testing during the discussion group meetings.

3.1.3 Membership profiling and database

The purpose of this element is to bring our existing database of individual members and member organisations up to date and to create member job role and professional qualifications as well as organisational segmentation categories or profiles that we can use for future mailing campaigns and promotions. This work is aimed at better understanding the membership and will provide the foundation for a more comprehensive online database which members can use.

The database is required in order to provide a sampling frame for this research project.

3.2 Primary research

The primary research phase will consist of both qualitative and quantitative elements:

3.2.1 Qualitative research

The qualitative elements of the research objectives will be addressed using a small number of discussion group meetings attended by a number of respondents taken from the membership database. Please refer to sampling section for further information on recruitment for the meetings.

The meetings will be conducted by a specialist research agency that has both the facilities to host the group meetings and the skills set and experience to ensure that this element is effectively executed.

The agency will prepare a detailed discussion guide for the sessions and they will use a number of projective techniques, aimed at exploring and gaining deep insight into the attitudes and opinions of the respondents. We are interested to understand their motivation for joining as well as any reluctance to fully participate in WRBSA activities and events. The meetings will also explore possibilities for other events and services that we could offer.

We will be able to covertly observe the discussion group meetings when they take place and we will have an opportunity to inject further topic areas/questions if necessary. The meetings will be videotaped by the agency for detailed analysis, post-meeting – the tapes will also be available for our own further analysis, should we require them.

3.2.2 Quantitative research

The chosen technique will consist of two web-based survey questionnaires that we will design, accompanied by an invitation e-mail message to encourage completion of the questionnaire. Web surveys have been chosen for their low relative cost and quick response. Prototype testing is also quick and easy. The surveys will be as follows:

- A current member survey
- A lapsed member survey

The surveys will be geared towards fulfilling the mainly quantitative research objects to determine attitudes, perceptions and reasons for current behaviour, for example why a member left.

The web surveys themselves will be hosted by a third party web survey hosting company. We will prepare and test the survey questions ourselves before conducting the survey.

3.2.3 Sampling

This research project is concerned with the attitudes, opinions and behaviour of members and so the WRBSA member database and associated profiles (please refer to Section 3.1.3) will be used to create a list of possible respondents for the research.

A sampling frame will be created using a numbered list of the individuals listed in the membership. Since we need to ensure that the respondents used are representative of the various types of company represented by the membership; the use of a probability (random) sampling technique, called stratified random sampling will be used. Each company type: B2B, B2C and not-for-profit will form different strata. We will also consider the use of sub-segment strata to break down these categories into small, medium and large businesses.

Respondents will be carefully selected to include a representative selection of the membership. A total of 24 respondents will take part in the discussion groups.

We will invite 200 members from each of the strata to participate in the current member web survey. This allows for sufficient coverage of smaller strata and to allow for non-response.

For the lapsed member survey, we will include every lapsed member on our database, limited to the previous two years.

Response will be incentivised using a prize draw. We plan to offer two Apple iPods as prizes.

3.2.4 Data analysis

Discussion groups

The agency appointed to conduct the discussion group research will transcribe and analyse the CCTV recordings from the meetings and then analyse and summarise the data to provide us with a list of findings and conclusions. They have also agreed to liaise with us when we prepare our final report.

Web surveys

Specialist software located on the survey hosting platform will provide detailed first-level analysis of the responses for us thus will include tabulation, cross-tabulation and various summary statistics. We will also have access to the raw data set which we can use for further analysis.

4 Timescales

The research report will be available, approximately 12 weeks from the board's approval to proceed. An outline schedule of activities is provided below:

Week No	Activity
1	Secondary research
2	Database profiling and membership segmentation
3	Design and produce discussion group guide
4–5	Conduct discussion group meetings
5	Design e-mail letter and web survey questionnaire
6	Pilot test questionnaires, modify if required
7	Conduct web surveys
8–10	Analyse data and prepare report
12	Final report and Presentation

5 Budget

The following costs are known at this time:

Discussion groups x 2, contracted to external agency £5000

Use of third party web survey hosting platform £100

Incentive prize draw for web survey x 2 £200

Part (b) Marketing activity plan

6 Segmentation

WRBSA have member organisations which fall into many different categories – it is useful to consider the variable which can be applied to the member organisations (and potential member organisations). The primary segmentation which has been used is organisation size, and we should continue to use this. However, we could also segment the market according to the usage the organisation makes of WRBSA, the type of business operated, geographical location and so on.

Segmentation will help us to develop strategies and tactics for the different services we offer to develop profitable business. The segments need to be considered carefully, and member companies can then be targeted with an appropriate marketing mix, probably developing one for each segment we identify. Our research should help us to identify segmentation variables which are appropriate.

7 Marketing mix

- o *Product* – We have a range of products (our services) and following research (plan outlined above) into member requirements we may wish to revise the range we offer. We should also be able to determine which of the services are more appropriate for the different segments. For all our services, quality and professionalism are paramount in the delivery, aiming to match the best available from commercial competition where it exists, and using this as a benchmark for other services.

  A new product we intend to offer is the member database. This will be a printed and online directory of member businesses which will be circulated amongst the membership and selected other organisations with the intention of enabling inter-trading between member organisations.

- o *Price* – We should continue with our current pricing structures from membership, but the sliding scale for pricing according to number of employees needs to be reviewed to check it is offering good value to those companies with over 20 employees. Pricing for services such as training and other events need to be reviewed in relation to commercial competitors to check we are giving value for money to our members, the prices currently represent good value for money, but the perceived benefits may not be high enough.

The member database will be free of charge for all member companies.

- o *Promotion* – We are good at promoting our member events to our membership, however, moving to electronic communication will assist us with targeting events to member segments more easily. In addition, more promotion externally will help us to achieve our objectives. We should increase our PR activity to enhance the awareness of WRBSA and show the benefits of membership. Attending events run by local professional organisations such as those organised by accountancy, legal and marketing institutes will help us to raise our profile and talk to potential member companies at relatively low cost. All enquiries we receive should be logged, from whichever channel we receive them, and wherever possible we should ask for permission to add details to our database for future marketing purposes.

  For the member database, we will need to contact all member companies to ask them for the information they would like to include about themselves in the database – this will include type of business, size, years established and so on. Non-respondents will need to be followed up.

- o *Place* – Having just moved to our new premises, physically we would not want to change the place where we deliver the majority of our services. We could, however, consider holding some of the events in different places throughout the region in which we operate. In addition, offering online booking services for all our events would be beneficial. We could also use our website for people to apply for grants which would save us time, and be more convenient for the applicant.

- o *People* – The quality of our service and customer care is of great importance to WRBSA so we need to ensure that all staff recruited are suitable for the organisation, and trained appropriately for the tasks we carry out.

- o *Process* – Our processes have to be as efficient and customer-focused as possible. Using our website for booking events will improve the process, making it less time-consuming and easy to use. IT systems used by staff throughout WRBSA need to be

437

reliable and comprehensive and staff need adequate training in order to use them. The systems should work to improve the service process for the customer, as opposed to causing them problems.

o *Physical Evidence* – Our new premises help massively with our physical evidence, however, they need to be well maintained to communicate to customers the high level of quality throughout WRBSA. We also have to encourage staff to reflect the required levels of physical evidence through their appearance, smart dress being a requirement for all staff.

8 Controls and measurement

We have set SMART objectives for both membership (maintain current levels of micro-business membership, increasing membership of organisations with more than 20 employees and increasing numbers of member organisations participating in events) and events (one member event per week, four days training per week and new types of event) will help us measure the results of the marketing plan and make any necessary amendments. All activities should also be budgeted carefully and expenditure matched against the budget.

Part (c) Selection and recruitment

Job analysis is the first stage in the selection of the two new marketing assistants – identifying the roles that need to be filled. This will enable us to define the job roles, produce job descriptions and look at the role within the team and the overall business. We are developing a small marketing team within the membership services department which will support the entire organisation.

When the job descriptions are complete they can be used to develop person specifications – identifying the characteristics of people suitable for filling the positions. The person specification profiles the characteristics of the individual most suitable for the role including factors such as attitudes, skills and knowledge (ASK). When we receive applications we can use this specification to measure the suitability of the person relative to the requirements.

The main method of attracting suitable candidates to the jobs will be advertising, both internally and externally. We can use our communication to our members to advertise the vacancies – this is a service we offer generally so it is beneficial to use it. The advert should communicate information about the job and WRBSA, the package offered – salary and other benefits and all necessary details about the application and selection process. The advert can be placed in local papers and we can also use the job centre to advertise the vacancies.

After applications are received they need to be assessed in relation to the criteria set out in the person specification to select those we should interview. References from sources other than current employers should be checked prior to interview. Our HR Manager should be involved in the recruitment and selection process, including interviews, she can also advise on any legal issues that we have to consider.

9 Induction

Upon appointment the new recruits should go through an induction process. Although the two will be job–sharing, the induction process is a good time for them to get to know each other as this will be important for the future when they work together but rarely see each other.

The induction should last two weeks and include:

- o Advising the team about the new employees to ensure they welcome them
- o HR issues – payroll, procedures and so on
- o Health and safety training
- o Team introduction – spending time getting to know the people working in the member-ship services department
- o Tour of the facility
- o Organisation introduction – spending half a day in each department to find out about the range of services we offer
- o Systems introduction – ensuring an understanding of our computer systems
- o Attending events and training – during the induction period the marketing assistants should attend any member events we are holding, including training course as this will enable them to see our operation in action and meet customers.

During the induction period any additional training requirements should be identified and discussed – hopefully we will be able to meet these through our existing training programmes.

Ongoing monitoring of the Marketing Assistants will be required.

PART B

Answer 2

Check your answer

A good answer is likely to:

   ☑

Use project planning tools for event management. ☐

Outline the activities to be carried out before and during the event. ☐

Consider who will be involved in the project planning. ☐

Specify who needs to be involved in the event from both within and outside WRBSA. ☐

Relate to a launch event. ☐

Use an appropriate format, e.g. a report. ☐

* * * * *

REPORT

To: Commercial Director

From: Membership and Marketing Manager

Date: XX/XX/XXXX

Subject: New premises launch event

1 Introduction

We are intending to hold a launch event for our new premises in three months' time – this should allow us to be settled in and working effectively from the premises. The event needs to be thoroughly organised and planned to ensure it is successful with the right people involved. This report details my proposals for the event.

2 Launch event planning

Planning for the launch event needs to be considered in four areas:

- Initiation
- Planning
- Execution
- Closure.

2.1 Initiation phase

This phase relates to the project construction and limits. For the Premises Launch event it is essential that everything required is completed by the event day.

The principle objectives for the Premises Launch event are:

- Raise awareness of WRBSA throughout West Rochshire through PR in the local media.
- Provide members the chance to see our new facilities.

2.2 Planning

The most critical stage for the Premises Launch event is:

- a team of staff members needs to be selected and created (see below for the content of the team)
- risk factors need to be taken into account, for example what would happen if our event clashes with something else locally
- decisions have to be made about budget and timings.

There are several project management tools, which can be to develop the schedule. PERT and critical path analysis (CPA) require that the tasks involved in the planning of our premises launch are treated as distinct events each of which has a time required allocated to it. The PERT method uses three time estimates for each task – pessimistic, optimistic and most likely, whilst CPA uses one fixed time duration.

Critical path analysis plots the tasks onto connected time lines, which highlights the 'critical path' – the tasks which have to be started and finished on time to ensure the project is completed by the scheduled finish time.

The same time information can be used to produce a Gantt chart to assist with scheduling. An outline Gantt chart for the events and activities required for our Premises Launch event is:

Activity/time	Month 1	Month 2	Month 3	Launch Day	Post-launch
Form project team	▓				
Establish theme	▓				

Determine invite list
  o staff
  o guests
  o media
  o members
		▓			

Create invitations		▓			
Invite media		▓			
Invite guests		▓			
Book caterers	▓				
Produce information packs			▓		
Develop presentations			▓		
Book photographer		▓			
Produce signage for the launch			▓		
Confirm attendances			▓		
The opening				▓	
Post-event team debrief					▓
Send out post-event press release					▓
Thank all staff					▓
Write to attendees					▓
Project team celebration					▓

2.3 Execution

This is the actual day of the Premises Launch event. Measurables for the day include:

- o establishing that all required equipment for presentations and so on works
- o all signage is in place
- o all staff are in attendance
- o visitor car park spaces are cleared
- o premises tours take place at the appropriate time
- o catering is available on time.

The success of the event depends upon the expected guests turning up and having an enjoyable, informative experience.

2.4 Closure

The success of our Premises Launch can be measured in terms of how well it meets our objectives of raising our profile within West Rochshire through the media, and giving members the chance to see our new facilities.

I think it is important that the project team have a discussion after the event to see how we all feel it went, and any lessons we have learnt. This should be followed by a celebration – probably a meal for the team and other staff members who contribute significantly to the success of the day.

3 Groups involved in the planning of the event

The key groups who need to be involved with the launch event are:

- o The senior management team – this team will need to approve the plans, and will be involved during the day giving presentations about WRBSA and being available to discuss our activities with all the guests.
- o The membership department – responsible for looking after the guests during the day and providing information for the media guests. The membership department will be sending out invitations and monitoring the replies received to create the final guest list.
- o All WRBSA staff – the tours will involve all areas of the premises so the entire staff have to be involved in planning as their work areas will be on display.
- o Our PR company – they will generate pre-event publicity for us, and assist in the production of press releases and materials.

4 Publics expected to attend the event

The key publics who we expecting to attend the Premises Launch event are:

- o The senior management team of WRBSA to give presentations and interviews with visitors
- o WRBSA staff – all staff should have a chance to attend the presentations throughout the day.
- o Member companies – it will not be possible to host all member companies at one event, we need to select 10 per cent of our member companies at random to invite them to the event. All member companies should be encouraged to visit the premises, however.

- o Media – local media (newspaper, radio, television, etc.) journalists who will hopefully feature us and our facilities in appropriate media to increase awareness of our activities.
- o Local businesses who are not currently members, but whom we would like to be.
- o Key suppliers – we should take the opportunity to invite our key suppliers to help build relationships with them.
- o Local educational centres – building links with local education providers will help increase awareness of our activities and should promote joint working on projects. The Premises Launch is a good opportunity to show them our capabilities.

Answer 3
Change management, e-communications

Check your answer

A good answer is likely to:

 ☑

Have clear objectives in mind. ☐

Focus on member needs, including offering higher level of service and information. ☐

Consider management aspects of the changes, e.g. the use of project management methodology, and the need for appropriate skills. ☐

Relate to WRBSA's specific circumstances. ☐

Use an appropriate format, e.g. a report. ☐

*   *   *   *   *

REPORT

To: Membership Director

From: Marketing and Membership Services Development Manager

Date: XX/XX/XX

Re: Conversion of WRBSA to E-Communications

1 Introduction

WRBSA has plans to increase its membership over the next two years and to boost the number of member events. At present all our communications to members are via hard copy but there are advantages for WRBSA in switching these communications to electronic methods. These include:

- ○ Reduced paper, copying, inserting and postage costs.
- ○ Ability to communicate at any time, for example on the day if, say, there is a late speaker change for a networking dinner.
- ○ Enhanced image – WRBSA is using 21st century communications technology.

This report looks at how the change to e-communications can be achieved.

2 The process

There are several steps in moving towards e-communications. Each is considered separately below.

2.1 Objective setting

It is important that appropriate objectives are set at the start of this project. Clear objectives guide decision-making throughout the process and give a yardstick by which to measure achievement both during and at the end of the project. Suggested objectives would relate to:

○ Persuading 90 per cent of the membership to receive regular communications (news-letters, event information, etc.) from us electronically;
○ Increasing the range of facilities and information available to members (thus, the move to e-communication can become part of a wider shift to providing a range of electronic member facilities);
○ Ensuring members perceive an increase in service levels from WRBSA.
○ These objectives would need to be refined and expressed in SMART terms (i.e. specific, measurable, achievable, realistic and time-bound).

2.2 Member research

It is important that WRBSA is seen to be a member-driven organisation. With this in mind at outset we should undertake research to identify what information and services members would like to receive, or have access to, electronically.

Research could take the form of a short questionnaire distributed with the next newsletter to all members. Answers to appropriately worded questions would enable us to identify the extent of member access to e-mail and the Internet, whether members have a preference for hard copy or e-mail communication from WRBSA, and what online facilities members would like to have available. We could also take advantage of one of our meetings to discuss the e-communications proposals, as interactive exchanges of ideas can often be very creative and constructive.

I suggest that we take the opportunity in the research to set out the benefits to members of WRBSA moving to e-communications. I see these as:

○ lower membership fees as a result of our reduced costs;
○ real-time access to the latest information;
○ ability to access a range of WRBSA information and services online.

Online facilities also enable us to create new opportunities for members to network, with online forums and discussion groups.

The research should act as the basis for development of our e-communication programme. Member suggestions would need to be prioritised, based on ease of implementation, importance to the membership and availability of in-house skills for development.

2.3 Implementation

This is covered in Section 3 below.

2.4 Communications to members

Changes to our communication processes should be clearly signalled to members in advance. This would include information in newsletters and at networking events. Members should be reminded of the benefits to them of e-communications and advised of the range of facilities that are being developed, based on the research feedback. As a member-driven organisation we should give them the option to opt out of receiving communications electronically – a few may prefer hard copy material – but we should encourage switching wherever possible. Offering an incentive to switch, such as a discounted membership subscription, would be a useful 'carrot'.

Care should be taken to ensure we comply with the Privacy and Electronic Communications Regulations 2003, with regards to the sending and receiving of e-mail. However, given that the organisation only has members who have *chosen* to belong to WRBSA, and given that the relations only apply to *marketing* messages this should not be a significant problem. Perhaps more importantly, if members are to be allowed access to the membership database for networking and marketing purposes then they must be reminded of the Regulations' requirements.

2.5 Monitoring

An important aspect of the e-communication development is that members perceive higher service levels as a result of the changes. Ongoing monitoring needs to be put in place to check this. Occasional questionnaires to a sample of the membership can give qualitative and qualitative information of members' attitudes. Less structured feedback can also be gained from meetings and written comments received. If members choose not to renew their subscription, reminder letters can include a question asking if they are dissatisfied in any way so that corrective action can be taken if appropriate.

3 Management of the e-communication project

Moving towards e-communication is a multi-dimensional and potentially complex task. I suggest that this is handled as a discrete project ('projects' can be defined as multifaceted packages of work that have a discrete beginning and end, and which must be accomplished to agreed standards). Project management methodology should be used, including the production of a number of key documents:

- ○ a Project Initiation Document (which clarifies the scope of the project and how it will be run);
- ○ a Project Plan (which details the activities to be undertaken and associated timescales, budgets, etc.)
- ○ a Post-Implementation Review held after the project to learn lessons to improve future project management.

I suggest day-to-day handling of this project is delegated to one of the two new marketing assistants, closely overseen by myself. This has implications for the recruitment process; the Person Specifications for the new positions should include: i) experience of working on, or preferably running, successful projects and ii) a good understanding of e-communications and the ability to work with e-communications software, for example to send bulk e-mails and to design and maintain web pages. If we are unable to recruit people with the appropriate level of skills then we need to support the new staff with development programmes. These could take many forms including external courses, computer-based training and a structured on-the-job coaching programme.

In addition we must ensure we have appropriate in-house hardware and software so that the online facilities can be created. We may need to talk to external consultants about this, but a good first move would be to trawl our database for member businesses which could provide these services at a discount in return for publicity for themselves.

I suggest that, while we are developing external communications facilities, we develop in-house facilities too. In particular an Intranet would enable WRBSA staff to share information quickly and easily, at any time.

4 Conclusion

In summary, moving towards e-communication is a constructive move for both the organisation and its membership. There is much to consider along the way but, very importantly, throughout the process we must remember that we are seeking to add value for members – increasing benefits to them and helping our own recruitment process.

I look forward to discussing this information with you in more detail.

Answer 4

Check your answer

A good answer is likely to:

☑

In the introduction, create the need for the information that will be needed to support the geographic and product expansion. ☐

In Part a, list and justify the types information that would will needed to ensure that training programmes are appropriate to the needs of businesses. Give reasons to justify why this information is required. ☐

In Part b, design a training course evaluation questionnaire. ☐

Adopt the role of the marketing and membership services development manager. ☐

Use Report format for 1(a) and a Research Questionnaire for 1(b). ☐

* * * * *

Part a)

REPORT

To: Managing Director

From: Marketing and Membership Services Development Manager

Date: XX/XX/XX

Re: Meeting Business Needs Through Training Course Development

1 Introduction

The sale of training course places forms a major part of the income of WRBSA. To ensure the continued growth of our training business, we need to ensure that our courses reflect current and future business and IT training needs.

This report identifies ways in which we can be both responsive and proactive in the development and delivery of our programmes. The report will focus on the information requirements to meet this objective.

2 Information gathering

This can be considered in terms of internal and external information sources:

2.1 Internal information sources

2.1.1 Delegate feedback forms

In order to track the attitudes and opinions of course delegates, we need to ensure that we capture adequate feedback concerning the quality and content of each training course. This information, although often subjective, and not necessarily reflecting the employer's opinions and requirements, does at least provides a good starting point. An example of an evaluation questionnaire is attached as an appendix to this report. The evaluation questionnaire, actually an external primary research tool, provides three types of information:

- o Course/tutor quality – The data collected allows us to address areas where we currently fall short of delegate expectations and to track quality improvement over time.
- o Course content – Delegates might spot gaps in the current content or suggest topics of importance to them that we were not aware of. This enables our existing programmes to be incrementally developed.
- o Suggestions for new courses – The form should provide an opportunity to capture additional ideas for courses that are not currently offered.

Analysis of the forms we have stored away in files (hence categorised as internal data) will greatly assist us in understanding our performance, content and quality.

We should bear in mind that course delegates are usually the end users or consumers of our training. The employer (and our member) is the buyer and decision maker. The feedback forms are insufficient in themselves and other collection methods will also be required.

2.1.2 Course attendance statistics

Since most of our courses are recurring, with many programmes running several times a year, we can monitor popularity by analysing attendance trends. At present this data is used only as a means of promoting less popular courses. We should use the data to trigger other information processes, aimed at improving or replacing programmes that no longer meet needs.

2.1.3 Tutor feedback

Many of our courses are delivered by external, freelance consultants. We can capture information and ideas from our tutor associates – this might be achieved using an ideas/suggestions scheme. Such information provides a different perspective.

2.1.4 Meeting reports

These should be completed whenever we formally meet or visit our corporate members. Training and development is an agenda item but, is again, mainly concerning with selling places on existing courses.

2.2 External information

2.2.1 External secondary research

Information that will assist us to identify and track changes and developments in the business and IT training world, available at low cost or free from a variety of published sources, including:

o Professional bodies such as the Chartered Institute of Personnel and Development, The Institute of Business Advisors and the Institute of IT Training, all have journals, forums, meetings and websites with rich sources.
o The Internet provides information on commercial providers of courses and various forums and sites provide insight into new ideas and developments in business models, management tools and IT. Microsoft's websites help monitor new developments.
o Magazines and periodicals in IT, management and training. *PC Pro, IT Training Magazine, Business Today, Harvard Business Review, Strategy and Business*; all sources of ideas and trends.

2.2.2 External primary research

This is research we undertake ourselves or commission others to do on our behalf, allowing us to overcome identified weaknesses of course evaluation forms.

Instead, we research the buyer directly (managing directors, business owners, IT managers, HR managers, and training managers) to identify their needs and ideas, opinions and perceptions. We can identify their future requirements, their business plans, and IT strategies. We can also obtain direct feedback regarding the effectiveness of any courses their staff members have attended.

o *Qualitative techniques* – executive depth interviewing by telephone or face to face, or the use of discussion groups. Both can be used to gain insight into the current thinking of employers. Discussion groups may prove less effective in this circumstance as topics might be commercially sensitive. Attitudes, opinions, ideas to explore; these are all possible areas that qualitative techniques could reveal.
o *Quantitative techniques* – surveys by telephone or via e-mail/the web. These can help us understand the types of course that would be of interest, assess likely demand and gauge the employers perspective on our training course quality and effectiveness in meeting the need of business.

3 Concluding remarks

A key objective for the new role of Marketing and Membership Services Development Manager is to develop our courses, grow sales and ensure that we meet the needs of our membership. The above hopefully demonstrates the steps that we can take to access a number of information sources to provide ideas and feedback for course development.

Part b)

We hope you have enjoyed the course and learned from it. Our aim is to provide a first-class service in all respects. To help us to ensure expectations are met please indicate your views below.

Training Course Evaluation				
1. To what extent have the course objectives been met for you? Fully ( ) Well ( ) Partly ( ) Poorly ( )				
2. How relevant was the course to your needs? Very ( ) Fairly ( ) Partly ( ) Slightly ( )				
3. How useful will you find the skills and knowledge gained from the course? Very ( ) Fairly ( ) Partly ( ) Slightly ( )				
How would you assess the following:	Excellent	Good	Fair	Poor
4. Presentation Content				
5. Presentation Materials				
6. Presenter's Ability				
7. Presenter's Knowledge				
8. Handout Materials				
9. Practical Exercises				
10. Support Materials – Videos, etc.				
11. Venue				
12. Food				

Which part of the course was most useful?	Which part of the course was least useful?
What other courses you would like us to run?	
Any other comments:	Name: Position: Company: E-mail:
Course title:	Date:

Thank You

Answer 5

Check your answer

A good answer is likely to:

☑

Consider the types of communication held with member organization. ☐

Outline team development activities for creating a cohesive message from the team. ☐

Consider motivational issues for staff. ☐

Relate to WRBSA's specific circumstances. ☐

Use an appropriate format, e.g. a report. ☐

* * * * *

REPORT

To: Commercial Director

From: Marketing and Membership Services Development Manager

Date: XX/XX/XXXX

Subject: Team development and staff motivation for customer service

1 Introduction

We have many people within WRBSA who communicate with our member companies for many different reasons – this ranges from the membership department who discuss services offered and actually sell the membership, we have the business advice department helping members with their own business issues, the payroll team, the funding team and the training department selling and advising on training courses. These teams all work individually at the moment, giving out their own message. Whilst this works well, it would be beneficial to ensure that the message which is delivered is consistent across all our departments.

2 Developing interfunctional cohesion

The individuals within WRBSA who communicate with our member companies currently work as a group – they all work for WRBSA, but effectively do their own thing. We need to bring these groups together to form a team which operates across the whole of WRBSA. In theory at least, a team that is working effectively can achieve far more than a group of individuals can for the organisation. They can:

o Perform tasks which require the skills, expertise, knowledge or physical ability of more than one person
o Test and verify decisions made outside the group/team
o Consult or negotiate to resolve disputes
o Create ideas
o Collect and transmit information and ideas.

Depending on the task at hand, the team can self-organise itself for the best results. For example, leadership can change depending on the person with the most experience in that area.

o Team members can support each other during difficult situations.
o Team members learn from each other, supplementing and extending their own skills through sharing activities.

Teams provide a means of gathering an extensive range of skills to bear on an issue. This can result in more innovative and wider ranging solutions than you would get from one individual. They are able to solve more complex problems than an individual working on their own.

What we need to do is to create an effective interfunctional team. The effectiveness of this team will be influenced by:

o The extent to which a common purpose is clear.
o The extent to which the team is effectively organised to meet its intended purpose.
o The extent to which the team contains the necessary constituent elements (team roles, ASK factors).
o The effectiveness of team interactional processes; often referred to as group dynamics.

These are vital factors to consider for developing a consistent message.

We need all the individuals who may talk to members to give the same message, and therefore we need to consider them as one team who have the ability to help each other. As an example, at the moment we have some staff who are unclear about all of the services we offer, and I have heard examples where members have been told to call back and ask if we can help. We should be able to offer a more seamless process than this.

The methodology I propose for creating an interfunctional team is:

2.1 Define the common purpose

o Ensure that all staff are clear about what WRBSA do and what our purpose is.
o Move on from this to ensure they know what their own purpose is within this.
o This requires communication which I propose to be through team meetings held within each department which I would like to attend.

2.2 Organise the team to meet the purpose

o   This stage will be harder to manage as it involves bringing all the departments together to ensure they deliver a consistent message

o   Initially this can be achieved through a team meeting of the managers of each department – getting them together to ensure they are all clear about the purpose of each others department.

o   This should then be followed up with meetings where representatives from each department meet – by the end of the process every member of staff should have attended a meeting at which there was a representative from every other department, where the purpose of the meeting was to find out what the other departments have to offer.

o   This should improve the team working, as the time spent will enable greater understanding of the team purpose.

2.3 Review team roles

o   It is important that all staff members are aware of the role they play in the larger organisation team than their own department.

o   We need to review training needs internally to ensure if we have the right balance of ASK – attitudes, skills and knowledge within each department to ensure team work across the whole organisation.

2.4 Ensure the group dynamic is appropriate

o   Through getting people together in groups, and opening up the channels of communication we should improve the interaction between departments, getting an appropriate group dynamic across the whole of WRBSA.

Beyond these activities, it is important to develop the message which we wish the staff to deliver and ensure this is understood by everyone. The message has to be conveyed to our members – to ensure this happens correctly we may need to run some training programmes for our own staff on communication skills, interpersonal skills and additional product knowledge skills.

3 Motivational issues

Beyond the process described above for ensuring all our staff have the knowledge and ability to deliver the messages we want, they also have to be motivated to do so. If they are not motivated to deliver the best possible advice to our members, then it will not happen

McClelland's motivational theory is based on three types of motivational needs which he says are found to varying degrees in all workers and managers.

3.1 Achievement motivation

o   This type of person seeks to achieve realistic but challenging goals, and also look for advancement in their job.

o   For these people we have to ensure we provide feedback about their achievements and progress.

o   They also need a sense of accomplishment.

3.2 Authority/Power motivation

o   These people need to be influential and effective to make an impact – they want what they do to make a difference.
o   The authority motivated person has a strong need to lead and for their ideas to prevail – we have to show that we respect their input.
o   These people are also motivated by increasing personal status and prestige.

3.3 Affiliation motivation

o   These people want friendly relationships and are motivated by interaction with other people.
o   We should recognise these people easily during the initial interfunctional team meetings as they will be very keen to get on with others.
o   They are motivated by the need to be liked and held in popular regard.
o   These people are very good team players and we need to encourage them to develop the skills in others.

McClelland states that most people exhibit a combination of these three characteristics, maybe with a bias towards one and a secondary need.

Work by Hertzberg identified the motivation factors which influence job satisfaction – things which we need to consider within our overall teamwork plans:

o   *Achievement* – ensuring that people can achieve what is asked of them, and that it is worth achieving.
o   *Recognition* – providing appropriate recognition for a job well done – this can be as simple as saying 'well done' to a staff member, but may involve more than this!
o   *Work itself* – the work itself should be rewarding and something people want to do.
o   *Responsibility* – people need to be given responsibility, and then left to do what they have been asked to do.
o   *Advancement* – seeing the ability to advance within the organisation is important for people.
o   *Growth* – personal growth through extra responsibilities and duties are rewording to most staff.

Combining these with McClelland's three factors will enable us to develop people who are highly motivated to provide excellent advice to our members.

4 Conclusion

Through the development of a team culture within WRBSA, and consideration of motivational methods for the staff we can improve the consistency of communication we have with our member organisations.

If you would like any further information about this please contact me.

SUGGESTED ANSWERS

PART A

Mini-Case 3: JJ Motorbikes (December 2005)

Answer 1 (Compulsory)

Segmentation, targeting, positioning and marketing plans

Check your answer

A good answer is likely to

	☑
	☐
Identify a range of segments appropriate for JJ Motorbikes	☐
Highlight the segments which should be targeted	☐
Outline a two-year marketing plan applied to JJ Motorbikes	☐
Use the case material and your own knowledge to produce a marketing audit	☐
Consider the extended marketing mix	☐
Define specific actions for positioning to capture the expanding female enthusiast segment	☐
Use an appropriate format, e.g. a report	☐

* * * * *

REPORT

To: Sales and Marketing Director

From: Marketing Executive

Date: XX/XX/XX

Re: Market segmentation, planning and targeting issues

1 Introduction

This is an exciting time for JJ Motorbikes with our move to Bike City and it is important that we take full advantage of the great opportunity it presents for us. To do this we need to ensure we know who are most likely to be our best customers through considering the segments available to us, we need a thorough marketing plan, and in particular we should consider the growing market for female bikers. This report aims to address these issues.

2 Segmentation

Market segmentation is the process of dividing a market into groups, or segments, of customers who have similar needs or characteristics and are likely to exhibit similar purchase behaviour. In segmenting the market the organisation acknowledges that different products or marketing approaches/marketing mixes will be required for different 'types' of buyers.

There are many ways to segment a market; typically they are:

- o *Demographically* – according to the age structure of the population
- o *Geographically* – by country or region or area
- o *Behaviouristically* – according to the nature of the purchase, the use the product is put to, the loyalty to the brand and so on
- o *Benefit* – according to the use and satisfaction gained by the consumer
- o *Socio-economically* – according to social class and income levels.

With the possible exception of geographical segmentation, all of these are applicable for ourselves. The fact-find you gave me segments our market around the criteria of behaviour – splitting our business between enthusiasts and utility riders. I agree that this is very important, but would suggest additional segmentation as follows:

- o *Age* – the age of customers will affect their likely purchase and their reason for purchase. Younger riders are less likely to be influenced by the classic motorbike display, and more interested in the latest technology.
- o *Type of product purchased* – whether customers buy new or second-hand products, and also whether they buy sports bikes, tourers or utility bikes. This categorisation relates to both behaviouristic and benefit segmentation for us – the different types of bikes are used for different purposes (benefit) and the nature of the purchase (behaviour) is likely to influence whether new or second hand.
- o *Sex* – there is an increasing number of female bikers who may have different motivation for buying particular types of bike – more information about this sector is included below.

From the knowledge I have so far, the segments which are likely to represent our best profit opportunities are:

- o Under 25-year olds – these customers are likely to be just setting out in biking and if looked after are likely to become repeat customers spending large sums in the future.
- o 'Born again' bikers – these typically represent customers with high disposable income (higher social classes), and they are likely to replace their bikes regularly which will make them profitable customers
- o Female bikers – this is a growing segment, currently not targeted by our competitors.

We need to create tailored marketing strategies for each of these groupings.

3 Outline a two-year marketing plan for bike city

3.1 Situational analysis

Macro-environment

Social – acceptability of motorbikes as a convenient city 'run-around' means of Transport
- increasing motorbike ownership by women
Legal – safety issues
- environmental (green) issues
Economic – increasing costs of car ownership, including taxation, fuel and parking charges
Political – limited car access to city centres with 'congestion charging' and parking limitations.
Technological – increasing technical sophistication of motorbikes makes quality servicing by professional technicians in well-equipped workshops important.

Competition

	Threat of new entrants Internet-based suppliers New clothing only suppliers	
Power of suppliers Reputation of JJ will help here. Limited number of bike manufacturers, large number of retailers	**Industry rivalry** Similar outlets local independent trainers specialists in motorcycle clothing – international chains, e.g. Damerell's car servicing centres	**Power of buyers** Increasing choice through Internet
	Threat of substitutes Alternative 'thrills' for born again bikers. Alternatives for commuters such as the Segway	

3.2 Objectives

- Increase visitor numbers by 100 per cent over two years
- Increase sales of bikes by 50 per cent over two years
- Increase accessory sales by 100 per cent over two years

3.3 Strategies

Product:
- We should continue with our current bike range – both in terms of the manufacturer brands and the types of bikes sold – sports, tourer, utility, new and secondhand.
- Our range of clothing and accessories should be increased.
- We can expand our off road training and tuition packages.

Place:

○ The main outlet for JJ Motorbikes will be the new Bike City complex.

○ The local race track should continue to be used for training and will help with promotion.

○ Create website for additional sales of clothing and accessories.

Price:

○ Our pricing has to be competitive, particularly for clothing and accessories, for the larger motorbikes we should command a small premium to reflect JJ's image and the service levels we provide.

Promotion:

○ Introduce loyalty card.

○ Develop business partner schemes for events such as the off road training.

○ Use the specialist bike press for advertising and PR.

○ Sales promotions in local press.

○ Utilise JJ's celebrity status for promotion – consider sponsorship of a local bike racer.

Physical evidence:

○ We have a great opportunity to develop very favourable physical evidence through the new Bike City complex. A common theme throughout the facilities – bike showrooms, accessories and clothing shop, café and service centre – should also be reflected in all promotional materials to generate a positive feel.

Process:

○ We need to ensure that our processes are efficient from a customer perspective. An area where this can be very important is in our service reception – we can consider introducing online booking for the servicing.

○ We will have to work with our bike suppliers to ensure the process for ordering new bikes is efficient for our customers.

○ If we develop online sales for clothing and accessories the process is important to deliver the purchases quickly.

People:

○ A major element in our success so far is the fact that JJ is a known biker which conveys an image of us as enthusiasts. It is important that our staff are knowledgeable bike experts as we are dealing with enthusiasts who will be well informed. Consideration has to be given, however, to the utility bike customers who will not want to be given lots of technical information.

Training for customer service across all departments is essential.

3.4 Implementation

The activities need to be staged throughout the two-year period to ensure the maximum benefit is gained. I would like to work with you and other departments to ensure we produce the most effective implementation plan possible.

3.5 Budgets and control

Throughout the plan, measures need to be included against which the implementation of the plan can be monitored and controlled. All areas need to have targets which can be evaluated and changed if appropriate – over the two years the environment will change and we have to be able to react to this. This can include areas such as monitoring the effectiveness of our promotion, awareness levels, measuring customer satisfaction and obviously sales and profitability levels.

I propose quarterly reviews of progress in all areas, with some elements such as sales being monitored more closely – weekly at maximum for clothing, accessories and bike sales.

I am currently working on a budget proposal for this plan, costing all elements of the mix and will present this to you shortly for approval.

4 The female biker market

A growing segment within the motorcycle market is that of the female motorbike enthusiast. Amongst others, Harley Davidson have identified this segment as important and have even considered the segment in terms of product design.

It is important for us, therefore, to consider this segment in our expansion plans and reflect this in our marketing activity. The following includes some of the areas I think we should consider.

4.1 Attracting female customers

We have to be careful to strike the correct balance between providing the information the female bikers need in an appropriate way without being patronising. Biking has predominantly been a male-orientated area so we have to ensure that females are not deterred from visiting JJ's to find out about, and hopefully purchase, bikes and accessories. The following are some of the specific areas we should consider.

Promotion via the women's pages of local media – many of the local papers and magazines have women's pages – we should invite the relevant journalists to a 'bike academy' specifically targeted at females. An ideal promotional tool would be to sponsor a female bike racer and gain publicity around this.

Service – we should ensure our service reflects the requirements of female customers – the motor industry in general is often regarded as not friendly to females, taking advantage of their lack of knowledge. Again, whilst being careful not to be patronising, we need to ensure our customers feel happy dealing with us – employing female technicians and sales staff would help here.

For our clothing shop to be appropriate, separate changing rooms need to be provided, along with female staff to offer assistance as required.

4.2 Retaining female customers

Just as important as attracting female customers is retaining them. I have proposed that we should introduce a loyalty card, and when we do it is important to provide tailored offers to our customers – this should include female customers and appropriate offers for them. We could offer the chance to attend female-only events at the local racetrack at reduced rates to our female customers.

In addition to the loyalty card offers, we should introduce a tailored newsletter for our female customers giving them information on more relevant products and services we can offer – this might include the introduction of basic bike maintenance classes for females which we could inform them about through the newsletter.

5 Conclusion

I hope that you will agree that through good segmentation of our customer base, the development and implementation of a marketing plan based around our move to Bike City, and targeting the growing number of female bike enthusiasts, we can build an even more successful business than we currently have.

If you would like any more information about my proposals please ask me.

PART B

Answer 2
Marketing communications activities for revenue generation

Check your answer

A good answer is likely to:

☑

Identify a range of activities, covering both internal and external communications. ☐

Suggest outline objectives for these communication activities. ☐

Relate the answer to the need for extra income generation and the need to make better ☐
use of the existing client base.

Relate to JJ Motorbikes' circumstances. ☐

Use an appropriate format, e.g. a report. ☐

* * * * *

REPORT

To: Sales and Marketing Director

From: Marketing Executive

Date: XX/XX/XX

Re: Marketing Communications Activities for Revenue Generation

1 Introduction

JJ Motorbikes is at an exciting point in its development, as it moves into larger, well-positioned premises. However, we need to generate more revenue and profits to meet our larger financial commitments and I believe effective use of marketing communications can make a substantial contribution to achieving our sales goals.

This reports sets out some appropriate marketing communications activities but first it would be helpful to set out the main objectives of these communications:

- o To raise awareness of JJ Motorbikes amongst potential buyers;
- o To develop relationships with existing customers to enable upselling (the buying of more expensive models or equipment) and cross-selling (buying of goods from other product categories);
- o To develop relationship with potential business partners;
- o To create an attitude amongst key stakeholders that JJ Motorbikes is *the* place for bikers to buy bikes and accessories.

2 Activities

A range of suggested communications activities is given below. Communications will fall into two phases: those for the launch and the ongoing activity after that, where appropriate. I will consider these separately.

2.1 Advertising

Creating awareness of the opening of the new premises is a vital first step, and advertising would be valuable as it can reach large audiences. We are appealing to a range of demographic segments within a local/regional market so appropriate media would include local newspapers, local radio and cinema – the latter would be particularly appropriate for the youth market. Roadside advertising should also be considered, particularly to reach the commuter market. Print advertisements should also be placed in specialist biking magazines and the local racetrack's race programmes. We should capitalise on our position next to the motorway with banner advertising, subject to planning regulations.

2.2 The Internet

Our site so far is only rudimentary; it needs to reflect the quality and diversity of the JJ Motorbike's offering. The site can be used to display our range of products and to raise awareness of our diverse facilities. The Internet can be a very visual medium showing pictures of bikes and accessories, and video clips of bikes in action. People need to have reasons to revisit the site so I suggest we include 'offers of the week'. We could also have some online games designed to add more fun to the site. Practical facilities like stock level enquiries, instore delivery times and even a home delivery service for accessories for more distant customers would all add value. We should ensure that there are links to our site direct from manufacturers' websites.

2.3 Public relations

John Jones is well known in the biking world and is a local celebrity. Combine this with the power and sex appeal of many modern bikes and you have an attractive PR cocktail. This should enable us to get good local and trade media coverage for the launch and, given the range of types of bikes and target segments, even to break into other media segments such as county lifestyle magazines. Regular post-launch events, perhaps featuring other stars from the biking world or launches of new models, would keep our profile high. We should also go out and create awareness and sales by taking display space at race events in the region. Race sponsorships would also boost awareness.

2.4 Customer relationship management (CRM)

We have a large customer base but, to date, have not managed this in any way. A starting point is to create a database to gather a) personal information such as addressees and contact numbers, b) purchase information – what, how much and when, and c) communication history including outbound and significant inbound communications. The database can become the basis for building an ongoing communications programme so that JJ Motorbikes remains front of mind for those interested in bikes. Communications could include information on events, model launches and special offers. A well-managed programme will help with retention and deliver cross selling and up-selling opportunities. Communications can be delivered by post and also by e-mail (subject to the recipient's prior consent). E-mails could give a hypertext link to relevant pages on our website.

2.5 Loyalty card

The development of the loyalty card would be closely linked to the CRM programme. Its aim would be to encourage people to continue buying from us rather than local competitors (such as Damerell's) or cheaper online stores. Encouraging buyers of bikes and accessories to complete a registration card enables us to collect data for the relationship programme. In return we can offers discounts on a wide range of goods and services as well as offer through selected business partners such as the racetrack.

2.6 Business partners

The link with the racetrack has proved successful so we should look to expand our business relationships. Links should mirror the likely interests of our target segments, for example clothing and music stores for the younger end of the market. Schemes could offer discounts at either partner based on purchases at the other and could be linked to the loyalty card offer. The schemes also offer opportunities to display goods at other locations. Business arrangements with loan companies or banks would help to make our products more affordable and attractive.

2.7 Internal communications

A significant amount of money has been set aside for internal communications and staff training. Staff attitudes can make a big difference to the customer's buying experience and can be a significant business differentiator, helping to build and maintain relationships and boost retention levels. Staff should be kept fully informed about business developments and communication programmes, and briefed on the importance of good service both for customer-facing staff and those with only internal customers. Some of the budget should go towards recognition and reward programmes – and fun days or evenings out, such as nights at the racetrack, would be good for team-building and motivation.

2.8 Branding

There is scope to develop a 'JJ' brand. This could be applied to selected clothing and accessories, and be used in all promotional activity. A distinctive company logo and house styling would be needed, with the brand standing for the quality and service for which JJ is well known. The brand would also reflect John Jones' own personality. As well as aiding consumer recognition of all JJ's activities, the branding would act as a differentiator from competing outlets, and help develop loyalty amongst the wide range of people who enjoy the JJ experience in one way or another.

2.9 Co-ordination

When a broad range of marketing communications activities is undertaken it is important to take a co-ordinated approach. Co-ordination means that consumers receive consistent, complementary and supporting messages – failure can lead to confusion and poor presentation of the JJ brand. The need for co-ordination is especially important at JJ with a diverse range of products, both launch and ongoing communications to manage, and promotional activities being undertaken by both Marketing and Sales personnel. This means that a properly Marketing Communications Plan needs to be developed.

3 Conclusion

By taking the initiatives suggested above, I believe we can make considerable progress in achieving the objectives stated at the beginning of this report. Awareness, retention and sales should all grow helping to consolidate JJ Motorbike's position as the leading local outlet for those with a love of motorbikes.

Answer 3
Change management and marketing orientation

Check your answer

A good answer is likely to:

	☑
Define marketing orientation and product orientation.	☐
Outline a change management process.	☐
Relate the change management process to the development of a marketing orientation.	☐
Consider internal marketing issues.	☐
Relate to JJ Motorbikes' circumstances.	☐
Use an appropriate format, e.g. a report.	☐

*   *   *   *   *

REPORT

To: Sales and Marketing Director

From: Marketing Executive

Date: XX/XX/XXXX

Subject: Becoming more marketing-orientated

1 Introduction

To date, JJ Motorbikes has been successful through adopting things which JJ has a personal interest in, and which our customers to date who are predominantly motorbike enthusiasts have appreciated. The success has been based on the products we sell, and developing a 'community' of bikers who meet at our premises for the products.

With the expansion plans we have we need to expand our appeal to people who have less enthusiasm for the product, but are still sufficiently motivated to purchase from us – we need to develop a marketing orientation rather than our current product focus.

2 Marketing orientation

In a company that is market-oriented, all departments (not just the marketing department) would be customer-focused, and the aim of providing superior customer value is seen as everybody's responsibility (i.e. everybody is seen as a part-time marketer).

Narver and Slater (1990) define the elements of marketing orientation as:

o *Customer orientation* – being concerned with understanding customers so that you can better meet their needs
o *Competitor orientation* – having an awareness of competitors' capabilities
o *Interfunctional co-ordination* – all aspects of the business striving to create value
o *Organizational culture* – a culture that facilitates organisational learning
o *Long-term profit focus* – as opposed to a shorter perspective.

Piercy (2002) suggests that for developing marketing orientation, managers need to concentrate on three key issues:

o *Customers* – understanding customers
o *Market strategy* – segmenting the market, selecting target markets and developing a strong competitive position
o *Implementation* – getting the strategy to the marketplace.

3 Changing to marketing orientation at JJ Motorbikes

Moving to a marketing orientation can be considered in two ways – the change process within the organisation, and the outcome of the change.

3.1 Managing the change

Invoking change within JJ Motorbikes involves marketing the required state, and the change process, to the people who will be impacted by it, this involves:

o providing people with the initial motivation to change
o making the change personal to the individuals
o honouring and recognising the previous contributions before expecting people to move on
o promoting the benefits of change as they are realised, to sustain motivation
o developing and continuing effective two-way communication – including criticism as well as praise

This can be expressed as:

o *Tell* – people clearly, realistically and openly
o *Sell* – the pressures which make the change necessary and desirable
       – the vision of successful, realistically attainable change
o *Evolve* – peoples attitudes, ideas and capacity to learn in new ways
o *Involve* – people wherever possible in planning implementation.

One of Narver and Slater's elements of marketing orientation is the long-term profit focus – this involves considering the long-term relationship we can have with customers. Therefore to develop a marketing orientation we have to consider how we can build relationships with customers so they continue to return to, and purchase from, us. The loyalty card I have proposed is just one element in the creation of these relationships – a large amount of it can come from our staff.

3.2 Making the change happen

The change to a marketing orientation requires changes in behaviour – using Lewin's unfreeze, change, refreeze process is an easy way to consider this and make it happen. An internal marketing plan to assist the process is:

Situation

- o We have been successful as an organisation so far. However, to expand we need to attract a wider range of customers who are less interested in the product, and more in the total package – in other words, we need marketing orientation to satisfy them.

Objectives

- o The objective of the change is to move to a marketing orientation, with the whole of the organisation focused on the customer.

Strategy

- o For the implementation of the change it is important that we recognise that some of the staff will be in favour of the change from the start, whilst others will be less favourable and there could be some who oppose it. These three groups can be considered as segment, and we have to deal with each of them in different ways.
- o We have a benefit that moving from our current premises to Bike City gives us an opportunity for a fresh start.

We need to consider how we are going to implement the change, and the marketing mix can be considered here.

- o *Product* – the product is the change itself – moving from product focus to a marketing orientation.
- o *Price* – there will be costs to the organisation and individuals within to the change. For us, the costs involve training and development of the staff. For the individuals, the cost can be the loss of security they may feel during the change. In addition to costs, there will be benefits – the main one should be increased profits, and therefore increased job security for the individuals.
- o *Promotion* – how we communicate the changes to the employees. We are a small enough business to be able to use direct, personal communication with everyone. I propose that we should launch the project with a relatively informal meeting of all staff, which is headed by JJ who can outline the vision for change. After this, the communication has to be tailored to each of the segments as identified, and we should aim to use those who are in favour of the change to assist in convincing the others that is a good change.
  Encouraging participation through rewards such as sessions at the local racetrack would help encourage staff to change (most of our current staff are assumed to be motorbike enthusiasts).
- o *Place* – essentially we can use our staff to deliver the change message, and support this through communication via an internal newsletter and notices in the staff room.

- o *People* – this change involves all staff, and therefore the people are an integral part of the process. In particular we need to consider those who will be implementing the change which will be the department managers.
- o *Process* – changing the orientation of an organisation is not an overnight process. We do have an advantage with our move that we have an ability to literally throw out the old and bring in the new, but this change relates to attitudes and behaviour which may be ingrained. Therefore, the process has to involve training programmes and monitoring of attitudes (this is the specific unfreeze, change, refreeze area).
- o *Physical evidence* – making sure the change is attractive in a way people can tangibly relate to it. Again the new premises will assist in this through the availability of a nicer working environment.

Actions and control

The training programmes mentioned are the main actions we need to take. Through monitoring customer satisfaction and repeat purchase behaviour we can see how effective our change is, and take any corrective actions necessary. Our systems can give us information which relates to the sales staff customers dealt with which should help us to isolate any staff who are not changing in the way we would like.

4 Conclusion

Our move to Bike City highlights the need to change, and also gives us a great opportunity to do so. Using the plan I have outlined above, I think we can achieve marketing orientation in a shorter time frame than is typically required.

Answer 4
Information to support website development decision, project management

Check your answer

A good answer is likely to:

                                          ☑

In the introduction. create the need for the information and research to support the project; justify your reasoning. ☐

In Part a, list and justify the types of internal/external information that would be needed to support the decision. ☐

Define the website as a project. ☐

Outline the project team to be involved. ☐

Apply appropriate project tools to the website launch programme. ☐

Adopt the role of the new marketing executive at JJ Motorbikes. ☐

Use Report format. ☐

*   *   *   *   *

REPORT

To: Sales and Marketing Director

From: Marketing Executive

Date: XX/XX/XX

Re: Information Needs for Website Development Decision

1 Introduction

The decision to re-develop and launch our website is a vitally important one, given the threat from web-based competitors who is offering clothing, accessories and bikes by undercutting our showroom prices. We also know that a number of our prospects use JJ's as the place to test bikes and get expert advice before buying online from a competitor.

The web development project will be expensive and we will require adequate information and analysis to support the decision. We also need information to help define the site's development, functionality and usability.

If we decide to go ahead with the development, a professional approach will need to be taken to ensure that the new site is delivered on time and within budget. Project management is addressed in the Section 3 of the report.

2 Information requirements

The acquisition of accurate, timely and relevant information will require a systematic approach, focusing on both internal and external sources.

2.1 Internal information

Internal information will relate to our current strengths and weaknesses with respect to the decision and development. Weaknesses will not necessarily prevent development, but key ones will need to be addressed. Internal information will answer the following questions:

- o Who will be responsible for the site, its development and maintenance? Do we have (or can we access) the necessary skills and experience for the project?
- o Associated costs can be high. What are these costs and do we have a budget, can we obtain ongoing financial support? What are the associated opportunity costs?
- o Can we obtain the necessary support and cooperation from other departments; would there be internal resistance and could we overcome it?
- o Do we have access to the equipment, Internet connections and software tools we will need to develop and maintain the site?
- o What is the strength of our relationships with various manufacturers and partners? Can we rely on these for financial, technical or marketing support for the project?
- o Do we have access to internal records and databases that will provide customer, market and competitor information in support of the external information needs?

The internal information requirement can be addressed using internal records, a focused internal audit and via consultation with various managers.

2.2 External information

External information helps identify key opportunities and threats and will be needed to provide answers to the following questions:

- o *Customers* – Who are they, will they use the site, how will they use it, and what facilities will they require? What will be the service emphasis? Is the current site adequate? Do they visit competitor sites, do they buy online? Can we segment them in terms of their online needs and behaviour? Is there scope to offer support for our training academy, to offer forums and user groups and to provide safety and other advice – will such features be positively perceived and used? Will they help build loyalty and sales?
- o We will need to investigate beyond JJ's normal catchment area, given the web's reach.
- o *Online competitors* – Who are they, what do they offer, what are their strengths and weaknesses? What facilities and features do they offer? Who are their customers? What do their customers like/dislike about the site? What gaps can we exploit? How does the online operation work alongside their bricks and mortar operation? What is their strategy for competing?
- o *Distribution channels* – How will the site support our conventional showroom route to market? Will we include e-commerce facilities for selling bikes and accessories, or will it be an information site? Can we link into the online channels of the manufacturers? How will the site work with our partner's operations – will it threaten existing relationships?

471

External information can be obtained using secondary (desk) research using internal records and databases plus access to published research and use of the web for competitor information.

Primary research will be needed to understand customers and competitors and to gain insight into needs and wants, attitudes and behaviours, as well as to identify gaps that we can address. This can be achieved using discussion group, competitor site analysis (mystery shopping) and e-mail/web surveys.

When we proceed with the web development, it will be vital to position the site correctly so that it supports and complements the new showroom facility and forms a key element of our marketing and communications strategy. Information will be required at all stages: analysis, planning, implementation and control.

3 Website project management

The website re-launch has to be considered as a project – some of the main project management areas which should be considered are:

- Understanding the nature of the project – this is moving from a basic website to a more dynamic one.
- The role of the project manager – this involves:

  - planning
  - organising
  - communicating
  - co-ordinating activities
  - leading.

- Setting up the project – assembling the project team.
- Planning a project – timing, budgets.
- Controlling a project – monitoring the project progress towards the objectives.
- Finishing a project successfully – delivering a new website on time.

3.1 The project team

The success of projects is generally down to the skills of the project team selected – we need a team made up of the individuals with required skills and personalities. For the website we have to consider:

- What skills are required to complete each task in the project?
- Who has the talent and skills to complete the required tasks?
- Are the people who have these skills and talents available and affordable and willing to join the project team?
- How much supervision will be required?

To gain full commitment from the team we select all the individuals have to be told why they have been selected. Inevitably, we may have to make compromises in the selection – the ideal skill set may not be available (possibly within the budget available). I hope it won't happen for this, but in extreme situations projects can be abandoned due to lack of availability of the required team members.

For this project we need to include the following team members:

- myself as the project leader
- representatives from new bike sales, second-hand bike sales, clothing and accessories department and the service department to give advise on the content on the site
- we need a technical website developer and need to bring in outside expertise to help with this – this person will be part of the team
- if possible, a customer representative should be included to advise on what they would like to see in the new website.

The creation of the team is one of the first stages of the project process. To ensure that we keep track of progress for each activity in the website development. I will use a Gantt chart – this will also show how the costs are running. Each activity will have a line on the chart, and show the time period during which it will be carried out. If necessary, we can move the time blocks around to report on actual activity versus planned, and to re-schedule, and to create new plan updates. The costs columns will show planned and actual costs and variances. I propose using a Gantt chart as they are the most flexible and useful of all project management tools, however, as they do not show the importance and inter-dependence of related parallel activities, and will not show the necessity to complete one task before another can begin, I will also use a critical path analysis.

3.2 Critical path analysis

Critical path analysis is a very logical and effective method for planning and managing complex projects. To create the critical path analysis for our new website we need to:

- Note down all the issues (resources and activities in a rough order):

  - appoint technical support company
  - assemble project team
  - establish website requirements and content
  - develop website
  - test website
  - pilot website with customers
  - publicise website
  - launch website
  - monitor response.

- Some of these activities must happen in parallel whilst some tasks must be started before others, and certain tasks must be completed in order for others to begin. The relationships between the tasks must be considered and checked to enable the process to continue effectively.
- The critical path analysis is produced to show a diagrammatical representation of what needs to be done and when. Timescales are applied to each activity and resource. In the early stages of this project, a carefully hand-drawn diagram can put 90 per cent of the thinking and structure in place.
- Critical path analyses are presented using circle and arrow diagrams. In these, circles show events within the project, such as the start and finish of tasks. Circles are numbered to allow identification. An arrow running between two event circles shows the activity which completes the task. A description of the task is written underneath the arrow. The length of the

task is shown above it. By convention, all arrows run left to right.

An example of a very simple diagram would be:

This shows the start event (circle 1), and the completion of the Develop website task (circle 2). The arrow between them shows the activity of carrying out the website development. This activity should take four weeks.

Where one activity cannot start until another has been completed, the arrow for the dependent activity starts at the completion event circle of the previous activity.

o   From the completed diagram we can see the critical path – the items which have to be completed on time to ensure the final project is delivered on time. The items on the critical path line are the ones which have to be monitored as if they get delayed the project will be delayed. Those not on the critical path have 'float' and can be started earlier or later than planned (within limits) without affecting the overall timing.

3.3 Managing the project team

Managing the team involves many activities – meeting, communicating, supporting, and helping others with decisions. A big challenge I will face as project manager will be deciding how much freedom to give for each delegated activity. Tight parameters need to be set and lots of checking will be necessary for inexperienced people, but less will be required for experienced, entrepreneurial and creative team members. I feel it is important to manage the team by the results they get – not how they get them.

The project manager's role is to enable and translate. Face-to-face meetings, bringing team members together, are generally the best way to raise and avoid issues. Communicating progress and successes regularly to everyone is very important. I will happily give the people in the team the recognition, particularly if someone likes you or JJ express satisfaction. Similarly, I will take the blame for things which may go wrong (although hopefully this will not happen).

It is important to remember that the team will go through Tuckman's development stages – forming, storming, norming, performing, adjourning – and the final one is important for the team, celebrating the success of the website when it has been completed.

3.4 Reviewing project performance

Checking the progress of activities against the plan is very important – I will regularly review performance and confirm the validity and timeliness of the remainder of the plan, if necessary adjusting the plan to reflect changing circumstances and new information. As necessary, the identification of new actions and informing both team members and those in authority about developments. Team review meetings will be planned.

4 Conclusion

Provided the project is carefully drawn up using appropriate tools, and the correct team is chosen, we should be able to deliver a very successful website on time and within budget.

If you would like any further information please do not hesitate to contact me.

Answer 5
Customer satisfaction and relationships

Check your answer

A good answer is likely to:

☑

Define links between customer service and long-term relationships. ☐

Consider the elements of service quality. ☐

Identify improvement areas to consider. ☐

Highlight where service issues could arise. ☐

Relate to JJ Motorbikes' circumstances. ☐

Use an appropriate format, e.g. a report. ☐

* * * * *

REPORT

To: Sales and Marketing Manager

From: Marketing Executive

Date: XX/XX/XXXX

Subject: Maintaining customer satisfaction in our service department

1 Introduction

When we sell a motorbike to a customer we are potentially only at the start of a relationship with them – they are likely to then need accessories and clothing which we can sell to them, but also, and most importantly, their bike will need servicing and repairing. This applies not only to people who purchase bikes from us, but also to those who buy bikes elsewhere – either from other dealers or via the Internet.

Servicing work gives us a great opportunity to build relationships with customers – they keep coming back if they are satisfied, and we can develop an understanding of their bike usage, how many miles they ride per year and so on. In addition, because the service department provides ongoing contact with customers, often at times when they could be dissatisfied (because a fault has developed on their machine, for example) the provision of excellent service (in a personal sense, rather than purely the mechanical repair service) is vital for customer relationships.

2 Service quality elements

The quality of service a customer receives is a perception that the customer has of that service. Customer service happens whenever there is what Jan Carlson (then president of SAS) called a 'moment of truth' – any contact with a customer. Whoever is involved in the moment of truth is the representative of the organisation during the contact, and their actions at the moment of truth should reflect the image the company wishes to portray and should be a positive action increasing the likelihood of continuing business from the customer.

Each time a customer interacts with us the interaction has an impact on their perception of the standard of customer service. We therefore need to:

- o Map the interaction between customer and organisation from the customer's point of view – the customer journey, more details below.
- o Determine the factors that add or detract value for the customer.

Understanding how we can influence these factors enables us to understand customer requirements and provide high standards of customer service.

2.1 The customer journey

Improvements in customer service can be generated at all stages of the customers' interaction with the organisation and its products; throughout the customer journey we should:

- o Identifies key processes at the customer interface.
- o Determine where improvements can be made to ensure positive experiences through understanding these processes.
- o Clarify customer needs and preferences.
- o Information we gather about the customer journey should be used for:

  - o Development of processes
  - o Staff training
  - o Product/service development.

2.2 Adding value to the customer experience

In order to improve customer service, we have to:

- o Identify customers
- o Establish customers true needs
- o Identify what they want in terms of service
- o Set customer service standards
- o Regularly monitor the actual service provided against standards.

And, vitally:

- o Take action to improve.
- o These steps are taken through service encounters, offering the opportunity to:
- o Build trust in the relationship
- o Build brand differentiation
- o Increase loyalty.

2.3 Service quality

Parasuraman et al. highlighted five main dimensions of customer service or service quality ('Servqual', as it is sometimes referred to). They are:

- *Reliability* – consistency and dependability of performance.
- *Responsiveness* – the ability and readiness to provide service.
- *Assurance* – guaranteeing the security and effectiveness of the deliverable.
- *Empathy* – the ability to communicate with, understand and deal with customers in an appropriate manner.
- *Tangibles* – the physical evidence of the service.

Therefore, monitoring the customer journey through our service department we might identify the following needs:

Stage	Reliability	Responsiveness	Assurance	Empathy	Tangibles
Initial booking	The duration between initial contact and the availability of a technician to carry out the repair work is important	We should be prepared to respond to customer requests – and avoid the 'they all do that' response some automotive repairers use	Customers have to be assured that the work will be carried out within the agreed time period	This is vital if the customer has a problem with their bike	A written acknowledgement of the agreed booking could be provided
Arrival for the work to be carried out	The service department should have all booking details to hand	Any additional information needs to be collected		A friendly manner will help at this stage	Tea and coffee may be provided
Collection after the work is complete	This should be able to happen at the agreed time	If necessary, we have to be prepared to be flexible as much as possible to meet changes to customer requirements	Evidence should be given to show we have done all the work required	If things are not complete, empathy is vital for any rebooking required	The bikes should be presented back to the customer fully cleaned and valeted
After the work is completed	The fault should not recur, or the bike should feel better for the service	Any customer feedback should be acted upon	A full satisfaction guarantee should be offered		Contact from us to check everything is satisfactory should be made

The above are suggestions only – we need to conduct customer research to find out what is actually required.

2.4 Identifying gaps in the service delivery

Another model we should consider is that of service quality gaps – identifying the gaps which can occur in five areas:

- o The gap between our perceptions of what customers want, and what they do want. Fortunately, as many of our customers are enthusiasts and visit us partly to socialise we have a chance to find out what they do want, care has to be taken to ensure we get a broad spectrum of views from across our customer base, however.
- o The gap between what we perceive our customers want and the service standards we set. We have to ensure the standards will deliver what customers want.
- o The gap between the standards and the delivery. Training and monitoring should ensure our staff deliver service at the level we want.
- o The gap between what we say we will deliver and what we do deliver. It is important not to promise higher service levels than we actually deliver.
- o Finally, and most importantly, the gap between what we actually deliver and the service the customer expects.

3 Conclusion

If we can ensure there is no negative element in the final gap (it is OK to deliver above expectations) then we should ensure that our customers will continue to use us and generate profitable business for us now and into the future, hopefully remaining loyal customers – prepared to pay extra for the service they receive.

SUGGESTED ANSWERS

PART A

Mini-Case 4: The Engineers' Store

Answer 1 (Compulsory)

Check your answer

A good answer is likely to:

☑

In the introduction, create the need for the information that will be needed to support the geographic and product expansion. ☐

In Part a; ☐

- o list and justify the types of internal/external information that would be needed to support the expansion
- o give reasons to justify why this information is required
- o describe the procedure used to collect this information.

In Part b; ☐

- o deliver an outline marketing plan
- o including brief environmental and SWOT analyses
- o emphasis on the objectives, strategies and tactics.

Adopt the role of the new marketing and relationship manager. ☐

Use Report format for 1(a) and a Marketing Plan for 1(b). ☐

* * * * *

REPORT

To: Managing Director

From: Marketing and Relationship Manager

Date: XX/XX/XX

Re: Information needs and data collection methods to support branch and product expansion

1 Introduction

We are about to embark on a programme of geographic market development combined with an expansion of our overall product range. The geographic development activity will centre on extending the total number of branches within the Company and by extending the active catchment area of a selected number of our existing branches. The actual method of expansion has yet to be determined – organic expansion and/or growth by carefully planned acquisition are the options actively being considered.

The expansion plan is ambitious and the geographic development especially will be very demanding of financial resources and considerable management time. In order to minimise the associated risks, access to the right information and at the right time will be essential. This report sets out to identify the information required and outlines the methods for collection of this information.

2 Information requirements and data collection methods for product range expansion

Here the focus will be on customer needs and competitor product portfolios. This information will be used, along with an analysis of our own product range, to identify product gaps that we can profitably address.

2.1 Customer information

We will use our sales order processing records and sales quotations to help build a picture of the current purchasing behaviour of each customer in terms of what they buy, when and how frequently. We will look at our record of special orders to identify frequently purchased non-stock items.

We will analyse customer feedback forms and complaints forms to identify product range deficiencies.

We have a high level of in-house knowledge about our customers in the form of marketing intelligence but much of this information is tacit and therefore not readily accessible for analysis. A key task will be to document key elements of this knowledge. This will be done with the cooperation of the branch salespeople who will be asked to provide written customer account summary reports; these will include details of the customer's plant assets and an overview of their forward business plans where possible.

We will also hold a number of internal sales meetings where individual salespeople and branch managers get together in a central location. A key agenda item will be to discuss staff suggestion for possible product range enhancements.

We will undertake executive interviewing by telephone with selected customers to identify their needs and to highlight their perception of any gaps in our current product range. We will also attempt to identify and understand any purchases that they regularly make with our competitors. We also need to understand their forward requirements, their plant asset replacement plans and maintenance budgets.

2.2 Competitor information

We will need to identify competitors on a branch-by-branch and national basis.

We will undertake desk research in the form of website and catalogue analysis to identify competitor product ranges. We will use accounts data from annual reports to ascertain average stock levels. We will also talk to our suppliers to see what intelligence we can gather with respect to each competitor's product ranges.

2.3 Internal stock audit

We need to audit our current product portfolio to identify gaps, taking into account the information and data collection referenced in the previous sub-sections. We also need to understand our inventory patterns to determine average stock levels using operations data held in our stock computer. Given that we carry high levels of stock, this exercise will serve the additional purpose of identifying rationalisation opportunities.

3 Information requirements and data collection methods total branch expansion

The information requirement in support of the branch expansion is more complex than for the product range expansion described in Section 2. Ultimately, there are two aspects:

- Where shall we site new branches for greatest return?
- Where can we actually establish new branches, based upon the availability of premises, the possibility of finding a viable green field site or the likelihood of identifying an ideally located competitor that can be acquired?

Acquiring a competitor is by no means straightforward or certain, since the ideally located competitor might not be willing to sell.

In this section, we will look at our requirements on the basis of internal and external information.

3.1 Internal information, possible sources and methods of collection

Information will be needed to answer the following questions:

- *Objectives* – What are the objectives for this project; how many new branches and over what period of time? We need to have access to the relevant SMART objectives from the business plan.
- *Strategy* – What is management's preferred method for growth? Organic growth will take longer to achieve and will require a different information gathering approach, starting with an understanding of the location and performance of our existing branches. Growth by competitor acquisition will start with production of a list of competitors, segmented by size, scope of activity and location.
- *Management* – Do we have the right skills and experience to manage the expansion; and can we release this individual(s) for a lengthy period to concentrate on the branch expansion project? HR will need to conduct an executive skills audit, perhaps using CVs and annual assessment records.
- *Financial* – What will this expansion programme cost and do we have access to sufficient funds? Where can we obtain funds? Internal or external sources will have to be identified. Our finance department should be able to provide management with this information.
- *Branch performance data* – size of premises, annual turnover and profitability data. We will use this information to provide productivity ratio data: sales or profit/square metre, for example. This should be available from internal sales and operational data.
- *Branch location data* – address, catchment in terms of number of engineering and related businesses (customers or potential customers) within a defined radius. This will require access to internal data about sales territories, if available. Otherwise external, secondary data need to be collected (see later). With this branch profile data, we can identify the business demographic for our highest performing branches. This information will assist us in identifying new locations on the basis of similar a demographic.

481

3.2 External information

Information will be needed to answer the following questions:

○ *Possible branch locations (macro level)* – Where shall we go? Geographic and demographic data will be needed to identify possible locations for new branches.
The branch profiles created above (see Section 3.1) will assist in this task, although it is by no means a precise science and management discretion, it will be required to establish a list of possible town/city/region locations. External data will be required concerning the number of businesses for all areas of interest. The data will include business statistics and business-type profiles. The UK Office of National Statistics provides some (free) data and reports on regional growth trends in industry, which would be a start point. Other sources of information will need to be collected from Business Links, local councils, regional development agencies, chambers of commerce, engineering trades associations. Local business libraries might also provide assistance, possibly by fax or e-mail.

○ *Competitor intensity* – How much competition already exists in each town or region? Business directories, industrial yellow pages and the Internet are all possible sources. Some of this data will be easy to find, since we know who our close competitors are and will be able to access branch location information from their websites.
On the one hand, we will want to avoid proximity of competition; on the other hand, the lack of a local supplier might indicate low demand in the area. This would need to be investigated using primary research. Quantitative telephone interviews with maintenance managers in engineering and manufacturing companies would be used to gauge levels of demand.
The competitor data we obtain will also provide a list of possible acquisitions for further commercial and legal investigate.

○ *Possible branch locations (micro-level)* – Where, within each area shall we go? This will require information on locations of trading estates and business parks with communications/transport route information to help determine accessibility. Local councils and estates management companies can provide such information.
A major factor here will be the availability of affordably priced and suitable accommodation. Commercial estate agents and estate management companies will be good sources. Business rates, availability of local grants and financial incentives will need investigation as this can reduce the establishment costs.

○ *Branch staffing* – How will we recruit staff? Sources and availability information will be needed.

4 Concluding remarks

The branch and product expansion plan will require access to a range of information, from a number of sources, both internal and external. When approaching this task, it is important first to define what is required and why (what decision will it help us take). It is also important to start with a search of information internally and then when this is complete to look outside. As can be seen from this report, secondary sources of information can be used to provide a very high proportion of the information and most of these sources are accessible via the telephone, Internet or fax. Some on the ground intelligence and research will be required and this should not be overlooked as it will confirm the findings of the primary research and provide management with the confidence to take a decision as to where to locate a new branch.

4.1 Marketing plan

Situational analysis

Political –There are few political influences which directly affect The Engineers' Store.

Economic – when the economy suffers, customers are likely to repair machinery rather than replace it, which can benefit companies like the Engineers' Store.

Social – as a business-to-business organisation, there are few social or cultural issues which affect us.

Technological – technology can replace some of our business, but has more impact in the way we do business. Customers placing orders have moved from the telephone to fax machines and are now looking at e-mail and web ordering.

Ecological – our products can be viewed as environmental as they are used for keeping equipment working, but some of the by-products such as the oils and rubber products (belts, etc.) have implications for disposal.

Legal – product liability is becoming a very important consideration. We have to be careful about making recommendations for product applications, but our authorised distributor status helps us.

Strengths	**Weaknesses**
o 50 years experience	o Lack of national presence
o High stock levels and availability	o Some stock is very old
o Authorised distributor status	o Poor visual image – premises and staff
o Good product knowledge	o Lack of online purchasing facility
Opportunities	**Threats**
o Product liability laws requiring traceability of supply through authorised distributors	o Longer life of components meaning reduced business
o Geographical expansion	o Specialised products not available for distributors

Objectives

- o Increase the turnover of all branches by 20 per cent over two years.
- o Increase profit margin by 5 per cent over two years.
- o Increase active customer base by 15 per cent over two years.
- o Gain authorisation from additional manufacturers.
- o Establish alliances with similar businesses in other geographical areas to enable national customer accounts to be served.

Strategies

Ansoff categorised potential strategies as:

		Products	
		Existing	New
Markets	Existing	Market Penetration	Product Development
	New	Market Development	Diversification

483

For ourselves, the best way to achieve our objectives will be a strategy of market penetration – developing business based on the reputation we already have. In addition to this, through additional suppliers we should be able to follow a process of product development.

Further, Michael Porter defines three generic strategies organisations can follow:

- o *Cost leadership* – being a lower cost provider than other organisations to enable pricing advantage
- o *Differentiation* – offering a product which is demonstrably different from others
- o *Focus* – targeting a particular segment of the market.

We do not have the scale advantages of some of our larger competitors, which would enable us to follow cost leadership. Following a differentiation strategy through the provision of service is very important for us, both in terms of customer service, and service availability through good stock levels and so on.

Segmentation

The main segmentation to be used is that of customer type – primarily relating to the reasons the customers buy the product and the type of product they buy. We can differentiate customers according to whether they produce a product and buy components for the product from us, whether they purchase for repairs to their own equipment, or whether they repair products on behalf of others. The main factor this affects is the urgency with which products are required from us.

Marketing mix

- o *Product* – increase the range of products supplied through additional partnerships with suppliers. The product mix may be tailored for each branch to relate to the requirements of their customer groups.
- o *Price* – our suppliers set list prices which are heavily discounted. We need to ensure that we price according to the benefits customers receive through our service rather than purely competing on price. This will involve being competitive, but with a small premium.
- o *Promotion* – the major focus of our promotional activity should centre on the proposed change in brand image. Advertising in relevant B2B magazines, trade directories/classified listings. PR opportunities where possible, particularly linked to service provision. Also develop a PR programme for national trade media, particularly as our growth programme develops. Local sponsorship opportunities to raise our profile, for example of local sports teams.
- o *Place* – we should continue with our current branches (the possibility of additional branches should be addressed separately) and develop an online ordering system.
- o *People* – our staff are critical to developing the service which we need to offer to our customers. They are already very good at building relationships, we need to ensure they also concentrate on developing business with these relationships. We will also need to implement training programmes to ensure the effective and consistent delivery of the service. We will provide staff with uniforms that identify them as the Engineers' Store staff.

o *Process* – we have very efficient processes at present, but will need to consider the adaptations needed to make these appropriate for Internet orders.

o *Physical evidence* – the proposed new brand image should address the issues regarding our current physical evidence. It is important that we ensure the premises are kept clean and in good condition once the new image is in place. The image also needs to be applied to all materials which may be seen by customers.

Control and measurement

The setting of specific SMART objectives for the development of business at each branch will help in measurement of the results of the marketing plan and in making any necessary amendments. The marketing plan will also be subject to strict financial controls due to the allocation of the budget for the promotion and development of each branch.

PART B

Answer 2
Marketing communications activities; evaluation of effectiveness

Check your answer

A good answer is likely to:

☑

Identify a range of activities, covering both internal and external communications requirements. ☐

Discuss what a corporate 'image' is. ☐

Include mention of 'current customers', and 'competitors'. ☐

Define/explain 'evaluation'. ☐

Relate evaluation to objectives. ☐

Identify several relevant measures. ☐

Relate to the Engineers' Store's circumstances. ☐

Use an appropriate format, e.g. a report. ☐

*   *   *   *   *

REPORT

To: Managing Director

From: Marketing and Relationship Manager

Date: XX/XX/XX

Re: Creating a Uniform Image for the Engineers' Store, and Evaluation of Communication Activities

1 Introduction

As part of my new role, I am keen to address the issue of corporate image. 'Image' is about how others – including customers, suppliers and competitors – perceive the business. A large part of this image is developed from corporate identity cues, that is the way we choose to present the business. At present there is no uniform identity across our nine branches. Each is presented and perceived as a stand-alone unit. This may be unattractive to some potential customers who may dislike dealing with what they see as a 'small' firm; they may also fail to recognise that we can take advantage of synergy between stores, exchanging stock and expertise. Also, the company is duplicating costs, for example for signage, stationery and sales materials, and failing to take advantage of economies of scale. All these factors could inhibit our future growth potential.

I suggest that we set an objective of aiming to create a uniform image across all our branches. This will:

- help retain credibility with key suppliers;
- create an image of consistency of service, and of size/strength with prospective and existing customers;
- reduce costs of duplicated activity.

It is important that any activity does not disturb the positive image held by our existing customers. We already have a good reputation which we want to build on, not lose.

2 Activities

The following range of activities is proposed.

Research: it is important that we begin with the correct understanding of stakeholders' perceptions of our business. This requires research which could be conducted informally via both our salesforce and through contacts with manufacturers. This will ensure understanding of our current image – both positive and negative aspects.

Internal Marketing: our staff are a very important part of our business and we need to ensure we have their understanding, co-operation and participation throughout this process. A comprehensive internal marketing programme is needed to ensure staff buy-in at every stage.

Creating a Brand identity: creating a uniform image will largely depend on presenting the business consistently. This means creating a single brand identity for the Engineers' Store – both physically, in terms of logos and so on, and in terms of what the brand stands for. We want to be known as reliable, responsive and offering a personalised service, whilst meeting 21st century needs. We may need to seek agency help for the design work at this stage, subject to budget considerations.

Applying the brand identity: the new corporate designs need to be applied to all relevant materials such as stationery, uniforms, signage and vehicles. We can also apply the branding to newsletters and sales presentation materials. To date, promotional literature has been manufacturer-led, but we should design our own based on an understanding (through research) of customer needs.

Customer and supplier communications: existing customers may be concerned about the changes – we need to provide reassurance through oral and written communications that service levels and existing contact networks will be unchanged. Particular attention will need to be paid to key accounts. We also need to retain and develop the confidence of suppliers, retaining the special status we have with many of them. We must be prepared for questions from customers along the lines of 'Why are you producing fancy signs rather than lowering prices?'

External communications campaign: Following the launch of our new identity we should mount an external campaign. Suggestions include:

- Advertising in relevant B2B magazines to introduce and reinforce our new identity; new advertisements to be placed in relevant trade directories/classified listings;

○ Seek PR opportunities. Have a launch event as each branch is re-branded, inviting key customers and other stakeholders; local media coverage should be sought. Also develop a PR programme for national trade media, particularly as our growth programme develops;

○ Investigate local sponsorship opportunities to raise our profile, for example sponsoring of local sports teams.

E-Commerce – Our Internet site needs to be re-developed to represent our new identity. We also need to introduce an extranet facility, making it available to selected accounts, with links to suppliers too.

Company standards: the re-branding activity will be wasted if customers still have very different experiences at each branch. Standards need to be produced, circulated and incorporated across the businesses, for example concerning facilities to be offered and standards of cleanliness. It is important that, whilst branches are refurbished, service levels are maintained.

The proposals above will help to create a uniform brand identity across the business, whilst addressing the needs of all key stakeholders. Carefully planning will be needed to ensure they are carried out effectively and efficiently. Effective implementation will strengthen our position against competitors and give a platform for future expansion.

3 Evaluation of effectiveness

Evaluation is an important part of any communications activity. An assessment is made to see to what extent the desired outcomes were achieved, and whether effective use was made of resources. Thus, we should assess both effectiveness – that is what is being done; and efficiency – that is the use of resources. Information from the evaluation exercise becomes an important input when planning future communications activity.

A key method of assessing any activity is against the objectives set at the outset. If SMART (specific, measurable, achievable, realistic, time-bound) objectives have been set then evaluation should be straightforward.

There are several other things we can measure in relation to the Engineers' Store re-branding to see how effective our activity has been.

We have a strong, loyal customer base which we wish to retain, so measuring retention levels are important. We also need to retain preferred distributor status for key suppliers – again, this can be measured. I suggest we have a programme to gather feedback from customers/ suppliers before, during and after the re-branding programme. This will enable us to identify their responses to our new image so that we can address any concerns immediately.

In terms of new business we can measure a) new customers gained, for example accounts opened, and b) sales levels. It is important to note that the effect of our re-branding on sales may take time to develop.

We can also measure the effectiveness of the individual communications tools that we are using. We can ask new customers where they heard about us, for example through advertising, trade directories, sponsorship, PR, word-of-mouth, signage, vehicles and so on. For PR activity we can count the number of publications we appear in, and column centimetres' coverage obtained.

Staff perceptions can be assessed through team meetings and occasional questionnaires. Any concerns need to be addressed immediately so as not to damage morale.

We should also put in place relevant measures for e-commerce, for example records of website visits, pages viewed, new (potential) customer information collected; extranet accounts opened and transactions conducted.

The above should give us a comprehensive set of measures but we must ensure that our evaluation process does not, itself, consume a disproportionate amount of resources.

4 Conclusion

This report has put forward a range of suggestions to both introduce and measure the effectiveness of a new identity for the Engineers' Store. I believe these provide a strong platform to drive the business forward and look forward to discussing them in more detail.

Answer 3
Recruitment, training and team building

Check your answer

A good answer is likely to:

☑

Identify the requirements for staff in a new branch. ☐

Consider the selection process for staff. ☐

Identify training needs for new staff. ☐

Explain the team building process for a new team. ☐

Relate to the Engineers' Store's circumstances – i.e. relatively small business. ☐

Use an appropriate format, e.g. a report. ☐

* * * * *

REPORT

To: Managing Director

From: Marketing and Relationship Manager

Date: XX/XX/XX

Re: Selection, training and team building staff during expansion

1 Introduction

Our longer-term expansion plans will require us to open new branches in geographical areas where we do not currently have coverage. This would involve us in recruiting new staff to work in the branch – to ensure the branch is successful we would need to carefully consider the recruitment, selection, training and team building needs of these new staff.

An outline of the main tasks involved in the process of recruiting staff is:

Deciding if there is a need → Conducting a job analysis → Producing a job description → Producing a person specification → Marketing the vacancy → Selecting the right candidate

However, the management process does not just stop once the candidate has been selected appointment, induction and relevant training are also required if the person is to fill the vacancy successfully.

2 Recruitment

An initial stage in the process, having determined the need for new staff (which opening a new branch will do), is to conduct a job analysis.

This involves describing the role in sufficient detail so that a job description can be filled out and the job evaluated.

A job analysis is designed to identify the:

- Objectives it has to meet.
- Performance standards.
- Relationships with other parts of the organisation, such as reporting and control mechanisms.
- Products and services it provides, such as information and projects. Resources it uses.
- Resources it controls.
- Levels of authority, accountability and responsibility.
- Processes, activities and tasks it carries out in order to meet the above requirements and their related performance standards.
- Core knowledge, skills and competencies required to deliver the above.

This is as true for an individual as it is for a team. A job analysis will lead to a record of all these elements. When conducting the job analysis we can get input from those who currently hold similar jobs in existing branches.

Following the job analysis we should produce a job description – this forms the basis of what the employee needs to do to perform the job successfully. A well-considered job description is useful in providing both us and the employee with a common understanding of what is expected from the job. It is important as a step in the recruitment process and later in job evaluation.

For a new branch opening we will need to produce job descriptions for each of the roles needed in that location – it should be based on the job analysis, and contents should include:

- Job title and grade.
- Working hours and arrangements.
- Reporting lines.
- Responsibilities and underlying tasks. These may be broken down by the percentage of time the jobholder is expected to spend on each part of the job.
- Authority – What levels of decision can they take without reference to someone else? What resources do they have control over?
- Accountability – What the jobholder will be held accountable for, including how performance in the role will be evaluated.
- Knowledge, skills and competencies (or Attitudes, Skills and Knowledge (ASK)) required from the jobholder. This aspect is sometimes called the 'job specification'.

The job description helps us to prepare the person specification – making decisions about what sort of person to target with the recruitment campaign, using the job description as input. A person specification details the essential attitudes, skills and capabilities required by the jobholder.

491

The contents of a person specification should be based on the attitudes or competencies, skills and knowledge of the job description.

We need to consider:

- o The assessment standards for each aspect of the job requirement:

    - o The standards against which candidates will be compared.
    - o They must be independently assessable and based purely on the requirements of the job.
    - o Often a scale with written assessment criteria for achieving each standard is used, for example scale of 1–5, person specification is Level 3.

A person specification will also include:

- o Essentials (must haves): if a person does not meet the standards, then they will definitely be unsuitable for the role. These are the grounds for rejecting candidates. Make certain that judgements are not based on poorly founded assumptions.
- o Desirables (nice to haves): all 'must haves' being met, these may be used to further decide between shortlisted candidates. For example, a desirable for us would be the knowledge of our particular industry. Such considerations have to be objective, based on organisational requirements, and be non-discriminatory.

Our next step is marketing the vacancy – my marketing experience is useful here. The requirement is to target as closely as possible those individuals who will be able to do the job *and* those who really want to do the job. We need to avoid temptations to overstate the benefits in advertising or selling the job during selection – mismatches will lead to demotivation and underperformance. The purpose of an advertisement is to attract suitable applicants, so it must contain sufficient information for potential candidates to identify if they are the right person to apply. Include details on the position, salary (if applicable), the organisation, contact details and what the applicant needs to do in order to apply.

Hopefully the marketing will produce applications from a number of suitable candidates form which we can make a selection. The candidates need to be compared against the person specification and job description/specification. Matching the two is very important.

- o We will have roles requiring someone with excellent telephone skills – for these interviewing face to face is insufficient, their telephone skills need to be tested.
- o For roles requiring specialist knowledge we need to arrange assessment by a qualified person.

Selection can be expensive, as can poor selection decisions. The applications should be considered using:

- o Pre-interview screening via application forms, CVs, telephone interviews.
- o Face-to-face interviews.
- o Demonstrations or tests of skills, such as presentation, telephone or IT skills.
- o We may want to consider psychometric tests for some of the more senior roles such as external salespeople. These can provide useful information for candidates and interviewers, but need to be used by a qualified person and should never be used on their own.

The selection interviews should be conducted in the most appropriate way to get the required information, this will involve considering:

- o The manner of the interviewers – tone, question phrasing and so on.
- o Questioning carefully so as not to confuse the candidates and get the most appropriate answers.
- o What questions are relevant (and appropriate and legal).
- o Ensuring the candidate gets the chance to ask questions.

Hopefully at this stage we will find a suitable candidate and be able to appoint them.

3 Induction of new staff

Once a new jobholder is appointed, and hopefully before the new branch opens an induction programme will need to be in place to:

- o Help them settle in and feel welcome (meet the rest of their colleagues, get to know the organisation, etc.).
- o Assist them to understand the requirements of their job (go through their job description so that they know exactly what is expected of them).
- o Deal with any queries they have.
- o Provide them with the development they need to perform their role effectively.

It is essential to have this planned well before they turn up for their first day at work. Their introduction to the organisation and/or their new job will have a big impact on their motivation to perform and their understanding of their work.

The following should be included in an induction programme, which should take place over two weeks at the start of employment.

- o Terms and conditions of employment.
- o Structure of the reward system, including wages and benefits, expenses claims.
- o Housekeeping and security issues, such as catering facilities and data protection.
- o Health and safety regulations.
- o Company policies, such as disciplinary and grievance procedures, equal opportunities.
- o Training and development opportunities.
- o Company profile and its markets, such as its mission statement, history, product markets, communications.
- o Job performance issues, such as job description, standards, reporting structure, appraisal and role within the department.

At this stage we need to consider the training of the new recruits. It is essential that they:

- o Understand the product range that we offer.
- o Understand how our computer systems work.
- o Recognise who our most important customers are.

These are areas in which we have to train people. We are lucky in that we can utilise our suppliers for much of the product training at no cost other than the time of our employee. For the computer system we are best to get the new recruits to work alongside their colleagues in existing branches, and this will have the added benefit of them getting used to the customers we have and the product range.

4 Team building

Bruce Tuckman identified the stages a team goes through during its development and life. These stages and their key features are:

- ○ *Forming* – a stage of awareness and becoming oriented. Resolving dependencies committed to group goals. Getting acquainted, setting goals.
  - – This process we can go through by getting all the staff for the new branch together about a month before the new branch opens, they can meet each other and get to know their roles.
- ○ *Storming* – a stage of conflict. Resistance, resolving hostility, confronting conflict, listening with understanding, clarification and belonging. Expression of opinions and a sense of belonging. As we will be forming teams before they are able to truly fulfil their roles (i.e. before the branch is open), we can hopefully go through the storming stage prior to the opening – it is an essential stage.
  - – Through the use of open communication we can hopefully resolve issues quickly, helping to build stronger teams as they go into the next stage.
- ○ *Norming* – a stage of co-operation, open communication, increased cohesion and decision-making. Respect for individual differences, involvement and support. Feedback and understanding.
  - – Hopefully, we can be entering this stage as the branch opens. It is important during the early period of the branch being open (and to continue it longer term) to have regular team meetings both in the premises and outside. The purpose of the meetings should be to raise any issues staff may have, discuss any problems which have arisen and celebrate successes.
- ○ *Performing* – a stage of productivity, problem solving, interdependence, achievement and pride. Collaboration and goal achievement, challenging milestones and celebration.
  - – Once we reach this stage we can be happy that the branch is performing as it should and the senior management team will need to be less involved than would be required up to that point – effectively the team has been built.
- ○ *Adjourning* – a stage of separation when the group reached the end of it's natural 'life'. Recognition and reward appreciation and future planning. A natural sense of closure.
  - – hopefully we do not need to worry about this stage!!

Specifically, I would recommend that the new teams are given the chance to get to know each other informally early in the process – allowing them time together during the training process will help with this. Depending upon the location of the new branches it may be that we will have to place staff in hotels during the training period and we should use this as a way to encourage the team to get to know each other.

5 Conclusion

New branch openings give us a great opportunity for recruiting excellent staff, giving them the knowledge required to perform well and having the ability to create a completely new team which will be able to perform well as soon as they are dealing with customers.

Answer 4
Project management, and associated problems

Check your answer

A good answer is likely to:

         ☑

Define or describe what a project is.   ☐

Discuss the stages of the project management process, and identify relevant tools that   ☐
could be used at different stages.

Identify difficulties and discuss how they can be overcome.   ☐

Relate to the Engineers' Store's circumstances.   ☐

Use an appropriate format, e.g. a report.   ☐

*   *   *   *   *

REPORT

To: Managing Director

From: Marketing and Relationship Manager

Date: XX/XX/XX

Re: Managing the Introduction of the New Brand Image

1 Introduction

The introduction of new corporate branding for the Engineers' Store is a potentially complex process with many strands. This needs to be managed effectively and requires the use of project management techniques. A project can be defined as a multifaceted package of work that has a discrete beginning and end, and which must be accomplished to agreed standards. This report outlines the key phases the project would comprise and the tools that can assist the process. It also considers some of the problems that may be encountered in managing the project and what can be done to overcome them.

2 Project stages and tools

Any project will have a number of stages. I will look at each phase in turn.

2.1 Initiation

This first phase starts the project off. Spending time getting things right here means that the rest of the project will proceed far more smoothly.

First, we need to get relevant authorisation to undertake a project, ensuring the project is allocated time and human resources for plans to be developed and that an appropriate budget will be made available. Typically, authorisation for a wide-ranging project such as the corporate re-branding will come from the company's senior executive team. A project sponsor also needs to be identified to whom the project team is accountable and who can give further authority where required.

An appropriate project team needs to be identified, with an appropriate mix of skills and experience. We may need to consult personnel records for this. The selection of a good project manager is an important aspect of this phase – he or she needs a diverse range of skills.

A project initiation document is a critical tool to be produced at this stage. This is a detailed specification of what is proposed so that all parties are agreed on what the project does and does not comprise. SMART (specific, measurable, achievable, realistic and time-bound) objectives need to be included.

I suggest we initiate a sub-project at this stage too relating to the selection, briefing and eventual presentation from the agency we wish to use to help develop the re-branding.

2.2 Detailed planning

With our team assembled and the project's scope agreed we can move on to detailed planning.

This will start with a Work Breakdown Structure which identifies separate project tasks (often called 'chunks'), allocates responsibility for them, and attributes budgets and timescales to each activity. Various tools can assist with this process, including:

- ○ Gantt charts: these plot activities and their timescales. They can be updated regularly to compare actual against planned achievement.
- ○ Resource histograms: these show planned resource utilisation at different times and help to identify shortfalls and surpluses.
- ○ Critical path analysis: this shows the relationships between activities and helps identify timescales for individual activities and the project as a whole. A variation on CPA – PERT – assigns probabilities to assist with estimating less certain timescales.

Modern software systems can help with all the above, but it is important to remember that software is a supporting tool, not a substitute for management skills.

Communication plans need to be agreed at this time too. This includes plans for communication between project team members, for example at meetings or by e-mail, and also plans to keep other key stakeholders informed such as the project sponsor and the business's staff generally.

All the above material will be collated into a Project Plan, available for consultation by all key stakeholders (I suggest we make it available on our Intranet site).

2.3 Implementation

If detailed planning has been undertaken successfully then everyone should be clear about responsibilities during the implementation phase. Ongoing internal and external communication will be needed to maintain understanding, buy-in and confidence of stakeholders.

The project manager will carefully monitor achievements against plan, based on pre-agreed reporting requirements (again software may help here) and will take corrective action when necessary. The manager needs to be resourceful and adaptable, and must keep his/her eye on the project objectives at all times. In particular it is important to avoid 'project creep' where the scope of the project expands incrementally in an unplanned, unauthorised way.

2.4 Completion

The project is not over when implementation is complete. It is important to check that all planned deliverables have been achieved to the required standards, and to obtain agreement from the project sponsor and any 'customer' of the project.

A post-implementation review (PIR) is an important final step, ensuring that lessons are learned which can improve the performance of future projects. Undertaking a PIR is an evidence of a learning organisation.

3 Possible difficulties

A number of problems may be encountered when implementing a project such as the Engineers' Store re-branding. These have been summarised in the table below, with suggestions made as to how these problems can be overcome.

Problem	How it can be overcome
Adverse reaction or lack of commitment from key stakeholders	Careful communications programme for key internal/external stakeholders, focusing on the need for change and the benefits.
	Demonstrable top-level commitment is needed from day one.
Project team problems – dynamics, delivery, etc.	Careful selection of team members based on knowledge, skills, experience, attitude.
	It may be possible to use techniques such as Belbin profiling, but its usefulness may be limited by the relatively small workforce from which to draw on and the need to ensure representation from all relevant areas.
	The project manager also needs appropriate skills including motivation, communication, problem solving, flexibility, planning, organisation, etc.
	The project manager must actively use his/her skills and avoid over-reliance on project management software.
Project creep	Accurate scoping is essential at initiation stage, and accurate planning at the detailed planning stage. If additional activities *are* identified there should be a rigorous procedure to ensure they are required, and will not distract from the original objectives. Project sponsor sign-off is essential for any additions.

Non-adherence to project plan	Realistic detailed planning is needed. The Project Plan must be continually monitored for deviations with corrective action taken as soon as any problems are identified.
Failure to learn from mistakes	No post-implementation review held and/or the outcomes not passed on. A knowledge management system is needed to ensure that information is shared across the business and over time.

4 Conclusion

I recommend that project management methodology is followed carefully to ensure that the corporate re-branding is implemented smoothly and successfully. We should ensure that suitable project management skills are available within the company, providing appropriate training if necessary.

I look forward to taking these suggestions forward.

Answer 5
Training programme for changing business emphasis

Check your answer

A good answer is likely to:

	☑
Define customer relationships.	☐
State the objectives for the training course.	☐
Outline the content and methodology for the training course.	☐
Relate to the Engineers' Store's circumstances.	☐
Use an appropriate format, e.g. a report.	☐

*   *   *   *   *

REPORT

To: Managing Director

From: Marketing and Relationship Manager

Date: XX/XX/XXXX

Subject: Creating more business

1 Introduction

We are known within the industry for our good customer relationships, however, having recently spent some time in our branches with the staff dealing directly with customers I have noticed that they are not taking full opportunity of some of the opportunities presented. In general terms, they are very good at passing the time of day, and getting to know the customers, but they are not as good as they could be at asking for business. This is not intended as a criticism of our staff, but it is something which I feel we could improve upon.

I would like to propose that we run a half-day training programme to develop proactivity in asking for business amongst the staff.

2 Training objectives

The main objective of the training would be to increase our sales. To create this the training objectives would be to:

- show where sales opportunities exist
- develop the skills required to take advantage of these opportunities
- enhance communication skills of our staff.

From my observations I think that this training programme if successful could add between 5 and 10 per cent to our turnover.

3 Training course outline

3.1 Who are customers and salespeople

This section would explore the role of salespeople and explain that all of our staff are involved in the sales process. In addition, it would highlight the fact that most of the people who visit our branches or telephone us are customers, even if they are not the decision makers within the organisations they work for.

This would be an interactive session using examples from staff experience which I propose to gather beforehand and ask for examples during the training.

3.2 Where sales opportunities exist

Highlighting that opportunities for making sales exist through both direct contacts with customers – when we are communicating with them directly either face to face or by telephone, or through indirect contact such as when we organise third party deliveries.

I am intending to use video taken in the branches to show some of the opportunities, being careful that it does not break privacy laws or single out any of our staff in particular. If this does not prove possible I will get transcripts of conversations with customers.

3.3 Products and services

It is important that the staff understand what our customers are buying – typically solutions to needs rather than the actual product itself – they are buying it for what it does, rather than what it is. This is the key to understanding the opportunities that are presented by customers.

Examples from staff personal experience could be used here, highlighting those situations such as when buying shoes being offered polish to go along with it, or times when we could easily be persuaded to buy things if the sales staff had expressed interest.

3.4 Communication

Understanding the communication process to take away the fears of upsetting relationships by talking about business is very important. This section would include developing an understanding of perceptions we have to build awareness, questioning and listening skills, and handling objections.

This section would use role-plays and other exercises to show behaviour and how small changes can make a large difference.

This section would also include a discussion on how to steer a conversation back to business when it has moved to more general issues.

3.5 Closing sales

It is important to take away the fear of closing sales, which even many experienced salespeople can have, but is almost certainly a major reason why the customer service team do not ask *for* business. It needs to be emphasised that if done correctly the sales add value to the business and increase customer satisfaction as we are seen to be the 'total solution' provider.

This section will be conducted using role-plays.

3.5.1 Course follow up

It is important that we do not look at the course as a one-off event. I see it as a basis for further staff development. It is certainly something we could use in the future as the basis for recognition of good practice.

I would like to run the course myself, and would then use it as reference for future training courses, which would build on the theme of relationships with customers.

4 Conclusion

Whilst this is only a short course, I feel that we could benefit substantially from it and would recommend that we start the process as soon as possible.

mastering the exam

So, your revision is out of the way and the big day has come. How are you going to make sure you perform at your very best in the exam? This section looks at some tips and techniques to make sure you achieve to your potential. It also includes discussion of the CIM's recently introduced 'Magic Formula' concept to help you understand what the examiners are looking for.

Getting the balance right

You need to do three things well to pass the exam.

Understand the theory – You need to be confident that you have understood all the relevant theory. You should have covered all this ground during your studies, and again during your revision. Use the checklists in the 'Key Concepts – Revision Checklist' to make sure you have covered the main concepts for each topic.

Apply your knowledge – It is vital to master the art of applying the theory to the specific business situation described in the exam question. Supplying theory without relevant application – 'theory dumping' – will generally lead to failing the question. Furthermore, you must be able to explain *why* you have reached a particular conclusion or proposed a specific action. Plenty of examples are given in the Suggested Answers in this text.

Get your exam technique right – Skills such as tackling the exam paper correctly, answer planning and time keeping are critical. This is what we will cover in the rest of this chapter.

The structure of the exam papers

To tackle the exam paper correctly, first make sure you are clear on the structure of each exam paper. Each one at the professional Diploma level has the same number of questions, discussed below.

Parts A and B

The question papers for all four subjects are split into two parts, 'A' and 'B'.

Part A includes a mini-case study, usually up to about 1000 words long, and then question one. This question is compulsory and offers 50 per cent of the marks for the entire paper. Question one could relate to any part of the syllabus for that Diploma subject, so it is a risky strategy going into the exam not having studied and revised all key topics.

Part B consists of four questions, from which you must select two. Each is worth 25 per cent of the marks for that paper. (Take care if you have previously studied the Professional Certificate in Marketing – you selected three questions from six at that level; that is *not* the case here.)

There are important differences between the Part B questions for the four Professional Diploma subjects.

For **Marketing Communications** and **Marketing Planning** in all exams to date the Part B questions have not related to Part A.

For **Marketing Management in Practice** all the questions, in both Parts A and B, relate to the mini-case described in Part A. You still, however, have a choice as to which two questions to tackle in Part B.

For the **Marketing Research and Information (MRI)** exam paper, *some* of the Part B questions will relate to the mini-case. Again you will still have a choice as to which two questions to tackle in Part B.

Tackling the questions

There are several techniques to use to ensure you tackle questions effectively.

1. Decide whether you want to start with Part A *or* Part B – For **Marketing Communications** and **Marketing Planning** you do not *have* to start with question one in Part A. Most people are nervous when they start the exam and a long mini-case followed by a compulsory question on a subject that perhaps they do not feel comfortable with can sometimes knock students' confidence. For this reason many people start with a Part B question on a topic they feel confident with. This eases exam nerves and gets the brain into the right gear. If you plan to adopt this approach, we suggest you ignore Part A when you first open the exam paper.

For **Marketing Management in Practice** and **Marketing Research and Information** you will need to start with Part A and Question 1. You may then wish to, or be asked to, build on what you wrote in the answer to Question 1 when you answer the Part B questions.

Whether you choose to start with Part A or Part B, do *all* of that section. Do not, for example, do a part B question, then Part A, then go back to Part B.

Also, whether you start with Part A or Part B, remember to **number your answers**. You are not going to get off to a good start with the examiner if he or she has to spend time trying to work out which question you are answering.

2. Choosing Part B questions – Read through all the questions. Put a cross on the exam paper by any you definitely do not want to do, and a tick by those you do. Use a question mark if you are not sure. If you end up with two ticks you are ready to start; if you have one, or even none, you will have to start weighing up the odds of success in one question versus those in another.

3. Preparing to answer the question – It is very tempting to quickly read the question and then immediately start writing the answer. But, if that is like you, hold yourself back! Do two things first:

a) Use the four-part checklist

When you have read through a question you have decided to answer, run through this checklist in your mind:

i) **Who am I?** Many questions will assign a character to you. You are, for example, 'a newly appointed marketing manager' or 'an account manager at an advertising agency'. Think yourself into that role and keep in it for as long as you answering the question. If, for example, you have been told to be an external marketing consultant then adopt the view of someone outside a company looking in. If the question does not specify your role then assume you are a Marketing Manager or someone similar.

ii) **What is the business context?** In other words, what is the business situation that is being described? It is vital to spend time on this point if you are going to show the examiner you can correctly apply the marketing theory you have learned to actual business situations. Start by asking what sector(s) you are working in – for example B2B, B2C, not-for-profit, services, FMCG. Think what it is like to work in that sector and then adopt the right attitudes and language – for example, a charity usually has donors and beneficiaries, rather than customers, and appropriate use of limited resources is likely to figure as a key theme.

Pick up on all the contextual information in the question – even in a short Part B question there are usually lots of important pointers.

Example of 'Business Context'

Take a look at Question 5 from the December 2005 Marketing Communications paper:

As a newly appointed marketing manager at an organisation that produces a brand of soft drinks, you have been asked by your Marketing Director to prepare notes for her use at a forthcoming meeting with the organisation's current advertising agency. She is concerned that there is too much broadcast media work and not enough new media. Prepare your notes in answer to the following questions:

a) Discuss the advantages and disadvantages of both new media and traditional broadcast media in the context of the soft drinks market. (10 marks)

b) Make recommendations concerning the type of media that the company might adopt when it wishes to launch a new brand. Justify your decisions. (10 marks)

c) Explain the key methods that the agency might use to measure traditional offline media effectiveness. (5 marks)

(Total 25 marks)

Start but getting a mental picture of this business; ask yourself, for example:

o What kind of soft drinks? Perhaps choose an actual brand from your own experience and base your answer around that.
o Who are your customers and main competitors? How do you distribute your products?
o Why might your boss feel, if there is 'too much broadcast media work'?
o What is your boss likely to be saying to the advertising agency and how are they likely to respond?

There is no need to write all this information down, but do think carefully about the situation you have been given and 'live it' for the duration of your answer.

iii) **How many things must I do?** It is surprising how often students omit to answer parts of the question. Inevitably this leads to loss of marks. First note how many sections the question has been explicitly broken down into. It is common for questions to be in two, three or four parts, labelled 'a', 'b', etc.

Second, study the mark allocation for the question. When it is split into sections, some parts will typically carry more marks than others. You should spend more time answering sections with the higher marks.

Finally, note how many things you must do within each part-question. It is a good idea to underline on your question paper each required item.

Example of 'How Many Things?'

The question above (Q.5, December '05) was split into three parts, 'a', 'b' and 'c' with 10, 10 and 5 marks, respectively. You would therefore allocate more time answering parts 'a' and 'b'.

Part 'a' asked you to 'Discuss the advantages and disadvantages of both new media and traditional broadcast media in the context of the soft drinks market'. Here there are, effectively, four requirements: advantages *and* disadvantages (2 items), for each of new media *and* traditional media (2 items).

The second part of the question said 'Make recommendations concerning the type of media that the company might adopt when it wishes to launch a new brand. Justify your decisions.' There are two requirements here – 'recommendations' and 'justification'. Note, incidentally, reference to a brand launch – some more important contextual information that you may wish to refer to.

---

iv) **What format?** The questions will often specify the answer format you must use, for example 'report', 'notes', 'memo', 'research questionnaire' or 'proposal'. Always adopt the format specified – *make it the first word you write at the top of your answer.*

If no format is specified always adopt 'report' format, addressing it to the recipient specified in the question or, if there is not one specified, a logical alternative, e.g. the 'Marketing Director' if you are the 'Marketing Manager'.

b) Planning your answer

Once you have carefully studied the question, *plan* your answer – do not write your answer in full yet.

Start a new page in your exam script or on a supplementary sheet given to you by the exam invigilator and make notes of the key points you plan to include in your answer. For each part of the question, jot down single words or short phrases, grouping them into logically connected ideas. (If you are familiar with the concept of 'mind-mapping' then this is an ideal technique to use here[1].) Thoughts might spring into your head in any order – if you first collect them together in your plan this is not a problem – it is better than writing your answer in full and then remembering you should have included something three paragraphs previously! By gathering

---

[1] See 'The Ultimate Book of Mind Maps' by Tony Buzan, published by Harper Thorsons, 2006.

random thoughts and grouping them logically, it helps to develop an appropriate answer structure, and to develop appropriate section headings and sub-headings – see page 508–9.

The CIM used to recommend that you cross out your planning after you have written your answer but this is no longer the case. Do not cross it out but label it as 'Rough Working' or 'Answer Plan' or something similar and draw an obvious line under it, making it clear where your actual answer begins. The benefit of this is that the examiner can take into account anything that is not crossed out; so he or she can see what you intended to put even if, for example, you did not have time to include it in your fully written answer. This could make all the difference to a candidate on the border between pass and fail – the examiner may be able to award an extra mark or two on the strength of what was included in the plan but which, for whatever reason, did not make it into the final answer.

4. Making sure you answer the question – A common student error is to answer the question they would like to have answered rather than the one examiner set. To avoid this:

- Pay careful attention to the specific words the examiner has used. If the examiner has said, for example, 'Explain' or 'Plan' or 'Compare' or 'Justify', then make sure you do whatever the word says.
- A useful tip is to try to use words from the *question* in your *answer*. For example, if you have been asked to recommend something make sure the word 'recommend' or recommendation' occurs in your answer; or, if the question is about marketing relationships, then you are unlikely to have answered it if you have not used the word 'relationship' in your answer at least once, probably more. Obviously the words must be used appropriately, but if you do so, it is likely you are answering the question in the right way.

5. Be ready to give examples – In some cases the question asks you to relate the situation to an organisation or country of your choice. If this is the case make it easy for yourself by choosing one that you are familiar with, e.g. the UK for UK-based students, or your own organisation if relevant.

Occasionally the question will ask you to choose examples from a sector that you are not directly familiar with. Such questions will usually relate to sectors that most students will have at least *some* passing knowledge of.

Whether prompted to do so or not, a student's ability to give relevant, brief examples from real life is always welcomed by examiners. Scripts that do so stand out and are likely to earn extra marks. They are further evidence of the ability to understand the *application* of marketing theory.

6. Use models and diagrams – but with Care! – Models and diagrams (or 'figures') are often valuable to support points made, especially to illustrate marketing theory. However there are two important caveats here:

- always put a short caption to a figure, as you would see in a textbook;
- very importantly, the model must a) be relevant to the question and answer and b) you must explain its relevance and relate it to what you are saying. Examiners dislike models that just 'float' within an answer and are not explicitly related to anything that is being said.

7. Use bullet points – but with Care! – Bullet points – a series of words and short phrases preceded by a symbol – are a common pitfall for unwary students. Bullet points encourage a list-based approach and too often lists are just a place for 'theory dumps' of material the students has learned by heart – short phrases often do not illustrate real understanding, and often fail to be applied to the relevant business context in the question. So, use bullets if you want – but make sure they are relevant and that they demonstrate real understanding. This will almost always mean expanding on the bulleted word or phrase, adding a line or two of explanation or discussion.

8. Be realistic – At the Professional Diploma level the examiner is expecting to be dealing with intelligent students operating at management level, or who are capable of doing so. So do avoid blowing your credibility by offering answers that are unrealistic. An international FMCG brand may be able to spend millions on an international advertising campaign, but do not say that a small local engineering business can. Or, recruiting a new marketing team may take months to do, and even more time to start delivering real results – so do not develop a plan that has an as-yet-unrecruited team firing on all cylinders within a month. You may laugh – but examiners will tell you that such claims are not unheard of in exam scripts.

9. Make reasonable assumptions, if necessary – It is impossible, and unnecessary, to give every relevant detail about each fictitious (or real) business in a question. Sometimes, to give a good answer a student may feel he or she needs to make an assumption about the business situation. This is acceptable practice providing:

○ the assumption is consistent with the rest of the question, and does not take you into new and unexpected territory that the examiner is unlikely to be interested in finding out about;

○ you explicitly state the assumption, so that the examiner can understand your line of thinking.

10. Do not copy out the question – Occasionally students write out the question – this simply a waste of time. More often they write out chunks of the question as part of the introduction to their answer, simply repeating long phrases as their justification for preparing a report. This is seldom helpful. It is often a good idea to briefly summarise the business situation at the start of an answer, but repeating large parts of the question adds no value.

Format and presentation

Well-presented and appropriately structured answers underline the professionalism of the candidate. Ten per cent of the marks for an exam answer are now available for good presentation and appropriate format – often the difference between pass and fail. So here are a few suggestions for good answers.

1. **Use the right format** – This was mentioned in the four-part checklist, on page 506. Make sure you deliver the answer format the examiner is seeking, or a report if no format is specified. All the answers in this text are written in the appropriate format for the question.

2. **Mirror the question** – If, for example, the question is in three parts then make your answer in three parts (plus, usually, an introduction and conclusion) each of which relates to one specific part of the question. The examiner does not wish to hunt through pages of unbroken text to try to work out which bits of an answer relate to which parts of the question.

3. **Use headings and sub-headings** – Each section of your answer should have a heading which, typically, will include key words or phrases from the question. There is often scope to use sub-headings as well.

Headings and sub-headings are valuable for:

- the student, helping to focus your thoughts on what you want to cover in each section;
- the examiner, so that he or she can quickly recognise that the student has adopted a logical, structured approach, with related ideas grouped together.

Example of Headings and Sub-Headings

A typical part-question from a Marketing Communications exam paper ask the students to 'Use appropriate criteria to compare and contrast the effectiveness of two promotional tools', say advertising and sales promotion.

A suitable heading would be:

'Comparison of Advertising and Sales Promotion'.

Then, after an introductory sentence or two, four sub-headings of 'Cost', 'Communication', 'Credibility' and 'Control' could be used.

These instantly indicate to the examiner that an appropriate approach to the answer has been taken.

---

4. **Use numbering in reports** – Appropriate numbering alongside headings and sub-headings should always be used in report format. Examples are given throughout this text.
5. **Write business English** – Prepare your answer as if you were going to give it to your manager. Write full, grammatical sentences, avoiding a short notes-type style that you might use if you were jotting down what someone is saying (even if the question asks for 'Notes' format, still use full sentences). Avoid txt language which some examiners have noted creeping in2 answers!

    The only time when it is appropriate to write abbreviated notes is if you are running out of time at the end of the exam. In this instance it is better to write your key ideas down quickly; the examiner is likely to award *some* marks for appropriate material in this instance, even if it is not fully written out.
6. **Do not be afraid of white space** – White space improves the presentation of answers. Leave blank lines before and after headings, space around figures and so on. (But do not artificially avoid writing up to the margins, which you will find on each side of the page in the answer book given to you in the exam.)

Time planning

Finally, some thoughts on time planning. It is critical to get this right – many otherwise excellent students have tripped up by failing to answer the last question adequately, or at all, because they ran out of time. Here are some principles of good time planning for the exam:

- Allow time for *planning* each answer. Do not expect to write full answers solidly for three hours. You are likely to write a better quality answer in shorter time if you have planned it first.
- Allow time for contingency and/or checking at the end of the exam.
- Very importantly, *stop writing at the end of the allotted time for each answer even if you have not finished it.* There is a temptation to keep on writing to the very end of each answer, but this steals a few minutes' answering time from the next question.

Cumulatively this could mean you end up having no time to answer all or part of the last question. So, stop writing at the end of the allotted time, whatever happens – bear in mind that you are more likely to pick up marks by covering at least part of a new answer than you are from neatly rounding off the previous one. If necessary, leave some space at the end of an answer so you can go back and finish it later if there is time.

Exactly how you structure your time will depend on whether you aim to tackle Part A or Part B of the exam paper first. Suggested exam timings for the two options are given below.

Suggested Exam Timing (Part B questions first)

	Elapsed Time[*]	Actions

1.	0.00	Don't look at Part A
		Read Part B questions
		  ○ select 'definites'
		  ○ eliminate 'definitely nots'

2.	0.03	Start first Part B question:
		  ○ 8 mins. planning
		  ○ 34 mins. writing

3.	0.45	Start second Part B question
		  ○ 8 mins. planning
		  ○ 34 mins. writing

4.	1.27	Start Part A
		  ○ 20 mins. reading/planning
		  ○ 64 mins. writing

5.	2.51	Contingency and/or checking
6.	3.00	It's over!

Suggested Exam Timing (Part A question first)

	Elapsed Time[*]	Actions

1.	0.00	Start Part A
		  ○ 20 mins. reading/planning
		  ○ 64 mins. writing

2.	1.24	Read Part B questions
		  ○ select 'definites'
		  ○ eliminate 'definitely nots'

3.	1.27	Start first Part B question:
		  ○ 8 mins. planning
		  ○ 34 mins. writing

4.	2.09	Start second Part B question
		  ○ 8 mins. planning
		  ○ 34 mins. writing

5.	2.51	Contingency and/or checking
6.	3.00	It's over!

[*]Time has been allocated in exact proportion to the marks available, so the timings are precise and sometimes give an odd number of minutes. Realistically, you are likely to round these times, if only to memorise the schedule for the exam.

The CIM's 'Magic Formula' Concept

To help students better understand what is required of them at all levels of examinations, the CIM has introduced the concept of a 'Magic Formula'. The Formula consists of four elements that examiners are looking for in students' answers. These elements are set out in Figure 1.

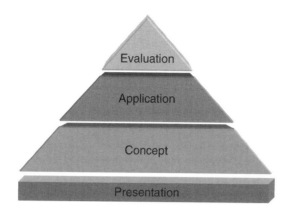

Figure 1 The structure of the CIM's 'Magic Formula'

At the Professional Diploma level marks will be awarded on the following basis:

30 % for **Evaluation**

- o This includes assessment of a course of action against a standard or set of objectives; in other words, what aims will it achieve?
- o This requires consideration of the wider implications of decisions
- o This requires justifying actions, reviewing whether the course of action taken was the right one and assessing whether resources have been used effectively.

30% for **Application**

- o This means relating marketing knowledge, models and frameworks to different scenarios and business settings.
- o This requires making and demonstrating associations between concepts according to set criteria.

30% for **Concept**

- o This is the knowledge of marketing terms, ideas, notions and principles;
- o This is an insight into marketing models and frameworks and how their effectiveness can be measured.

10% for **Presentation**

- o This includes format, presentation, Harvard referencing, evidence of wider reading and effective communication.

The 30% weighting applied to both Concept and Application underlines the point made before in this chapter that, to succeed in the exam, you need to balance both theoretical understanding with the ability to apply it to the situation described. In addition, the weighting for Evaluation means that it is important to say not only what you have done or are proposing, but also why – so reasoned argument is essential.

Examination rules

Finally, it is important that you do comply with the rules of the examination, for example in relation to what you can and cannot take into the exam room and what forms of identification you will need to show the invigilators. This information will be sent to you with your 'Summons letter', sent four weeks prior to the exam, but if you want to check anything out beforehand go to the Rules for Examainations at:

http://www.cim.co.uk/mediastore/Qualifications/Rules_for_Examination_Candidates_0905.pdf

Examination rules

CIM information resources

Studying members of the Chartered Institute of Marketing have access to a range of information resources to help them with their studies. These are available in person at Moor Hall, via its Library Services, and are also now available electronically via the Knowledge Hub www.cim.co.uk/knowledgehub.

Electronic services

Business source corporate

Studying members have FREE access to over 3000 journals in full text and another 7000 in abstract form via www.cim.co.uk/knowledgehub.

The database is searchable by topic, by author, publication and a whole range of other identifiers. Results are listed and the format shown (whether the item is available as a PDF or HTML or as an abstract).

The list can also be reordered to show different media types, e.g. academic journals, trade journals and so on, and a recently introduced feature now means that the literature selected can also be searched by cluster headings – in the case of a search on 'viral marketing', it will cluster the responses under *electronic mail*, *Internet advertising*, *word-of-mouth advertising*, etc. This cluster can be seen graphically if you use the *Visual Search* tab at the top where the results are literally displayed in graphical clusters*.

As well as journals, there are reports on countries, industries and companies.

Company profiles have key personnel, biographies, company history, company news, SWOT and key competitors of the global top 10 000 organisations.

Get the benefits of the whole world of marketing thought without leaving your desk!

Note – Occasionally there are problems with access to Business Source Corporate. Problems sometimes arise if you are running Norton Internet Security and there have also been some reports of problems with AOL. If you are experiencing any problems accessing Business Source Corporate then please contact library@cim.co.uk or call 01628 427333 and we will do our best to resolve the issue for you.

*****NB** Java will be required to utilise this function. Java reader can be downloaded for free from www.java.com

Cutting Edge

Cutting Edge is a weekly round-up of pertinent marketing and business news.

Written in a chatty, accessible manner, it will help you keep up to date with the marketing world. Each week more than 30 sources are used to write the abstracts, saving you the time and trouble of trawling through the marketing and business press.

Studying members can sign up for an alert of the six top stories at www.cim.co.uk/cuttingedge. When the alert is received you know the full version is available on the website.

A list of the marketing profession's major events and awards are also available on open access on the above website page.

Library catalogue

Studying members can use the library catalogue to obtain an instant list of references for any marketing or business subject, product or brand. The catalogue is updated on a daily basis.

Studying members can access a web version of the catalogue at www.cim.co.uk/library, or alternatively, CIM staff can create listings and e-mail these directly to the studying member.

The catalogue may also direct studying members to a third party website where further information is available.

Fact files

Fact files provide studying members with a brief introduction to different marketing subjects. They provide comment on the subject, links to websites, and links to other organisations that may be of assistance, and are written on an ongoing basis.

Titles such as International Financial Reporting Standards, Public Relations and Codes of Conduct are all available.

Agenda papers

Every six months the Chartered Institute of Marketing presents a new Agenda, which addresses a major topic for marketers today.

The Agenda sets out the issues, and analyses the drivers, implications and solutions. During each agenda, a paper is published, drawing on the best new ideas from academics and practitioners from around the world.

If you want to keep up to date with the latest thinking and developments in marketing, make sure you read CIM's Agenda Papers.

Current and past papers can be viewed on the Knowledge hub: www.cim.co.uk/knowledgehub.

Personalised research service

Moor Hall Library

Over 120 journals, 4000 text books, market research reports (including Mintel, Key Note and Snapdata), conference proceedings, and an extensive range of other reports, pamphlets and directories are all available at the Chartered Institute of Marketing's Library.

Located at its head quarter in Moor Hall, Cookham, the Library is open to visitors Wednesday–Friday, 9.00–5.00.

Researchers are on hand to assist studying members in finding the information they need – saving you time and effort in finding what you need.

Do not forget that these facilities exist to help CIM members in their studies and jobs. Copyright laws will differ if you are working for your company, but these can be explained to you at the time.

Remote research assistance

The library at Moor Hall is also at hand to answer individual enquiries from studying members. Staff can help you navigate the electronic services, assist with extracting information from library stock, or direct you towards other resources that will be of use. This could be a book loan, or articles being photocopied, or a list of relevant websites.

Photocopying is permitted within the Copyright Law and agreements have been reached with market research suppliers to allow photocopying of small sections of market research reports [charges apply].

Telephone and e-mail access is available Monday–Friday, 9.00–5.00.

For further information about our library services please go to www.cim.co.uk/library.

Note – details correct at time of going to print.

The CIM Information and Library Service
Moor Hall
Cookham
Maidenhead
Berks SL6 9QH

Tel +44 1628 427333
Fax +44 1628 427349
E-mail: Library@cim.co.uk
Website: www.cim.co.uk

bibliography

Aaker, D. (2001) *Strategic Market Management*, Chichester: John Wiley & Sons.

Bacal, R. (2000) 'Understanding the cycle of change and how people react to it', www.work911.com/articles.html.

Berry, L.L. (1981) 'The employee as customer', *Journal of Retail Banking*, 3 March, pp. 25–28.

Brassington, F. and Pettit, S. (2006) *Principles of Marketing*, London: FT Prentice Hall.

Buzan, T. (2006) *The Ultimate Books of Mind Maps*. London: Harper Thorsons.

Carlzon, J. (1987) *Moments of Truth*, New York: Harper & Row.

Christopher, M. (1995) *Relationship Marketing for Competitive Advantage*, Oxford: Butterworth Heinemann.

Christopher, M., Payne, A., Clark, M., and Peck, H. (1995) *Relationship Marketing for Competitive Advantage*, Butterworth Heinemann.

Christopher, M., Payne, A. and Ballantyne, D. (2004) *Relationship Marketing: Creating Stakeholder Value*, Oxford: Elsevier Butterworth Heinemann.

Davidson, H. (1997) *Even More Offensive Marketing*, London: Penguin Books.

Dibb S., Simkin, L., Pride, W. and Ferrell, O. (2001) *Marketing Concepts and Strategies*, Boston: Houghton Mifflin.

Gronroos, C. (2000) *Service Management and Marketing: A Customer Relationship Management Approach*, John Wiley & Sons.

Gronroos, C. (2004) *Service Management and Marketing: A Customer Relationship Management Approach*, Chichester: John Wiley & Sons.

Herzberg, F. et al. (1959) *The Motivation to Work*, New York: John Wiley & Sons.

Hughes, G. and Fill, C. (2005) *Marketing Communications*, Oxford: Elsevier Butterworth Heinemann.

Johnson, G., Scholes, K. and Whittington, R. (2005) *Exploring Corporate Strategy*, London: FT Prentice Hall.

Kotler, P. (1999) *Principles of Marketing*, London: FT Prentice Hall.

Kotler, P., Armstrong, G., Saunders, J. and Wong, V. (1999) *Principles of Marketing*, FT Prentice Hall.

Kotler, P. and Armstrong, G. (2005) *Marketing: An Introduction*, Pearson Prentice Hall.

Kotler, P. and Armstrong G. (2006) *Marketing: An Introduction*, London: Prentice Hall.

Kotler, P. and Keller, K.L. (2006) *Marketing Management*, London: Pearson Prentice Hall.

McClelland, D. et al. (1953) *The Achievement Motive*, New York: Appleton Century Crofts.

McDonald, M. (2002) *Marketing Plans*, Oxford: Butterworth Heinemann.

Narver, J.C. and Slater, S.F. (1990) 'The Effect of a market orientation on business profitability.' *Journal of Marketing*, 54(4).

Parasuraman, A., Zeithaml, V.A. and Berry, L.L. (1985) 'A conceptual model of service quality and its implications for future research.' *Journal of Marketing*, 49, fall.

Payne, A. and Christopher, M. (1995) *Relationship Marketing for Competitive Advantage*, Oxford: Butterworth Heinemann.

Piercy, N.F. (2002) *Market Led Strategic Change*, Oxford: Butterworth Heinemann.

Tuckman, B.W. (1965) 'Developmental sequences in small groups', *Psychological Bulletin*, 63, pp. 384–399.

Wilson, A.M. (2003) *Marketing Research: An Integrated Approach*, London: FT Prentice Hall.

Index